Project Management for Information Systems

Visit the *Project Management for Information Systems* Companion Website at **www.booksites.net/cadle** to find extra question material and answers for **students**, to help test learning, and also lecturers' quiz questions and PowerPoint slides to accompany the book.

Fourth Edition

Project Management for Information Systems

Edited by

James Cadle
Director of Assist Knowledge Development and an independent
consultant in IT analysis and project management

Donald Yeates
Independent consultant and associate client director,
Henley Management College

FT Prentice Hall
FINANCIAL TIMES

An imprint of **Pearson Education**
Harlow, England • London • New York • Boston • San Francisco • Toronto • Sydney • Singapore • Hong Kong
Tokyo • Seoul • Taipei • New Delhi • Cape Town • Madrid • Mexico City • Amsterdam • Munich • Paris • Milan

Pearson Education Limited

Edinburgh Gate
Harlow
Essex CM20 2JE
England

and Associated Companies throughout the world

Visit us on the World Wide Web at:
www.pearsoned.co.uk

_____

First published 1991
Fourth edition published 2004

© Pearson Education Limited 1991, 2004

ISBN 0 273 68580 5

British Library Cataloguing-in-Publication Data
A catalogue record for this book is available from the British Library

Library of Congress Cataloging-in-Publication Data
Project management for information systems / edited by James Cadle and Donald Yeates.—
    4th ed.
        p. cm.
    Includes bibliographical references and index.
    ISBN 0-273-68580-5
        1. System analysis.   2. Management information systems.   3. Information resources
management.   4. Project management.   I. Cadle, James.   II. Yeates, Donald.

    HD69.P75P72865 2004
    658.4′038′011—dc22

                                                                2004043345

10 9 8 7 6 5 4 3 2 1
08 07 06 05 04

Typeset in 9.5/12.5pt Stone Serif by 35
Printed and bound by Ashford Colour Press Ltd., Gosport

The publisher's policy is to use paper manufactured from sustainable forests.

Contents

Contents

7 The profile of a project 100

8 Project planning: understanding the work 120

9 Project planning: estimating 144

Companion Website resources

Visit the Companion Website at **www.booksites.net/cadle**

For students
- Extra question material and answers to help test learning

For lecturers
- Quiz questions and answers
- Powerpoint slides that can be downloaded and used as OHTs

Preface

This is now the fourth edition of *Project Management for Information Systems*. As with its predecessors, we have had three groups of people in mind when preparing it:

- *IS project managers and systems developers who find themselves responsible for managing systems projects.* Newcomers to this activity will find much that will be of help to them; and we also hope that older hands will find some new ideas to help them tackle the job with new enthusiasm.
- *Students of information systems and project management.* Not everything can be learned from books. Oscar Wilde said that 'experience is the name everyone gives to their mistakes', and throughout the book we have included advice based on experience gained the hard way.
- *Part-time developers.* Many people are drawn into the development of application systems and have no need to understand all the duties of the project leader. Selected reading can, however, help you in understanding how your activities fit into the whole scheme and will, we hope, lead to better project management.

To our 'traditional' audience, however, we would now like to add a fourth group:

- *People working in programme and project support offices.* Programme and project support offices (PPSOs) are an increasingly common feature of project organisations and many people find themselves working in a PPSO role without much or any experience of projects or project management. For them, we have created a new, specific chapter (Chapter 5) and we feel that the rest of the book should be accessible to them and will perhaps fill in some of the gaps in their understanding of information systems project management.

So what is new or different about this fourth edition? The main changes are these:

- Additions to Chapter 1 (Managing Change) to address multinational and multicultural projects.
- More discussion of strategic analysis tools in Chapter 2 (Business Strategy and Information Systems).
- A new Chapter 3 on the business case.
- A review of different organisational models (functional, matrix and so on) and how these fit in with projects for Chapter 4 (The Organisational Framework).

- A new Chapter 5 introducing the role and responsibilities of the programme and project support office.
- Additions to Chapter 6 (Development Lifecycles and Approaches) to cover extreme programming, Soft Systems Methodology and the socio-technical approach.
- Revisions to Chapter 7 (The Profile of a Project) to present a more generic process model and to discuss some of the stages in more detail.
- In Chapter 8 (Project Planning), discussion of the organisation breakdown structure and its link to the work breakdown structure/product breakdown structure.
- Some additional methods are considered in Chapter 9 (Estimating).
- A more detailed treatment of earned value analysis in Chapter 11 (Monitoring Progress).
- A major revision to Chapter 14 (Quality) to focus on more current initiatives and to discuss the quality plan and quality control methods in more depth.
- Extended discussion of vendor assessment in Chapter 19 (Managing Suppliers).
- Material on 'virtual teams' added to Chapter 22 (Project Teams).
- A new chapter (Chapter 25) on the range of project management qualifications available today.
- A survey of relevant bodies of knowledge and standards in the new Chapter 26.

In addition to the above, we have moved the references to Further Reading sections at the end of each chapter and provided an extended glossary of project management terms at the end of the book. Finally, a supporting website will contain answers to the questions posed in the text, downloadable PowerPoint presentations and more besides.

As ever with these publications, the authors owe much to their long-suffering wives, who have to put up with our being closeted in our studies at nights and weekends as we laboured on the revisions. We would also like to thank Alan Paul, a very experienced information systems project manager who has worked in both the public and private sectors, for contributing the new chapter on the programme and project support office. Finally, thanks to Jacqueline Senior, Amanda Thompson, Heather Fyfe and others at Pearson who have kept us going with their usual mixture of cajoling and threats!

James Cadle
Donald Yeates
February 2004

Disclaimer

The publishers and authors do not accept responsibility in any way for the failure of any project carried out based on ideas in this book or following your reading of this book. Whilst the ideas and good practices are based on hard-won experience, they need to be applied with skill and understanding and take account of project circumstances.

Acknowledgements

We are grateful to the following for permission to reproduce copyright material:

Figure 1.4: copyright ©1998, 2003 by Rob Goffee and Gareth Jones. Reprinted by permission of HarperCollins Publishers Inc. and Profile Books; Figure 2.2: from Gordon Greenley, *Strategic Management*, 1989, Prentice Hall. Copyright ©Gordon Greenley; Figure 2.5: adapted with the permission of the Free Press, a Division of Simon & Schuster Adult Publishing Group, from *Competitive Advantage: Creating and Sustaining Superior Performance* by Michael E. Porter. Copyright ©1985, 1988 by Michael E. Porter. All rights reserved; Figure 2.6: with permission of Robson, W. (1997), *Strategic Management of information systems*, 2nd Ed., Prentice Hall; Figures 6.1 and 6.5: from ©2004 IEEE; Figure 6.2: with permission of N.D. Birrell and M.A. Ould, *Handbook for Software Development*, 1985, Cambridge University Press; Figure 6.3: reproduced with permission of the National Computing Centre Limited from the STARTS *Guide* 1987, which was supported by the Department of Trade and Industry; Figure 18.1: Charles W.L. Hill and Gareth R. Jones, *Strategic Management: An Integrated Approach*, 5th Ed., Copyright ©2001 by Houghton Mifflin Company. Adapted with permission; Figure 18.2: from Johnson & Scholes (2002), *Exploring Corporate Strategy; Text & Cases*, 6th Ed., Financial Times Prentice Hall; Figure 20.2: from Adair J., *Great Leaders*, Talbot Adair Press; Figure 20.3: reprinted by permission of *Harvard Business Review*. From "How to Choose a Leadership Pattern" by Robert Tannenbaum and Warren Schmidt, May/June 1973. Copyright ©1973 by the Harvard Business School Publishing Corporation; all rights reserved; Figure 21.2: reproduced with permission of Henley Management College.

In some instances we have been unable to trace the owners of the copyright material, and we would appreciate any information that would enable us to do so.

1 Managing change

Introduction

All new information technology (IT) systems bring a range of associated changes with them. These may be changes to business processes and procedures, new roles and responsibilities, organisational restructuring, new equipment or facilities, or new skills to learn. All of these involve people, and it is the people within any organisation who are the key to the success of any IT implementation. No matter how well designed the new system and how well planned the implementation, only with proper consideration of the 'people issues' will your project succeed. Managing change is all about dealing with the people issues, and about involving people at every stage in the project to help ensure it realises the full business benefits. Information systems are only tools to enable people to take better decisions, so getting the commitment of the people who will use the system is central to the success of your project.

Managing change means being proactive in identifying and planning for the changes that need to take place within the business to support the new system. Many post-implementation problems are caused by users not having been adequately prepared for the change – for example, a lack of training or communication, or failure to get support and commitment to the changes from key users. These problems can be avoided by planning a change programme at the start of the project and running the programme throughout the life of the project and for some time beyond it.

Organising the project so that there is a user project manager with a responsibility for managing the change can be a great help in enabling these people issues to be tackled.

Key considerations for a change programme are:

- Plan the change programme in the same way as you plan the development and implementation of the system itself – these processes are integral to the project and not separate from it. Choose development methods that enable the people who will use the new system to play a part in its development. Joint Application Development (© IBM) techniques could be considered in this context.
- Ensure that the change programme not only includes communication and training but also considers the impact of the change on the users: the

1

timing and methods used to implement the system should be planned to make the transition as easy as possible for the user.

■ Phase the introduction of change to ensure that people are not bombarded with too many changes at once, and allow for periods of consolidation to enable people to become comfortable and confident with new responsibilities, processes or environments.

■ Involve users in planning and implementing the change programme because they understand the issues in the user community: this will help to ensure that those in the business are in control of the change, and are managing it, rather than being helpless bystanders to something that is imposed on them.

This chapter explores some of these issues in more detail, and gives some practical advice on how to plan and run your change programme.

1.2 Organisational change

Business change is all around us and the pace is ever increasing. The time to market for new products is decreasing year on year, privatisation has brought radical change to public institutions, and increased globalisation in many sectors has brought the challenge of managing across national boundaries and cultures. Organisational change is now commonplace and, given this, you might be tempted to suppose that some universally applicable rules would have emerged to guide you when planning a new IT project within a changing business environment. However, on closer examination the main lesson seems to be that there is not one easy prescription for managing change: there are many complex influences on the way people react to change and in any given project their behaviour is not easy to predict. Fortunately there are some patterns that can be found buried in the mystery of organisational change.

The first thing to look for is the business context for your project: what is really driving the investment of all this time and effort in delivering new IT systems? There is further discussion about this in the next chapter, but it is enough for now to note that there are four broad reasons for organisations to invest in large-scale corporate IT development programmes. They are:

■ Business survival
■ Improved efficiency
■ Potential competitive advantage
■ External factors, such as legislative change, privatisation, merger and so on.

The business context will have a major influence on your tactics for taking people with you throughout the project lifecycle, and on how you prioritise the efforts of your project team. Let us examine each of the four different reasons.

Business survival In this context, time is often the key success factor. To hit deadlines you may need to compromise on the specification, marginalise people who resist the change, and focus on delivering the essential functionality to those users who are key to the business. Production automation systems and workflow systems often fit this category.

Improved efficiency In some situations the increase in operational efficiency may come from the design of the system itself – through decreased processing time, for example – but these situations are rare. In most cases it is the ability of management to make better decisions based on the information provided by the systems that results in increased efficiency. In this context you have to take people with you and to be sure that they know what a *better* decision is, are able to access and interpret the data which informs that decision, and are motivated to take it. Management information systems (MISs) and office systems are often the products of this sort of business context.

Competitive advantage The key here is to encourage innovation and new ideas throughout the project lifecycle. If the way forward were clear at the start of the project then most of the competition would have thought of it too and so there would not be much advantage in progressing it. Rapid prototyping and end-user solutions are tactics that often have value in this context.

External factors Here, where the specification is not under your own control, you need to be ever mindful of the external stakeholders who have to be satisfied by what you are doing. Involvement is a key process here to ensure that all of the key players, internal and external, are taken along every step of the way. You need to avoid unhappy surprises at the implementation stage but be ready with contingency plans for when the ground rules change under you. It is not enough to comply with the letter of the law, you need to continually test that all parties have a common understanding of what is required. It is unlikely in these circumstances that firm requirements specifications will be available and it is therefore essential that users and computer people move together flexibly towards the target system. **Risk profiling** techniques are particularly useful tools here. Risk is covered in more detail in Chapter 15.

Once you have established the business context for your work, the next priority is to be clear about the pace and the scale of the change that is required for a successful completion of the project. Simply, this means looking at how many people are affected, how radically they have to change their attitudes and behaviours, and how long you have to bring about this change. Again the answers to these questions will point to very different tactics for managing the people side of the project. Programmes that have to deliver radical changes in short timescales usually require changes to staffing either through hiring and firing or through the acquisition of new organisations that contain the needed skills. If timescales are longer, but the changes are still large and far-reaching, then you can look at fundamentally re-engineering business processes to deliver the potential of the new systems and have the time to develop existing staff to run the processes.

If the scale of change is incremental or affects only small numbers of people then tactics borrowed from the **total quality management** (TQM) world are

Type of change	Short-term (3–9 months)	Long-term (1 year +)
Radical	Restructuring and redeployment of staff	Business process re-engineering
Incremental	Process automation and refinement	TQM, innovation schemes

Figure 1.1 Time and change matrix

often appropriate (see Figure 1.1). Quality circles or focus groups can both increase buy-in and also generate ideas for process improvements. They can be used throughout the design and development phases and, particularly after implementation, to manage the requests for enhancements to the original functionality. However, our experience shows that it can take more than two years to set up these mechanisms, embed them into the culture and generate worthwhile returns on this basis.

Having looked at some large-scale strategic issues that you need to bear in mind when planning the project, we should now consider briefly some issues concerned more specifically with project management. In a book about the project management of IT projects it is tempting to believe that change projects will follow the same pattern, that traditional project management approaches are always the best approaches for change management projects. The standard disciplines of planning and measuring, of estimating effort, of leading teams and of involving users are still valid, but the overall reductionist approach to work or product breakdown structures does not suit a change programme. Just as software development projects differ from engineering projects, so change management projects differ from software development projects. Some of the important differences are as follows:

- The goal may not be the same for everyone. We are talking about a 'future situation' where working is different and where people behave differently, rather than a new system with measurable goals.
- With this in mind, the creation of a formal estimated and timed project plan against which progress can be measured is unrealistic.
- The goalposts keep moving as people react differently to the change programme. The programme itself will uncover new ideas and views and reactions about where the programme should be going and how it should get there.

This is not to suggest that no project management should be done, but rather to indicate that it needs to be different. A plan is essential but it will not be a detailed plan that shows how something will be built and implemented. The most likely plan will have detail at the beginning followed by key events which are planned but which wait to be triggered.

There will be constraints, but not as formal as the 'triple constraint' which is referred to later. Managing stakeholder expectations becomes more important therefore. A change project is unlikely to be closed down if it is making progress even though the progress may be slower than originally planned or not exactly the kind of progress envisaged. Different project lifecycles could be appropriate – such as the Outcomes Development Method, which identifies desired outcomes and their realisation, and measures progress as these outcomes are achieved. In the next section we move on to the personal issues. What does it feel like to an individual user who may be part of the target audience for your system, and what might be their reactions to the project?

1.2.1 Resistance to change

How did you feel when you last experienced a major change? Stressed? Unsure of the future? Worried about how you would cope? Unprepared? Confident? Organised? Ready for anything? Your personal reaction to any change dictates whether you will be receptive or resistant to it. The changes resulting from information systems (IS) projects often meet resistance because the project managers have not anticipated the personal reactions to change they might meet from the people affected by a new system.

The Chinese ideogram for change is made up from two symbols: one that represents danger, the other opportunity. And that is one of the paradoxes of change: any new situation contains within it some danger, some loss, but also the potential for new opportunities. Daryl Conner and others have done work in developing questionnaires to classify people as D-type or O-type: Danger people or Opportunity people. Not surprisingly, most project leaders and business managers are O-type; they have got to their current position by seizing new opportunities. But the majority of users who are targets for a new system are probably D-type people, and they may well see threat in the change and seek ways to resist it.

Resistance to change can be active or passive. If it is active, the resistance is explicit and obvious. For example, when a dairy introduced a new computer system designed to improve the way milkmen recorded their deliveries, some milkmen put diesel fuel into the milk to sabotage the project. The most obvious way some other workers express resistance to a new project is to go on strike. Passive resistance to change is harder to recognise but can have effects just as devastating on IS projects as active resistance. People involved in the project might agree to functional specifications and then argue later that the system is not what they wanted. Staff sit in meetings, agree solutions and then insist that their interpretation of the proposals was different from yours. Alternatively, they agree with proposed project plans and then sabotage them more subtly. For example, a manager in a building society agreed to provide an individual to become a trainer for a new insurance system, then changed that person four times during the project. Each time, the new person had to be trained in the skills needed to become a trainer, the training approach and the new insurance system: this had time and cost implications that affected the whole project. You can get some insight into the likely forms of resistance by conducting a change readiness assessment with your users at the start of the project.

Before you work out how to deal with resistance to change, you need to understand the pattern of ups and downs that characterises behaviour during

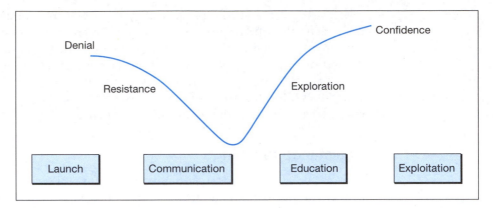

Figure 1.2 The phases of change

the lifecycle of an IS project. The change curve in Figure 1.2 shows early enthusiasm for change gradually falling off as problems surface, and then accumulating strength again as people lift themselves out of the 'dip'. The point is that, whatever the type of change brought about by your project, you will have to drive individuals and groups along this curve. In planning for this, the first thing to realise is that

being right is not enough.

The quality of the design of the solution may affect the final level of performance but the time taken to get there and the depth of the dip in performance during transition will depend on how well you deal with the people issues. Let us look at the phases of change in more detail.

Denial At the start of an IS project, people may feel challenged and apprehensive about the new system, but confident that they can apply current skills to a new situation. They deny the need to change.

Resistance Then, as people gain more information about the system, they may feel a loss of self-esteem because the job is broader than they expected; a loss of confidence in their ability to perform against the demands being made. They might exhibit signs of stress, such as working longer hours and being indecisive.

Exploration Gradually, people confront their difficulties by talking them through with colleagues or by trial and error; their self-confidence grows.

Confidence Over time, people become more responsive, decisive and assertive. They take responsibility for and pride in the exploitation of the benefits that the system can bring.

1.3 Organisational culture

The impact of the change curve on your project and the tactics you can employ to drive people along it depend on the culture of the organisation in which you are working.

There is more discussion about organisational culture in later chapters, but here we shall use a model of different organisational cultures based on the work of Charles Handy which classifies organisations according to the degree of centralisation and the degree of formality in the way things are done. Organisational cultures are shown in Figure 1.3.

To help to remember them they are characterised with the names of Greek gods. You may be able to identify organisations that operate in these ways. When you run up against them you will find the following suggestions helpful in dealing with them.

Zeus or power culture Here, obtaining and demonstrating sponsorship is the key. Everyone looks to those with the power to supply the answers and sanction actions. Owner-managed businesses often fall into this category. But in larger organisations any department with a charismatic leader can develop a power culture. Unless you get the explicit backing of the people in power you may find that you get low participation at user workshops and review sessions where you want a cross-section of users to express their own opinions. You also need to be aware that, whatever formal sign-off route you have agreed, no significant products will really be approved until the person at the top has said yes.

Apollo or role culture Here the culture is formal and centralised. Everyone has a role, a job description and a formal relationship with others in related roles. Public sector organisations and large financial institutions are often bureaucratic role cultures. The watchword here is to play by the rules but also to be aware that there is probably a parallel informal set of relationships that people use to 'get around the system' and to 'get things done'. If you can identify this and tap into some key contacts you can often get access to information and opinions much more

Power-based culture	Bureaucratic culture
• Centralised and informal • Get and demonstrate sponsorship	• Centralised and formal • Play by the rules but also use your network

Task-based culture	Individualistic culture
• Devolved and formal • Regular use of project teams and task forces	• Devolved and informal • Everyone has an opinion • Consensus needed

Figure 1.3 Organisational cultures

quickly than by going through the formal channels. But remember that when it comes to spending money or other decisions that need to be defensible later you need to have covered the formal systems as well.

Athena or task-based culture
Here tasks are devolved to the lowest practical level but there is still a formal framework for reporting and decision making. Organisations like this are used to forming taskforces and problem-solving teams. Modern manufacturing companies often fall into this category. In many ways it is the easiest culture in which to run a project as many of the traditional disciplines of project management such as planning and control and team responsibility are embodied in a task-based culture. The main source of difficulty here is that user staff may want to get too involved in the running of the project, to question all the internal working arrangements of the project and to be engaged throughout the lifecycle rather than just providing input or review at a specific stage.

Dionysus or individualistic culture
Here the organisation is so informal and decentralised that people often do not like to think of it as an organisation at all. In general, professional organisations often best fit this category. Lawyers may talk of their practice or chambers and designers talk about their studio; people working in a Dionysus culture may say things like, 'we all think of ourselves as a family here'. In a culture such as this, everyone has a distinct voice and all opinions deserve to be aired. This type of organisation can be a very challenging place in which to run an IT project. The watchwords are to use the formal mechanisms, such as the baselining of specifications and plans, sparingly. But when you do, make a big show of it. Make it very clear to all concerned why you, as the project manager, need to go through this process in order to do your job properly, and try to win their respect as a fellow professional. Also spell out the consequences of going back on a decision once agreed and highlight any forthcoming decision dates well in advance.

More recently than Handy and Harrison, Gareth Jones and Rob Goffee have offered an alternative but connected analysis of organisational culture which, from personal experience of its use, really lights up the bulbs in people's heads when they consider their unit's culture. They say that the character of an enterprise, a division, a department or a project can be described by identifying its

■ Sociability, and its
■ Solidarity.

These terms need some explanation. *Sociability* is a measure of friendliness. It is the same in our personal lives and at work. It means that people relate to each other in a friendly, caring way; they 'look out' for each other. Project teams with high sociability play together outside work, invent their own language and develop their own team characteristics. The benefits at work that come from high sociability are often those associated with high team spirit, the sharing of information and ideas, and a willingness to work beyond normal limits. The kind of atmosphere found in start-up companies is often high on sociability where high creativity and a commitment to performance are essential to establish and grow the business.

Sociability is not a universally good dimension: it has a dark side. High sociability can lead to friendship becoming more important than performance. There can be too much tolerance of poor performance or disagreements, with colleagues being unwilling to criticise or disagree. The result is that the best solution never gets implemented; life is all about compromise. In large organisations, high sociability can lead to the establishment of cliques, 'kitchen cabinets' and 'in-groups' where those 'in' disempower those who are 'out'.

If we think of sociability as a heart thing, then *solidarity* is a head thing. It is concerned with the tasks of project management: common goals, common tasks and mutual interests that affect everyone. You do not have to like everyone on your project but you do have to focus to get the job done. In high solidarity organisations, poor performance is not tolerated and poor performers are shown the door – and no one misses them when they are gone. No doubt a project team's customer would rather see this kind of climate than one high in sociability where compromise rather than goal achievement is the norm.

But would anyone want to work in solidarity-focused project teams? Too much focus on the goals can lead to an unfeeling atmosphere where performance is the only thing that counts and there is little inclination to explore the reasons for poor performance so that they can be addressed.

These two dimensions – sociability and solidarity – give rise to the matrix shown in Figure 1.4 with the four different cultures.

Let us look briefly at these four different cultures; remember that each has positive and negative aspects which are displayed in various ways.

Networked cultures

In networked cultures:

- People know each other at work and outside work. They like each other and help each other.
- There is openness, trust and tolerance.
- Poor performance is managed in the ways described in Chapter 21 on performance management.

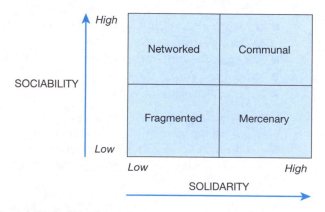

Figure 1.4 Sociability/solidarity matrix

(Based on Rob Goffee and Gareth Jones, *The Character of a Corporation*, 2nd edition, Profile Books, 2003)

■ Development is encouraged and there is an open approach to developing careers and moving people around.

■ People deal well with complexity and uncertainty; they can 'feel' their way towards a solution.

On the other hand, networked cultures can be over-tolerant of poor performance, there can be over-reliance on consensus, and too much focus on process and discussion rather than on outcomes and results.

Mercenary cultures

In mercenary cultures:

■ There is strong agreement about targets and goals.
■ There is a real sense of purpose and drive.
■ Work is very important and there is great task focus.
■ Socialising has a purpose: to talk about work.

On the other hand, it is a ruthless place to work. There is no peace or sympathy, and people who do not deliver are a 'waste of space'. Managers think short term about meeting results and there is little inclination to help anyone else.

Fragmented cultures

In fragmented cultures:

■ People work for themselves and not for the organisation.
■ High performance is everything; it is not who you know, it is what you deliver that counts.
■ There is a lot of freedom; you do not have endless consultation (high sociability) or constant reminders of corporate goals (high solidarity).

On the other hand, it is not a particularly friendly place to work, a fragmented culture is the culture of the individual. This often makes it a culture found in legal practices, consultancies, journalism – print, radio and television – and the academic world.

Communal cultures

People in communal cultures:

■ Have a high level of commitment to each other. There is friendship as well as high energy and focus on the goals.
■ Are focused on the product or service; there is no need for personal agendas.
■ Work in teams all the time.
■ Support the leader.

On the other hand, communal cultures absorb all of your time. Either you are goal-focused (high solidarity) or you are colleagues-focused (high sociability). It is a great place to work if you believe in the brand and want to belong, but not if you want time to think your own thoughts or have a life outside work.

Finally, some overall comments about organisational cultures. It would be neat and tidy if an organisation had only one culture and, whilst it is true that organisations can be characterised by a single culture, for example individualistic (using Handy) or fragmented (using Jones), most organisations can demonstrate several different cultures at the same time. For example, the human resources department might be networked, the consulting division might be fragmented and the sales division might be mercenary. Also, no single culture is good or bad by definition. It all depends on what is right or appropriate for the competitive climate and the work context. For example, if the IT department has a networked culture and you are leading an external consulting team there, you will need to accommodate your culture and the way you work to your client's needs.

1.4 The project manager and change

Most information systems are a tool for people to use to support them in their job, therefore to implement the change successfully you have to ensure that people are using the system effectively and efficiently. Just because the system is available does not mean that people will use it. Therefore, a change programme that combines training, awareness, communication and business process design activities is crucial to the success of an information systems project. Armed with a knowledge of the business context for the project and an understanding of the organisational culture you are working within, you can design and manage a change programme which takes the users with you and ensures that the project as a whole delivers what the business needs.

There are four overlapping stages in such a change programme:

■ Launching the project
■ Winning hearts and minds
■ Skilling the end-users
■ After go-live.

1.5 Launching the project

As soon as the project is launched, find a sponsor from the business who will act as the change manager; they will need to be credible and influential rather than senior. You need to work in partnership with this sponsor because you need them to visibly sign up to decisions and take a leading role in bringing about the change. You also need to raise their aspirations so they become a radical champion for the project. Manage their expectations of the technical difficulties, as well as the people difficulties, in implementing the new system so they do not become disillusioned when the going gets tough.

You will need help from other people as well, so try to identify champions and change agents throughout the organisation and get commitment for their involvement from their line managers. This group will need training and support to develop new skills to carry out change programme tasks. For example, you might need to train people to become system trainers or run user acceptance tests. Remember, though, that delegation of tasks does not mean abdication of responsibility: you should provide ongoing, active support and monitor people to ensure that their learning is positive and effective. For example, you might review a training guide or observe a practice training session and then provide constructive feedback. You must focus on the business benefits of the change you are introducing, and as a team share the responsibility for achieving them.

Having prepared the sponsor and the user side of the project team, you then need to launch the project to a wider user audience. At this early stage in the system's project lifecycle you probably will not have many facts about timescale or functionality, and the temptation is to say nothing in case going public means you will be held to account later. In fact the greater danger is that by saying nothing the grapevine will run riot and the rumours that spread about what the system can or cannot do could cause far more damage to your future reputation. Typically, at this stage what people want to know is: why the system is being introduced, who is responsible from the business point of view for making it work, when it will affect them, and some broad indications about what it could do for the business and how this could be measured. Wherever possible you should try to ensure that these messages are delivered down the management line – starting with your sponsor rather than from the IT department.

Do not be afraid of saying 'I don't know', but be clear about what is known, and give dates that you are prepared to stick to regarding when you will be able to give more information. A 'countdown to go-live' chart is a good way of preparing people for a fairly lengthy build-up before they get their hands on the system. You might want to consider giving the project and the system a name and a visual branding, such as a logo, at this stage. This gives people something more tangible to identify the project by in the months before any new systems actually hit their desks.

Winning people's hearts and minds is the next step in implementing successful change. The key is to involve customer staff in the change. With help and coaching from the project team, users can find facts, analyse data, investigate needs, brainstorm solutions, produce reports and prepare training and communications materials. A powerful way to start this process is to involve users in preparing a risk profile for the project. Inevitably, the pre-emptive actions for many of the risks will fall to the users themselves, and immediately they are engaged in making the project work.

Winning hearts and minds also means communicating widely with everyone who will be affected by the new system. First, there needs to be a consistent way of describing the need for change. This often means finding ways of describing the problems with the present situation – what is pushing us towards a new system – and the vision, the opportunities offered by the new system – what is pulling us towards the new. You also need to plan the right vehicle for the communication. For example, use 'hot' vehicles for sensitive or significant information, and 'cold' vehicles for uncontroversial or detailed messages. Typical hot vehicles are face-to-face events like conferences and seminars, presentations, roadshows, team briefings and regular management meetings. Cold vehicles are impersonal things like paper or electronic media such as videos, notices, posters, emails or the internal mail. Most of all, remember that communication is a two-way process: you need to make time to listen as well as to inform.

There is a useful model to remember when trying to win hearts and minds. It is not quite as simple as ABC, but it is as straightforward as AABBCC!

AA Identify audiences and the actions you want from them. *Audiences* and *actions*.

BB Identify the barriers which audiences might have that may prevent them from delivering these actions and tell them about the benefits that will come from the actions. *Barriers* and *benefits*.

CC Choose the communication channels to each audience and the controls and measures that you will use to check that the messages have been received and understood. *Communications* and *controls*.

Sometimes it will be necessary to take a clinical look at the people involved in the change project. There will be supporters and blockers, keen but incompetent people and so on. After a while it become clear that not all of these individuals are best treated in the same way. A framework for making a preliminary classification is shown in Figure 1.5.

People are categorised according to their competence – their ability to make changes, implement them and carry others along with the process, and by their commitment – their belief in the necessity of the change and their demonstration of that belief. People therefore can be grouped in one of the four quadrants of the matrix.

■ In the top left we have highly competent people who are able to play an important part in the change process or in the development of the new project, but for some reason are unwilling to do this or feel insecure about it. This frustrating situation needs investigation. Do they have underlying concerns about the development that have not yet surfaced?

Figure 1.5 The change competence/commitment matrix

- In the top right are people who are able, willing and confident about the change. These are the people who can be the change leaders or who can be positive influencers in new developments.
- In the bottom left are people who appear both unwilling and unable to make the change. Sooner or later – and probably the sooner the better – they have to be moved out or moved to one side.
- The people in the bottom right are keen and motivated but do not have the competence to lead change and implement it. Consider giving them some training, provide supportive supervision or provide a coach for them.

1.6 Skilling the end-users

You need to continue winning hearts and minds right from when you first launch the project through to go-live and beyond, but as the systems get nearer to live use, the emphasis of user activities has to move from giving information to building new skills and knowledge: from communication to training. The two sets of activities must be closely linked, and it is often a good idea to use the same team to develop and deliver both.

The key to effective system training is to base it around the business tasks that users will perform, not just around the menus and functions of the system. Make the training examples as realistic as possible, use a copy of the live data if you can. By doing this people see the context in which the system will be used and you minimise implementation problems later. Do not be constrained by thinking just of conventional classroom training; consider delivering training in the workplace, possibly using key users – but make sure you select these people carefully and invest enough time in building their training skills. One successful approach is to create a model office in which you can run past 'real work' scenarios using the new systems and procedures. Well designed, these events can give the two-fold benefits of having powerful impact on the people involved (who have now been part of the future, for a few hours at least, and can then act as powerful advocates of the change with their peers) and also giving valuable feedback on the dependencies between the various technical parts of the project. Finally, make sure that training materials and user guides look professional. The quality of these printed materials will play a large part in forming users' initial expectations of the quality of the system itself.

1.7 After go-live

As far as the system is concerned you may think your job is almost over as soon as it goes live, but for the users the job is just beginning. For users to make the most of the potential benefits of the system and for the project to achieve its business objectives, users still need your support after go-live. The job is much easier if the training has been designed to produce self-supporting groups, people who are confident in using the paper-based and on-screen documentation and know which of their colleagues to turn to for local advice. But in setting up a support system, there are a few broad lessons to bear in mind. Make sure that each level of support filters problems and resolves those that are their responsibility and does not just pass them on. Monitor help desk calls, and when you find repeated problems produce short, targeted 'best practice' user guides to educate users to solve them themselves. Make sure that new recruits are properly trained in the current best practices and not just left to find their own ways of doing things. If staff turnover is high, computer-based training is an effective way of coping with new joiner training.

Finally, make sure you stop, review the benefits that users are delivering against the original objectives, and acknowledge the contributions that people have made. Because large projects never have a clear end-point, it is all too easy to forget the need to celebrate successes, to identify what remains to be done and to learn the lessons for next time.

The four-phase model of managing business change is summarised in Figure 1.6.

Figure 1.6 Four-phase model of managing business change

1.8 | Avoiding failure

The aim of this book is to help project managers and to prevent them having to answer the question: 'Why has your project failed?' In truth, everyone involved knows two things:

- Many projects do fail or are deemed to have failed; it is just a question of how much failure can be tolerated and the project still be called a success.
- Everyone knows the golden rules but thinks that, this time, there is a super-ordinate reason for breaking the rules and that 'it will be all right on the night'. In other words, a good project manager ought to be able to sort it out; it is what he is paid for, after all.

There is a variety of project health checks and diagnostic tools to gauge the likelihood of success or failure, and we might therefore say that getting appropriate scores will bring success – but some of the health checks have around a hundred questions! They can, however, identify the parts of the project management process that need attention; they identify the risks. Two interesting ones have been created by Turner and by Wateridge and are referenced in the Further Reading at the end of this chapter. However, let us begin with a definition of a successful project: it is one that delivers to the customer everything specified, to the quality agreed, on time and within cost.

Three pieces of research are now quoted to show how often this is achieved. Perhaps most widely known are the surveys by the Standish Group in the USA. They classify projects under three headings:

- Successful
- Challenged
- Impaired.

Successful projects were those that met the definition above. Challenged projects were those where the project was completed and became operational but cost more, overran on time and delivered less functionality. Impaired projects were cancelled during the development stages. Overall, only 16 per cent were deemed to be successful, 53 per cent were challenged and 31 per cent were cancelled. If one were to present this in a positive light, however, people could say that 69 per cent of projects were successful.

The survey report does not pretend to know all of the answers but it does offer a 'success potential' chart citing user involvement, top management support and a clear statement of requirements as the three most important factors for success. It also says that

smaller time frames, with delivery of software components early and often, will increase the success rate. Shorter time frames result in an iterative process of design, prototype, develop, test, and deploy small elements. This process is known as 'growing' software, as opposed to the old concept of 'developing' software. Growing software engages the user earlier, each component has an owner or set of owners, and expectations are realistically set. In addition, each software component has a clear and precise statement and set of objectives. Software components and small projects tend to be less complex. Making the projects simpler is a worthwhile endeavour because complexity causes confusion and increased cost.

The problem is, we do not learn from our experience or, if we do, we are unable to get our sponsors, clients or users to take notice of it. The House of Commons Public Accounts Committee in the UK sums it up by saying: 'of particular concern is that problems continue to occur in areas where this Committee has made recommendations in the past'. The Committee, which examined 25 public sector projects, drew attention to the importance of senior management's role, noting that the big decisions about IT systems are likely to be business based rather than technical decisions. They also emphasised the interconnectedness of IT systems and wider changes in the environment – very often political decisions in the public sector – and the need for good change management.

In contrast, information from a continuing survey published on the internet at www360.com and carried out by staff from Templeton College, Oxford,

> seems to indicate that project and programme performance in the UK is today better than has typically been supposed. Most of us read in the media about the big failures, but need to remember that in-house projects still represent a substantially higher proportion of the total than projects for external clients, and the content of most projects appears to follow the classic sequence of requirements identification, design, integration and testing.

Let us finish, then, with something about change management and relate it to the difficulties associated with achieving a successful project implementation. The change curve in Figure 1.2 still holds true, but if we follow Kotter's eight reasons why change fails, what do we find?

1 There is not enough sense of urgency. There are not enough people who want to make the change. In project management terms this means that there is no top management driving force behind the need for the new system and no sense of urgency – 'the sooner we get this system implemented the sooner things will improve.'

2 There are not enough interested parties pushing for the change; it is not important enough to a wide cross-section of management and users. How many projects dealing with customers actually involve customers on the steering committee? What a powerful force that could be. Does the development of hospital systems involve doctors, nurses, patients, general practitioners, administrators, laboratory technicians and members of the hospital trust?

3 There is no vision. In change management terms, vision clarifies the direction in which the organisation needs to move. In project management terms it is a combination of the business case and the scope. In a study carried out by Andrew Taylor, poor scope management and poorly defined objectives were highlighted as common reasons for project failure.

4 Under-communication. Business change is not achieved in the short term and the same is true of IT systems developments. Throughout the development

lifecycle everyone needs to believe that useful change is possible, that the new system will work and that it will deliver the promised benefits. There are many things that can be done to make communication effective, and later parts of this book suggest some of these. But it is not just the project team that needs to communicate; user management, sponsors and key users need to communicate positive messages about the systems change all the time.

5 'Leaving an elephant in the way.' Successful systems change involves many people. Good communication means the people get positive messages about the new system and its benefits, but obstacles always appear. They may be organisational obstacles or they may be managers who refuse to let their staff participate in activities connected with the development process. Whatever they are, they need to be removed or else they give the wrong message: one of 'talking positive and acting negative'.

6 There are no short-term wins. In other words, the project waits for the big finish when all results are delivered at once and users are expected to keep the faith until the day of deliverance. This is what the Standish report called the old concept of developing software. Creating short-term wins means growing the solution so that a series of successes demonstrates the beneficial effect of the systems development project.

7 Declaring victory too soon. It is easy to believe that development is complete when systems testing is going well. The IT director of a well-known engineering firm regularly told his fellow directors how good the test results were and why they should accept the new system into operation. They told him about all the errors uncovered by their users' departments and enquired when all of the changes they had requested would be implemented.

8 Not cementing the changes into everyday life. Systems change should never stop. The implementation process should be pursued rigorously to make sure that all parts of the system work and that everyone can use them. This then becomes the new baseline from which the backlog of changes can be tackled before development moves on to deal with new requirements from a changing business environment.

So, how can we conclude our review of why systems projects fail? Instead of talking about failure, let us put the summary in a positive framework. Successful projects have:

- A strong business commitment to making them work. They are business and not technology driven.
- A clear, detailed scope and requirements that are agreed and enthusiastically supported by everyone concerned.
- A clear process for dealing with project changes. The project is not constantly following moving goalposts.
- Requirements that can be delivered through a series of staged products and deliverables.
- Proactive project management good at managing the client and the project team.

1.9 Summary

There is not an all-purpose, simple way to implement and manage change. Key ingredients in a change programme are to plan it properly as a subproject in its own right, to ensure that communication and training work together to reinforce the messages of the change – the benefits of the new system. Involving the users throughout, so that they manage their change rather than become victims of it, is essential. Some final pieces of advice would include:

- Treat everyone with equal respect, making an effort to understand their motivations, viewpoints and perspectives.
- Being right does not count. You need to take people with you to get their commitment, their buy-in.
- Always maintain your focus on the business benefits of the change.
- Take advice from, and use the help of, experts. You do not have to do it all yourself!

Questions

1 Figure 1.7 shows how bad an implementation can become. Action needs to be taken to prevent this kind of situation. What would you recommend should be done?

2 You are the project manager for a new management accounting system that will provide monthly profit and loss accounts to a chain of 30 computer dealerships, each of which is franchised to its local owner-manager. They have all done their own accounting before. What change issues would you expect to encounter? Does the fact that they are PC dealerships make any difference? Why might they have joined together in the chain?

3 Consider the organisation that employs you or where you study. What is its culture? Why does it have that particular culture? What organisational culture would give you most satisfaction as an employee? Where might you find such an employer? Given your preferred organisational culture, what would it mean for you as an employee in terms of your responsibilities and obligations?

4 You have to design a 'hearts and minds' programme connected with the implementation of a new system for the recording and management of stock in a book publishing company and for the supply of books to booksellers. What would be the main stages of such a programme?

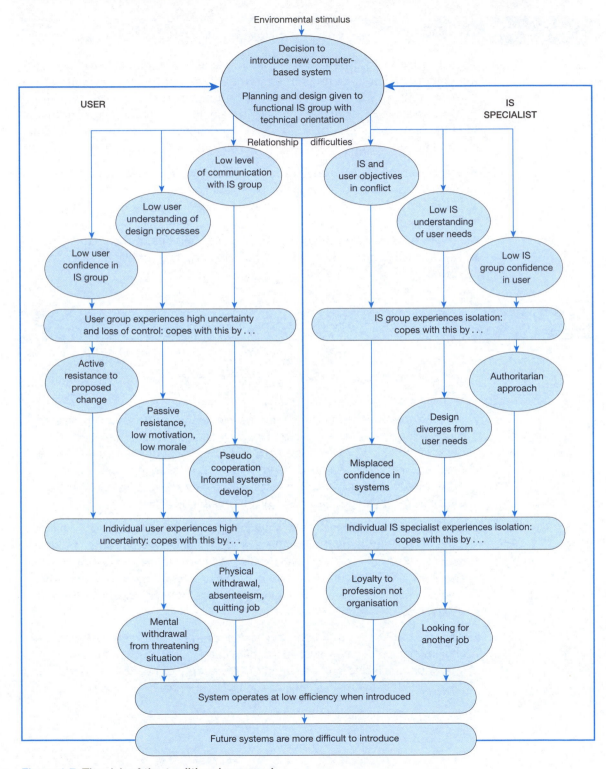

Figure 1.7 The risk of the traditional approach

Case study

Introduction

The case study running through this book illustrates how the ideas and principles set out in the text could be applied in practice to IS projects. The case study itself (and the organisations referred to within it) are fictional but it does illustrate the issues and problems that the authors have encountered or witnessed in many real-life projects.

Background

France Vacances is a UK-based travel agency that specialises in the rental of high quality self-catering accommodation in France. For the summer months, it offers a wide selection of *gîtes* (holiday cottages) and, for the winter, apartments and chalets in various ski resorts.

The company was founded by two friends who still own it, David Martin and Jean-Pierre Massenet, and has been in business since 1993. It has grown rapidly to achieve a turnover of some €6.75 million per annum and employs 85 staff at two offices, one in the Greater London area and one in France.

France Vacances currently uses two main sales channels:

- Direct selling to customers through mailshots of its brochures and customer support centres (70 per cent of sales).
- Sales via high street travel agents (30 per cent of sales).

However, the company is aware from press coverage and from surveys among its own customers that there is a growing public demand to be able to book holidays via the internet. This is particularly true as its customers are precisely the sort of people who are 'net aware'. France Vacances does have a website but this is really just its latest brochure in electronic format and it does not have links to up-to-date availability data or the facilities for customers to make secure bookings online.

Consequently, France Vacances has decided to implement a new internet-based booking system. This will be linked to its existing computerised booking system, which contains data on the availability of properties, and to its customer database as well as having secure links over which credit card data can be received. In addition, the company wants its management information system (MIS) enhanced so that it can trawl its databases and send targeted information to customers on properties that are likely to be of interest to them.

▶

Case study continued

Figure 1.8 Organisation of France Vacances

France Vacances organisation

The current organisational structure of the company is shown in Figure 1.8.

In essence, the two founders have divided the business between them. David Martin (who has a sales background) looks after the sales and operations side, and Jean-Pierre Massenet, an accountant, takes care of finance and administration.

The small IT department within the administration function consists of the IT manager, Peter Clay, three analyst/programmers and a computer operator/trainee programmer.

The project

Because of the small size of its IT department, and since the department lacks skills in the design of e-commerce applications, France Vacances has decided to entrust the development of its internet service to a consultancy company, E-Con. This firm has tendered for the following services:

■ Analysis of the requirements.
■ Production of a detailed requirements specification.
■ Design, development and implementation of the internet systems, including a new website and secure communications links.

Case study continued

- Training France Vacances staff in the use of the new systems.
- Specification of the interfaces required from France Vacances's existing customer database and booking system (the development of the links at the France Vacances end to be done by its own IT department).
- Specification of the additional hardware required to support the new system (to be obtained from France Vacances's usual suppliers, the procurement to be managed by the IT department).
- 'Skills transfer' to France Vacances's IT department, so that ongoing maintenance and development of the new system can be handled in-house. The development of the MIS aspects of the new system will be dealt with by France Vacances's IT department.

The date now is 1 April and France Vacances wants to have the new system up and running for the start of the winter season's bookings at the end of June.

Organisational issues

Imagine that you work for E-Con and that you are part of the team assigned to the project for France Vacances. Because of your special skills and experience you have to write a background paper and brief your project colleagues about France Vacances – the kind of organisation it is and its organisational culture. You also need to give your colleagues a few tips to help them to fit in with France Vacances.

What are some of the things that you would do to uncover the information to give to your colleagues and what results would you expect to find?

A useful technique to get rough-and-ready but fast information about priorities is the critical incident technique. A group of people representing the target population is asked about the topic to be investigated or about the way they would respond to specific circumstances. For example, a services company might spend 80 per cent of its training budget on technical training because it believed that it was important to be a technological leader, and 20 per cent on project management and interpersonal skills. If a critical incident survey and analysis showed that fewer than 25 per cent of the project overruns were caused by technical issues and that about 75 per cent were caused by poor sales and customer management, then the training budget should perhaps be reallocated.

In a cultural analysis context you might explore how E-Con handles success and failure, change and innovation, opportunities and threats. So what critical incidents could you pose to your group of representative France Vacances people? You would need to find ways of identifying networked, communal, mercenary or fragmented cultures if you were to use the Jones and Goffee model. This would mean exploring the extent of solidarity and sociability at France Vacances. Let us take as an example how the different

▶

Case study continued

cultures might react at pay rise time – surely a critical incident if ever there was one. Someone receives a really big rise. What does it mean and how do the different cultures react?

- Networked people either want to be in their network (a good place to be because they are obviously going places) or assume that she has pulled off a confidence trick and been unfairly rewarded (a negative response).
- Mercenary people might work harder so that they get a similar rise next time, or they might concentrate on defeating the successful person or bringing them down in some way.

Try working out for yourself how a fragmented culture (low solidarity and sociability) and a communal culture (high solidarity and sociability) might react.

Just one critical incident is not enough to tell you as much as you need to know about France Vacances's culture. You would need ten or a dozen to give you a reasonably accurate picture. Try devising some more critical incidents for success, failure, change and innovation, opportunities and threats.

Further reading

Carnall, C (1999), *Managing Change in Organisations*, 3rd edn, Prentice Hall

Connor, D (1992), *Managing at the Speed of Change*, Wiley

Goffee, R and Jones, G (2003), *The Character of a Corporation*, 2nd edition, Profile Books

Handy, C (1995), *The Gods of Management: The Changing Work of Organisations*, Arrow

Kotter, J (1996), *Leading Change*, Harvard Business School Press

Taylor, A (2000), 'IT project management: sink or swim', *Computer Bulletin*, January, British Computer Society

Turner, R J, 'Project success and strategy', *Handbook of Project Management*, 3rd edn, Gower

Various (1998), *The Harvard Business Review on Change*, Harvard Business School Press

Yardley, D (2002), *Successful IT Project Delivery*, Pearson Education

Wateridge, J H, 'IT projects: a basis for success', *International Journal of Project Management*, Vol. 13

2 Business strategy and information systems

2.1 Introduction

This chapter is all about context: the business context within which systems projects are created; how the **strategy** of an organisation determines its shape and how that shape determines the business processes and their systems. This context begins with a 'systems planning activity' that determines which projects are started according to the needs of the enterprise. The systems planning function enables business plans to be translated into developed computer systems to meet business goals. Typical business goals might be related to profit, or growth, or market share but could also focus on customer services, safety or staff development. Business goals lead to the identification of key result areas (KRAs) which specify in turn the need for new systems. Information systems management is therefore concerned with the development of new systems to contribute to the achievement of the business's key result areas. Figure 2.1 shows how this systems planning process can take place and how it can produce a range of possible systems projects.

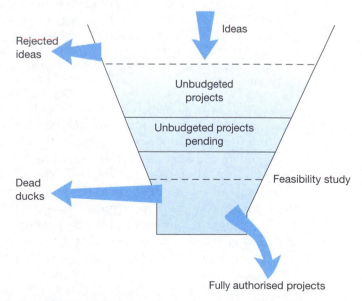

Figure 2.1 Planning for projects

We now want to look at what happens before the systems planning activity and address some of the issues around an organisation's strategy. With increasing expectations that computer people – especially analysts and project managers – will have an understanding of the wider environment within which organisations operate, it seems even more necessary to explore the wider context of how information systems fit into business strategy.

2.2 What is strategy all about?

Firstly then, what is strategy? It is not some twentieth-century idea coming out of big business or the business schools, even though big business and the business schools have taken it to their hearts. We come across the concept of strategy in the development of military strategies in the time of the ancient Greeks over 500 years BC. First of all the word described the role of the general of an army – what the general did – then it became a civilian activity, but still in a national context, where it was concerned with a system of government, and finally it moved from the military and diplomatic or government worlds into business. Secondly, strategy is not an exact science. Indeed, some writers have said that 'there is no single, universally accepted definition of strategy'. If this is true – and judging by the number of books and articles about strategy it certainly seems to be true – what can we usefully say here to give us a foundation for thinking about business strategy? We can begin with some general definitions of aspects of strategy and identify the components of an effective strategy.

James Quinn (1991) makes the following observation about strategy:

Strategy is the pattern or plan that integrates an organisation's major goals, policies and actions into a cohesive whole. In other words, it pulls together and gives meaning to everything an organisation does. A well formulated strategy helps to organise resources into a unique and viable force based on the competences and shortcomings of the organisation, on anticipated changes in the environment and activities by competitors.

In other words, strategy is the result of a careful analysis and it is purposeful; it is a plan for achieving something. The problem with strategy, though, is that it cannot be a plan for everything. How could it be possible to know all of the environmental changes that might take place in the lifetime of the strategy? How can the strategic planners know what competitors will do? Henry Mintzberg, a leading American thinker and writer about strategy, says that strategies can emerge: they are not all formulated by strategic planners in quiet offices on the top floor but are formed by events that fall into patterns that are then recognised and developed. Consistency of behaviour then becomes a strategy even though that is not how it started out. It is almost a post-event rationalisation of what looks like intuitive actions. This is why 'strategies' change and why strategic plans and the IS developments that support them get thrown out of the window and why systems projects are shut down for what seem like arbitrary or irrational reasons. 'We're killing this project, the strategy's changed.'

We might find it difficult to define 'strategy' but we know a good one when we come across it. A good strategy is:

- *Clear*. The overriding goals for all units of the enterprise are clear enough to give continuity and cohesion to all of the tactical choices made during the lifetime of the strategy. Managers can answer the question: 'Does what I do now move us towards the strategy?', and answer it correctly.
- *Keeps the initiative*. A good strategy preserves freedom of action, supports empowerment and enhances commitment. It sets the pace and determines the course of action. Consequently people feel in charge and motivated to achieve.
- *Concentrated*. A good strategy concentrates resources at the place where and the time when they will generate maximum advantage. A good strategy defines what will make the enterprise superior to its opponents and organises the resources to achieve that advantage.
- *Flexible*. This is not about changing the strategy but about being well balanced to take advantage of changes that occur. Is the opposition kept on the run by our consistent innovation?
- *Well led*. Successful strategies require commitment, not just acceptance. Good leadership is needed to turn a strategy into competitive advantage.
- *Full of surprises*. Our strategy is seeking to gain an advantage for us. We are in competition with other organisations, other ideas, other projects. We gain advantage out of proportion to the effort expended by doing the unexpected.

Just as we can recognise the criteria for a good strategy, it is possible, according to Mintzberg, to see strategy as:

- *A plan*. People talk about having 'a strategy' for this sales visit, or for this meeting or for this game. Really it is just a plan or a consciously intended course of action to deal with a situation.
- *A pattern*. This is different from a consciously intended course of action. Strategy as a pattern means that, intended or not, we consistently behave in a certain way and that leads us to formalise this pattern of behaviour into a strategy.
- *A position*. Our strategy describes how we position ourselves in our market. It therefore enables us to exclude areas of possible activity: 'Our position is here and we do this kind of thing, so we can't consider doing that'; 'We intend to be active in the public sector but not in local government'; 'Our position is that we do business analysis, project management and high-level design; even though we could do a lot of programming on this project, we don't, so we subcontract it out'.
- *A perspective*. This is really attempting to describe strategy as a set of values. Strategy in this respect is the organisation's character or culture and it means that individuals are united by common thinking or behaviour. Strategy as a perspective can easily be applied to a project team which can

create a shared vision of how the project team will behave and work together. So, in spite of the rather grand overtones that strategy formulation may have, you can use it directly on a project yourself.

2.3 Developing a strategy

Knowing about strategy is useful only if we need to understand the strategy of the organisation for which we are developing new systems. To understand that strategy, it is helpful if we are clear, at least in outline, about how strategies are developed. If we look at the stages we go through when making a decision, we first of all:

- Investigate the situation to collect as much data as we can about the facts of the case, and people's views and feelings about them.
- Then we develop some alternative courses of action based on what we know about the situation under review.
- Next we evaluate these decisions in terms of their likely outcomes and consequences.
- Then we choose the decision to be implemented on the basis of the outcomes or consequences. We take account here as well of the likely risks associated with our choice.
- Finally, we implement our decision or solution and follow it up.

We can use this simple process to help us to develop a model of strategic management. Referring to Greenley's model in Figure 2.2:

- *Analysing the environment* is concerned with investigating the internal and external environments and developing a comprehensive understanding of our business, its strengths and weaknesses, our competitors and the market within which we all operate.
- *Planning the direction* determines the future that we want for our business. We might create a vision for the kind of business we want to be, our overall philosophy for doing business and the range of activities that are to be considered. This planning might be done at the corporate level, the division level and even at lower levels.
- *Planning the strategy* is all about designing the means for going in our planned direction. It addresses the issue of how we will achieve our goal. We might have several alternative approaches and we might pursue more than one of them at the same time. Organisational structures influence decisions taken here and, equally, organisational structures may be changed to speed up moves towards the planned direction.
- *Implementing the strategy* is putting it all into action and monitoring and controlling the implementation.

There are many analytical tools to help in this strategic management process, but most are concerned with offering ways of analysing the current

Figure 2.2 **A model of strategic management**
(Gordon Greenley, *Strategic Management*, Prentice Hall, 1989)

situation of which the SWOT (strengths, weaknesses, opportunities and threats) analysis, the PESTEL analysis, the Balanced Business Scorecard and the Boston Consulting Group matrix are well known.

A **SWOT** analysis identifies the strengths, weaknesses, opportunities and threats that face an organisation. Strengths and weaknesses are an assessment of internal factors, whilst opportunities and threats are ways of defining the

Figure 2.3 **A SWOT matrix**

external environment. A SWOT matrix would show strengths and weaknesses as in Figure 2.3.

In segment A, for example, we identify those activities in which we are strong and where good opportunities exist. We are playing from our strengths into a receptive market so our strategy for these activities is to overcome external threats that may arise (because the market is attractive to others) by eliminating any weak aspects of our overall performance. In segment B we identify that we have weaknesses internally even though there are external opportunities. Without some strategic internal action to eliminate these weaknesses, the opportunities will be taken by our competitors. Segment C is the worst place for a product or service; we are weak and there are external threats from competitors or the environment. We might decide to take action to reduce both the weakness and the threat – a difficult strategy to follow – or we might choose to discontinue our product or service, or leave this market. Finally, in segment D we are strong but face external threats. A strategy here could be to use our strength to deflect the threat. It is generally not advisable to engage in unnecessary competitive battles. Overall, the strategic actions taken by an enterprise are the result of this kind of SWOT analysis and could lead to new system developments.

The **PESTEL** analysis – or **PESTLE** analysis depending on how you choose to order the constituent terms – is a popular method for examining the external factors that affect an organisation now or may affect it in the future time period within which strategic options are strategy, and the possible external trends that could be significant in the future. PESTEL is an acronym for Political, Economic, Socio-cultural, Technological, Environmental and Legal, and in considering these aspects of the external world their impact on all stakeholders is taken into account.

Political Political decisions affect all businesses. Government attitudes towards private and state-owned enterprises; international politics; the impact of conflicts and variations in the price of oil and raw material supplies are among the many factors that can alter the future performance of an organisation.

Economic Economic factors are closely related to the political influences. Interest rates and currency exchange rates will affect home and international markets. Consumer expenditure is related to inflation and the amount of disposable income present within the different economic groups within a society. This too affects long-term planning. The profitability of the organisation, its market share and the predictions about these will also influence the planning process. Decisions taken to enlarge the European Union in 2004 will have a profound impact on organisations in the joining countries and on those already part of the EU.

Socio-cultural Socio-cultural aspects may include demographic changes and the changing perceptions of the population; lifestyle changes and changes in working conditions. Education, transport and family responsibilities are all examples of social issues that can impact on an organisation. An aging population offers an opportunity to the healthcare sector yet threatens the capability of economies' welfare structures.

Technological Technological factors include the availability of new ways of delivering a service through the use of technology; the use of technology to obtain and exploit marketing information; and the ability to extend choice and communicate readily with suppliers, customers and other agencies through the use of internet technology.

Environmental Climate change and the impact of pollution come under the environmental heading. Sustainability of raw material supplies, the use of energy, regional variations of climate and the impact of the environment on the individual's lifestyle will also affect the way the organisation plans its growth.

Legal Legal issues link closely with the political, social and environmental aspects of the PESTEL analysis since the constraints that occur under these headings are enforced through law. Anti-trust and monopoly legislation can be viewed as a political issue or as a legal issue, and similarly laws aimed at the reduction of pollution may be cited as environmental issues or may appear under the legal heading. Specific legislation may impact upon an organisation on account of its location. Planning restrictions may apply to organisations in green belt areas and specific taxation legislation and controls may be applied to financial institutions.

How might all this affect a project manager's work? It can change the view that organisations have about their strategy and where they will invest. Changing the investment pattern will lead to different systems being developed, developments being given different priorities and projects being curtailed. It means that you need to be aware of the external factors affecting your organisation and how they might change IS developments so that you can inform yourself about new applications that might be useful.

Having decided on a strategy, we need to monitor our progress towards its achievement. Mostly we find that organisations' operational and management control systems are built around the achievement of financial targets and, whilst this is essential, it is not enough to give a complete picture. Accounting measures show how well an organisation has invested in physical assets such as plant, machinery, stock and so on, and how well these assets have been managed, but do not address the ability to exploit intangible assets such as customer loyalty, people skills, innovation and so on. Consequently, in 1992, Robert Kaplan and David Norton proposed a solution to this dilemma in the *Harvard Business Review*. This solution was the Balanced Scorecard – now often called the **Balanced Business Scorecard**. Kaplan and Norton described it as supplementing 'traditional financial measures with criteria that measured performance from three additional perspectives – those of customers, internal business processes, and learning and growth.' They said that the balanced scorecard

> retains traditional financial measures. But financial measures tell the story of past events, an adequate story for industrial age companies for which investments in long term capabilities and customer relationships were not critical for success. These financial measures are inadequate, however, for guiding and evaluating the journey that information age companies must make to create future value through investment in customers, suppliers, employees, processes, technology, and innovation.

The three views the Balanced Business Scorecard gives of an organisation, in addition to the financial view, are the customer perspective, the internal business perspective and the employee perspective. Each of them has goals and measured achievements. For example:

- The customer perspective looks at how customers see the organisation. The measures might include growth in market share, customer profitability, response and delivery times, defect rates and so on. Customers are surveyed to find out what it is like to be a customer of our organisation. Are we achieving our service levels, are we responsive, do we have a 'can do' attitude, are we positive in the advice we give?
- The internal business perspective looks at how well our business is running. How efficient are we at creating new courses to meet client demands? Is there always confusion about getting the notes, handouts, visuals, exercises and lecturers in the same – and right – place at the same time? What processes must work excellently if we are to exceed our customers' expectations?
- The employee perspective – often called the 'learning and growth' or 'organisational growth' perspective – is the foundation for working smarter and not harder. It is about the constant development of employees and is much more than just training. It includes the provision of learning support mechanisms – human and technological – mentors and e-learning and the ease

Figure 2.4 **The BCG matrix**

with which individuals can communicate and cooperate with each other to meet new customer demands.

Having carried out various strategic analyses, there will be a need to evaluate the organisation's current product and service offerings. The Boston Consulting Group (BCG) analysis technique is one tool for doing this. It models the relationship between a product or service's current and future potential and how management wants to deal with it. It is therefore a marketing analysis tool, with market growth along one axis and market share along the other, and it shows the products that are cash generators and cash consumers. Each of these will need to be managed differently and supported by different kinds of systems. Figure 2.4 shows how the BCG matrix works.

Wild Cats are the potential good businesses of the future. They are usually new products or services with a low market share but with a high potential for growth. *Stars* are the products that are profitable now and are expected to do well in the future. They are market leader products in growth markets needing investment to keep them there. It is hoped that as many Wild Cats as possible will become Stars. It is likely that organisations will invest in new systems for Stars. *Cash Cows* are the current high income earners. They provide the majority of current profit and are a source of investment funding for Wild Cats and Stars. They are not expected to provide significant future revenues, and investment in information systems will be around increasing the profit – by greater cost control perhaps – or by increasing their market share so that the Cash Cow can move back to becoming a Star. Finally, the *Dogs* are those products and services that make little or no contribution to today's profits and are not expected to make much contribution in the future. These are typically products that have lost market share to competitors or are in declining markets.

There is, then, a process for the development and implementation of business strategy, and a range of tools and methods to help in this process from which come the different types of systems projects that project managers are required to develop. We cannot, however, leave this overview of business strategy analysis without considering the influence of Michael Porter's work and the impact that this has on IS development.

2.4   Competition and strategy

Porter's view is that, 'the essence of strategy formulation is dealing with competition'. He sees the competitive world as a violent environment within which the business position of an organisation is determined by five forces acting on it. Porter's **five forces model** is shown in Figure 2.5. The first force is the *rivalry* between existing competitors. This rivalry can be intense if there are many organisations of a similar size and there is often fierce price competition. We saw just this situation in the UK in 1995 with *The Times*, the *Daily Telegraph* and the *Independent* all fighting each other for market share and making aggressive price changes in the process.

- *New entrants* also pose a threat. If the marketplace looks good and competition is weak, new entrants will want to enter the market. The seriousness of the threat they pose depends on the barriers that prevent them from joining, their determination to get over those barriers and the potential retaliation from the existing competitors in the marketplace.
- *Substitute products or services* also threaten the existing competition. The advent of the word processor and then the powerful word-processing packages on the latest-technology personal computers wiped out the typewriter industry. Technological change is often the driving force behind the arrival of substitute products.
- *Suppliers* can exert pressure on participants in an industry by reducing the supply of the product and by increasing prices. Suppliers are powerful if there are few of them and if they are bigger and stronger than the enterprises in the industry to which they sell.
- *Buyers* can also influence competition if they purchase in large volumes. We see this particularly with large supermarket chains and major retailers such as Marks and Spencer which are able to put competitive pressure on the suppliers competing for their business.

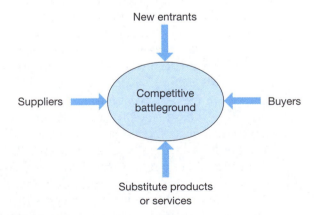

Figure 2.5 Porter's five forces model

(Michael Porter, *Competitive Strategy: Techniques for Analyzing Industry and Competitors*, The Free Press, 1970)

Figure 2.6 Robson's analysis of the five forces and IS opportunities

(W Robson, *Strategic Management and Information Systems*, 2nd edn, Prentice Hall, 1997)

This five forces model of industry competitiveness offers a way of asking general questions about the role that information systems could play in generating competitive advantage. Wendy Robson has modified Porter's five forces model to show the opportunities for information systems. This is shown in Figure 2.6. The Porter analysis would identify the major threats and then an analysis could be made of how information systems could be used to minimise these threats. For the Royal Bank of Scotland, the use of ISs to support the Direct Line insurance business enabled the bank to generate new products and services. For the UK's supermarket giants, the Tesco Clubcard and equivalent products elsewhere use information systems to increase the cost to the customer of switching to a rival.

Taking the Porter analysis further, Robson identified three generic business strategies to respond to the five competitive forces:

- To go for a low-cost strategy and seek to be the overall cost leader and use ISs to reduce overall costs.
- To distinguish or differentiate products and services from the competition's offerings and aim to use ISs to enhance this differentiation and add additional features to the product or service.
- To concentrate on a particular market segment and to use IS to identify and support activity in these market segments or niches.

Robson also lists the IS applications that might support low-cost and differentiation strategies. In pursuit of a low-cost strategy in manufacturing we might see process control system applications, stock planning and stock control. In sales and marketing, there could be applications to prioritise calls and to track advertising and sales promotion activities; and in finance there might be applications for planning and budgeting and for controlling costs. For businesses following a differentiation strategy, the manufacturing area might support total quality management systems; in sales there could be order entry systems, order query systems and total customer care systems. In finance there could be office automation and business integration systems. Strategic direction therefore directly influences application development.

Finally in this section, what of generic IS strategies for organisations? Gregory Parsons offers six strategies for the development of information systems in organisations. These are:

1 *Centrally planned* – where the planning cycles for business and IS are closely linked and where IS strategy is embedded in the planning of the business strategy. The IS function is a service provider and closely linked to the users it serves. We might regard this as an ideal model where it would be a pleasure to manage the development of IS projects.

2 *Leading edge* – where there is a belief that innovative technology can create organisational gains and that risky investment can generate big paybacks. The IS function is therefore the promoter of new ideas and technologies, always watching technological developments – but never realising the benefits perhaps?

3 *A free market* – where users make the decisions since they are the ones who have to live with the results and deliver the profits. The role here for the IS department is to behave as a competitive business unit – perhaps even a profit centre – achieving its financial targets through charging its users and relying on its knowledge of the business to give it an edge over external competitors. This has proved to be a popular strategy in the 1980s and early 1990s as companies reorganised themselves into flatter structures with greater autonomy. However, it can also be seen as a move by top management to distance itself from the IS function by simply following the rule of 'if they balance their books and there's outside competition, everything is bound to be all right; we'll get a good deal'. There is unlikely to be a long-term corporate plan or use for IT, and the IS department may well find itself outsourced.

4 *Monopoly* – the opposite to free trade. This strategy for IS development is founded on the belief that information is a corporate asset that should be available across the whole company and that this will happen only if there is a single supply source that everyone is obliged to use. The danger for the IS department is that it becomes slow-moving and unresponsive to customers, concentrating on the delivery of large, integrated systems that take a long time to deliver, by which time users' needs may have changed.

5 *Scarce resource* – where the scope of the IS function is deliberately limited by budget constraints and users' projects compete for service from the scarce resources using strict cost/benefit criteria. This strategy has a negative impact on the development of information as a resource.

6 *Necessary evil* – where organisations see the development of ISs as a necessary evil and believe that information is not important to their business. The IT department's role is to provide a minimum level of resources and skill: not an attractive place to work.

Reviewing competitive strategies, and the IS applications that may result from them and the overall profile of the IS department itself, will give you an overview of the climate for development of information systems in the organisation, and of the context in which your project should be managed and in which it will be evaluated.

<table>
<tr><td>2.5</td><td>Strategy and culture</td></tr>
</table>

2.5 Strategy and culture

Although we have recognised that the development of business strategy and information systems is an imprecise science, this chapter has nonetheless depicted the activity as scientific rather than emotional. In this final section we want to redress this balance by addressing some strategic human issues that influence the way organisations are structured and managed and consequently influence how projects could best be managed in these environments. Later in the book, in Chapter 20, we consider the leadership role of the project manager; here we are concentrating on the context for leadership.

We begin by considering how strategy interacts with the way an organisation is structured, the systems it has and the style in which it operates: in other words, how strategy and systems link with organisational culture. The best way to do this is through an examination of the 7-S model developed by McKinsey, the management consulting firm. The 7-S model proposes that there are other factors in addition to strategy that make an organisation effective. It may be that strategy is not the most important. In order to achieve better performance – and that is why we have new systems developed – organisational change depends on the relationship and interactions between:

1 Strategy
2 Structure
3 Systems
4 Style
5 Skills
6 Staff
7 Shared values.

In this McKinsey model, *strategy* is the action that an organisation takes based on its assessment of the environment which it defines as its customers and its competitors. Its strategy defines how it aims to improve its position against its competition. Clear ideas about strategy can enable organisation *structures* to be created that in turn enable the strategy: a strategy of diversity may call for a decentralised structure for example. The model warns, however, that setting the structures that fit the strategy is not the only thing that has to be done. To understand how an organisation really works, you have to look at the *systems*. These are the things that keep the organisation going, day by day. Organisations can be changed by changing the systems without disruptive restructuring. A strategy to become more customer oriented can be implemented much more easily by discussing customers and markets at management meetings – and taking follow-up action – than by trying to reorganise the structure and create new marketing departments. How does *style* fit into all of this? We should recognise the importance of management style and the power that it has in shaping the strategy and culture of an organisation. How managers spend their time shows what they think is important; is it poring over figures or out with customers? All of the strategy, structure, systems and style in the world will not deliver the results without people and without the fifth S – *skills*, which here means the dominating attributes or capabilities of the organisation. In the *staff* dimension we can talk about recruitment, appraisal, pay scales, etc. and we can talk about morale, motivation, attitude, commitment, etc. Often, top management is reluctant to get involved with these issues, yet top-performing companies pay extraordinary attention to managing the development and progress of tomorrow's managers. The final S is *shared values*. These are the guiding concepts, the values and aspirations that make us want to work here, that give meaning to what we do.

You will have seen that four of the variables of an effective organisation are soft, informal variables – systems, style, skills and shared values. Each of them plays a powerful part in determining organisational success and, taking the project as an organisation, each lies in the gift of the project manager. Taken together they establish the culture of the organisation and are the elements that make project staff want to work for you again.

Let us finish this chapter, then, with some summarised ideas about organisational culture. An organisation's culture is an important feature of its life. You may well have experienced cultural differences yourself between one organisation and others. Do you think that Marks and Spencer's culture is different from Dixon's? Is BT's culture different from that of NTL or of Orange? In working with different organisations, knowing just the technical aspects of the new job will not be enough. Charles Handy (1995) has suggested that cultures are deep phenomena in organisations:

> In organisations, there are deep-set beliefs about the way work should be organised, the way authority should be exercised, people rewarded, people controlled. What are the degrees of formalism required? How much planning and how far ahead? What combination of obedience and initiative is looked for in subordinates? Do work hours matter, or dress, or personal eccentricities? Do committees control an individual? Are there rules and procedures or only results? These are all part of the culture of an organisation.

What is this thing called organisational culture? It reflects the underlying assumptions about the way work is done, what is acceptable and what is not; what behaviours and actions are encouraged and discouraged. It is often thought to be the part of the organisational iceberg that lies beneath the surface and to consist of unwritten rules. More and more organisations are, however, writing down these unwritten rules and we recommend that your project does the same. Your project's mission will be well known to everyone: to achieve some deliverables within a time and within a budget. But does your team know the spirit with which you want them to work, do they see your vision, do they share it, for how you want your project to feel? It is not only captains of industry who need to give a vision; leaders at all levels need to do it. There is more about this in the leadership chapter later.

2.6 Summary

In this chapter we have been addressing the topic of business strategy and how it is linked to IS strategy.

Regarding the nature of business strategy and the characteristics of a good strategy, we saw that strategies can be created from the top down, but they can also emerge.

There are tools to help in the analysis of business, which is the starting point for the development of a strategy. The SWOT analysis, the PESTEL analysis and the Balanced Business Scorecard, the Boston Consulting Group matrix and Porter's five forces tools were described. This led into a review of strategies for the development of IS functions and the impact of organisational culture on strategy.

Questions

1 Why is it important for project managers to understand the strategy of the organisation that uses their services?

2 If you knew about an organisation's strategy, could you suggest IS applications that would support it? For example, how could a large supermarket chain use information systems for cost reduction, or for a strategy based on differentiation?

3 If you had to develop a strategy for a small software house employing 50 or so computer professionals, how would you go about it? What criteria would you use to test whether or not the strategy was sound?

Case study

The internet booking project is a result of a recent strategic review of France Vacances undertaken by its senior managers – the two directors and their direct reports.

The SWOT analysis showed that France Vacances has a good reputation in its marketplace and a lot of 'brand recognition' by its target market. However, this target market (reasonably affluent professionals) does make extensive use of the internet and it was felt that being unable to offer this service would increasingly become a weakness. At least one of France Vacances's competitors already has an internet booking service (albeit not a very good one) and others are sure to follow in the near future.

Applying the internet to France Vacances's position using Porter's five forces model also produced some interesting results. The internet tends to

Case study continued

increase the power of buyers (as they can shop around more easily) and lowers the cost of entry for new competitors. In addition, the suppliers (the owners of the *gîtes* and chalets) can also set up their own websites, thereby cutting out brokers like France Vacances and increasing their own relative power.

The conclusion of the strategy review was, therefore, that not setting up an internet service was not a viable option. Also, since the competitors' sites were not very good at present, it was felt that creating a very good and user-friendly site would provide a source of competitive advantage (at least in the short to medium term).

Further reading

Handy, C (1995), *The Gods of Management: The Changing Work of Organisation*, Arrow

Greenley, G R (1989), *Strategic Management*, Prentice Hall

Kaplan, R and Norton, D (1992), 'The Balanced Business Scorecard', *Harvard Business Review*, Jan/Feb

Kaplan, R and Norton, D (1996), 'Using the Balanced Scorecard as a strategic management system, *Harvard Business Review*, Jan/Feb

Mintzberg, H (1987), 'Five Ps for strategy', *California Management Review*, Fall, reprinted in *The Strategy Process* (1991), Prentice Hall

Parsons, G (1983), *Fitting Information Technology to the Corporate Needs: The Linking Strategy*, Harvard Business School Press

Porter, M (1979), 'How competitive forces shape strategy', *Harvard Business Review*, March/April, reprinted in *The Strategy Process* (1991), Prentice Hall

Quinn, J B (1991), 'Strategies for change', in *The Strategy Process*, 2nd edn, Prentice Hall

Robson, W (1997), *Strategic Management and Information Systems*, 2nd edn, Prentice Hall

3 The business case

3.1 Introduction

No project should be undertaken without first establishing a business case for it – without, in other words, showing that it is justified. The business case defines what is to be done, why, and what are the timescales and costs involved.

Whether the project manager is involved in creating the business case depends on the organisation concerned. In some organisations, the project manager is appointed early in the lifecycle and so would have a major input to, even if not total responsibility for, the business case. In other situations the project manager may be appointed only after the business case has been approved and the project has got the go-ahead. However, in either situation, project managers need to have a good understanding of what goes into a business case, as, once the project starts, they will have a major influence on whether the business objectives are achieved and these will be used by stakeholders to measure success. At some time or other, most project managers are asked either to provide input to, or to review, business cases.

Once a project is under way, its progress should be measured against the business case to make sure, for example, that costs or timescales are not being exceeded or that business benefits are not being eroded. The business case thus provides the base for business-level monitoring and control and, ultimately, for assessing whether the project was worth undertaking at all.

3.2 Content and format of a business case

The format of business cases varies quite widely between organisations. Some like to have multi-volume documents, with all the facts and figures carefully recorded, whereas in other organisations a single-page format is mandated. (Although the latter may seem a rather cavalier approach to what can be major business decisions, it should be borne in mind that the only people who can make such decisions are usually (a) very senior and (b) extremely busy and hence do not have the time to wade through vast business case documents. Such people need the basics presented simply, briefly and clearly. If a large document is unavoidable, then even more attention has to be paid to the management summary, of which more shortly.)

If the format varies widely, the content of a business case is rather more predictable and, in the sections that follow, we outline the major elements that are needed in all business cases.

3.2.1 Introduction and background

Usually, a business case opens with a short introduction setting out what the document is about and sketching any background to the proposed project. This may refer to previous work, particularly if a feasibility study has been undertaken to establish the prima facie case for the project.

3.2.2 Management summary

In many respects, the management summary is the most important part of the business case. As we have already seen, the people who can make important business decisions are usually very busy and so the management summary is the first part of the business case they will turn to – and perhaps the only part of it that they will read properly. So, it is vital to make the management summary sharp, punchy and clear.

We have seen so-called management summaries that ramble on for dozens of pages and we have wondered who the writers think will read it all. Although not always practical, the ideal management summary would have three paragraphs only:

- A statement of what is the problem or opportunity that the project is intended to address.
- A résumé of the options considered and why those not chosen have not been recommended.
- A statement showing which option has been recommended, why, and what business benefits are expected to flow from it.

Although this ideal cannot always be achieved, every effort should be made to give the management summary as much impact as possible, so as to allow the decision-makers both to see clearly what decision they are being asked to make and to understand the consequences.

3.2.3 Description of problem or opportunity

There should be a description of the problem that the project is designed to solve or the opportunity it should address. Although enough detail needs to be provided to enable the decision-makers to see what is the point of the project, brevity is again the ideal here. Often, decision-makers complain that they have to read dozens (or hundreds!) of pages that tell them what they know already.

3.2.4 Options available and considered

In most cases, there are various options that could be proposed to deal with the problem or opportunity – including, of course, that of doing nothing at all.

Those that are not to be recommended should be described briefly and the reasons for rejecting them should be made clear. The option that is to be recommended should be described in more detail, to allow the readers to see what exactly is being proposed.

Often, there will be sub-options as well. There may be a basic option, which deals only with the most pressing issues or, in the case of a computer system, provides the most important functionality, and then there will be additional options that offer enhanced features or facilities.

3.2.5 Cost/benefit analysis

The **cost/benefit analysis** part of the business case presents a description and, where possible, a quantification of the costs of carrying out the project and of the benefits that are expected to flow from it. As Figure 3.1 indicates, costs and benefits are often presented as a 'balance'. In addition, costs and benefits are:

- Tangible (which means they can be plausibly quantified in some way) or intangible (which means that they cannot be so quantified), and
- Incurred/enjoyed immediately or in the longer term.

Many business cases fail because of the careless treatment of intangible benefits. For example, having 'better management information' will obviously be of benefit, but how much is it actually worth? Putting spurious valuations on what are, in fact, unquantifiable benefits often leads to their being questioned by the decision-makers and may also lead to doubt about some of the more justifiable benefits claimed. With intangible benefits it is usually better to explain what they are and to let the decision-makers place their own valuation on them.

Getting reliable information on costs and benefits can be challenging, and input from the organisation's management accountants is invaluable here. Costs for elements such as new hardware or packaged software are usually not too difficult to obtain, but some sort of preliminary project plan may be needed for the costs of systems development work.

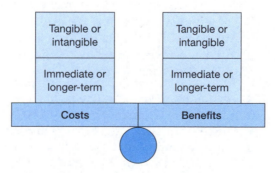

Figure 3.1 Costs and benefits

43

3.2.6 Impacts and risks

Impacts may have costs associated with them but they also include hard-to-quantify things like the need to adopt a different management culture or to manage suppliers in a different way. Impacts, in short, are changes in the way an organisation thinks and acts and are worth spelling out in a business case so that the decision-makers can judge whether the proposed changes are feasible or not.

All projects involve risk of some sort and the subject of risk management is covered in detail in Chapter 15. In a business case, an outline of the principal risks associated with the recommended option (and also, perhaps, of doing nothing), together with the proposed measures for either avoiding or mitigating them, will raise the confidence of the decision-makers that the proposal has been thought through properly.

3.2.7 Conclusions and recommendations

Finally, the recommended way forward should be described and the decision that is needed should be set out clearly.

3.2.8 Other possible inclusions

The sections above describe the basic elements of a business case. However, the PRINCE2® project management method suggests that an outline project plan should also be included to enable the decision-makers to see when and how the project would be implemented if approved. This is a good idea if a credible plan can be generated at this early stage.

3.3 Investment appraisal

Various methods are used to assess the financial implications of a business case and fuller information on these can be found in many textbooks on accountancy. However, we outline here three of the most popular methods: payback, discounted cash flow and internal rate of return.

The simplest approach is to calculate the *payback*, and the technique is best illustrated by an example. Let us suppose that we are trying to justify a project to install a new computer system that will completely eliminate some clerical jobs. The basic facts are these:

- The hardware will cost £500,000.
- Hardware maintenance will cost £50,000 per annum.
- The software will cost £180,000 initially.
- Software support will cost £20,000 per annum.
- We expect to save 11 junior clerical posts which, with overhead costs included, are worth £20,000 each per annum (£220,000 per annum overall).

Table 3.1 Payback projection

Item	Year 1	Year 2	Year 3	Year 4	Year 5
Hardware purchase	500,000				
Hardware maintenance	50,000	50,000	50,000	50,000	50,000
Software purchase	180,000				
Software support	20,000	20,000	20,000	20,000	20,000
Cumulative total costs	750,000	820,000	890,000	960,000	1,030,000
Staff savings per year	220,000	220,000	220,000	220,000	220,000
Cumulative savings	220,000	440,000	660,000	880,000	1,100,000
Cumulative savings less costs	−530,000	−380,000	−230,000	−80,000	+70,000

The payback projection for the project is shown in Table 3.1. We can see from the table that in the first four years the costs of the project outweigh the savings but that, from year 5 onwards, the project is cost-justified.

The problem with a payback calculation, however, is that it takes no real account of what is termed the *time value of money*. What this means is that £100 spent today will cost more, taking inflation into account and the rate of return that it could have earned if invested, than the same sum spent in five years' time. In investment appraisals therefore, especially when comparing the merits of competing projects, it is desirable to use some method of calculation that takes account not only of how much is paid out and received but of exactly when these inward and outward cash flows occur. A technique that addresses the time value of money is **discounted cash flow** (DCF) and this produces a **net present value** (NPV) for the project. The NPV takes into account the cost of borrowing the money needed to finance a project or, alternatively, the interest forgone by investing in the project; in other words it reflects what else could have been done with the money. Applying this method to the example will make the situation clearer.

The net cash flows for our project are as follows:

Year 1	−530,000
Year 2	+150,000
Year 3	+150,000
Year 4	+150,000
Year 5	+150,000

The NPV calculation uses tables of discount factors, which depend upon the interest rates currently being used. If the discount rate is 20 per cent (that is, we would have to pay 20 per cent interest for the money being used on the project), then the discount factors to be applied for years 2 to 5 are 0.833, 0.694, 0.579 and 0.482. Using these factors, the calculation of net present value is:

$$-530,000 + (0.833 \times 150,000) + (0.694 \times 150,000) + (0.579 \times 150,000) + (0.482 \times 150,000) = -£141,800$$

The general convention is that a project is justified if it produces a positive NPV. On this basis, our project cannot be recommended. Now this is a rather different result from that given by our simple payback calculation and illustrates why a DCF calculation is desirable. In our simple payback example, it appeared that our project was cost-justified, albeit that we had to wait five years for a positive result. But the NPV calculation indicates that there are probably better things that could be done with the funds needed to invest in the project. The result of the NPV calculation does rather depend on the period over which it is made; if the example had been calculated over eight years instead of five, it would have shown a positive NPV of £41,850. But every organisation will have some rules about the length of time over which an investment must be justified, and five years is a typical period.

Sensitivity analysis can be applied to DCF/NPV calculations to see what would be the effect of using different discount rates. In our example, using a discount rate of 15 per cent produces a net present value of –£101,600 and a discount rate of 10 per cent would have given an NPV of –£54,650. So, it appears that the negative result for this project is relatively insensitive to rather large changes in interest rates.

Of course, not all projects are justified solely on grounds of cost. Installing an expensive scanner in a hospital, for example, would probably be justified in terms of the improvements in patient care that could be made with it. Even so, the NPV calculation does enable the decision-makers to see the true financial costs of their decisions.

The third measure, **internal rate of return** (IRR), in effect stands the DCF/NPV calculation on its head and asks 'what discount rate would we have to use so that costs and benefits precisely balance out over the defined assessment period?' There is no formula for calculating IRR and it has to be found by trial and error, usually using a computer spreadsheet: One tries different discount rates until an NPV of zero is achieved and, in our example project, the IRR is 5.136 per cent. Managers like IRR because it gives a simple, single number that can be used to compare different projects to see which ones are most worth investing in. So, all other things being equal, a project with an IRR of 10 per cent would be better than one with an IRR of 5 per cent. However, all other things are seldom equal and a problem with IRR is that it does not take into account the sheer size of the competing projects. For this reason, the accounting textbooks seem to agree that DCF/NPV is the better measure to use, whilst acknowledging that many managers like to use IRR.

3.4 Presenting the business case

Once the components of the business case have been assembled, they need to be offered to the decision-makers in an attractive and persuasive way, in the form of some sort of written document often supported by a formal presentation.

Thinking first about the report, a simple four-part formula is to consider the following issues:

- *Aim*. What decision needs to be made?
- *Audience*. Who are the decision-makers and what are they interested in? Some people are captured by a grand vision and others by the careful accumulation of facts and figures, and it is important to understand which category (or categories) the decision-makers fall into.
- *Arrangement*. Using a logical order to present the materials, probably following the order given in section 3.2 above.
- *Appearance*. The decision-makers have to be induced to read the document and it must be easy for them to find what they are looking for. Therefore avoid lots of densely packed text and try to have plenty of white space and diagrams (ideally in colour).

If giving a presentation, remember that a presentation is usually a supplement to a written report, not a substitute for it. The format of the presentation should follow that of the management summary: describe the problem, outline the options, present and 'sell' the proposed solution. The presenter(s) should select the main points to present but have the full 'chapter and verse' available to answer questions and to enlarge on topics if requested.

3.5 Benefits realisation and management

In recent years, there has been growing interest in the subjects of **benefits realisation** and **benefits management**. The reasons for this are not hard to find: too many projects have been completed without the expected benefits being achieved. Benefits realisation and benefits management aim to manage the project in such a way as to maximise the chance of the benefits being achieved.

Figure 3.2 provides an example of a basic benefits realisation and management process.

The key to any benefits realisation effort is the business case as this is where the benefits have been identified and, where possible, quantified. From the business case, a set of criteria should be developed against which the achievement of the benefits will be measured.

Once the project is under way, one of the key control criteria applied by the project sponsor or project board (see Chapter 4) should be 'is this project on target to achieve the business benefits?' Any projected overrun of cost or timescales could jeopardise these benefits, as could changes in the scope, so the baseline established by the business case should be used to evaluate any such alterations in the project's planned progress.

Once the project has been completed, and perhaps after a sufficient interval has elapsed to allow the new systems to bed down, a formal review should be carried out to see if the expected benefits have been realised. This will have to

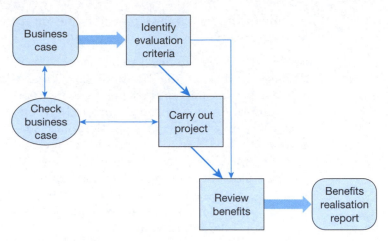

Figure 3.2 Benefits realisation and management

use the original business case as its starting point and will have to take into account any changes in the business climate that may have affected the ability of the project to deliver the business benefits. The purpose of the review is to ensure that lessons are learned that can benefit future projects.

3.6 Summary

The compilation of a business case is essential before any project is undertaken as it will define the scope of the project in broad terms and establish what are the costs and benefits of undertaking it. Ideally, the project manager should be involved in preparing the business case, or at least should have significant input to it. The business case provides a baseline against which possible changes to the scope or direction of the project can be evaluated and decided on.

Questions

1 At what point in the project lifecycle should the business case be prepared?

2 What should be the role of the project manager in relation to the business case?

3 Explain the term 'cost/benefit analysis'.

4 What do you understand by the terms 'tangible' and 'intangible' when applied to costs and benefits?

5 What is meant by the term 'benefits realisation' and why is it important?

Case study

The SWOT analysis conducted by France Vacances has already shown that not having an internet service is not a viable scenario, since so many of the company's customers now regularly use the internet. However, the issue still arises as to how much it would be worth investing in the project, and this means that the company has had to develop a business case for undertaking the internet development.

Jean-Pierre Massenet, as the accountant, has undertaken production of the business case and he has identified three main business options that could be considered:

1 Building an internet booking system for France Vacances and interfacing that with the company's existing systems.
2 Building a standalone internet system and operating the internet booking as, in effect, a separate subsidiary business.
3 Finding a partner organisation with an internet booking system and interfacing France Vacances's system with that.

The third option is unattractive as the customers of the booking system would not be France Vacances's own and this is considered very important. Massenet also rejected the second option as it is likely that the company's customers would sometimes use the internet and sometimes book over the telephone and having two sales channels would go against the principle of being a 'one-stop shop' for all the customers' requirements.

Consequently, the business case has been built around the first option, adding a web-based booking front-end to the existing booking system.

Massenet has used France Vacances's salesforce to conduct a telephone survey of existing customers, and that has suggested that an additional €50,000 of business might be secured each year via the internet. Assessing the likely amount of additional business (from new customers) is more difficult but a recent travel industry survey concluded that firms could attract 10–15 per cent new customers through e-commerce. If true, this would mean that France Vacances could obtain between €68,000 and €100,000 per annum more business through web bookings, but the directors, wishing to be cautious, have opted for the lower figure. In total, then, it seems as if the internet booking system should secure an additional €118,000 worth of business annually. The directors want to break even on their investment in three years and so this suggests a maximum cost for the internet development of €354,000. Initial discussions with various potential software vendors, including their preferred partner E-Con, suggest that a system could be developed for €350,000. On that basis, the directors approve the business case.

Further reading

Boardman, Anthony E, Greenberg, David H, Vining, Aidan R and Weimer, David L (2001), *Cost–Benefit Analysis: Concepts and Practice*, 2nd edn, Prentice Hall

Remenyi, Dan, Money, Arthur, Sherwood-Smith, Michael with Irani, Zahir (2000), *The Effective Management and Measurement of IT Costs and Benefits*, 2nd edn, Butterworth-Heinemann

Various (1999), *Harvard Business Review on the Business Value of IT*, Harvard Business School Press

4 The organisational framework

4.1 Introduction

This chapter considers the organisational structure for project work and also examines various types of organisation within which a project may take place. It discusses the framework which is needed around the project if it is to be a success. It is vital that this framework is established at the outset and well understood by all concerned since otherwise it will be impossible to get important decisions made and adhered to. Too many projects have set out with no clear idea of who the customer is and who is empowered to take these important decisions, and a project which starts in this way is bound to encounter severe difficulties along the way even if it does not end in total disaster.

Consider this scenario. The IT director of a retail business engaged a systems consultancy to study the company's current systems and develop proposals for a new, integrated system that would enable the firm to manage its resources better and respond to changing market conditions. The IT director reported to a main board member who was not interested in IT matters. For the purposes of the project, another senior director was to act as the main user. Who was the customer in this scenario? The IT director? The main board member? The retail director? All of them? This lack of clarity bedevilled the whole project and meant that the consultants were unable to secure agreement on either the business or the technical requirements of the new system.

Consider another scenario, from the public sector this time. A public utility wished to introduce a corporate personnel system. The driving force behind this was the management services director, who held the budget. But each of the various personnel managers in the organisation had a different view on what the system should do. It proved impossible to get consensus on a requirements specification, so eventually a package was bought which at least delivered something in a measurable timescale. The organisation then spent the next five years, and a great deal of money, trying to adapt the package to meet its real requirements. Who was the customer here? The management services director? The personnel managers?

These two examples show why establishing a sound organisational framework is so important. In this chapter, we consider organisation from a general perspective and then look at the structure offered by the PRINCE2® project management method.

Figure 4.1 Functional organisation structure

4.2 Introduction to organisation structures

Here, we shall examine some of the main organisation structures that may be encountered and explain how these relate to – and sometimes clash with – project organisations.

Functional organisation

A **functional structure** is the most basic and probably the most common form of organisation that is encountered, and a simple example is shown in Figure 4.1.

In essence, with a functional structure, the organisation is divided into a number of departments, each specialising in one aspect of the business. Our example involves a manufacturer of computer printers which has a marketing department, departments focusing on mechanical, electrical, chemical and software engineering, a production facility and a procurement (purchasing) department.

The advantage of functional organisations is that they encourage the development of a high degree of specialist skills. Also, people in the functions report to managers who understand their fields and can provide relevant advice, guidance and support. However, a great problem with functional organisations is that people can develop a 'silo' mentality – being more concerned with departmental objectives than with the needs of the organisation as a whole.

'Pure' project organisations

One answer to the 'silo' problem of functional organisations is to set up projects to carry out specific tasks, drawing team members from across the functions. Once the project is over, everyone goes back to their 'home' departments (or perhaps on to another project). An example of such a structure is given in Figure 4.2.

Figure 4.2 shows a team set up by our printer manufacturer to develop a new product, and it has representation from all the main functions. The great advantage of the **project structure** is focus: everyone on the team is there for one purpose, to carry out the project. However, there are some problems as well, not least that the team members may get out of touch with what is going

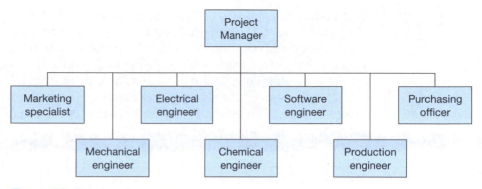

Figure 4.2 'Pure' project structure

on in their 'home' departments, including important and useful technical developments. In addition, functional managers may feel that they have little control or influence over what project teams are doing and this makes it difficult to impose functional policies across an organisation. But perhaps the biggest problem with 'pure' project teams is that they can be rather inefficient in their use of resources, especially people. For example, it may be that the main issues to be addressed for the new printer are mechanical and electrical, and there is little for the chemical and software engineers to do. If this is repeated across the whole organisation, there may be a lot of people sitting around without full-time jobs.

Matrix organisations A **matrix organisation** attempts to balance the benefits of the functional and the pure project structures, and an example is shown in Figure 4.3.

With a matrix organisation, people have more than one boss. In our example, they report to the head of their function (as far as professional issues

Figure 4.3 Matrix structure

are concerned) and also to a project manager for project-related issues. We can see that project A requires full-time mechanical and electrical engineers but only half-time commitment from other team members. Project B (which has been set up to iron out some software and production issues relating to an existing product) does not require all functions to be involved.

The matrix structure is clearly more resource-efficient than the pure project since resources can be shared between projects. Also, functional managers can have some input to projects since it is 'their' staff that work on them. But managing their time can prove a major headache for people in matrix structures, since they may have several bosses, with conflicting deadlines, pulling them this way and that.

Organisational issues for project managers The starting point for project managers must be to understand the organisational structures within which they are working. Have they been given a dedicated project team or is there a matrix structure, where they must share resources with others? Is the project being run from one function, with others providing input on an 'as needs' basis (in which case, adapting some of the supplier management approaches discussed in Chapter 19 may be appropriate)? If there is a matrix structure, the project manager must realise that team members will have commitments other than to this project – and he or she may have to negotiate with other project managers to agree what proportion of a person's time they can have, and when. If there is a dedicated project team, it may be seen as elitist or outside the normal organisation and hence be resented, in which case the project manager must make positive efforts to sell the project within the organisation. Finally, as the project nears its conclusion, team members will be nervous about what happens to them afterwards and the project manager must take steps to reassure them and to find them satisfactory follow-on assignments.

4.3 Project roles and responsibilities

Here we shall examine the principal roles encountered within an information systems project. In real projects, the people concerned may not be known by these titles but it is important to establish who they are nevertheless. Figure 4.4 is an organisation chart containing these roles but this is only a typical example and actual organisation structures will vary from this generic example; in many cases, roles may be combined, especially on smaller projects.

Sponsor The **sponsor** is the person who is accountable to the business for the investment represented by the project and for the achievement of the project's *business objectives*. The sponsor therefore will:

■ Define the business aims of the project.
■ Justify the project to the board, or whatever the overall management body is called in the particular organisation.

Figure 4.4 Generic project organisation and roles

- Define the project's objectives and its priorities in terms of the 'triple constraint' of time, cost and quality/performance.
- Specify the minimum requirements that the project must meet if it is to achieve its business objectives.
- Obtain approval for any capital expenditure involved.
- Initiate the project and appoint the project manager.
- Monitor the progress of the project from a business standpoint.
- Monitor also the business environment to ensure that the project still meets the business needs.
- Keep the board or higher management informed of progress.
- If necessary, terminate the project.
- Account for the success of the investment.
- Provide high-level support as a champion for the project.

The sponsor is thus the 'owner' of the project as a piece of business and the sponsor will, ultimately, be responsible for its success or failure in delivering business benefit to the organisation. The sponsor does not necessarily need to be a user of the proposed system and, in some ways, it is preferable if the sponsor is not, as they will then be better able to make disinterested value judgements on whether a particular feature or facility is essential. The sponsor must, however, have the necessary authority to make major decisions on the project and this implies that the sponsor should be a senior manager or director in the organisation.

User The user is the person who will make use of the facilities of the system in their everyday work and is therefore the person most directly affected by the project. The user will:

- Define the detailed requirements for the system to the developers.
- Review the developers' specification to ensure that it supports the business functions.
- Work with the developers in introducing the system into the organisation.
- Conduct, or at any rate witness, the acceptance tests to ensure that the system meets its specified requirements.

The user therefore requires a detailed understanding not just of what processes are to be included in the system but also of how they work. This often means that there is not one but several users with whom the project team must communicate in order to define the system. Inevitably, different users will have different requirements of the system and they will also adopt varying attitudes towards it, from warmly supportive to overtly hostile. The developers will try to reconcile these differences themselves but, at the end of the day, it may be necessary to refer contentious issues to the sponsor for resolution.

Project manager The **project manager** is appointed by the sponsor and is responsible for the management of the project on a day-to-day basis and for the achievement of the *project objectives*. The project manager's role is to:

- Achieve the project's objectives within the time, cost and quality/performance constraints imposed by the sponsor.
- Make or force timely decisions to assure the project's success.
- Plan, monitor and control the project through to completion.
- Select, build and motivate the project team.
- Keep the sponsor and senior management informed of progress and alert them to problems – especially if these could have an impact on the project's achieving its business objectives.
- Recommend termination of the project to the sponsor, if necessary.
- Serve as the principal point of contact between the sponsor, management and contributors.
- Select and manage subcontractors.

The project manager's role and responsibilities are considered in more detail in Chapter 24.

These are the principal project roles but, within the project, other roles may be encountered. Not all of these will be found on every project, and several roles may well be combined, but the main responsibilities are as follows.

Risk manager On a large project, risk management may be a significant part of the project manager's work and it may be necessary to appoint someone to assist with this. The project manager retains overall responsibility for project risk but the risk manager will control the process of identifying, classifying and quantifying the risks and for chasing people to carry out their risk reduction actions. Risk management is discussed more fully in Chapter 15.

Quality manager Again, on a large project, it could be worthwhile to appoint someone as quality manager. Under the guidance of the project manager, this person will write the quality plan, develop the quality control procedures, check that these procedures are being followed and provide advice and guidance to team members on quality-related issues. Quality is the subject of Chapter 14.

Chief analyst This is a senior and experienced business or systems analyst who will, under the direction of the project manager, lead the analysis work. The chief analyst will advise the project manager and project team on analysis methods and techniques and, with the quality manager, ensure that appropriate standards are being followed. It is useful to have as chief analyst someone with extensive experience of the *type of business* being studied who can authoritatively discuss business issues at the highest levels in the user organisation.

Chief designer Like the chief analyst, the chief designer works under the direction of the project manager to control the work of the design team, and probably that of the programmers as well. The chief designer will have extensive experience of the *technology* being used and can provide advice and guidance to the project team as well as develop any project-specific standards that are required.

Database administrator The database administrator will be the principal custodian of the database and of its supporting data dictionary. The database administrator will develop and enforce standards for the use of the database product, the naming and placement of data items and so on. Usually, the database administrator will work closely with the chief designer in the development of the design and with the programming teams in using the database.

Configuration librarian Configuration management is discussed in Chapter 14. Someone needs to assume responsibility for operating the configuration control procedures and, on a large project, this is often a full-time role.

Team leader The project manager is responsible for the overall direction of the project, but detailed management of the staff is often delegated to a number of team leaders. Typically in charge of a small group of, for example, programmers, team leaders plan and direct work on a day-to-day basis and either review or organise reviews of the team members' work.

Project office A project office provides administrative support to the project manager. This includes such things as the collection and recording of timesheets, the organisation of meetings and the dissemination of information. It is quite common to find a project office that supports a number of discrete projects.

4.4 Organising the roles

The various roles we have described may be organised in different ways, depending on a number of factors, including the type of project, whether the work is being done in-house or under contract, and the culture of the organisation. In the simplest case, the sponsor appoints the project manager and these two, plus the user, make the important decisions for the project. Usually, though, the situation is more complex than this, and other bodies that may be encountered are the steering committee and the user group.

The steering committee A **steering committee** is set up to control the development of a particular project – or perhaps a group of related projects – and has representation from the various interested parties. Typically, it might have a senior user representative, or representatives if there are multiple users, plus people from other departments or functions affected by the project – finance, purchasing, personnel and so on. A steering committee is a fine idea provided that either it, or one of its members, possesses the authority to make decisions on the project. Unfortunately, this is not always the case and sometimes one encounters steering committees that lack one vital member: the project's sponsor. Where this is the case, the steering committee risks becoming a 'talking shop' which has to refer all real decisions to the sponsor or some other authoritative person or body in the organisation.

The user group Where there are several users for a planned system, it is sometimes useful to create a forum where they can come together and discuss and reconcile their disparate requirements. Unless the sponsor is a member of the user group – perhaps chairing the meetings – this body's role will be advisory only and the final decisions will have to be made elsewhere in the organisation. What usually happens is that low-level decisions – for example on the layout of a proposed report – are made at the user group, and more fundamental policy issues, probably involving the project budget, are referred upwards. Quite often, the user group will continue to meet after the project has been delivered and will then become the conduit through which changes and enhancements are passed to the maintenance and support team.

The risk management committee On large projects, the management of risk can assume great importance. Rather than burden the steering committee or user group meetings with another large agenda item, it may be found useful to form a committee expressly to review and control the project's risks. Typically, the function of this group would be to review the current status of risks, assign owners to the risks and check that the identified avoidance or mitigation actions are being carried out. It should be noted that the risk management committee does not remove overall responsibility for managing risk from the project manager but acts in support of the project manager.

There are other bodies that may be encountered on projects or set up on an ad hoc basis, for example a technical committee or a quality assurance group. The important point, however, is that the project manager must ensure that the final responsibility and authority for the project is clear and unambiguous. There must be an identifiable sponsor who will decide what the project must do and the constraints within which it will operate. Without this, there are bound to be problems of direction and authority and it will be difficult, if not impossible, to secure sign-off for the project at the end.

| 4.5 | Programme and portfolio management |

Programme management

This book is primarily about *project* management, but in recent years increasing interest has been shown in the related field of *programme* management. Although there is not enough space here to cover programme management in detail, some introduction to the subject would seem to be in order. Readers wishing to pursue this subject are referred to the publications listed in the Further Reading.

Various definitions of the term **programme** have been proposed, including the following:

- Whereas one of the defining features of a project is that it has a definite end-date, a programme may well be a continuing endeavour with no such finite conclusion.
- With a project, the project manager is usually responsible only for the achievement of the narrow project objectives (see Chapter 7), but in a programme the programme manager may well be responsible for realising the business objectives as well.
- A programme is a series of projects that together contribute towards the achievement of some overall business or organisational objective.
- A programme is a very large project with a number of subsidiary projects involved.
- A programme is a set of projects which share a fixed pool of resources.
- A programme is a group of projects undertaken for a single client.

This lack of an agreed definition is one of the reasons why there is confusion about the term 'programme management' and a lack of understanding of how it relates to project management. For our purposes, however, and within the confines of project management for information systems, it would seem that a workable definition of a programme might be:

> *A set of IT projects that are undertaken within an overall strategic business framework that together will contribute to meeting business/organisational objectives and which involve the sharing of a relatively fixed pool of resources in terms of people, equipment and supporting services.*

This definition is probably best understood through an analogy. Let us imagine an in-house IT department for an organisation that has decided to make the use of information technology central to the way it does business in the twenty-first century. The IT director will have agreed with the organisation's senior management a set of projects that will be undertaken as and when resources and finance permit. The overall aim of all of these projects will be to advance the organisation's business strategy, but each will, in addition, have more narrow project objectives.

Each project will have its own project manager whose focus will be on achieving their own project objectives. In doing this, each project manager will need people, finance, equipment, office space and so on, and since the size of the IT function is fixed, they will be in competition with each other for these scarce resources. What is more, precisely because project managers are judged on the success of their individual projects, they will tend to pursue project objectives to the possible detriment of the wider organisational goals.

In this situation, it makes sense to group all of the projects into a programme with an overall **programme director**. The objectives of this person will be:

■ To decide on the relative priority of the projects on a continuing basis. This may mean giving precedence to project A at one stage and to project B at another.
■ To arbitrate between project managers in their demands for resources and, where necessary, decide who will have use of resources at each point.
■ To ensure that the utilisation levels of the resources are kept as high as possible, thereby ensuring that costs are kept strictly under control.
■ To keep a careful watch over the organisation's strategy and ensure that all the projects continue to contribute to the achievement of those objectives. The issue here is not just that projects can drift off course but also that the strategy itself will change as the organisation adapts to changing circumstances.
■ To act as overall champion for the programme within the organisation.

Programme management can thus be seen to be an extension of project management though on a larger scale and with, perhaps, even greater focus on the business objectives of projects. Programme managers will typically be experienced project managers who can take an overall view of the situation and shift resources from project to project as seems necessary to achieve the best return for the organisation. Other senior managers, often without a project management background, are sometimes appointed as programme managers. This has the advantage that they are usually business-oriented and well positioned to act as programme champion, but some exposure to project management is useful in the role if only to understand the issues raised by individual project managers.

Portfolio management Portfolio management represents a slightly different situation from that described for programme management. As we have seen, the main issue in programme management is that the various projects that make up a programme lead to some common objectives. However, the situation also arises where resources have to be shared between projects that do not have the same objectives; indeed the projects may be for different clients altogether. In this scenario, someone is usually still needed who can arbitrate between the competing projects and decide, on a day-to-day basis, which shall have the (usually scarce) resources. This role is referred to as portfolio management.

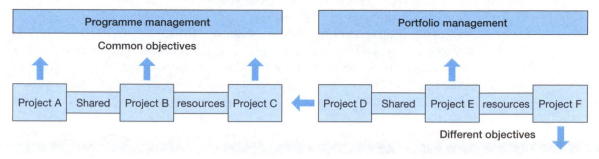

Figure 4.5 Programme and portfolio management

The differences between programme and portfolio management are illustrated in Figure 4.5.

4.6 PRINCE2® organisation structure

PRINCE® is an acronym for Projects in Controlled Environments. PRINCE® is a structured approach to project management developed for and championed by the UK government. PRINCE® was originally intended for the management of IS projects, but most of its principles have always had broader applicability and **PRINCE2®**, launched in 1996, is specifically designed to be useful to a wide range of project situations. PRINCE2® offers a number of features that are of benefit in the management of IS projects:

- A defined management structure
- A system of plans
- A set of control procedures
- A focus on product-based – that is deliverables-based – planning.

We examine each of these features of PRINCE2® in this book, starting with the PRINCE2® management structure, which is illustrated by Figure 4.6.

Figure 4.6 PRINCE2® organisation structure

At the top of the PRINCE2® hierarchy is the body that sets the overall objectives for IS projects within the organisation. PRINCE2® refers to this level as corporate or programme management, reflecting the fact that the fulfilment of this role varies between organisations. It is probable that major decisions on which projects to undertake will be made at a high level in the organisation, perhaps by the board of directors. As we have seen, too, individual projects may form part of a programme and, in this case, it is likely that whoever is directing the programme will have a major influence on which projects are undertaken and how.

We now come to the top level of management for individual projects, which PRINCE2® calls the project board. The **project board** represents the three main constituencies that are interested in the project:

- The **executive** chairs the project board. This person is appointed by the organisation's senior management and represents the business interests of the organisation. The executive provides overall guidance throughout the project and is 'first among equals' on the project board.
- The **senior user** represents the interests of the business areas that are affected by the new system and has the authority to speak for all users of the system.
- The **senior supplier** represents the developers of the new system. Probably, someone like the organisation's IT director or systems development manager would assume the senior supplier role, though, if the development were being done by outside consultants, perhaps the consultants' account manager or managing partner might be more suitable.

An important issue to grasp, however, is that PRINCE2® is a flexible method and the 'standard' project board structure may be varied to suit the requirements of specific projects. For example, it is quite possible to combine the executive and senior user roles if the senior managers are sure there are no major conflicts between the perspectives of the organisation and the user community. There could be more than one senior user if there were several differing perspectives to be accommodated. Or, there could be more than one senior supplier if, for example, several companies were involved in a project. The important point is to have a body that can understand and, vitally, *decide* on critical project issues and that is not, perhaps, so large that it risks degenerating into a debating society.

The day-to-day management of the project is the responsibility of the **project manager** and one or more **team managers**. The project manager's role is what one would expect, but the team manager perhaps requires some explanation. It is assumed that a PRINCE2® project will go through several **stages**, with each stage being signed off and the plans reviewed before moving to the next stage. Since a different blend of skills may be required at each stage, it is possible that a different team manager will be required for each. Alternatively, there could be several teams working within the project (for example, software developers, hardware engineers, networking experts) and each may have its own team manager. In practice, there are several ways the project manager/team manager roles could be operated:

- There may be one project manager throughout the project, with a different team manager for each stage.
- The project manager may also assume the team manager role.
- A succession of team managers may be appointed, with each also assuming the project manager role for that stage.
- In a customer and supplier context, the customer may supply the project manager, with the supplier providing the team manager or managers.

The project board needs to decide on the project manager and team manager responsibilities with regard to the size and cost of the project, the technical complexities involved and the availability of suitable personnel.

The project manager is given authority to manage the project within constraints of time, cost and quality set by the project board. The project board will also assign some tolerances around these constraints within which the project manager may make adjustments to the project if necessary. Tolerances are discussed in more detail in Chapter 8. The project manager may retain control of these tolerances or may delegate some to team managers.

In PRINCE2® as well, there is the concept of **project assurance**. The project board has ultimate responsibility for ensuring that the project meets its business objectives (executive), the users' needs (senior user) and relevant technical standards (senior supplier) but board members are likely to be senior managers with only a part-time involvement in the project. So they can, if they wish, delegate their quality assurance role to others who constitute the project assurance team. There are three aspects to the project assurance work but the project assurance team may have more or fewer than three members. The three aspects are:

- *Business assurance* – evaluating the business aspects of any proposed changes to the project and ensuring that the project continues to be viable in business terms.
- *User assurance* – representing the interests of the system's users, ensuring that the users' requirements are properly addressed, establishing the acceptance criteria for the project, assessing changes and assisting in the quality review of products from the users' perspectives.
- *Technical assurance* – assisting in defining the technical strategy for the project, advising on quality criteria and other technical methods and standards and ensuring that these standards are being adhered to.

The project manager and team manager(s) may also have assistance from a **project support office** (PSO). This assists the project manager in preparing the plans and collects the project monitoring information on the project manager's behalf. It also assists the project manager and team manager(s) in the preparation of reports and keeps the detailed plans up to date. Where an organisation is conducting a number of projects simultaneously – perhaps within the context of a programme of projects – it is often a good idea to establish a central PSO to provide shared services to project teams and to allow information from all the projects to be coordinated. Chapter 5 discusses the concept of a project support office in more detail.

The PRINCE2® structure provides a sound basis for the management of an IS project. It ensures that projects have as their primary focus the achievement of business objectives and it ensures that IS projects grow out of the business strategy. It also ensures that the interest groups affected by the IS project are properly represented and that there is a proper decision-making body that can control and direct the progress of the project.

4.7 Summary

It is vital to the success of an IS project that there is a clear understanding of who the customer is, who will make the major decisions about the scope and direction of the project and who will ultimately accept responsibility for the project.

It is necessary, in particular, to identify the sponsor of the project within the organisation. Various bodies may be formed to guide and advise the project, including the steering group, the user group and the risk management committee.

A programme is a group of projects that together contribute towards the achievement of some overall business objective and which involve the sharing of resources. The programme director will act as arbiter between projects and champion for the overall programme.

The PRINCE2® project management method offers a convenient and effective structure for the management of IS projects.

Questions

1 How many different types of customer may there be for a systems development project? Who are they? What kind of relationship and reporting arrangements should the project manager have with the sponsor?

2 Describe the roles of (a) the sponsor and (b) the project manager.

3 What are the principal problems of managing projects within a completely functional organisation structure?

4 What are the pros and cons of a 'pure' project organisation compared with a project operating within a matrix structure?

5 In a PRINCE2® project structure there are formal committees, a project board and specific roles. What is your opinion about the value of this kind of arrangement? How do you see it working in large and small projects? Could it be useful for projects outside IT?

Case study

E-Con, the consultancy firm engaged by France Vacances to develop its internet-based system, has recommended the use of a PRINCE2®-type structure to manage the project.

The project board will be made up of:

- David Martin, one of France Vacances's directors, as executive
- Jean Hunt, France Vacances's customer services manager, as senior user
- Barbara Currie, E-Con's account manager, as senior supplier.

The project board will meet on a Thursday afternoon every two weeks during the project.

There was some argument about how the role of project manager should be filled. Peter Clay, France Vacances's IT manager, thought that he should take this position, with the E-Con project manager being a team manager. However, E-Con argued that, as it was doing most of the development work, it would make more sense for E-Con to provide the project manager. In the end, David Martin agreed with E-Con and so the project manager will be Richard Vaughan, an E-Con principal consultant. He will manage two teams, one led by Peter Clay which will develop the MIS aspects of the new

Figure 4.7 France Vacances internet project structure

Case study continued

system and the other led by E-Con's Siobhan Reid which will develop the internet software.

E-Con will also provide the project support functions, as it has a project support office that works with all of its projects.

The project assurance functions will be discharged by a small team comprising:

- Helen Winter, one of Jean Hunt's sales supervisors
- Mark Southam, one of the resort managers
- Gail Hardie, France Vacances's management accountant
- Norman Pierce, E-Con's quality assurance manager.

The organisation chart for the project is shown in Figure 4.7.

Further reading

Office of Government Commerce (2002), *Managing Successful Projects with PRINCE2*, 3rd edn, The Stationery Office

Reiss, Geoff (1996), *Programme Management Demystified*, E&FN Spon

Shafto, Tony (1990), *The Foundations of Business Organisation*, Stanley Thornes

Turner, J Rodney and Simister, Stephen J (eds) (2000), *Gower Handbook of Project Management*, 3rd edn, Gower

5 The programme and project support office

5.1 Introduction

In Chapter 4 on the organisational framework, we considered a number of different roles and responsibilities, and organisation structures that were used in helping to ensure that our projects were successful. One of the support areas is the programme and project support office, or PPSO. The principle of having a support office for project-related work is widely accepted and in the context of this book also covers the terms project support office, project office and programme office. The terms tend to be used interchangeably to a certain extent and the precise definition of what they cover depends on the organisation within which they operate. The PRINCE2® method uses the term project support office, and its documentation provides a definition of its scope within a PRINCE2® project environment. On the other hand, the Information Systems Examination Board (ISEB), part of the British Computer Society, currently offers certificate examinations for programme and project support office (PPSO) work. For this book we shall stick to the term PPSO but it should be borne in mind that the other terms are also well-used. The activities of the PPSO will be covered at a high level only as many of their tasks are described in some detail in later parts of the book.

5.2 Evolution of the PPSO function

The role of the PPSO has evolved over time from humble beginnings. At one time, it may have been that an organisation had embarked on a major project and decided that the project required some administrative support. A number of staff may have been seconded to the project to assist. They would probably have been released at the end of the project back to their previous administrative duties. Their duties tended to be centred on the 'donkey work' – the mundane, day-to-day work that the project manager perhaps lacked the time to do. Typically this would involve tasks such as taking notes at meetings and updating project plans with information from timesheets.

As organisations began to use project-oriented structures more widely, and the number of projects increased substantially, the PPSO became more of a permanent fixture and helped to service a number of projects rather than working exclusively on one. This in turn changed the nature of the relationship between project manager and PPSO staff. Although the PPSO staff would generally be more junior than the project managers on whose projects they were working, they found that they had a number of masters who inevitably had conflicting views about the relative priority and importance of the support work that related to 'their' projects. This resulted in PPSOs having their own management structure, independent of the project managers. This in turn led to PPSOs having a reporting role involving the collation of individual project progress reports and the assembly and distribution of this information to management.

It became clear, as project management disciplines became more widely used and with project working becoming an increasingly common way of life, that there were many other activities that were common to all projects and that could more easily be carried out by centralised 'specialists' rather than being reinvented by each new project. Hence PPSO has moved from a purely administrative and support role to, in some cases, being at the centre of the control and direction of the organisation's project and programme portfolio. We shall look in a little more detail at some of these PPSO activities and at the changing role of PPSO within organisations. With the advent of change programmes and the use of techniques such as business process re-engineering (BPR), the role of PPSO has moved outside the IS/IT arena in some organisations. However, as this book is concerned primarily with project management for information systems, the remainder of the chapter concentrates on PPSO work with IS/IT projects and programmes.

5.3 Functions of a PPSO

The range of functions carried out by a PPSO varies from organisation to organisation. The depth of each function may also vary, with a PPSO being heavily involved in some functions, less so in others. It may be useful to look at the complete range of possible PPSO activities across the project lifecycle and explain how a PPSO may play a part. The project lifecycle is more fully explained in Chapter 7 of this book.

As far as PPSO is concerned, the project lifecycle may be divided into a number of main stages:

1 PPSO work prior to formal initiation of a particular project.
2 Work carried out as part of project initiation.
3 Activities that take place to support the main delivery phase of the project (analysis, design, build, test, implement, and so on).
4 Work carried out after completion of the project, i.e. after 'go-live'.

Figure 5.1 sets out the possible functions that could be carried out by a PPSO at each of these stages.

Figure 5.1 Possible functions of a PPSO

5.4 Pre-initiation stage of project

Project approval process
The PPSO may be responsible for the process of bringing projects into being. In other words, it may control the requests for new projects (or programmes), the prioritisation of these requests, the subsequent placing of a project within a programme, and overall resourcing in terms of manpower and cost. In other organisations, PPSOs may not become involved at all until the project has been formally given the go-ahead.

Business case preparation
PPSOs may provide expertise in the preparation of business cases. The business case is a key product that sets out the justification for a project based on the anticipated business benefits and the estimated costs. No project should be considered without a supporting business case. The PPSO's role may involve outright ownership of the business case, or providing guidance through the use of specialised techniques such as investment appraisal and discounted cash flow (see Chapter 3 for more on this). Alternatively, the PPSO's role may be simply to assist with formatting, possibly using previous business cases as models.

5.5 | Project initiation

Initiation of a project, after it has been given formal management approval to proceed, is one area where a PPSO is usually heavily involved. This is the stage where the **project initiation document** (PID), the project plan, the quality plan and the risk management plan are all produced for the first time. The PPSO will probably have standardised formats for all of these documents.

Planning In many organisations, the PPSO is treated as a 'centre of excellence' for planning matters (and project management in general). This usually involves having skill and expertise in the use of planning tools and packages. In the past, the PPSO was viewed perhaps as a training ground to develop planning expertise, with staff ultimately moving on to become project managers. A fuller planning role has become more prevalent in recent times as organisations have moved to using project structures more frequently and as many types of project, in addition to IS/IT ones, have formed part of the organisation's project portfolio. This has led to the project manager role being carried out by business managers, often with limited project management experience. This has placed a greater responsibility for the planning on the PPSO staff and has led to greater dependence on their services by the project managers.

Risk management Many of the risks faced by projects have been met and dealt with on previous projects. Hence the PPSO is well placed to provide input to the project's risk management plan, using the case histories that have been amassed. Some organisations, and industries with safety-critical projects, take risk management very seriously and may have risk specialists attached to the PPSO whose sole job is to assist with risk management.

Resourcing The allocation of staff to projects, especially those responsible for project management, may also form part of the PPSO. In some organisations, all project management staff are employed through the PPSO and are 'contracted out' to projects. The PPSO can act as a clearing house for all project staff, although this is less usual.

5.6 | Main delivery stages of the project

This covers the main development stages of the project and includes many of the day-to-day ongoing support tasks. Where an organisation has a limited PPSO, the following are likely to be the main areas where the PPSO comes into play.

Reporting The collation of progress reports, highlight reports and financial reports plus any other reports required by the project manager will be carried out on a regular basis, for example weekly or monthly. The PPSO will ensure that the requisite information is being provided by the projects, when required, and arrange for dissemination to interested parties. The distribution lists for reports of this nature may be quite extensive and circulation has been facilitated in recent years by the use of email. The PPSO may also summarise the reports for the benefit of management, highlighting areas where projects are off track.

Time recording Issuing timesheets and updating project plans on the basis of the completed timesheets is often part of the PPSO's work. Sometimes this work is carried out by the PPSO itself (although less so nowadays); sometimes it merely controls the process, with project staff entering the data.

Documentation library The PPSO may act as the repository for all project documentation by holding the master copies and providing a library facility for interested parties.

Configuration management **Configuration management** (CM) is the ability to identify the components of a system at any given point in time and of knowing the status of each of these components. For our purposes this applies to all the components of the project: hardware, software and documentation. The topic of CM is discussed more fully in Chapter 14. The role of PPSO with regard to CM takes a number of forms and, once again, may be fully centralised in PPSO or shared with the individual projects. The documentation library may come under CM and all documents may have to be formally booked out if they are to be changed or updated. Similarly, the updated version may only be accepted back into the library after the appropriate quality reviews have been carried out. The software (source code and object code) may be managed in the same fashion as documentation. The PPSO may also be responsible for assembling 'releases', that is sets of hardware, software and documentation which are consistent with each other and together have a defined purpose. For example, a release could be the set of system components put together for a particular round of system testing.

Monitoring and control Following the regular updating of the project plans, as described above, the PPSO may be responsible for monitoring progress against the baseline plans and advising the project manager, or others, of project activities that are late starting, are likely to overrun, or are late finishing. The PPSO may also provide separate monitoring for management, independent of the normal project reporting.

Financial Part of the process of capturing actual effort spent on projects, via time recording, may involve the calculation of project costs. This may form part of general project reporting, or, where the project work is being carried out for an external (or internal) customer, may be used for charging and invoicing purposes.

Stakeholder management In some instances, particularly where the PPSO acts as a powerful programme office, all communication with the project stakeholders may go through the PPSO rather than the individual projects. This ensures a consistent approach and uniformity of treatment of all stakeholders.

Business case monitoring It is important that the business case is revisited during the course of the project to ensure that it is still valid. This generally takes place at the end of project stages, although it can be done at any point if considered necessary. The PPSO will undertake the same tasks as outlined in Chapter 3 on business case preparation. Clearly, if the business case is found to have changed such that there is no longer justification for the project, the decision may be taken to abandon the project.

Change control Change control (see Chapter 12) covers a large area, and part or all of the change control process may be administered by the PPSO. At the project level, the PPSO may assist by logging requests for change and recording information about the change, for example impact assessment in terms of cost, effort and time. It may also record the status of the change as it progresses, for example raised, being analysed, awaiting decision, rejected and so on. On a wider scale, the PPSO may handle changes that have an impact outside the immediate project, perhaps on other projects in the programme, or with other systems in the organisation. In this situation the impact of the change on all the affected projects/systems has to be fully assessed and PPSO analysts may be employed to carry out this work.

Assurance The project assurance function may be carried out by a centralised PPSO. This is independent of the project manager and is designed to give senior managers confidence that the project is being managed competently and that nothing is being hidden from them that could affect the ultimate success of the project. The assurance may take different forms and may focus on elements of the project management, such as risk or issue management, or on adherence to standards or quality procedures. It may also include a full project audit where the whole project is subjected to a stringent examination.

Procurement Procurement activity is sometimes handled by individual projects although some organisations have a centralised function with specialist procurement and contract staff. In some organisations this is a separate management service, but in others the function is part of the PPSO.

Training/ mentoring Training may be carried out directly by members of the PPSO or may be managed on behalf of project staff. In some organisations, particularly those who use the 'centre of excellence' concept, the PPSO staff may act as mentors to the project managers working on the projects.

5.7 Post-project

Once the project has been completed there are a number of areas where the PPSO may play a part.

Post-project reviews When a project finishes, the staff involved often move quickly to other projects. It is important that the experience is not lost and that any lessons learned, good or bad, are recorded. This information can then be used to guide future projects. The PPSO has an independent role in ensuring that this type of exercise does not become an opportunity to rewrite history, removing the less successful parts, but accurately reflects what happened. The report would then be held by the PPSO as part of its records.

Benefits realisation Benefits realisation takes place after the products of the project have been in use for a period. Users' experiences of the new system are used to determine whether the business case is being, or has been, met. Benefits realisation may continue for some time after completion of the project and can be an extremely complex activity. PPSO activity in this area is usually to support the business in carrying out the work, although, with a powerful programme office type of structure, the PPSO may itself drive the exercise. Benefits realisation may be treated as a separate project in its own right.

5.8 Ongoing PPSO activities

In addition to the specific PPSO functions carried out to support projects directly, there are a number of areas where the PPSO may be involved on a continuing basis. The PPSO may be the custodian of the standards to which projects are expected to adhere. These standards may have been developed by the PPSO and the PPSO may be responsible for their maintenance, or this work may have been subcontracted elsewhere. These standards may be very detailed or relatively high-level – once again it depends on the organisation. The quality standards are likely to be included in this set. The overall project support infrastructure, with a set of procedures, report templates and the like may be defined and maintained by the PPSO.

5.9 Benefits of a PPSO

The reasons for having a centralised support group are varied but derive mostly from the fact that projects, by their nature, are not permanent. Most organisations find it useful to have a means of ensuring consistency in their approach to projects and in having a repository for information about past projects. The main benefits to an organisation are as follows.

Information on past projects Information on past projects enables metrics to be kept and used on future projects to improve the quality and accuracy in areas such as estimating. It allows less effort to be spent on future projects by not having to reinvent processes each time. Projects should not repeat the mistakes of earlier projects if this base of project information is maintained.

Consistency If all projects adhere to the same standards and processes then staff transfer from one project to another is easier and faster as staff do not have to learn different ways of working.

Independence Some of the functions of a PPSO provide independence from managers of the individual projects and enable senior management to take a clear view of the status of each project.

Specialism Many of the functions of a PPSO are specialised and it makes sense to maintain, and increase, that expertise in a central location. Otherwise the experience may be lost if only used on isolated projects.

Centre of excellence A PPSO can act as a centre of excellence in project management matters and provide expertise and consultancy support to project managers.

5.10 Summary

The programme and project support office plays a key role in many organisations. That role can vary considerably from one organisation to another. In some, the PPSO provides only administrative support on request from the project manager; in others it is central to the overall control of the project or programme portfolio.

The use of PPSOs has become more widespread as organisations have accepted the need to retain information on their projects and to learn from their experiences. The PPSO has become the central repository for this knowledge. Many activities are common to all projects and the PPSO can provide specialist skills and expertise in areas such as planning, reporting, configuration management, documentation library and change control.

One of the advantages of having a PPSO is that it can provide senior management with an independent view of projects, separate from the projects' own management.

Questions

1 Explain why the concept of the PPSO arose in the first place.

2 What are the advantages to an organisation of having a PPSO?

3 What conflicts are likely to arise between project managers and PPSO staff?

4 What skills are useful when working in the PPSO?

Case study

As was mentioned in the previous chapter, E-Con has a well-established project support office function that is used for all its projects. The PPSO contains specialists in business case development, estimating and planning as well as administrative support staff.

At the start of each project, the project manager agrees with the PPSO manager the type and amount of support that will be required and this is then the subject of an internal service-level agreement. These agreements allow the PPSO manager to assess the resource requirements for the coming periods and to balance the use of PPSO resources between the various projects that are in progress at any one time.

E-Con's PPSO also has an audit function, in that it monitors the progress reports emanating from projects and provides independent progress assessments to the E-Con account manager, in this case Barbara Currie.

E-Con has found that the availability of PPSO resources frees their project managers from much routine administrative work and allows them to concentrate on the more active aspects of project management, especially managing the key stakeholders and the projects' human resources.

Further reading

Marsh, David (2000), *The Project and Programme Support Office Handbook: Foundation*, Project Manager Today

Marsh, David (2000), *The Project and Programme Support Office Handbook: Advanced*, Project Manager Today

Office of Government Commerce (2002), *Managing Successful Projects with PRINCE2*, 3rd edn, The Stationery Office

Turner, J Rodney and Simister, Stephen J (2000), *Gower Handbook of Project Management*, 3rd edn, Gower

6 Development lifecycles and approaches

6.1 Introduction

In this chapter we consider the project lifecycle and the various approaches to system development which can be used on IS projects. These approaches are sometimes more formally termed 'lifecycle models'. Various models exist, many of which are developments or refinements of earlier ones.

It is important to define the terms 'system development lifecycle' and 'project lifecycle'. Generally speaking, the system development lifecycle covers the whole life of a system. This will cover not only feasibility study, analysis, specification, design and development but also the operation, maintenance and enhancement aspects which take place after the system has been accepted by the end-users.

A project can be defined as 'a management environment set up to ensure the delivery of a specified business product to meet a defined business case'. In terms of systems development, this can generally be taken to mean the delivery of the specified IS within given constraints of time, cost, resource and quality, but a project may not cover all stages of the system lifecycle. As a project is defined as something which has an end, it is unlikely, although not impossible, that ongoing maintenance would be included in the scope of a project. Similarly, the objective of the project may cover only the delivery of a specified product, for example a feasibility study report or requirements definition. In other words, the project lifecycle covers the delivery of whatever has been defined as constituting the end-product of the project.

There is another important difference. The system development lifecycle often covers only the technical deliverables whereas the project is concerned with all aspects leading to the delivery of the project's objectives. This therefore includes not only the delivery of technical products but also the associated management and quality aspects necessary to a successful project.

The government-sponsored project management method known as PRINCE2® explicitly divides the project lifecycle products into two groups:

- *Specialist* products. These products are concerned with the actual deliverables for the IS – the software, user manuals and so on.
- *Management* products. These are used to manage the project itself – the organisation, plans, reports and so forth. Management products also

include the *quality* products which are used to define the required quality criteria and the controls to be applied to the project and to its deliverables.

Many of the system development lifecycle models, particularly the earlier ones, were concerned solely with the work required to produce the actual system; elements such as quality, planning, control, risk analysis were not covered or were fairly superficial. This is now changing and these areas are increasingly being incorporated in development approaches.

The selection of an appropriate system development lifecycle model is important for the project. It is probably true to say that it is useful to have a defined lifecycle for systems development. It is better to go into the project with a clear idea of the general form that the development is going to take. The decision as to which 'model' to follow may not be in the hands of the project manager. The project may be handed over to the project manager with the development approach already set out, possibly in the project's terms of reference or in the initiation document. The organisation for whom the project is being carried out may have sets of standards in place which dictate how system development is to take place. Another possibility is that the project may form part of an overall strategy in which a number of systems are being developed and this strategy may have defined the approach to be followed.

Alternatively, and this is rather less likely nowadays, the project manager may have the power to decide on the most appropriate development model to be used for the project. In this selection there are many factors which have to be taken into consideration to determine the best approach. In any case, whether the project manager gets to choose or not, the project has to be planned with the system development approach in mind.

There are only two basic system development lifecycle models: the waterfall model and the spiral model. All other well-used models tend to be variants or refinements of these two. This chapter looks at these models and how they can be used in a project context. It describes them along with their strengths and weaknesses in order to assist the project manager in their selection and use. The chapter also considers a number of development approaches which make use of the basic models in various ways.

6.2 The waterfall model

In the early 1970s, it became apparent, following a number of high-profile failures, that computer projects required a greater degree of formality than had previously been the case. The waterfall model was originally published in 1970 by W Royce in order to introduce this level of formality, and the original is shown in Figure 6.1. In the waterfall model, system development is broken down into a number of sequential sections or stages represented by boxes, with each stage being completed before work starts on the following one. The outputs from one stage are used as inputs to the next. This is illustrated by the

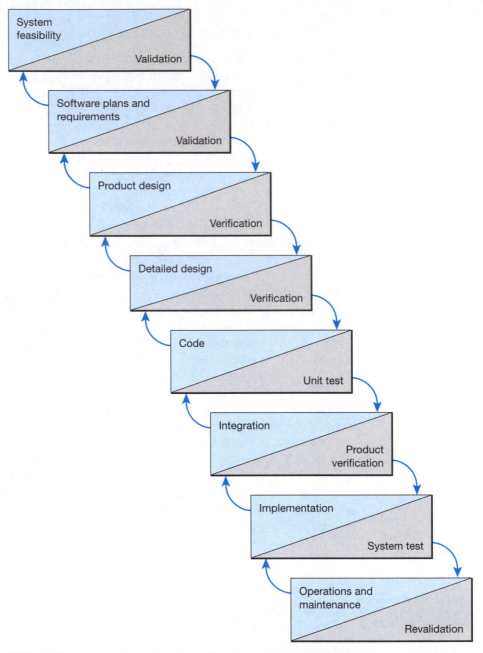

Figure 6.1 The waterfall model of system development lifecycle

(*Computer*, May 1988, © 1988 IEEE)

'flow' from one stage to the next. For example, using Figure 6.1, the Product Design products are completed and accepted before being used as inputs to the work of the next stage, Detailed Design, and so on.

Each stage is divided into two parts: the first part covers the actual work being carried out in the stage; the second part covers the 'verification and validation' of that work. *Verification* is taken to mean establishing the correspondence between a product and its specification – in other words, are we building the product in the right way? *Validation* is concerned with whether the product is fit for its operational mission – in other words, are we building the right product? Typically, there is a degree of iteration of work and products within a stage but very little between stages. Rework, where necessary, is carried out in succeeding stages and the original stage in which the product was produced is not revisited. For example, if a new requirement is identified during the Detailed Design stage, the project will not return to the Software Plans and Specification stage but will incorporate the reworking within the current stage. This may mean that some of the previously delivered products need to be amended, however.

Nowadays, the waterfall model is generally taken to mean any sequential model divided into consecutive stages and having the attributes of the original model. The identification and naming of the stages are not fixed and can be modified to suit particular project characteristics.

The model has a number of good points. Apart from the sequencing of activities, it addresses elements of quality management through verification and validation, and configuration management by baselining products at the end of the stage. It does not have explicit means for exercising management control on a project, however, and planning, control and risk management are not covered. Nevertheless, the stage-by-stage nature of the waterfall model and the completion of products for the end of each stage lend themselves well to project management planning and control techniques and assist in the process of change control. Many projects still use versions of the waterfall model, generally with some of the shortcomings of the original one addressed, and the model is used as the basis for many structured methods such as SSADM (structured systems analysis and design method).

Waterfall models work best when the level of reworking of products is kept to a minimum and the products remain unchanged after completion of their 'stage'. In situations where the requirements are well understood and the business area in general is not likely to undergo significant business change, the waterfall model works well. In situations where the business requirements are not well understood and where the system is likely to undergo radical change, a different approach from that suggested by the waterfall model may be more appropriate.

6.3 The 'b' model

One of the weaknesses of the waterfall model is that the maintenance phase is not adequately covered. Operations and Maintenance is treated as a separate stage as if it had a separate start and finish like the other stages. There is no acknowledgement that maintenance is different in nature from the other stages in that it is ongoing and open-ended. It should be borne in mind that most of the effort which is expended on a system over its whole life is

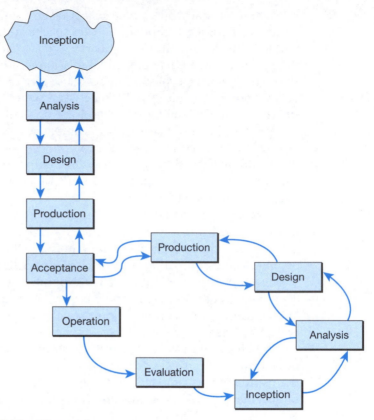

Figure 6.2 The 'b' model

(N D Birrell and M A Ould, *A Practical Handbook for Software Development*, Cambridge University Press, 1985)

expended during maintenance and that it can typically represent more than 70 per cent of total lifecycle costs. The 'b' model, illustrated in Figure 6.2, was devised by N Birrell and M Ould to address this shortcoming in the waterfall model. It takes its name from its distinctive 'b' shape, with the maintenance and enhancement of the information system shown as a series of cycles each of which follows the same general sequence as the original development. In other words, each change or correction to the system will go through feasibility, analysis, design, production, acceptance and finally operation. These changes may not be implemented separately, of course: they may be combined into 'packages' for implementation.

6.4 The 'V' model

In this model, which is another variation of the waterfall model, the successive stages are shown in a 'V' formation. An example of the 'V' model is shown in Figure 6.3. On the diagram, the left, downward leg of the V shows the progress

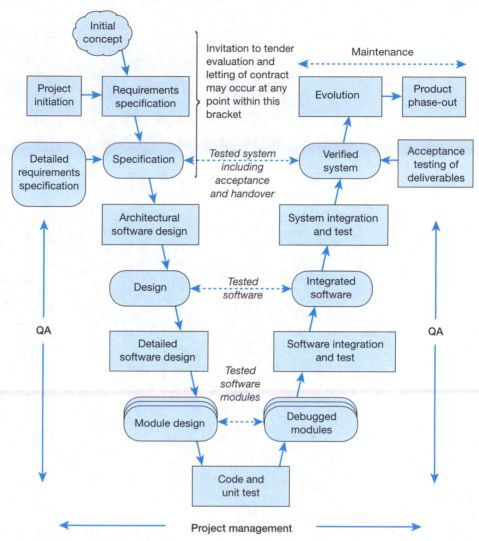

Figure 6.3 The 'V' model

(Reproduced with permission of the National Computing Centre Limited from the *STARTS Guide*, 1987, which was supported by the Department of Trade and Industry)

from analysis to design to programming and the increasing breakdown of the system components. The right, upward leg shows the progressive assembly and testing, culminating in the delivered product. The important feature of this model is that it shows correspondence between the different stages in the project. For instance, the individual programs or modules are tested against the individual module designs, the integrated set of software is system-tested against the system design and the final system is user-acceptance-tested against the requirements specification. This model demonstrates elements of quality assurance (QA) in its treatment of this correspondence.

The 'V' model also introduces something else of interest to the project manager. In the situation where the development work is being provided by

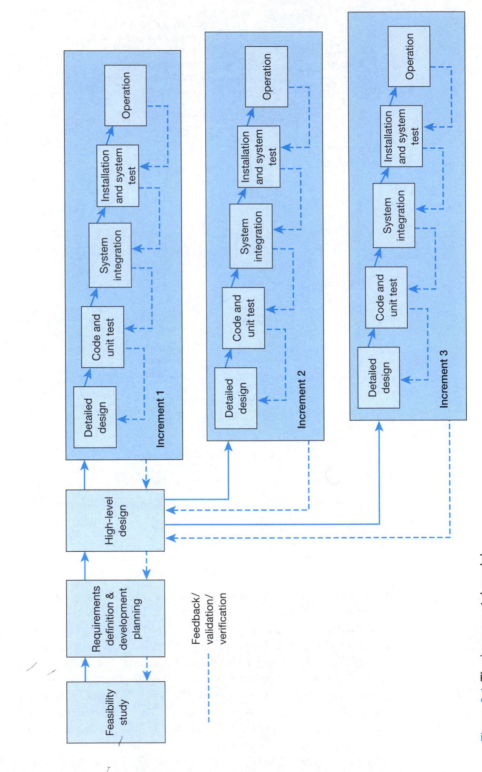

Figure 6.4 The incremental model

external contractors, it enables the procurement and delivery stages to be clearly defined and the deliverables of each stage to be validated. This model is used in the next chapter where a particular project is examined in some detail.

6.5 The incremental model

The incremental model is another variant of the waterfall model and is illustrated in Figure 6.4. This model is used where the total functionality of the system is to be delivered in phases over a period of time and it is sometimes termed 'phased delivery'. This makes the delivery and testing more manageable as it introduces the new system to the organisation over a period of time, allowing familiarisation with the changes. It can be difficult to break the delivery of systems down into phases which are internally consistent and it does introduce overheads in that the latest phase has to be integrated with the earlier ones and the whole system retested. Incremental delivery is an implementation issue and the total scope and definition of requirements must be completed before the increments are defined. The incremental model is not appropriate where the scope of the project is poorly defined or undecided, or where there is lack of clarity of some of the requirements.

6.6 The spiral model

The spiral model differs from the waterfall model in that it introduces an evolutionary or iterative approach to systems development. The waterfall model concentrates on a stage-by-stage process with the end-products from one stage being finalised before the next stage is begun. This works reasonably well where the requirements of the system are well understood by the users and the environment is stable. There are often occasions where the requirements are not well formed or understood by the users, where it is difficult to specify the requirements, or where it is difficult to determine how a proposed solution will perform in practice. In this situation, an evolutionary approach may be appropriate. This involves carrying out the same activities over a number of cycles in order to clarify the requirements, issues and solutions, and in effect amounts to repeating the development lifecycle several times.

The original spiral model was developed by Barry Boehm and it is shown in Figure 6.5. The project starts at the centre of the spiral and progresses outwards. At the centre, the requirements will be poorly understood and will be successively refined with each rotation of the spiral. The total cost of the project will increase as the length of the spiral increases. The model is divided into four quadrants:

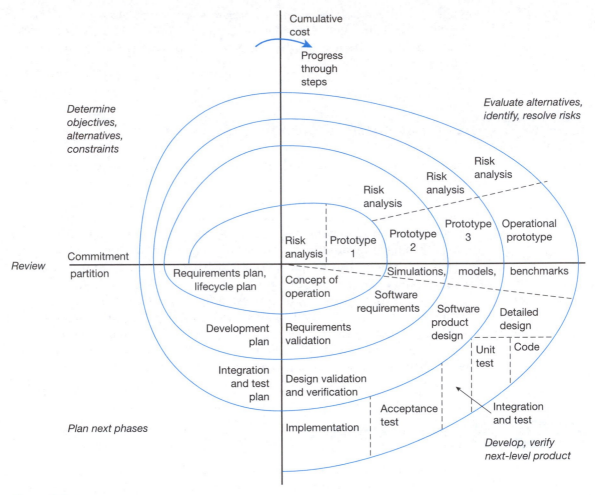

Figure 6.5 Boehm's spiral model

(*Computer*, May 1988, © 1988 IEEE)

- The top left quadrant is where the objectives are determined and the alternatives and constraints identified.
- The top right quadrant is where the alternatives are evaluated and the various risks are identified and resolved.
- The bottom right quadrant is where the development takes place. This in effect covers the same area as the more conventional waterfall model.
- The bottom left quadrant is where the next phase or iteration is planned.

The Boehm spiral introduces the important concepts of objective-setting, risk management and planning into the overall cycle. These are all very desirable from a project management point of view as they apply explicitly to factors which may affect the timely delivery of the system within its defined constraints.

6.7 The traditional approach to systems development

In this model, 'traditional' tends to mean unstructured and somewhat non-specific and most traditional approaches are based on variations of the water-fall model. Although the overall picture will probably be familiar, the actual methods of developing the systems are almost as numerous as the projects themselves. A diagram of a representative traditional approach is shown in Figure 6.6. This shows three of the stages:

- *Analyse requirements*. In this stage the analyst considers the current system and investigates any problems associated with it. The users are also interviewed to obtain their views of the problems and to get their ideas for improvements. Other sources of information about the system and the new requirements would also be investigated at this time. The output from this stage would probably be no more than a set of notes put together by the analyst.
- *Specify requirements*. In this stage the analyst considers the information that has been accumulated and produces a requirements document. This is likely to be a mix of business requirements, functional and non-functional requirements and an overview of the proposed hardware and software. Elements of the physical specification in terms of screens and printed output reports might also be included.
- *Produce high-level design*. The designer would consider the requirements document and, on that basis, produce a high-level design for the system setting out the database design, the input and output specifications, the menu structure and the overall program design and breakdown.

This approach is characterised by the lack of user involvement, the use of text-based, as opposed to diagrammatic, documentation and an emphasis on *how* things are going to be achieved rather than *what* is going to be achieved. Although there is a stage-by-stage approach, it is difficult to see how the stages link together or to follow an audit trail of individual requirements. Typically, in project management terms, there is no business case or defined acceptance criteria for the system, which makes it difficult to gauge success or failure. The lack of user involvement is demonstrated in many ways. The users would be involved at the initial analysis stage but the only point where they would be formally required to review anything would be when the requirements specification has been completed. Following this, their next contact with the computer system would probably be when the system is delivered.

On the other hand, this method of working suited many analysts and users. It allowed the analyst to use 'intuitive' methods of working and made limited demands on the users' time. The documentation was relatively easy to understand, being mostly in English, and there were no special techniques to be learned in order to understand it. Unfortunately, text tends to be ambiguous and interpreted differently by different people and misunderstandings were common. This lack of user involvement and 'ownership' of the system often resulted in a poor quality system and an abdication of responsibility by the users and blame for the developers.

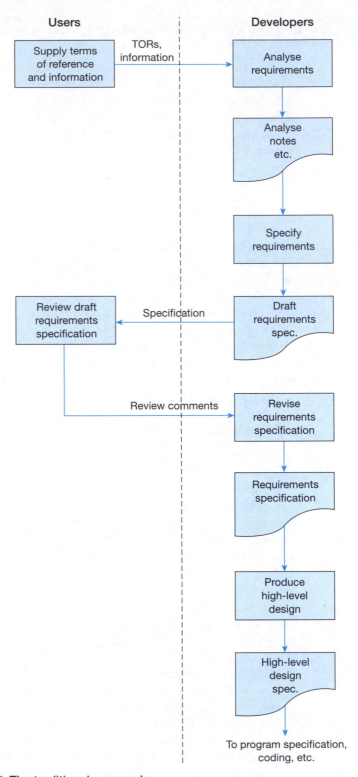

Figure 6.6 The traditional approach

6.8 Structured methods

Structured methods have largely taken over from the traditional approach in the development of IS projects. Most of these methods offer a set of techniques and tools to carry out the systems development work within a defined framework. Structured methods are characterised by:

- *User involvement.* The users are involved with the review of the products throughout the project and with formal agreement or acceptance of them.
- *Separation of logical and physical.* There is a clear separation in the design of the system between *what* is to be achieved and *how* it is to be implemented. This has the advantage of allowing business benefits to focus on, rather than being diverted by, physical implementation issues.
- *Emphasis on data.* Most structured methods concentrate on the data rather than the processing required by the system. This is because the data tend to be more stable and less likely to change over time.
- *Diagrammatic documentation.* Diagrams rather than text-based documentation are used as much as possible to avoid the problems inherent in large textual documents.
- *Defined structure.* Most structured methods have an overall structure associated with them which ensures a more consistent and complete approach to the work. This allows progress in the work to be fully charted and there are no sudden unconnected and unexplained jumps between stages or activities.

In general, structured methods are considered to offer improvements over traditional methods but there are drawbacks and criticisms. The users and analysts/developers need to be trained to understand the documentation; this is important as there is no value whatsoever in producing documentation to be reviewed and signed off if it is not fully understood. The users also need to accept that the amount of time required from them will be much increased. This is a project management issue, and full user commitment must be obtained if the final system is to be a success. However, the major criticism levelled against structured methods is that they lead to increased levels of documentation and therefore of bureaucracy. Unfortunately, there is an element of truth in this as, in inexperienced or ill-informed hands, the use of structured methods can lead to the adoption of a 'cookbook' approach. This is where the various steps and activities of the method are followed blindly without considering the reasons why they should be carried out. The needs of the particular project should always be examined before embarking unthinkingly on the use of a method in order to ensure that best use is made of the method. It is usually disastrous to assume that the method, rather than the analyst, will do the work.

6.9 SSADM

The structured systems analysis and design method (SSADM) is an example of a structured method. It is a non-proprietary product and was originally developed for use by the UK government in 1980. It has been widely used in all areas of business and commerce in the UK. SSADM covers analysis and design but does not cover the whole system development lifecycle, providing only a general approach to feasibility and ending with physical design. It generally conforms to the structured method description in section 6.8 and additionally has links to the project management method PRINCE2®, although it may be used with other project management methods. The method has been developed over several years and includes a comprehensive set of techniques. The major techniques include business activity modelling, logical data modelling, data flow modelling, entity behaviour modelling – incorporating entity life histories, function definition and conceptual process modelling. These techniques provide alternative views of a system that cross-check each other to ensure that an accurate and complete picture of the system is formed. We do not go into any detail on these techniques in this book but several good books exist which explain the method fully.

SSADM has a 'default structural model' which suggests an order to the system analysis and design work to be carried out. The default structural model consists of five modules:

- Feasibility
- Requirements Analysis
- Requirements Specification
- Logical System Specification
- Physical Design.

Each module is decomposed into one or two stages, each stage into a series of steps and then the tasks of each step are defined. The default structural model is based on the waterfall model. There is also a product breakdown structure which shows the composition of the products to be delivered. For an explanation of product breakdown structures, refer to Chapter 8 on project planning.

In response to accusations of an over-prescriptive and bureaucratic approach, SSADM4+ (released in February 1995) highlighted the need to tailor the method for individual projects. It has introduced the concept of a template of activities known as the system development template. The system development template defines a number of areas of activity where work must be carried out during the development of a system. This template shows the interaction between techniques during the analysis and design of a system. Along with the default structural model, this template provides a mechanism for developing an approach for the analysis and design of a particular system. This has to be done with care, however, and ideally should be carried out by people experienced in the use of the method. SSADM also proposes the use of prototyping at various places and may involve a limited use of the spiral model in order to elicit and clarify requirements.

6.10 | Rapid application development

Rapid application development (RAD) is an approach which has gained in popularity. With business changes taking place at an ever-increasing rate, traditional organisational structures being redrawn, technology continuing to change quickly and user expectations of information systems increasing, there is pressure to do it 'quickly'. There are many RAD approaches and some are more formalised than others. The one thing that all RAD approaches appear to have in common is the 'rapid' part and RAD has become popular because of the commercial pressures to provide a competitive advantage by putting in a system quickly, often accepting that the implemented system may not be perfect. In the same vein, a business opportunity may arise which has a fixed and limited life and which, if missed, will render the development a waste of time. An advantage of developing systems rapidly is that external changes are reduced and are made easier to control as there is less elapsed time for change to become necessary than with a conventional and longer development cycle. The spiral system development lifecycle model is generally used for at least part of the project.

Other circumstances justifying a RAD approach – ones that we have alluded to before when discussing the spiral lifecycle model – are when the customers are unable to provide a complete and detailed specification of their requirements at the start of the project. This can happen not only because they just cannot think through the issues but also when they are themselves moving into a new and unknown business area. So, instead of trying to develop the whole system in one go, the system is divided into a number of iterations, each adding some functionality or perhaps improved performance to its predecessor(s). As the business and technical requirements and possibilities become better understood – by both customers and developers – so additional iterations can be scoped and carried out to enhance and improve the system.

Generally, the RAD approach involves a number of techniques which enable the requirements, and subsequently the system, to be developed via a series of iterative activities generally involving the use of prototypes. The use of prototyping does not necessarily imply RAD, however, as prototyping techniques may be used in other types of development approach. Within a RAD project, prototyping may be used in many ways, including:

- Assisting users to define and confirm requirements by demonstrating possibilities.
- Investigating the effectiveness of novel methods of working.
- Testing performance implications.
- Assisting in considering work practice.

Once developed, prototypes allow the system to be examined and reviewed by the users and modifications and refinements can be made quickly and easily. The prototypes then become the final delivered system. One of the major differences between RAD and the more conventional structured methods is that iteration and rework are seen as being an integral part of the RAD approach and not something to be avoided if possible, which is the view of most structured methods.

There are several schools of thought on RAD. One says that RAD should only be used where there is a completely stable environment in that:

■ The application is not complex and the scope is well-defined.
■ The organisational environment is fixed and mature.
■ The technical environment is neither technically advanced nor novel.
■ The application fits in well with the existing infrastructure.

Another RAD school of thought is more radical and advocates a truly evolutionary approach to development. In this situation, the requirements may not be clearly defined and even the scope of the project may be 'fuzzy'.

Practical experience of the use of RAD approaches suggests that they are best suited to situations where the overall system is not too large and where the number of stakeholders (with potentially divergent views) is fairly small. For larger and more complex projects, it is probable that one of the more conventional approaches will prove easier to manage.

Most RAD approaches do have a number of things in common:

■ The success of the approach depends on users and technical staff being empowered to make decisions without having to obtain explicit approval from their senior managers.
■ All deliverables are reviewed for their business fitness rather than their adherence to a 'requirements' document. The reason for this is that requirements are often not completely accurate and this may ultimately lead to a poor system.
■ Testing is seen as being an integral part of the iterative cycle.
■ All changes are viewed as being reversible. This means that going down a dead end is not seen as being a mistake but rather as an integral part of the process.
■ Incremental delivery is acceptable and so a partial system may be implemented initially and refined by subsequent increments.
■ The concept of a 'timebox' is used to develop a system with a predefined scope within a short time limit. The limit for each timebox is set before work starts and delivery is limited to what can best be achieved within each timebox.
■ Joint Application Development (© IBM) brings together the system developers and all key stakeholders from the user organisation. Typically, workshop-type methods are used to develop requirements and agree priorities.

A more formalised approach for RAD is the Dynamic System Development Method (DSDM), which sets out nine key principles in a framework for this type of development. These principles, which are set out briefly below, are broadly in line with those in the previous discussion of RAD.

■ Users must be actively involved.
■ Teams must be empowered to make decisions.
■ Products are delivered frequently rather than perfected.

- Each product should be fit for its business purpose.
- Iterative and incremental development is an integral part of the approach.
- All changes are reversible.
- The high-level scope of the system should be agreed at a level which does not make it difficult to change it later in development.
- Testing is an integral part of the lifecycle.
- All stakeholders must cooperate and collaborate.

The final thing to be said about RAD is that it can create difficulties for the project manager. RAD methods imply speed and, to a certain extent, a lack of structure to the development. The lack of clearly defined requirements, possibly even of the overall scope of the project, and the iterative nature of the specification and development process, make it very important that control is properly exercised if the project is to deliver the 'rapid' benefits of the approach.

6.11 Object-oriented development methods

Object-oriented (OO) approaches represent a radically different and, many people would claim, a more natural and 'organic' view of the construction and development of software. The basic concept of an object is that it is a package of software that contains both data (*variables* in OO terminology) and processes (*methods*). So there may be an object in a system that draws shapes: its variables would be the size and type of shape and its methods the actual processes used to draw the shapes. Objects communicate with each other via messages so, to continue our example, the drawing-control object may send a message to the shape-drawing object saying 'Draw circle 25 mm in diameter'.

The reason why it is claimed that OO methods are a more natural approach to software development is because the real world is made up of independent objects that communicate with each other via messages. Consider a cricket match where the batsman-object has just hit the ball and the bowler-object shouts 'Catch it' to a fielder-object; the bowler does not have to tell the fielder *how* to catch the ball since that is one of the methods that the fielder knows perfectly well how to carry out.

Objects, in addition, can be grouped into classes and, indeed, these can be used to build a hierarchy. So both bowlers and batsmen would be grouped into the class Cricketers, and cricketers, footballers and tennis players can be put in the superclass of Sportspeople. Some of the methods for objects can be defined at a high level, so that sportspeople can all run around, train and drink beer in the pub afterwards. Members of the class Footballers have some specific methods, like shooting at goal and falling over pretending to be hurt, whereas cricketers can sit around waiting for the rain to stop. Classes inherit some behaviours from superclasses and objects inherit behaviours from the class. In software terms, this means that many methods and variables can be defined at class or superclass level, leaving only the more specific behaviours to be defined for the individual objects.

The relevance of all this in software development terms is to do with the way that systems are developed and maintained. One of the main problems of building systems – particularly large ones – has been how to coordinate the efforts of lots of programmers to build a coherent system. The larger the system, the harder this becomes. In addition, to go back to our shape-drawing example, what happens if there is suddenly a need to draw a new shape like a dodecahedron? In conventional systems, there would probably have to be a new routine written and fitted into all the places in the system where this new shape was needed. In an OO system, all that is changed is the shape-drawing object, and all other parts of the system can send it messages asking it to draw the new shape; only the shape-drawing object has to know how the shapes are produced.

Object-oriented methods originated in the early 1980s with various developers who were building simulation software, and one of the earliest OO languages was called Simula. More commonly used languages include Smalltalk, C++ and, in recent years, Java.

Initially, the OO approach was largely applied to the programming effort, the analysis being done in the usual structured fashion. However, there are some problems with this as, with structured methods, data and processing are typically analysed separately, though cross-checked against each other, whereas with OO we need to consider an object's methods and variables together. Consequently, some OO approaches to analysis (such as those advocated by Peter Coad and Ed Yourdon) have now been established.

After some years of competing ideas and standards, a more-or-less standardised approach has emerged for OO projects with the Unified Modeling Language (UML) and the Unified Process (UP). UML provides a visual language for OO projects and UP supplies a process model. Although UP is an 'open' (non-proprietary) approach, Rational Corporation of the USA has, through its Rational Unified Process, offered a commercially available and well-developed set of processes and tools which are becoming widely used and are developing into an embryonic de facto standard.

In essence, there are four phases within the Unified Process: inception, elaboration, construction and transition. Within each phase, there are five 'workflows': requirements, analysis, design, implementation (building the software) and test. So, the Unified Process can be represented by a two-dimensional grid, with the four phases along one axis and the five workflows along the other. This provides a sound basis for the management and control of an OO project.

6.12 Component-based development

Objects, as we have seen, are small-scale components of an information system. However, some organisations have been experimenting with something called 'component-based development' which is not quite OO but has some similarities to it.

The objective with component-based development is to try to avoid the tendency in IT projects to keep on 'reinventing the wheel' and instead to reuse already available software. The idea is that, over time, it will be possible to develop a large library of standard software components that can be assembled in various ways to produce a range of applications. For example, there may be a standard routine to access a database and produce a file of employee information, and this routine can be used in the personnel system, the payroll system and the pensions system. So, in time, instead of systems needing to be handcrafted, they can be assembled from a kit of standardised parts. If achievable, the advantages of the component-based approach would appear to be considerable:

- In the long run, development costs should fall, as more and more reusable components become available (but see the warning below).
- There should be greater consistency in the presentation of data between different systems. For example, employee information would be identical whether it is being used by payroll or personnel.
- Development times should be reduced since not all of a new system will have to be built from scratch.

The problem here is that the benefits will only be realised in the long term. In the short term, development of the individual components will probably be more expensive since instead of, say, just thinking how a routine will be used in the personnel system, the developers will have to consider the needs of payroll and pensions as well. Moreover, technology is developing constantly and rapidly, which means that components will have to be continually redeveloped to keep up with the latest advances.

Nevertheless, it is likely that most large IT organisations – including the consultancy firms – will devote some effort to component-based development in the next few years in an effort to control development costs and improve the quality of software.

6.13 Extreme programming

Extreme programming (or 'XP' as its proponents call it) is a rather extreme form of the rapid application development approach. It was created to deal with the common project problems of rapidly changing requirements, challenging deadlines and working with new or unfamiliar technologies. As we have seen in our discussion of RAD, there is no attempt to scope the whole system at the outset and, indeed, it is suggested that XP will work best on relatively small projects, or at least projects that can be undertaken by small, tightly focused, teams of software engineers.

The XP concept is of the small team of developers working hand-in-glove with their customers to create, test and implement relatively small pieces of software against deliberately challenging timescales. The developers work in pairs, at the same computer, checking and testing each other's work. Software is created from user 'stories' and is tested as it is built. There are frequent small releases. The customers must be available at all times and there must be well-established standards for code that are adhered to to ensure consistency.

Although this might sound somewhat anarchic, in fact there is a good structural model to support it. Each piece of work is treated as a 'mini-project', with its own stages and tasks. Many of the traditional disciplines of project management, such as creating estimates and schedules before starting work, apply, but on a smaller scale – and therefore, possibly, with a greater chance of success.

The main drawback would appear to be that the approach cannot be 'scaled' to handle very large projects, although it may be that many large projects could be broken up into smaller subprojects and handled using the XP method.

6.14 Package-based IS projects

All of the development methods described so far have one thing in common: an assumption that the organisation undertaking a development project will create the software from scratch. However, organisations are trying increasingly to find packaged software to meet their needs, since such software provides some important business advantages:

- Introduction of the new system is likely to take less time.
- Cost is likely to be lower, since the costs of development of the package are, in effect, shared between all the package users.
- Ongoing support and system enhancements are usually readily available.

However, there are some potential drawbacks associated with the packaged solution:

- The package may not be a perfect fit with the organisation's requirements.
- The best package in functional terms may not run on the organisation's hardware or fit with its software strategy.
- The organisation is in the hands of the package supplier in terms of getting changes and enhancements made.

In addition, adopting a packaged solution is unlikely to provide competitive advantage, since other organisations can easily buy the same package. Often, therefore, organisations will try to use packages for 'bread and butter' applications, like accounting or payroll, and will develop specific applications in areas where they think IT can provide a competitive edge.

An organisation considering using a package needs to make a very fundamental decision as to whether the solution will be package-constrained or package-based. With a *package-constrained* solution, the organisation should analyse the requirements in some detail and find the package that is the best fit with those requirements. Then, in areas where the package works differently from the organisation's processes, it is the processes that are changed to fit the package rather than vice versa. For this to be viable, the package must be a very good fit in the first place, with the differences being in areas of marginal importance. With a *package-based* solution, the organisation selects a package that provides most of the required functionality and then either commissions or develops additional functionality on top.

The danger with the package-constrained approach is that the organisation selects a package that detrimentally constrains the way it works but it has the advantage of minimising costs and timescales and making ongoing support relatively straightforward. With a package-based approach, the organisation gets a solution that better fits its requirements but at considerably greater expense and with some increased difficulty in terms of supporting the hybrid application. In addition, experience tends to suggest that extensive customisation of a package (say more than 30 per cent) can, in the long run, work out more expensive than developing the whole application from scratch.

The project manager needs to bear the following points in mind when managing a project where a packaged solution is preferred:

- There is still a need for proper analysis of requirements, at least to the level of detail where the evaluation of potential packages can be undertaken.
- Business and user management need to be clear about whether they are going down the package-constrained or package-based route. Whatever the decision, the role of the sponsor is going to be vital in keeping minds focused on the implications of the chosen approach.
- Although all project management is about orchestrating the efforts of several disparate specialist groups or individuals, this is even more so in the case of a package-based project. The project manager will have to make sure that all the interested parties – the package vendors, hardware suppliers, in-house IT department and so on – are aware of the overall plans and direct their efforts in line with them.

6.15 Soft Systems Methodology

Strictly speaking, the Soft Systems Methodology, or SSM, is not an approach to information systems development, and therefore we could regard it as outside the scope of this book. However, IS projects are rarely concerned purely with technology and they have cultural, human and organisational dimensions as well and it is in these areas that SSM can be of use to the IS project manager. Soft Systems Methodology originated in work undertaken at Lancaster University in the 1970s and 1980s, led by Professor Peter Checkland. Checkland and his team were interested in the world of 'systems' in its widest sense and they recognised that the universe is full of systems – natural systems (like human beings), designed physical systems (like computers), designed abstract systems (for example, mathematics or logical positivism) and, finally, 'human activity systems'. The problem with the traditional approaches to human activity systems – represented, for example, by conventional systems analysis techniques – is that it assumes a crisply defined problem and clearly stated requirements for change. Since, in the real world, problems are seldom well-defined and there is usually a lot of argument about what the problems actually are, and since getting clear requirements is notoriously difficult, the SSM people concluded that what they called the 'hard systems thinking' approach often led nowhere. Instead, they proposed an alternative approach they called the Soft Systems Model which accepts the inherent 'greyness' of real-world situations and proceeds, through a series of steps, to identify the problems and suitable solutions:

1 The 'problem situation' is stated but perhaps in an unstructured way.
2 'Root definitions' – in effect the perspectives of the system's stakeholders – are collected and explored, to find out what people believe about the system.
3 Based on the root definitions, a series of conceptual models are built that show what a human activity system would look like if built from each model.
4 The various conceptual models are compared and discussed and agreement is sought on a model that all the stakeholders can agree represents the way forward.
5 Real-world constraints – such as time, cost, culture and politics – are considered to see what changes are desirable and feasible.
6 Actions are generated to implement the change.

In an IS situation, the SSM approach can be used to great advantage in the early stages of a project where the requirements are not at all clear, or are in dispute between the project's stakeholders. The conceptual models can be used to explore different business scenarios and to facilitate agreement about the way forward. Once this has been accomplished, more conventional – 'hard systems' – techniques can be used to detail the actual IT system requirements, as a basis for systems development. Alternatively, SSM can be used in conjunction with a RAD or extreme programming approach to incrementally develop an IT system to meet the business needs.

6.16 Socio-technical approach

The socio-technical approach is, again, not really an IT approach but, like SSM, it does offer some useful concepts of value to the IS project manager. The socio-technical approach, developed by the Tavistock Institute in the UK, is concerned with change and its impact on people and organisations. New technology invariably involves changes to work processes and to the organisations within which they take place – and both of these have a knock-on effect for the people concerned. Technology projects that fail to recognise and deal with this reality are going to run into difficulties, at the least, and possibly fail altogether. The socio-technical design process is similar to business process re-engineering (see next section) but places greater emphasis on designing processes for people as well as efficiency, the philosophy being that high job satisfaction leads to high performance and therefore to superior economic achievement.

6.17 Business process re-engineering

Business process re-engineering (BPR) originated in the early 1990s with the publication of *Reengineering the Corporation: A Manifesto for Business Revolution*, by two American consultants, James Hammer and Michael Champy. Their philosophy was basically that, although some improvement in business performance can be achieved through marginal changes to systems and organisations, real, large-scale gains only result from a fundamental rethinking about what is done and how it is done. The idea with BPR is to ask: If we were starting this organisation today, what would we do? How would we do it? What systems and processes would we need? What skills would be required to operate these processes? The process models that result from this 'green field' approach are usually very different from what the organisation does now, and the challenge then is to get as close to the 'ideal' model as is possible, given real-world constraints.

In most BPR initiatives, IT emerges as a key enabler of change, with new and more integrated systems allowing things to be done faster, better, cheaper and in more places. So, many IS projects are either part of, or result from, BPR exercises.

Unfortunately, BPR has become associated with 'downsizing', as many organisations have used the technique to make themselves leaner for a more competitive environment. However, the most successful organisations – Wal-Mart supermarkets and Dell Computer are good examples – have used technology-driven process improvements not to shrink their workforces but to grow the size and profitability of their businesses.

6.18 Summary

It is important to appreciate the difference between the project lifecycle and the system development lifecycle. Although this book is primarily about project management, the project manager needs to have an appreciation of the different models used in developing systems as it may be necessary to select an appropriate system development lifecycle in order to meet the constraints of time, cost, quality, resources and risk which have been placed on the project. In any event, the project manager will need to have a knowledge of the problems, pitfalls and good points of managing a project using each of the lifecycles.

There are basically two system development models: the waterfall and the spiral; most other models are based on these. The waterfall model adopts a stage-by-stage approach with each stage being carried out once only and a stage starting only on completion of the one before. The spiral model is iterative in nature with several cycles being carried out in succession with the system under development being refined at each cycle.

The 'b' model, the 'V' model and the incremental model are variants of the waterfall model.

There are many approaches that have been used, and are being used, to develop information systems. Most structured approaches make use of a waterfall model but the spiral, iterative, approach forms the basis of rapid application development (RAD) and extreme programming. Object-oriented approaches are growing in popularity and the Unified Process and Unified Modeling Language offer structure and tools for OO developments. Finally, IS projects usually take place within a wider organisational context and here approaches such as the Soft Systems Methodology, the socio-technical approach and business process re-engineering are very relevant.

Questions

1 You have been asked to take charge of a system development where the customer requires about 50 per cent of the functionality very urgently to meet a business opportunity but where the remaining functions can be delivered over the next few years. Which of the various development lifecycles do you think would be most suitable for this project and why?

2 What would you say are the principal advantages and disadvantages of the sequential approach to system development offered by the waterfall and 'V' lifecycle models?

3 Some critics have said that the use of structured methods, such as SSADM, increases both delivery time and bureaucracy. Do you think these criticisms are justified and what are the claimed advantages in the use of structured methods?

4 Increasing interest is being taken in the use of rapid application development. Why is this, and are there any dangers associated with the RAD approach?

5 Consider how you would organise your project team for a RAD-type project. What leadership practices would it require from the project leader and what would the team members have to do? How, and at which points, would you involve the users?

6 What have RAD and extreme programming got in common? What are the claimed advantages of these approaches?

7 Why are approaches such as the Soft Systems Methodology, the socio-technical approach and business process re-engineering relevant to IS project managers?

Case study

Richard Vaughan, the project manager for the France Vacances project, has decided to use a waterfall lifecycle for the development with the following stages:

1 Analysis of requirements and production of requirements specification
2 Technical design
3 Code and test of programs
4 Integration and system test
5 User training
6 Acceptance testing
7 Implementation.

For stages 1 and 2, the two development teams will work together, then stages 3 to 5 will be undertaken as two parallel projects. Finally, stages 6 and 7 will be done as one project. This lifecycle is illustrated in Figure 6.7.

Figure 6.7 France Vacances internet project lifecycle

Further reading

Arlow, Jim and Neustadt, Ila (2002), *UML and the Unified Process*, Pearson Education

Checkland, Peter (1993), *Systems Thinking, Systems Practice*, Wiley

De Marco, Tom (1982), *Controlling Software Projects*, Yourdon Press

Gilb, Tom (1988), *Principles of Software Engineering Management*, Addison-Wesley

Hammer, Michael, and Champy, James (1993), *Reengineering the Corporation: A Manifesto for Business Revolution*, HarperCollins

Mumford, Enid and Beekman, Geert Jan (1994), *Tools for Change and Progress: A Socio-Technical Approach to Business Process Re-engineering*, CSG Publications

Yeates, Donald and Wakefield, Tony (2003), *Systems Analysis and Design*, FT/Prentice Hall

7 The profile of a project

Introduction

In the previous chapter we looked at a number of system development life-cycles and considered some of the general project management issues that affected them. In this chapter we look at a particular project in some detail and at the work involved at each stage of the project. We then examine a generic 'process model' which can be tailored to suit the project in question. Rather than looking at an 'in-house' project where the information system is to be developed for the organisation by internal staff, we are going to consider the situation where an external supplier will carry out the technical development work alongside the company's users. In the remainder of the chapter, therefore, we shall use 'customer' to mean the organisation commissioning the work and 'supplier' to mean the external company brought in to carry out the development work. Even if you work for an in-house IT department, it is not a bad discipline to think of the relationship between yourselves and your internal clients as a customer/supplier relationship, as this provides a sound framework for the governance of your projects.

The IS project to be considered is the delivery of a specified information system within given constraints of time, cost, resource and quality. We shall assume that a feasibility study has been carried out and that the scope of the project and the overall requirements have been specified as part of the pro-curement process to select the supplier. The project will come to a conclusion with the acceptance of the system by the customer and there will then be some element of ongoing maintenance or enhancement as part of the project. The work will be carried out by the supplier on the customer's premises and will be developed, tested and finally installed on hardware owned by the customer. Any additional hardware procurement will be handled by the customer and will not form part of the remit of the supplier.

We also look in this chapter at the issues involved in systems delivery with this type of arrangement as the views of the customer and supplier can be rather different and it is useful to be aware of both sides, irrespective of which 'side' the project manager represents. Obviously the overall objective is the same from both sides: the delivery of an information system acceptable to the customer in terms of quality and delivered by the supplier within the allotted budget and timescale.

Projects of this type are usually carried out in one of two ways: 'fixed-price' or 'time-and-materials'. In a **fixed-price** contract, the cost of the work is agreed at the outset and is based on delivery of the stated requirements. A time-and-materials contract is less rigid and means that the supplier is paid on the basis of the effort which is put into development. There are pros and cons to each arrangement which are different for customer and supplier. Fixed price means that the requirements need to be specified to a high level of detail in order that both customer and supplier have a clear understanding of what is to be delivered. The risk with this kind of project is carried by the supplier as it receives the same amount in payment irrespective of how much resource has been put into delivering the system. If the supplier underestimates the amount of work involved, its profit will be reduced or even eliminated. Conversely, if the supplier can deliver the project efficiently, there is scope for maximising the profit. This type of arrangement also means that change control is very important; the customer is likely to find that the cost of the project is increased with every change which is required to the original requirements specified at the outset. From the customer point of view, this can be frustrating and lead to a deterioration of working relations with the supplier, perhaps unfairly. **Time-and-materials** arrangements, on the other hand, mean that the customer is required to pay for all effort expended by the supplier and leave the customer exposed to inefficient and poor quality work by the supplier. The advantage of this arrangement for the customer is that it is more flexible, allows the requirements of the project to be varied more easily and minimises reworking and renegotiation of the contract.

7.2 The process model

Although all projects are different and have unique features, there are elements which are common to most. The concept of a 'process model', which shows a generic framework, can be useful. A process model needs a set of features which:

- Are adaptable to a wide range of applications.
- Provide a complete and adequate definition of any project to which they are applied.
- Are easy to assimilate, with the key tasks and points of interest highlighted.
- Are suitable to act as a memorandum and checklist to ensure that everything is covered.
- Do not impose any unnecessary constraints on the use of tools, techniques or methods during a project.

A typical process model is shown in Figure 7.1. This model shows the project divided into a number of stages which are followed in sequence from start to finish of the project. Several of the stages are carried out in parallel with the main stages and these are also shown. The major deliverables from each stage are indicated by the round-cornered boxes.

Figure 7.1 Generic process model for software development

A process model can be helpful to a project manager in planning the project but obviously cannot be followed blindly and must be tailored to meet the requirements of the project. Not all of the elements of the process model will be appropriate, but the model can be used as a checklist to ensure that nothing important is missed from the project. Within the process model, the system development lifecycle must be considered and an appropriate model chosen. This was discussed in some detail in the previous chapter. The process model is also used to help define what is required of the project manager at each stage in the project and to define the inputs and outputs of each stage.

The process model shown perhaps implies a waterfall-type system development lifecycle (see Chapter 6) owing to the sequential nature of the activities. However, the model does allow a number of different system development lifecycles within the Development process box. This typically covers the analysis, design, programming and testing aspects of IS development but does not prescribe how, or in what order, these activities should take place. For example, a full waterfall model approach would have analysis, design, programming and testing carried out in sequence with each activity starting only when the preceding one had been completed. With a phased delivery approach, the analysis and high-level design would be completed followed by sets of detailed design, programming and system testing for each delivery phase. Similarly, if a spiral model approach were adopted, the analysis, design, programming and testing would be repeated for each turn of the spiral. The generic process model would cater for all of these different approaches without substantial modification.

We now look in some detail at a number of the stages of our project and how they relate to the process model. These stages are:

■ *Pre-project work* – including initial client contact, evaluation of tenders and agreeing a form of contract.

- *Start-up or Initiation stage* – this includes the Project Start-up stage on the process model.
- *Development stage* – this includes the Development stage on the process model.
- *Completion stage* – this includes the Delivery to Customer, Staff Training and Familiarisation, Acceptance Testing, System Commissioning and Customer Takeover stages on the process model.
- *Operational stage* – this includes the In-service Live Running, Warranty Support and Maintenance, and Enhancements stages on the process model.
- *Post-project review stage* – this involves auditing the project after it has finished, to capture any lessons learned from it.

7.3 Pre-project work

Prior to the development project starting, there will have been extensive discussions between the customer and supplier to establish the objectives and scope of the project and to agree a suitable contractual framework within which the project will take place. Very often, the customer will have prepared a specification of their requirements and will have issued invitations to tender (ITTs) to suppliers it thinks may be able to carry out the project. The suppliers will then respond with their tenders and the customer will subject these to a detailed evaluation process. Once the chosen supplier has been selected, negotiations will take place to agree a suitable form of contract for the project. As we have seen, if the requirements are tightly defined, a fixed-price contract may be appropriate, but if much detail remains to be agreed, a time-and-materials contract may be more suitable. The supplier, too, may have to agree subcontracts with other suppliers (perhaps hardware vendors) if it is not doing all the work, or providing all the infrastructure, itself.

7.4 Project start-up

7.4.1 The importance of this stage

Project start-up covers the work which is carried out at the beginning of the project when the basic framework is put in place. The stage is also called the Project Initiation stage, particularly in the PRINCE2® method. Start-up is an important stage of the project as it is the stage where the foundations for success, or failure, are laid. Much of the future work of the project is based upon these foundations and the importance of the Start-up stage should not be underestimated. There is often pressure at this point to start the 'real' work; this should be resisted as time spent in getting the basic infrastructure of the project correct is always time well spent.

A lot of the issues to be addressed here, and particularly those summarised in the project initiation document (see below) should have been covered in the contract. However, even with the utmost diligence shown at the contract stage, it is surprising how many details are still unresolved when the actual project starts, and it is up to the project manager to wrestle these to the ground during start-up. (If the project is being carried out in-house then there is unlikely to be a contract as such, and the project initiation document then has to act as an internal contract between the 'customer' and 'supplier' departments.)

It is instructive to look a little more deeply into the overall organisation of the project as, in a sense, there are likely to be two project managers involved. The *customer project manager*, or project director as this person is sometimes called, is responsible for the overall project which involves coordination of the customer/user resources and all issues relating to the customer's liaison with the developer or supplier. This person's responsibility is to arrange for the appropriate user involvement, specifically during the production of the requirements specification, and for customer acceptance of the system. The users may be required to be involved at other times too. Prototyping, training and production of user manuals are some of the other activities requiring user input.

Depending on the terms of the agreement between customer and supplier, there may also be an ongoing review of products by the customer's staff other than the users directly involved in the project. This may be considered necessary by the customer as part of the general assurance of the project, to make sure that it is on course and continuing to meet the business objectives and to ensure that certain standards, technical policies and strategic aims are being adhered to. In a PRINCE2® project, this work could be carried out by the project assurance team reporting to the project board. In terms of the overall organisation of the project, the project director should be in overall charge as the project is owned by the customer, not by the developer or supplier. It is important also that the customer side is involved in planning work, as many projects fail not through technical problems but because of a lack of available user resources at key points.

The *supplier project manager* is responsible for the delivery of the technical products which make up the information system. As described in Chapter 4, this role can, in PRINCE2®, be taken by a team leader responsible for one aspect or stage of a project. There may be a number of stages in the project for which a supplier is responsible and the supplier may use the same manager for all stages or change managers to meet the differing technical requirements of each stage.

In the remainder of this chapter we refer to the customer project manager as the project director and to the supplier project manager as just 'the project manager'. Both managers have responsibilities which relate to project management and it is important that the boundaries between their roles and their respective responsibilities are clearly agreed and documented; failure to do this often leads to misunderstandings and problems later in the project.

It is useful to look at the different elements of project start-up under the headings of what, why, who, how and when:

- What is to be carried out?
- Why is it being done?
- Who is going to do it?
- How is it to be accomplished?
- When is to be done?

What? We need to know what objectives, scope, constraints and interfaces apply to the project. Most of this information can be gleaned from other sources such as a feasibility study report, project brief, project terms of reference and contract documents. It is important to re-examine this information, however, and to confirm that it is still accurate and consistent.

Why? Every project should have a business case which sets out the main problems or opportunities which are to be addressed. The main part of the business case contains details of the costs of developing and maintaining the system as against the benefits it is expected to produce. This provides a justification for the project and can be used at any point in the future to check that the benefits can still be cost-justified. This is important as circumstances can alter, and changes to the business requirements or in development costs can result in the project no longer being a cost-effective proposition. Many projects in the past have continued with open-ended development when a reappraisal of the business case – assuming one existed – would have made it obvious that the project should have been terminated. There is more detail on constructing a business case in Chapter 3.

Who? This covers the project organisation. It is particularly important that the roles and responsibilities of customer and developer or supplier are clearly set out to avoid arguments clouding the project later.

How and when? These elements are covered in the plans for the project which are developed at this stage. The planning process is described in detail in Chapters 8, 9 and 10. It is usual at the start-up stage of a project to produce a high-level plan for the whole project and a more detailed plan for the first stage. As each stage is approached, the overall plan is revised and a detailed stage plan is developed. In reality, there is more than one plan and the following aspects should be covered in some form or other:

- A general plan description which, as well as a narrative description, details the project prerequisites, the external dependencies and the planning assumptions.
- A technical plan which sets out the products to be delivered, the activities required to produce them, the times, dates and durations of each activity and the dependencies between activities.
- A resource plan which identifies the type of resource – analyst, programmer, user and so on – and the amount of effort required from these resources to carry out each activity. 'Non-people' resources, including the provision of

computers, desks, CASE (computer-aided software engineering) tools and other items, should also be included.

- A project quality plan which sets out the quality strategy to be followed and cross-references any quality management system, quality manuals and development approaches which the organisation has decided are to be used. The quality plan should also set out the quality criteria which are to be applied to each of the products.

- A risk analysis which sets out the probable risks to the project and identifies actions to prevent them occurring or minimise their impact if they do occur. Risk management is covered in Chapter 15.

- The configuration management plan which defines how control is to be exercised on the products of the project and how changes to these products are to be managed. Configuration management is covered in Chapter 14.

Resources should be addressed as early as possible in the project, especially when particular resources are required. From the customer perspective, the project director has to ensure that the appropriate end-users are available at the right times. This may involve negotiating with their managers who may not be keen to have their staff diverted from their normal duties. The project director has to assemble the 'experts' in the various assurance activities if their experience is to be used in monitoring the project. Some organisations have dedicated groups for this purpose. The project manager is responsible for locating the development resources and making sure that these are available. There may be competition between different managers for specialist resources and the use of contract staff may have to be considered to make up any shortfall.

Ensuring that resources other than people are available is important and often overlooked. Because of the limited life of a project and the varying number of people involved at different stages, accommodation can be a troublesome issue and ensuring a suitable place for all to work can be difficult. Similarly, an adequate infrastructure for the project is needed if time and effort are not to be wasted. Analysts probably need access to CASE tools and PCs to produce the project's documentation. The development environment also needs to be ready for the programming staff, with appropriate support tools for building and testing modules. The list of possible resources is long and needs consideration if nothing is to be overlooked.

7.4.2 The project initiation document

This important document is the product of the Start-up stage and encapsulates its main decisions. It should be produced by the project manager and approved by the project sponsor (see Chapter 4).

The format of a project initiation document (PID) will vary from organisation to organisation and the PRINCE2® project management method has a detailed product description for it. However, a simple but effective format for a PID is given through the mnemonic OSCAR, as described below. Completing the sections of the OSCAR format will ensure that the most important project start-up issues are addressed.

Objectives Two types of objective need to be defined. The *business objectives* are what has ultimately justified the business case for the project, for example 'to increase our market share by 25 per cent', or 'to enable us to handle 25 per cent more patients without an increase in manpower'. The *project objectives* are narrower and specify exactly what the project itself is to deliver, for example 'to implement an e-commerce trading system', or 'to implement an automated appointment scheduling system'. Project objectives are often defined in terms of the 'triple constraint' of the time they should take, what they should cost and the product/quality to be delivered.

The reason for making this distinction is that, whereas the project manager is responsible for delivery of the project objectives, he or she cannot be responsible for achievement of the business objectives. It is perfectly possible for a project to be delivered to its time/cost/product definitions and yet for the business objectives not to be achieved; sales may not, for instance, rise by 25 per cent as expected. However, it is still useful for the PID to specify the business objectives as these will help the project team to understand what they are contributing towards, and failure to deliver to time/cost/product can certainly lead to the business objectives not being met.

Scope Scope defines the project objective in more detail in terms of what is included in the project. This is best achieved by defining the principal deliverables from the project. It is also important, in order to avoid confusion, misunderstanding and argument later, to define anything that is *not* included in the project. For example, a patient booking system project may include analysing, designing, building and implementing the software but not installing the infrastructure on which it will run.

Constraints Constraints dicate not so much what is done on the project but how it is done. They may therefore include the methods and standards to be used, the hardware and software platforms that will be involved and any legislation or organisational policy that must be complied with.

Constraints can also include time, for example that a system must be available by some date. Resources, such as people, equipment or money, may also be constraints but these are probably best dealt with under their own heading (see below).

Authority It is vital to define who is the customer for this project, that is who can authorise it in the first place, sanction changes to it and accept is as finished at the end. Although this sounds fairly obvious, it is surprising how many projects have got into difficulties precisely because of a failure to define who has this authority. Whoever it is, they have some specific responsibilities:

- To agree the PID and any subsequent amendments.
- To resolve (or adjudicate) any differences between users.
- To make financial and other resources available to the project.
- To support and promote the project to senior managers in the customer organisation.
- To accept the project on completion.

Because of this, the authority for the project is likely to be a senior manager in the customer organisation. It may well be the project sponsor, as defined in Chapter 4. In a PRINCE2® project, the authority will be the project board or, more specifically, whoever takes the executive role within that board.

Resources The resources – people, money, equipment and so on – required to execute the project should be defined. The project manager should take particular care to ensure that the amount of user and customer management involved in the project is defined properly and that the authority is fully aware of this.

Depending on the type of project and the amount of information available, the basic PID described here can be supplemented by an outline project and quality plan, a risk assessment and so on.

In developing the PID, it is often necessary to make assumptions. There is nothing wrong with this so long as the assumptions are clearly stated. For example, the amount of effort required for analysis may have been calculated on the assumption of the need to interview six people in one location and it may turn out that twenty people need to be seen, located throughout the country. If the assumptions are clearly set out in the PID, then one of two things can happen:

■ The authority may challenge them and the project can be replanned and the PID rewritten.
■ The assumptions are left unchallenged and, when they prove to be wrong, the project manager has a good case for asking for more time, money or resources to complete the project.

Once the PID is complete, it should be signed off by the project manager and the authority.

7.5 Development stage

The Development stage of the project is where most of the supplier's work is carried out. Although overall control of the project should be exercised by the customer's project director, many of the activities are under the day-to-day control of the supplier project manager. If we assume that the system development lifecycle approach in our project is based on a waterfall model, then the analysis, design, programming and system-testing activities come into this stage. It should be noted that these activities are more likely, particularly on a medium or large project, to be divided into separate stages themselves in line with the boxes in the waterfall model.

It is instructive to consider the 'V' model again as this is a frequently used model in the type of customer/supplier situation in our example. The 'V' model is shown again, in a slightly modified form, in Figure 7.2. This version shows more explicitly the products that link the production activities of the left-hand part of the 'V' with the validation and verification activities on the

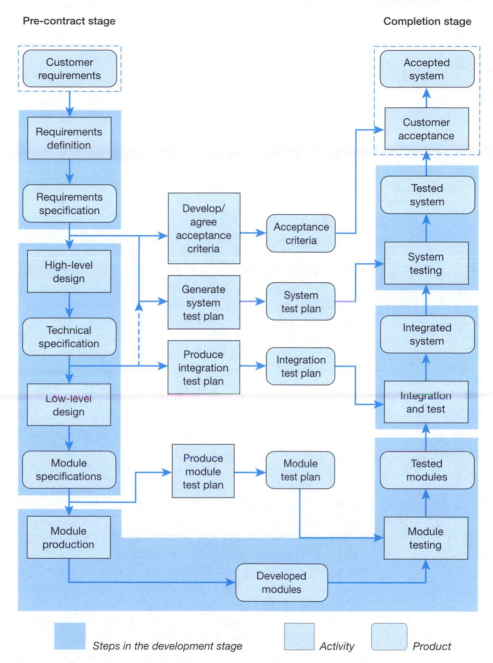

Figure 7.2 The 'V' model (modified)
(© Sema UK Ltd 1992)

right. These validation and verification activities are largely carried out by the supplier although, as stated previously, the customer may wish to apply checks and assurance procedures on these products.

The Development stage has several distinct parts and these have varying amounts of user/customer involvement. The different parts of the

Development stage are set out below. All projects will vary to some degree depending on the precise nature of the project, but the following is fairly typical of a customer/supplier type of project. The parts considered here are:

- Requirements definition
- Design
- Implementation
- Integration and testing
- System testing.

Requirements definition

In the requirements definition part of the project, the customer's requirements are specified in detail. Much of this information will have been supplied in some form in earlier documents, perhaps the initial contract documents, and confirmed in the Start-up stage output document. The purpose of this work is to ensure that all the requirements are captured and documented, that the requirements themselves are complete and consistent with each other, and that they are recorded in a precise and unambiguous manner. These requirements must be in a form such that it is possible to tell at a later date whether they have been met by the information system which is delivered.

The representatives of the customer, the users, will be much involved in this part of the project and it is imperative that these users are able to commit the required time to carrying out the work properly. This issue should have been addressed in the planning activity of the Start-up stage.

From the customer point of view, the requirements should be framed to support the overall business needs for which the system is being developed as well as meeting the needs of the end-users of the system. The supplier will be looking at the requirements from a slightly different point of view. If the project is being delivered on a fixed-price basis, the supplier will need to check whether the requirements are in accord with what was originally agreed in the contract documents and that the customer has not increased the overall scope of the project.

A good requirements specification is the foundation of all the rest of the development stage work and the work of the project manager should from now on be relatively straightforward, at least in the sense that the target has been clearly defined. This requirements specification document will be a major deliverable for the customer as it will form the basis on which the delivered system will be accepted, or otherwise, by the customer. The specification should include acceptance criteria which set out in a clear and unambiguous manner what the information system is expected to do. These acceptance criteria should link with the requirements themselves and be stated in quantitative terms wherever possible to avoid later disputes on the acceptability of the system.

Design

The design is the first part of the project which addresses *how* the requirements of the project are to be met. As we saw earlier in Chapter 6, most projects now adopt a structured approach to systems analysis and design, and one of the key points of structured methods is the separation of logical and physical designs.

It is important that all design work stems from the requirements specification and that there is a clear link, an 'audit trail', from requirements to the design components. The techniques used to produce the design and the form which the documentation of that design takes will be determined by the method or approach being used. The design will be broken down into smaller, more manageable components which will form the basis of the program or module specifications. It must be possible to identify easily how these low-level components fit together to form the overall design – the audit trail again. In terms of the 'V' model, the design will be used to form the basis of the integration tests and system tests later in the project.

Implementation The implementation part of the Development stage is where the programming and unit testing take place. This will depend to a great extent on the programming environment to be used on the project and is probably the part where the customer has the lowest level of involvement in the delivery of the products. This is not to say that the project director will not be continuing to monitor progress and to take corrective action when necessary, as the overall progress of the project is the project director's responsibility, even if the day-to-day control of the technical work is being carried out by the project manager. At the end of the implementation part there should be a complete set of modules which have been tested and signed off as conforming to the specification to which they have been built.

Integration and testing This part is concerned with integrating the individual components and checking that they work properly together. For instance, it is essential that the data passed from one module to the next is in the form that the second module expects. Integration testing must be designed to ensure that all components communicate in the expected way.

System testing System testing is carried out by the supplier to check that the whole system behaves according to the specification in the design documents and meets the requirements specification. The supplier should also check that the acceptance criteria set and agreed in the requirements definition have been met, as there is little point in delivering the system to the customer for deficiencies to be pointed out when the system is subjected to acceptance testing by the customer.

There remain a number of issues that are relevant to all parts of the Development stage. Change control is an important issue if the project is not to be allowed to overrun its time or cost constraints. The project should have a procedure for dealing with change in all its forms. It should be remembered that changes can arise at any stage of a project. Although the general procedure to be followed should be much the same, whatever the stage at which the change occurs, the impact of such a change is likely to be considerably greater the later that it takes place in the project. As an extreme example, a change which is raised late in the project could necessitate a reanalysis of the requirements for consistency, a major redesign and attendant modifications to a number of programs and the rerunning of system testing.

The need to make changes to project products can arise in a number of ways. There may be a genuine change in the requirements raised by the users because some element of the business has changed, or simply because the customer has realised that something necessary has been omitted from the requirements. When this happens it is necessary to carry out a thorough impact analysis to ascertain what effect the implementation of this change will have on the project. The impact analysis will need to take into account the effort, time and cost of reworking any components which have been completed, of specifying and building any new ones, and of modifying any which have still to be constructed. It is important to identify every component affected by the proposed change and to estimate the likely cost of modification. The total cost of implementing the change must be calculated along with the probable delay to the project. The authority for accepting changes is generally the steering committee or project board or whoever has been given executive authority for the project. It is usual, however, for the project director to be allowed a tolerance of time and cost for each stage of the project and to be able to authorise the implementation of changes of this nature as long as the tolerance is not exceeded. Tolerance is generally agreed at the Start-up stage of the project and may be defined as an amount of money or a number of days' effort. In a fixed-price contract, a change of any significance is likely to increase the cost of the contract if it leads to more work being carried out by the supplier.

Changes may be required to products for other reasons. Errors may be discovered during integration testing or system testing, which will result in reworking components, retesting them and possibly revising estimates for other uncompleted components. Errors of this type become progressively more expensive to put right the later they are discovered and therefore it is sensible to attempt to eradicate them as early as possible. The general procedure to be followed is similar to that for changes to requirements. The contractual position regarding who has responsibility for paying for this type of correction will depend on what was agreed between the customer and the supplier at the outset of the project.

Configuration management is another important element of any project and is closely related to change control. The configuration management plan should contain details of how this is to be handled. Configuration management is concerned with managing the numerous components – plans, program code, technical documentation and management documents – which will be in varying stages of development or change throughout the project. Configuration management is concerned with four basic disciplines:

- *Configuration identification* – the process of uniquely defining each component, or configuration item.
- *Configuration control* – the mechanism for controlling change to configuration items and for recording their status, for example undergoing development, baselined.
- *Configuration status accounting* – the means of extracting information about configuration items such as the number of outstanding changes.

■ *Configuration audit* – for verifying the completeness, accuracy and security of the configuration items.

Throughout the whole of the Development stage the project director and project manager will have paid particular attention to tracking the progress of the work, monitoring this progress against the plans, taking action to resolve problems as they arise and modifying the plans accordingly. If it appears, at any time, that the stage is going to exceed its agreed tolerances in terms of cost or time, a report should be prepared for the project board or steering committee in order that they can consider the continued viability of the project. At the end of the stage a report will be produced for the project board or steering committee setting out the cost, time and resource figures for the stage.

7.6　Completion stage

The Completion stage begins when the information system has been completed by the supplier and has been subjected to the full rigours of a system test and every error and problem eradicated. The associated technical documentation, user manuals, operating instructions and any other documentation should also have been finished. This stage is where the customer receives the finished product and carries out a number of examinations and tests in order to confirm that the system meets the specification which was agreed between customer and supplier. This culminates, hopefully, in the acceptance of the completed system by the customer.

There are a number of steps in the completion stage:

■ Delivery to the customer of all the elements of the system including software and documentation.
■ Training and familiarisation for the end-users, system administrators and operators.
■ Carrying out of acceptance tests by the customer on the delivered products.
■ Acceptance by the customer.
■ System commissioning.
■ Final takeover by the customer.

Not all of these steps will necessarily take place. For example, the customer may wish to carry out the training without assistance from the supplier. Similarly, commissioning the system in preparation for live running may be implemented directly by the customer using internal resources. It all depends on the agreement between the customer and the supplier or on the terms of the original contract.

Delivery to the customer Delivery to the customer should take the form of a formal handover with all the deliverables being held under configuration management. Software should be available in an appropriate electronic form together with paper records of source code or whatever was agreed in the project plans. All documentation should be handed over as agreed, with appropriate numbers of copies, and generally should be in electronic as well as paper form.

Training and familiarisation

Training and familiarisation may have been taking place over a period of time as it is generally unwise to leave all training until the last minute. If the supplier is to be responsible for training and for the production of user and operator documentation, the numbers of staff involved and the definition of the training will have been agreed beforehand.

Acceptance testing

Acceptance testing involves the customer applying a series of tests to the delivered system and associated documentation to check that they meet the specification. These tests will take a number of forms and can be divided into four categories:

- *Functionality testing*. This will check that the functionality specified in the requirements definition document has been delivered. The customer will consider the requirements and the acceptance criteria and carry out a full test to confirm them. The 'V' model shown in Figure 7.2 illustrates the correspondence between the requirements specified for the system and the customer acceptance testing.
- *Performance testing*. This will check that the system meets its performance criteria in terms of response times at terminals, numbers of transactions handled per hour, numbers of users logged on, or whatever. Recovery testing should also be included. If the system is running under test conditions which are different from live running conditions, the results of these tests must be treated with care, by both supplier and customer.
- *Interface testing*. This will confirm that the delivered system works with other systems with which it has interfaces and that the communications between the systems are functioning correctly.
- *Environmental testing*. This relates to power consumption, heat dissipation, noise and other environmental factors.

User acceptance testing is the responsibility of the customer and should be planned and managed in the same way as any other part of the project and not allowed to become open-ended. There should be a formal procedure in place for reporting faults and errors – or more correctly, issues, as they may turn out not to be faults at all – and proper records should be kept on progress to resolve them. When there are faults to be corrected, the supplier manager should plan the redelivery of the system in a sensible fashion. For instance, it would not be wise to redeliver the system in response to each individual fault, unless perhaps the number of faults was very low indeed.

Acceptance by the customer

When all of the above tests have been successfully passed, or the number of faults is low enough to be acceptable – this will have been defined in the acceptance criteria – the system will be officially accepted by the customer, probably through signing an acceptance certificate.

System commissioning

Following acceptance of the system by the customer, the system will be set up in its final environment for live running, connected to other systems and loaded with real data. Many of the tests previously carried out during acceptance testing will be repeated as, in some instances, these tests can only properly be carried out in a production environment. For instance, capacity and stress testing are better carried out in conditions which are as close to live running as possible. In some cases acceptance testing and system commissioning will be combined in order to save time. This is probably what would happen in the example project described in section 7.1 as all development and testing is being carried out on the customer's premises and using the customer's equipment, and there would be limited benefit in repeating much of the testing.

Final customer takeover This is the point where the customer formally accepts the system and the project comes to an end. It is possible that the system will be accepted with some minor faults on the basis that they will be corrected within a specified time. The project director should prepare an end-of-project report for the project board or steering committee which is responsible for officially accepting the system. The report should set out in summary form information relating to the whole project and whether the time, cost and quality objectives have been met.

The project director also prepares a second report on the project, from the project management point of view, in order that the organisation benefits from this experience. The focus of the report should not be on allocating blame for anything which went wrong but on lessons for the future. This is sometimes called a *project evaluation report*.

7.7 Operational stage

The Operational stage takes over when live running begins. This stage does not form part of the project as such, unless some type of guarantee or support arrangement has been negotiated between the customer and supplier. Business requirements change, however, and it is likely that the system will require maintenance and enhancement. Faults will arise during live running which were not discovered during testing of the system. Perhaps the system will be used in a way not envisaged by the designers and this may lead to faults becoming apparent. Changes to requirements or additional requirements will become necessary with the passage of time. The management process of applying these changes in a controlled way is essentially the same as when the project was being developed, and the documentation produced during the project phase should be maintained and kept up to date.

7.8 Post-project review

Some time after live running has started, usually at about six months, a post-implementation review should be carried out. This reconsiders the business case produced at the beginning of the project and assesses whether the business objectives of the system have been met. This concentrates not so much on whether the requirements have been met as on whether the organisation has achieved the business benefits from the system which it expected.

In addition, the post-project review should address the following issues:

■ The technical methods and standards used, and how effective these proved.
■ Project risks – how effective were the methods used to identify, assess and manage risks.
■ Contractual issues – what they were and how they were resolved.
■ Customer/supplier relationship issues.
■ Stakeholder management issues.
■ Team resourcing issues.
■ Project performance against plans, with a view to updating and improving the planning and estimating methods used.

The aim of post-project reviews is not to 'hunt for the guilty' (although often they do deteriorate into this), but to capture experience and make it available for the improvement of later projects.

7.9 Summary

In this chapter we have looked at a particular project from beginning to end. We have considered the use of a generic process model and identified the likely stages of a project. These stages are:

■ *Pre-project work*, which is concerned with establishing the requirements, identifying and selecting a supplier and agreeing a contract.
■ *Start-up or Initiation stage*, which is more concerned with 'pure' project management than with direct delivery of IS products. The start of a project was looked at under the following headings:
  – *What?* The objectives, scope, constraints and interfaces.
  – *Why?* The need for every project to have a business case.
  – *Who?* The project organisation to define the roles and responsibilities on the project.
  – *How and when?* The plans which need to be developed to ensure that the project has a firm base.
■ *Development stage*, which is concerned with the traditional analysis, design, programming and testing aspects of system development.
■ *Completion stage*, which is where the finished product is delivered by the supplier, and tested and accepted by the customer.
■ *Operational stage*, where the information system goes into live running.

For each of these stages, project management issues which are likely to be encountered have been discussed and considered from the viewpoint of the customer and the supplier and we have noted areas of possible dispute.

Questions

1 What work goes on prior to project start-up?

2 Describe the products that typically result from the following project stages: Project Start-up; Analysis of Requirements; Design Integration and Testing.

3 Explain the incremental approach to testing represented by the sequence: unit (module) test; integration test; system test; acceptance test.

4 From what product should the acceptance criteria for a project be derived and why?

5 Why is it important that the project team and the users develop and agree a process model for a project?

Case study

Richard Vaughan, the project manager for the France Vacances project, has created a project initiation document as follows.

Objectives

■ *Business objective.* To increase sales of France Vacances's products by 20 per cent through the introduction of an internet-based booking system and to convert 20 per cent of existing telesales business to internet bookings.
■ *Project objective.* To introduce an internet-based booking system for France Vacances and to provide facilities to deliver management information on the usage of the internet-based system.

Scope

The following are *included* in the scope of the project:

■ Analysis of the requirements.
■ Production of a detailed requirements specification.
■ Design, development and implementation of the internet systems, including a new website and the secure communications links.
■ Training France Vacances staff in the use of the new systems.
■ Specification of the interfaces required from France Vacances's existing customer database and booking system (the development of the links at the France Vacances end to be done by its own IT department).
■ Specification of the additional hardware required to support the new system (to be obtained from France Vacances's usual suppliers, the procurement to be managed by the IT department).
■ 'Skills transfer' to France Vacances's IT department so that ongoing maintenance and development of the new system can be handled in-house.

▶

Case study continued

The development of the MIS aspects of the new system will be dealt with by France Vacances's IT department, supervised by E-Con.

Constraints

■ France Vacances wants to have the new system up and running for the start of the winter season's bookings at the end of June.
■ The project shall be managed using the PRINCE2® project management method.
■ Specifications and other deliverables shall be produced according to E-Con's established quality system.

Authority

The authority for the project will be David Martin, director of France Vacances, who will work with a project board that also includes Jean Hunt, France Vacances customer services manager, and Barbara Currie, E-Con account manager. The authority's responsibilities will include:

■ Approving this PID and subsequent amendments.
■ Authorising changes to the project.
■ Providing resources for the project.
■ The reconciliation of conflicts between users.
■ Final acceptance of the project.

Resources

E-Con will provide the following resources:

■ Project manager (Richard Vaughan)
■ Team manager (Siobhan Reid)
■ Project analyst (David Cooper)
■ Analysts (Pam Stephanou and Don Short)
■ Web developers (Greg Martin and Janet Vine).

France Vacances will provide the following resources:

■ Team manager (Peter Clay)
■ Analyst/programmer (one – name to be agreed)
■ Reasonable access to other personnel for fact-finding, training, testing etc.

A fixed price of €300,000 has been agreed for those parts of the project being undertaken by E-Con. France Vacances has been advised to budget up to €50,000 for the work being undertaken by its own IT department and for user and management involvement in the project.

The PID is put before the project board on 5 April and approved.

Further reading

British Standards Institution (2002), BS 6079–1:2002 *Guide to Project Management*, BSI

International Organisation for Standardisation (2002), ISO/IEC 12207 Amendment 1 *Information Technology – Software life cycle processes*, ISO

Turner, J Rodney and Simister, Stephen J (2000), *Gower Handbook of Project Management*, Gower

8 Project planning: understanding the work

8.1 Introduction

In this chapter and the two that follow we examine some of the steps involved in planning an IS project – or most other types of project for that matter. We present a systematic model for the development of sound and practicable project plans and we contrast two approaches to breaking the project down into controllable chunks: the work breakdown structure and the product breakdown structure.

A First World War general once remarked that 'no plan survives first contact with the enemy'. Translated into the more peaceful sphere of project management, this might become: 'no plan survives the start of actual project work'. If this is the case, the question might be asked, why do we bother to plan at all? Why do we not just roll up our sleeves and get on with it, a project management approach that has been called JDI – 'just do it'? Although this might seem like a silly idea, the fact is that many – too many – IS projects have been attempted using JDI and most of them have ended in disaster. Project managers come under a lot of pressure to JDI, not least from their customers who want to see some 'real work' in progress.

So why do we need to plan? There are some compelling reasons:

- Developing an information system is a complex undertaking, generally involving the synthesis of various elements – hardware, software, data capture, user training and so on. Making something of this complexity is likely to succeed only if it is planned carefully in advance.
- The people involved in a project need to know exactly what their role is, what they are expected to produce and when it is wanted. The project plan communicates this information to all concerned.
- Customers want to be confident that the developers know what they are about. The plan is a tangible demonstration that thought has gone into the work and that the developers have a clear idea of where they are going.
- Unless there is a plan, how can the project manager know whether the project is on schedule, ahead or behind, and whether corrective action is needed?

This last reason explains why a plan is needed even though it will not survive first contact with the enemy. If there is no plan, the project manager has no information on which to base their management actions – it is rather like driving a car with one's eyes closed, not knowing whether one should be steering to left or right, or even putting on the brakes.

Three chapters are devoted to project planning. In this chapter, we examine how to break down the project into manageable chunks that we can plan and estimate. We also discuss the dependencies between activities and introduce the concepts of the network diagram and the bar chart. In Chapter 9 we review some different methods available for estimating the work to be done, and in Chapter 10 we see how the estimates and the dependencies are combined to create workable schedules for the project.

One final point. The planning *process* itself has a value irrespective of the plan that results. This is that it gives the project manager the opportunity to sit down and *think* about what the project is about and how it is to be achieved. What are the deliverables and when are they wanted? What skills do we need and where do we get them? What are the problems we are likely to encounter and how shall we tackle them? What are the risks involved and how shall we manage them? Risk management is such an important subject that it gets a chapter to itself later in the book. Planning for quality, too, is addressed as a specific topic. In the rest of this chapter, we consider how to develop the basic project plan, specifying the work to be done, the sequence in which it will be performed and who will undertake it.

8.2 Understanding the requirement

The starting point for a good project plan is a proper understanding of the requirement: what is it *exactly* that the project is supposed to achieve? If an IS project is to be successful, then all concerned must know *in detail* what they are trying to do. Unfortunately, in too many instances, this is far from being the case.

In an ideal world, the project would start with a requirements specification of some sort. Exactly what this covers, and the level of detail involved, will depend on where we are in the project lifecycle. For example:

- If we are about to start an IS strategy study, then the requirement may be very broad indeed – for example, the study might be to include all activities that contribute towards the business's market strategy.
- A feasibility study would have a narrower focus – for example to examine the practicality of automating stockchecking in a warehouse.
- A full IS project covering the analysis, design, specification, development and implementation of an information system requires a much more precise definition of the requirements from which to start.

It is evident, then, that the further along the IS lifecycle we are, the more precision we require in order to get going. The very generalised briefing given for a strategy study is quite inadequate for a development project. It is the project manager's responsibility to ensure that the requirement is specified in enough detail for the project to get off to a clear start.

But what if the specification is not detailed enough? What if you are a systems company, or an in-house IT department, that has been asked to quote for a development project against a very high-level specification? The logical response to such a situation would be to decline to bid and to ask the customer to define their ideas more precisely and come back later. But we live in the real world and developers are often forced through commercial pressures to tender against quite inadequate specifications. The practical answer is that the project manager must conduct a thorough risk analysis of the project and identify where there are holes in the specification. These holes must then be discussed with the customer and any assumptions must be documented and accepted by both customer and project manager. This is not a trivial activity and probably involves some hard bargaining, but it is essential if the interests of all parties – the customers in getting what they want and the developers in limiting their exposure – are to be protected.

This analysis of the work is the first and perhaps most important stage in the planning process. At the end of it, the project manager should have a pretty clear idea of what the project is supposed to achieve, its business objectives and the assumptions inherent in the proposed approach.

8.3 Breaking down the work

Having looked at the objectives of the project, it is time to consider what needs to be done to meet those objectives: what are we trying to produce and how shall we go about it? There are two basic approaches to this: the work breakdown structure and the product breakdown structure, but, as we shall see, these converge in developing a detailed list of the activities needed to execute the project.

8.3.1 Work breakdown structure

Work breakdown is the more traditional approach and has been widely used in many industries for a long time. The basic idea is to take the overall 'work' – the project – and to break it down progressively into smaller and smaller chunks until we end up with individual tasks, or work packages, that we can estimate sensibly and assign to team members.

To understand how this works, let us consider a small IS project, say a feasibility study in a builder's merchant to see if there is scope for introducing a computerised stock control system. If we consider the project as a whole, we might decide that the work breaks down into two main components, as shown in Figure 8.1.

If we look in more detail at the first of these components – conduct investigation – we could break it down further, as shown in Figure 8.2.

We now have five work packages but these are still too large to estimate properly or to plan from. So we need to subdivide some more, as shown in Figure 8.3. And we might decide to subdivide each interview once more, as shown in Figure 8.4.

Figure 8.1 **Work breakdown structure: top level**

Figure 8.2 **Work breakdown structure: second level**

Figure 8.3 **Work breakdown structure: third level**

Figure 8.4 **Work breakdown structure: bottom level**

Actually, in this case we probably would not subdivide the work this far. We would probably decide that a single interview – conducting it, writing it up and reviewing the results – is a small enough work package, say a day's work. But this does illustrate the principle involved.

The idea, then, is that we continue to break down each activity until we arrive at tasks that are:

■ Fairly atomic, that is do not readily lend themselves to further subdivision or to assignment to more than one person.

■ Small enough to estimate with reasonable accuracy, say are about half a day to two days' duration.

Some IT departments and system companies have developed standard work breakdown structures (WBSs) based on their experiences over a number of projects. If these are available, they provide a useful starting point for the creation of a project-specific WBS and they make it more likely that the project manager will not forget something. The danger of using a standard WBS (or a standard anything else for that matter) is that each project has some distinctive features and it is important not to try to fit the project to a standardised approach; if anything, the standardised approach must be customised for each project.

8.3.2 Product breakdown structure

In recent years another approach to project planning has emerged based upon the idea of considering the products that will result from the project. This approach underpins the PRINCE2® project management method. There are several advantages claimed for the **product breakdown structure** (PBS), including:

- It ensures that the project's focus is on *what* is to be achieved rather than how, in other words on the ends rather than the means. This is valuable in that projects are not undertaken for their own sake but to achieve some wider purpose, and keeping their eyes on the **products** helps remind the project team of this fact.
- When approaching a new area of work, it is sometimes difficult to envisage exactly what one needs to *do* – in other words, the work. However, it is somewhat easier to consider what one has to develop – the products – and starting from the product end is more productive.
- Project managers who have used the product-based approach report that it is less easy to forget something in the plans than it is when using a work breakdown approach.
- Once all of the products have been identified, then other things can be associated with them. What quality standards will be applied? Who shall review them? What will be the configuration management regimes? And so on.

As with a work breakdown structure, product-based planning works by progressively decomposing the project products into smaller products until a sensible, unitary product level is reached. To illustrate this, we shall use the standard PRINCE2® approach.

In PRINCE2®, the top level of products is known as 'project products'. These subdivide into two main categories as shown in Figure 8.5.

Management products are those products associated with the planning and control of the project. They include, for example, the project initiation document (PID), the project plan, the quality plan, the acceptance criteria, the regular checkpoint reports and so on. Management products also include the *quality products* which are associated with the definition and control of quality and include the product descriptions, quality review reports and project issue reports. *Specialist products* are those things that the project has been set up to create. In the case of our example project, the top-level specialist products might be those shown in Figure 8.6.

Figure 8.5 PRINCE2® product breakdown structure: top level

Figure 8.6 Product breakdown structure: second level

Figure 8.7 Product breakdown structure: third level

Figure 8.8 Product breakdown structure: bottom level

We could subdivide the analysis products further, as shown in Figure 8.7.

Finally, the products may be subdivided one more time as shown in Figure 8.8.

At the bottom level, we find an individual product for which we can write a **product description**. We discuss this in more detail in section 8.4.

Once we have completed our PBS we have a complete list of the products that the project will develop. Some of these will be final, deliverable products such as the feasibility study report. Others will be transitional products, created on the way to our final product but not deliverable. A good example of this might be the minutes of weekly team checkpoint meetings.

With our list of products, we can now consider the work we will need to do to create the products. PRINCE2® uses a technique known as a **product flow diagram** for this. The idea is simple enough: we look at the products in relation to each other and consider how one product is transformed into another. For example, let us say we have conducted our interviews for the stock control feasibility study. We have our interview notes and we need to transform them into entries in our requirements catalogue and into data flow diagrams (DFDs). We can represent this as a product flow, shown in Figure 8.9.

In this diagram we can see that our interview notes are transformed into requirements catalogue entries by the activity *Create requirements catalogue*. Similarly, the draft DFDs are transformed by the activity *Review DFDs* into a set of agreed DFDs.

The product flow diagram provides two important inputs to the planning process:

- A set of activities, for which we will need to estimate effort.
- An understanding of the dependencies between activities.

We discuss dependencies more fully in the next section. Before moving on, however, there are a couple more points to make in relation to PRINCE2® and products. The PRINCE2® manual and many of the textbooks on PRINCE2® provide outline PBSs for projects. These are quite detailed in respect of the management/quality products, less so for the specialist products – necessarily since all projects are different. However, when PRINCE2® is used in association with the structured systems analysis and design method (SSADM), then SSADM provides a more detailed PBS for its specialist products, as well as detailed product descriptions. Thus, a project manager using both PRINCE2® and SSADM will have available a very good general product breakdown structure from which to develop a project-specific structure. Even if you are not using SSADM, the SSADM PBS provides some guidance on the types of product that you are likely to develop in any IT project.

Figure 8.9 PRINCE2® product flow diagram

8.4 Product descriptions and work packages

8.4.1 Product descriptions

Once the bottom level of the PBS has been reached, we are in a position to create a description of each project. There are two main reasons for doing this:

- It encourages us to think through *exactly* what we want this product for, what form it should take and what quality and completion criteria should apply to it. Once we have a proper understanding of these things, we will be in a better position to develop accurate estimates for the development of the product.
- It provides, as it were, a detailed specification of work for the project team member who will ultimately be asked to develop it, leaving them in no doubt about what is required from them.

Each product description should contain, as a minimum, the following sections:

- *Purpose*. Why the product is required.
- *Composition*. What are the elements that make up the product. As we have seen, we develop our understanding of products through a process of decomposition but, at some stage, we reach the point where it is not sensible to decompose further as the product represents a coherent piece of work. However, even then, a product may have sub-components; a report, for instance, will contain a number of sections.
- *Derivation*. The product flow diagram, which we met in section 8.3, illustrated the principle that a project consists, in effect, of a number of transitions, where one product is transformed into another. So, for each product, it is useful to record which previous products it will be based on or, perhaps, where the information needed to develop it will come from.
- *Quality/completion criteria*. This part of the product description is very important. The project manager (or whoever is planning the project) really needs to think through what is wanted, to what standard; and the person who is going to be asked to do the work needs to know exactly what is expected. Where a project is being undertaken within a defined set of procedures and standards, then often the product descriptions need only to make cross-references to these standards; otherwise the quality/completion criteria will have to be defined specifically for each product.

In addition to the above, it can be useful to define the following:

- *Format*. What format should the finished product take. Again, if there are standards or templates available, reference can be made to these.
- *Related products*. Often, there are products that need to be developed together, or at least kept in step with each other and, if so, it is worth recording the fact here. (We shall have more to say about this in the next section about work packages.)
- *Review methods*. It is a good policy to decide in advance what method/s will be used to review the finished product, for example management review or

formal inspection. There is more information on possible review methods in Chapter 11.

Clearly, creating all the product descriptions is not a trivial task but, at the end of it, the project manager will have a much better understanding of what is involved in the project; and the project team members will have a clear view of what is expected of them

If a project is being undertaken using PRINCE2®, then the PRINCE2® manual contains detailed product descriptions for the management/quality products and these definitions can either be copied into the relevant product descriptions, or cross-references can be made to the manual.

8.4.2 Work packages

At some point, the project manager has to assign specific pieces of work – **work packages** – to individuals. A very simple, and non-bureaucratic, way of doing this is to treat each product as a work package. All that then needs to be done is to add three sections to the product description:

- *Effort estimated*. How much effort has been estimated to produce the product.
- *Date required*. A date when the finished product is needed.
- *Allocated to*. The name of the person who has been tasked with developing the product.

However, sometimes it makes more sense to group a set of products together into a work package and this is illustrated in Figure 8.10.

In Figure 8.10, we show some of the products identified for developing a training course. We could treat each product as an independent work package

Figure 8.10 Work packages for a training course

but, in fact, it would be much better for the person developing each session of the course to take complete responsibility for all the products for that session; these include the trainer's notes, the exercise, any supporting handouts and the audio-visual materials as well. So, the products of each session have been grouped into work packages that can each be assigned to one person – with an effort estimate and a deadline for completion.

8.4.3 Work package assignment to roles or individuals

Once the work packages have been identified, the project manager can give some thought as to who is going to do what in respect of each: who will produce it, who review it, who approve it and so on. In the early stages of planning, assignments will probably have to be by role, as the individuals filling each role may not yet have been identified.

An excellent way of summarising who does what is to use a 'linear responsibility chart' as illustrated in Figure 8.11.

A linear responsibility chart is a two-dimensional grid with the list of products or work packages on one axis, and the roles identified in the project organisation chart on the other. Where each work package and role intersect, we record that role's responsibilities.

In Figure 8.11, we present two possible schemes for defining responsibilities. In the first, the role is said to be:

- Responsible: For actually creating the work package.
- Accountable: Managing creation of the work package.
- Consultation: Will provide information for creating the work package.
- Information: Will be kept informed about progress.

Organisation breakdown

R = Responsible / A = Accountable / C = Consultation / I = Information	Project sponsor	Project manager	Analysis team leader	Chief designer	Development manager	Test manager	Project support assistant	Senior user	OR, could use: I = Initiation / E = Execution / A = Approval / C = Consultation / S = Supervision
Interview notes	I	A	R	I				C	
Requirements catalogue	I	A	R	I				C	
Use case diagram	I	A	R	I	I			C	
Package review	I	A	R	I	I	I		I	
Report text	I	A	R	I				I	
Report illustrations	I	A	R					I	
Report appendices	I	A	R	I				I	

Product/work package breakdown

Figure 8.11 Linear responsibility chart

In the second scheme, we use five categories to define the responsibilities:

- Initiation: Starts the process off.
- Execution: Carries out the work.
- Approval: Reviews the results.
- Consultation: Is consulted during the work (and/or provides information needed to carry it out).
- Supervision: Manages the work.

The initial assignment of work packages to roles may have to be revisited later in the planning process, when the workloads on individuals, and their capabilities, are better understood.

8.5 | Understanding dependencies

Dependencies are fundamental to planning a project and, later, in understanding the effects of any problems encountered. Yet many IS project managers do not conduct a proper analysis of project dependencies, arguing that for most IS projects they are obvious: one has to analyse a requirement before specifying a solution and write a program before testing it. Although this is true enough in this case, these arguments apply only to simple projects, with a few people involved in them. Where – as is often the case nowadays – there are several teams at work, each of them developing a specific part of a system, the need to understand the often complex dependencies becomes paramount.

In essence, understanding dependencies is simple. If activity B can begin only when activity A is complete, then we have a dependency. In our example project, we can begin to develop DFDs only once we have conducted our interviews. However, dependencies are often more complex than this. Do we, for example, need to have completed all of our interviews before we start any of our DFDs? Probably not. Quite possibly, we could produce a high-level DFD after we have interviewed the managing director and then develop it further as other interviews are completed. With multiple teams operating, dependencies become more complex still as we need to know exactly which components from one team are required before that, or another, team can start on something else.

We can analyse dependencies using a **network diagram**. A network diagram for our example project is shown in Figure 8.12.

This diagram has been drawn using a format known as *activity-on-arrow*, which means that the lines represent project tasks and the circles the connections between tasks. From the diagram, we can read the following:

- Once the project starts, we have two activities – *Conduct interviews* and *Investigate other systems* – that can proceed in parallel.
- But the results of both activities have to be brought together before we can start the next three activities – *Analyse requirements*, *Investigate packages* and *Investigate hardware*. We show this bringing together by using a 'dummy' activity, one with zero duration, indicated by the dotted line.

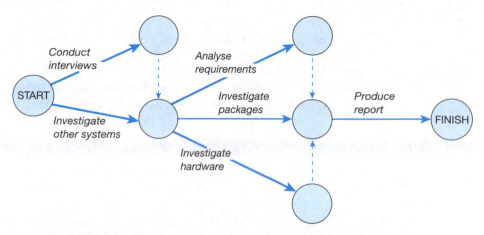

Figure 8.12 Network diagram (activity-on-arrow format)

■ The three activities are then brought together – again using two dummy activities – before we can start the last task of our project, *Produce report*.

This very simple structure has already told us one important thing about our project: we can use more than one person on it if we wish, working independently until such time as their work must be brought together.

Once we have estimated the effort involved in each activity, we can use the network to establish another important feature of the project. Let us suppose that we have estimated the effort for each activity as follows:

Conduct interviews	8 days
Investigate other systems	4 days
Analyse requirements	3 days
Investigate packages	8 days
Investigate hardware	5 days
Produce report	5 days

Using this information, we can enhance our diagram, as shown in Figure 8.13.

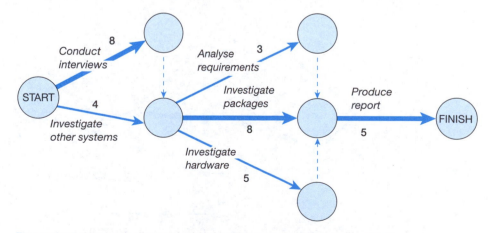

Figure 8.13 Network diagram with durations and critical path added

131

This now shows those activities that are on the **critical path** of the project: in other words, those that, if they are delayed, will delay the whole project. For example, *Conduct interviews* will take eight days whereas *Investigate other systems* will take only four days; so a delay of up to four days in *Investigate other systems* will not delay the start of the three successor activities. In Figure 8.13 the critical path has been indicated by the use of thicker lines. We know, too, that if we wanted to shorten the project we would need to shorten the critical path tasks – perhaps by adding an extra analyst to *Conduct interviews* and *Investigate packages*.

On a small project like this, we could probably have a good guess at the critical path activities without constructing the network diagram. But what about the project illustrated in Figure 8.14?

It would be rather difficult to spot the critical path through this project without a network diagram and it would be practically impossible to work out what would be the effect of slippage on the non-critical activities.

The usefulness of the network diagram becomes clear once the project gets under way and snags are encountered – as they surely will be. If an activity gets behind schedule, the network lets the project manager assess the effect on other activities and on the final outcome of the project. If the late activity is not on the critical path, and there is enough slack to accommodate some delay, then perhaps the project manager just needs to keep a careful eye on it to ensure that it does not slip further. But if it is a critical path activity, then the project manager can consider adding more resources, or assigning more experienced staff, or otherwise taking action to bring the activity back on schedule. We shall have more to say on this in Chapters 11 and 12 on monitoring progress and exercising control.

The other method of producing a network diagram is a convention known as 'activity-on-node', where boxes represent the activities and the arrows simply represent the dependencies between them. This method is becoming the more common today as it forms the basis of many of the most popular project planning software packages, such as Microsoft® Project and Niku's

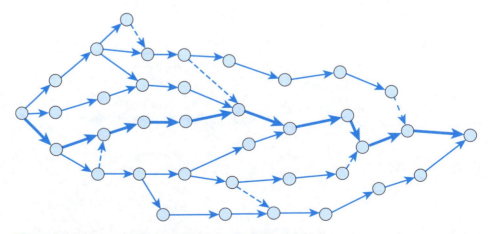

Figure 8.14 Network diagram for more complex project

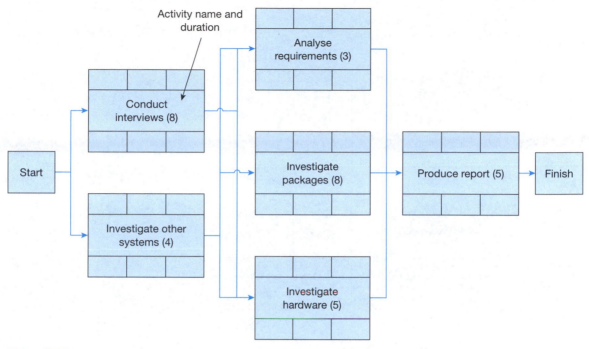

Activity name and duration

Figure 8.15 Network diagram (activity-on-node format)

Project Workbench®. Figure 8.15 is Figure 8.13 redrawn in the activity-on-node format.

With the activity-on-node method, we analyse the critical path by making two passes through the model. In the forward pass, we establish the *earliest start time* (EST) and *earliest finish time* (EFT) for each activity, and we do this by addition, as shown in Figure 8.16.

We record the EST for each activity in the top left-hand box and obtain the EFT by adding to this the duration of the activity. The result is then recorded in the top right-hand box. Moving through the model, the EST for an activity is the same as the EFT of its predecessor. Where an activity has more than one predecessor – as does, for example, *Produce report*, then we take the highest of the possible EFTs, in this case 16 from *Investigate packages*. The reason for this is fairly obvious: since *Produce report* is dependent on all three previous activities, it cannot begin until the longest of them is complete, which is *Investigate packages*. We know from the forward pass that the shortest time in which the project can be completed is 21 days.

Next, we perform a backward pass through the model to establish the latest start time (LST) and latest finish time (LFT) for each activity, this time by subtracting durations from our EFT for the whole project of 21 days. This is illustrated in Figure 8.17.

The LFT for each activity is recorded in the bottom right-hand box and the LST is arrived at by subtracting the duration of the activity from the LFT. The LFT for an activity is the same as the LST of its successor on the model. Where

Figure 8.16 Network diagram after forward pass

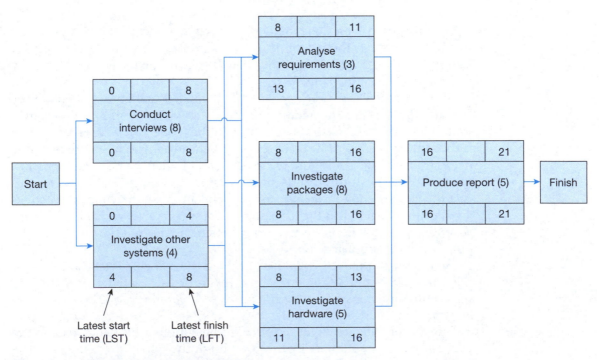

Figure 8.17 Network diagram after backward pass

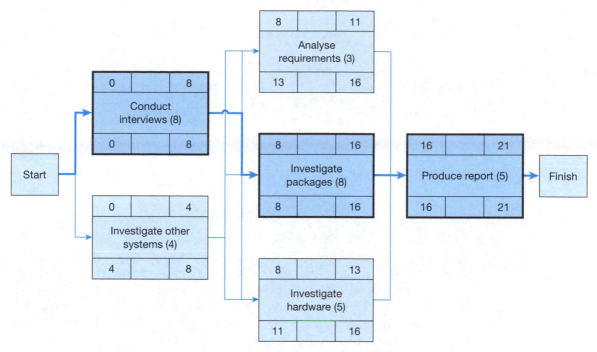

Figure 8.18 Network diagram with critical path activities highlighted

an activity has more than one successor – as does, for example, *Conduct interviews* – the LST used is the smaller of the alternatives on offer, in this case 8 for *Investigate packages*. Again, a moment's thought will reveal why this is so: if a larger figure were used, then the start of *Conduct interviews* would be delayed.

We are now able to calculate the critical path by subtracting the EST from the LST for each activity or – which amounts to the same thing – by subtracting the EFT from the LFT. If there is no remainder from the subtraction, the activity is on the critical path; if there is a remainder, then this is equivalent to the float or slack there is in the activity. Figure 8.18 shows our network diagram with the critical path highlighted.

The advantage of the activity-on-node approach now becomes apparent since we know not only which activities are on the critical path but also how much float there is on other tasks. In other words, we know by how much these could slip before they impact on the end-date of the project.

8.6 Bar charts

Another widely used planning tool is the bar chart, often called a Gantt chart after H L Gantt, an industrial engineer who pioneered their use during the First World War. Bar charts provide a highly visual way of illustrating the sequence of activities in a project but, because they do not show dependencies very readily, they are less useful for managing progress on a project. Figure 8.19 is a

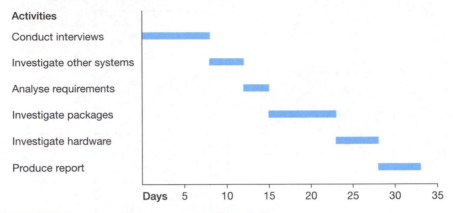

Figure 8.19 Bar chart showing sequential activities

bar chart of our feasibility study project. We have drawn it on the assumption that one analyst will be performing all the work and that therefore the activities are arranged in a simple linear sequence.

In fact, of course, we know from our network diagrams that some activities can proceed in parallel and this is shown in Figure 8.20, along with the float for each activity which is indicated by the dashed lines.

This illustrates well why bar charts are so poor for indicating dependencies. Although the bar chart seems to indicate that *Analyse requirements* cannot start until *Conduct interviews* is complete, this may not in fact be the case; the chart might just be reflecting the fact that the person who is to carry out *Analyse requirements* is not available for a few days.

Some project planning software tools try to show dependencies on bar charts but the result usually ends up looking messy, as in Figure 8.21.

Generally, it is much better to construct a network diagram to indicate dependencies and to use bar charts for what they are most suited for: as a means of indicating to those involved in the project the overall sequence of activities. We return to bar charts in Chapter 10 when we consider how they are used to create the schedules for the project.

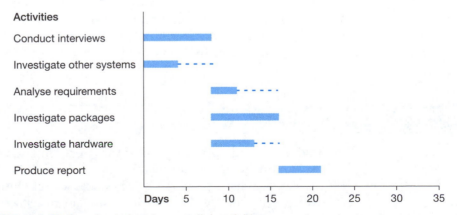

Figure 8.20 Bar chart showing parallel activities

Figure 8.21 Bar chart showing dependencies between activities

8.7 Planning for quality

So far, we have mainly discussed what is to be done on the project – what activities are required and the order in which we shall carry them out. But this is only part of the planning process. We also need to decide *how* we shall carry out the work, in other words what methods and techniques we shall use and what quality standards we shall apply to our work.

Chapter 14 discusses the issue of quality in some detail. For now, we need to note that planning for **quality** is an important element of the planning process. The quality plan may be a document in its own right or it may be part of the project plan, but whether there are two documents or one, the essential thing is that quality must be considered when planning the project's activities since quality reviews, inspections and rework arising from inspections are tasks that must be planned for like any others. Moreover, the nature of the project needs to be considered: a critical piece of command software for a nuclear power plant is likely to need more rigorous quality control applied to it than a little spreadsheet-based system to support a local cricket club.

8.8 Tolerances

The PRINCE2® project management method uses the idea of **tolerances**, and we explore these now.

Projects are set up in order to achieve certain objectives and these are usually expressed in terms of the triple constraint of time, cost and quality, for example:

- The new system must be in place in two months.
- The budget for the project is £1 million.
- The system must enable us to process 500,000 transactions per week, with an average transaction time of two minutes.

However, the three criteria quoted are all absolutes and we need to know whether there is any latitude associated with them. Would the system still be worth having if it took three months to develop? Or four? Would the cost justification for the project be compromised if the final cost were £1.1 million? Or £1.2 million? Would a transaction time of 2.5 minutes be acceptable? There may, in fact, be some flexibility in these criteria and they may be interlinked. For example, it may be acceptable for the budget to rise to £1.2 million provided that the system was delivered in two months.

It is important that: (a) it is known what tolerances there are in a project, and (b) it is clear who is allowed to use the tolerances. A PRINCE2® project is 'owned' by the project board which delegates authority to run the project to the project manager – along with some tolerances within which they must work. This gives the project manager some flexibility to make adjustments to the project as necessary whilst keeping overall control within the business. If it looks as if the tolerances might be exceeded, the project manager must return to the project board and present a case for exceeding them – to which the board may or may not assent.

8.9 Using planning tools

It will probably have occurred to you by now that creating the various diagrams and charts for a project is likely to be a time-consuming business. In addition, as we have said, plans are not produced at the start of a project and then engraved in stone; they will require constant adjustment and revision as the project progresses. All of this points towards the use of computerised planning tools to take the drudgery out of the planning work and to make replanning less of a chore.

There are many project planning tools on the market. Most of these have been created for use on personal computers but some of the most powerful tools require a mainframe computer. In a book such as this, it would be impossible to present a proper survey of the available tools – and it would become out of date as soon as it was published. Instead, we consider some of the pros and cons of planning tools in general.

8.9.1 Advantages of planning tools

Ease of replanning Plans are generally created iteratively. We produce a project breakdown, create estimates and produce a schedule. This does not work, so we reschedule. We go back and review our estimates and produce another schedule. And so on. If we are drawing our plans by hand each time, we will soon run out of patience and settle, perhaps, for a less than optimal solution. With a planning tool, however, there should be no such reluctance and we can make minor or major adjustments to our plan at will. The result should be that we plan more thoroughly and produce a much better end-product.

Quality of presentation A plan is a means of communication from the project manager to the project team, to the users, to senior management and to customers. Planning tools generally have flexible presentation and reporting facilities capable of producing high-quality output in a variety of formats. Although presentation is not everything, the fact is that a well presented plan is both easy for its audience to assimilate and has greater credibility than a hand-drawn plan.

What-if analyses Perhaps the most valuable feature of a planning tool is the ability to perform what-if analyses of various scenarios. What if the activity *Investigate other systems* takes more than four days? What if we do not get information on packages in time to complete *Investigate packages*? What if the customer asks us to conduct an extra four interviews? Without changing our working plan, we can model the effects of each of these changes and decide how we would handle them. It is difficult to do this without planning tools and, without them, project managers' responses to change are likely to be based on instinct and feeling rather than proper analysis.

Tracking progress Most planning tools have facilities to track progress on a project. The data may have to be input manually by the project manager or support staff or, if they are lucky, it may be possible to link the tool to a time recording system and capture the input that way. In either case, though, the project manager will be able to compare the actual progress with the plan, to identify where problems seem to be arising and to investigate them and decide how to respond to them.

8.9.2 Disadvantages of planning tools

Planning tools have some disadvantages too, of which we would mention two.

Hard to use Although very powerful, some project planning tools can be difficult to use. Indeed, there is the usual trade-off between ease of use and functionality. Some products, too, are rather finicky about the sequence in which the plan is set up: if you start out the wrong way, it can involve a lot of hard work to reshape the plan later. The answers to this are to read the manuals thoroughly, get properly trained and, best of all, find a local 'expert' who can help you out when you get stuck.

Means become ends There are some project managers who become quite besotted with their planning tools. They sit at the screen day after day, tuning and tweaking their plans and trying to achieve perfection. In the meantime, the project is proceeding merrily – or probably quite disastrously – without them. This is not an exaggeration and, with all the facilities available on some packages, it is quite easy to see how IS project managers – who probably started out as technicians – get hooked on their use. However, the planning tool is a means to developing a workable plan more quickly and not an end in itself, and the project manager needs to keep this in mind.

8.10 Summary

Planning is essential to the successful execution of an IS project. Planning involves thinking hard about the project, what it is to achieve and how the team will go about it. The starting point for a good plan is a proper understanding of the requirement and the project manager must ensure that this is available before planning begins. The work to be done is analysed using either a work breakdown structure or a product breakdown structure. In either case, the product is a set of activities that will need to be performed to complete the project. With the activities identified, the next step is to understand the dependencies between them. A network diagram shows these dependencies and can be used to identify the critical path through the project. Bar charts provide a visual means of showing the sequence of activities in a project, but are less useful for assessing the progress of work overall. The project manager needs to understand the tolerances – of time, cost and quality – within which the project must operate. Project planning software can take much of the drudgery out of the planning process, produces high-quality output and facilitates what-if analysis of various scenarios.

Questions

1 Give three reasons why it is essential to plan an IS project in detail before starting work on it.

2 Ideally, the requirement for an IS project would be specified in some detail before planning begins. If the requirement is not detailed enough, what steps can the project manager take to improve the likelihood of the project's success?

3 In essence there are two basic ways of breaking down a project into plannable chunks: the use of a *work breakdown structure* or a *product breakdown structure*. Contrast the advantages and disadvantages of these approaches.

4 What do you understand by the term 'dependency'? How can project dependencies be represented for planning purposes?

5 Define the terms 'product' and 'work package' and explain how these are related to each other.

6 Network diagrams and bar charts have different parts to play in planning a project. Where is each of these tools used and what does it show?

Richard Vaughan, the E-Con project manager, has developed an overall product breakdown structure, as illustrated in Figure 8.22.

The management and quality products are a subset of the full PRINCE2® products. Richard has decided to combine the project and quality plans. Checkpoint meetings will be conducted with the two team managers weekly and checkpoint reports will be produced for the project board. The method of delegating work to team members will be via short, written work package authorisations.

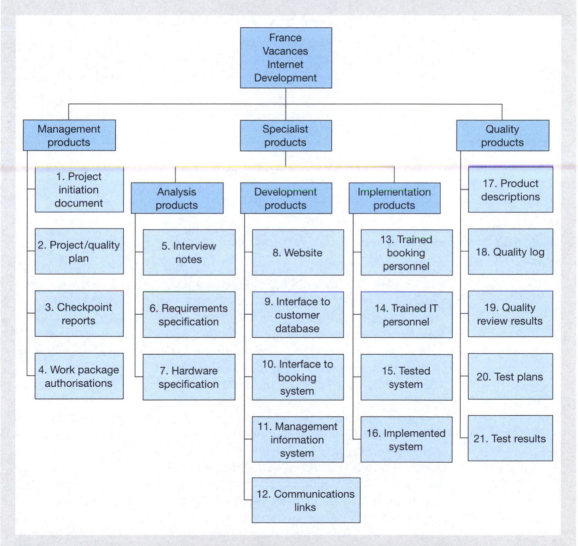

Figure 8.22 Product breakdown structure for France Vacances internet project

Case study continued

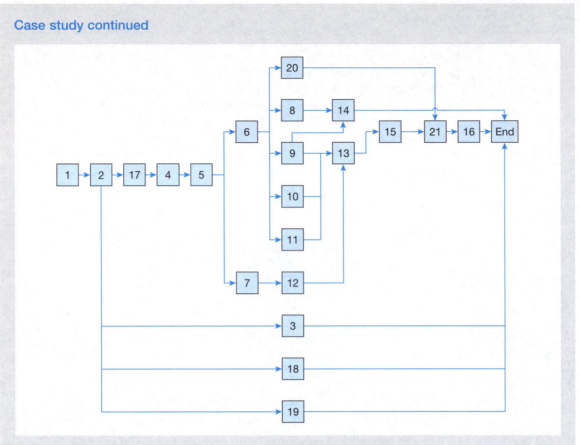

Figure 8.23 Dependency diagram for France Vacances internet project

Product descriptions will be developed for all products and the products themselves will be checked using reviews (for such things as the requirements specification) or through testing (for the software products).

Many of the specialist products (for example the website itself) will require a lower level of decomposition but detailing this will only be possible once the requirements specification is complete.

The dependencies between the products/deliverables are illustrated in Figure 8.23.

It will be noticed that three deliverables (3, Checkpoint Reports; 18 Quality Log; and 19, Quality Review Results) have been shown as dependent on deliverable 2 (Project/Quality Plan) and then feeding into the end of the project. These deliverables are of the 'recurring' variety, that is they occur at several points during the project. There are two ways of representing this situation: as shown here, or by breaking them down and trying to show exactly which other deliverables they relate to. The second approach tends to lead to a very fussy network diagram which obscures rather than illuminates the plan. Unless the amount of work involved in these deliverables is

Further reading

Case study continued

very large – which here it is not (see the case study for Chapter 9), it is probably better to leave these deliverables off the network diagram and show them as a 'continuing' activity on the bar chart (see the case study for Chapter 10).

Further reading

Maylor, Harvey (2003), *Project Management*, 3rd edn, FT/Prentice Hall

Office of Government Commerce (2002), *Managing Successful Projects with PRINCE2*, 3rd edn, The Stationery Office

9 Project planning: estimating

9.1 Estimating for IS projects

We need to admit at the outset that the reputation of estimating for IS projects is not exactly glorious. Too many projects have gone badly over time and exceeded their budgets and the blame has often been put on the original estimates. Before we look at estimating methods, therefore, it might be as well to consider the special features of IS projects that make estimating for them so difficult.

The first, and perhaps most important, characteristic is that IS projects tend to be one-off affairs. The project is undertaken to achieve some specific business objective, very often to secure some competitive advantage, and this means that there will always be a degree of innovation involved. The project may be using familiar methods and standards, established programming languages and proven hardware but it will almost certainly be using these components in a combination that is in some way unique. The implications of this are obvious, in that it will be difficult to obtain reliable experience on which the estimates may be based. In addition, there will very likely be no metrics available to assist the estimators or, if there are, they will have to be examined carefully to ensure that they are suitable for the new project.

The second feature of IS projects is that the initial estimates are often prepared long before there is a detailed specification of the requirement on which to base them. In commercial systems development, for example, companies are often asked to tender for a development based upon a 'user requirement specification' which is a long and ill-defined 'wish list'. Even where in-house IT departments are planning for projects, they are frequently asked to prepare budgets long before the detailed specification of the system has been pinned down.

A third aspect of IS estimating is that it is seldom performed by professional estimators. Generally, estimates are prepared either by the project manager, by salespeople or by any staff who are spare at the time. Although one could argue that estimating is a project management skill, the fact is that a project manager is not a disinterested party. Still less impartial are salespeople, and the fact that someone happens to be available does not mean that they possess the skills and experience to create realistic estimates.

There are some additional factors that can influence the estimating process and these are considered later in this chapter. Before proceeding, however, it is worthwhile to compare the approach found in IS with that of a more established profession, to see if there are any lessons we can learn.

9.2 Estimating in engineering disciplines

In order to see how IS estimating might be done better, we could look at civil engineering, to see how the practitioners there go about things.

The first thing we observe is that, usually, civil engineering projects use well established techniques and equipment. This permits the use of generally agreed and reliable metrics. There is, for example, hundreds of years' experience available of bricklaying, with bricks of all types used in all conditions and positions. The result is that an estimator can go to a 'blue book' of metrics for various building operations and find out, to a very reasonable degree of accuracy, how long it will take to perform such-and-such a task in a particular set of circumstances.

Now, it is clearly nonsense to claim that civil engineering projects do not involve innovation. Many do – for example the Sydney Opera House and the Channel Tunnel. It is noticeable, though, that where, as in these two projects, there is a large degree of innovation, the civil engineers prove no better at producing accurate estimates than do the information technologists. Nevertheless, a civil engineering project can usually be broken down into components for which reliable metrics can be found. However, an important aspect of civil engineering estimates is that they are prepared against detailed specifications. The architects and structural engineers will provide a comprehensive design and the estimators will stick rigidly to that. If, subsequently, the design is changed, then that will trigger a variation to the contract. Finally, estimating is a distinct specialism in civil engineering. An estimator does nothing else and is judged, and rewarded, according to the accuracy of the estimates produced. The result is that there is greater professionalism in civil engineering estimating than is usually found in IS.

The lessons for estimating for information systems are therefore:

■ We need to identify the known, rather than the innovative, components of our project and base our estimates around them.
■ We should be very careful that firm estimates are offered only on the basis of firm specifications.
■ We should be more active in compiling metrics on our projects, to help progressively to improve our estimating accuracy.
■ An effort should be made to achieve a degree of specialisation in IS estimating.

All of these things are more easily said than done, but project managers can help themselves by taking a tougher attitude towards estimating and insisting that it be done as well as possible before signing up to an incompletely defined commitment.

9.3 | Estimating methods compared

In the following sections, we examine a number of the most commonly used methods for preparing estimates for IS projects. Clearly, in a chapter of this size we cannot provide an exhaustive treatment of each method but we do aim to give an outline of each approach and to set out the pros and cons of each. For more detailed treatments of the methods, you are recommended to obtain some of the books mentioned at the end of the chapter. A word of warning, though. All estimating methods are prone to error and all depend to some degree on subjective views of the size and complexity of the task ahead. No single method is going to give a 'right' result and, in fact, a 'right' result is probably unachievable. Estimates are a means by which the project manager can get a notion of the scale and scope of the project and make important decisions on how it will be tackled. Inevitably, factors will arise that will invalidate many of the estimating assumptions and there will be a need to revisit the estimates for the later project tasks once work is under way. So do not expect the methods described here to produce the correct result for your project every time. Use them as a means to an end, as a pointer to the development of your own approach to project estimating.

9.3.1 Analogy method

The analogy method is one of the oldest, but one of the most reliable, of methods and depends on finding a project similar to the current one which has already been undertaken in the organisation. The similarity should ideally extend to:

- The type of business involved.
- The overall size of the applications.
- The general scope of the systems – for example, the ratio of online to batch functions, whether there is a major communications component and so on.
- The technical methods, standards and languages used.

Where there are differences in any of these areas, suitable adjustments must be made. For example, if the historical project was developed in COBOL, but the new one is to use a fourth-generation language (4GL) and perhaps a code generator, then the programming effort – though not the analysis or design – should be less this time.

In addition, some judgement needs to be made if there are likely to be other significant differences between the historical project and the new one, for example:

- The customer's company culture.
- The customer's level of computer literacy.
- The degree of management support for the project.

The major advantage of the analogy method is that it enables a broad-brush estimate for a whole project to be developed fairly quickly, perhaps during the preparation of a bid or a proposal. The great danger is that there are actually fewer similarities between the two projects than initially appears to be the case. If the older one turns out to have been much more complicated or broader in scope, then the result might be an overestimate which could make the bid uncompetitive. If the newer project is the more complex, perhaps involving new and untried techniques, then an underestimate might be produced, resulting in loss if the company wins the business.

9.3.2 Analysis effort method

The analysis effort method is most suited to producing the initial estimates for a project, probably before detailed analysis has begun. The general idea is to estimate the effort required to perform the analysis work for an assumed number of project functions and then to derive the estimates for subsequent project stages via the use of ratios to the analysis effort. For the purposes of this method, a somewhat simplified systems development lifecycle is assumed:

- There is some analysis work, leading to a functional specification.
- Design work, resulting in a system design, is followed by the writing of program specifications.
- Programs are coded and unit tested (CUT).
- The programs and modules are combined and subjected to an integration test and finally full system testing is performed.

As a starting point, some idea is needed of the overall range of functions which are to be provided. This overview could have been obtained from a feasibility study or from the invitation to tender, supplemented by further questioning of the prospective customer. Once the functions have been identified, the estimator assesses the effort needed for the *analysis* of each function. This should include *only* the analysis effort itself, not ancillary activities such as familiarisation, training or project management; these are examined later in this chapter. In producing the estimates, the estimators will use their own skills and experience, discuss their ideas with others and, perhaps, use statistics from previous projects which have tackled similar functions. With the analysis estimates available for the individual functions, these can be totalled to give figures for functional areas – groups of functions – for subsystems and for the overall system.

The next step is to make some assessment of three key factors which will apply to the project in terms of its size, familiarity and complexity. Each of these will need to be classified in some way, for example:

- *Size*. The size, or S, factor relates to the number of people who, it is expected, will be involved in the project at its peak. A suitable scale might be:

  S = 1 One-person project.
  S = 2 Small project (up to 4 people).
  S = 3 Medium project (up to 12 people).
  S = 4 Large project (up to 30 people).
  S = 5 Very large project (more than 30 people).
  S = 6 Size cannot be determined at this point.

- *Familiarity*. The familiarity, or F, factor concerns the familiarity that project staff are likely to have with the type of work and with the business and technical environments. These may be classified as:

  F = 1 All factors known by the people likely to work on the project (usually because it is similar to a previous project).

  F = 2 Application or techniques well known to the developers but using unfamiliar hardware, operating system, language or other software package.

  F = 3 Unusual application or specialist techniques known only to a few people within the development organisation and who are unlikely to work on the project, but using familiar hardware etc.

  F = 4 Application or techniques new to the developers but more common in the IT industry generally, on familiar hardware etc.

  F = 5 Application or techniques new to the developers but standard in the IT industry, using unfamiliar hardware etc.

  F = 6 Large element of innovation with considerable uncertainty over outcome.

  F = 9 Familiarity cannot be assessed at this time.

- *Complexity*. The complexity, or C, factor takes into account the types of technical issue likely to be associated with the project. Definitions might be:

  C = 1 Straightforward algorithms, simple data structures, few files, few interactions.

  C = 2 One of the above factors not true.

  C = 3 Two or more of the above factors not true.

  C = 4 Severe constraints on storage, timing or performance.

  C = 5 Complexity cannot be assessed at this time.

Using the S, F and C factors, tables are used to determine the ratios between analysis – for which an estimate is now available – and design, CUT and testing. These ratios can then be used to calculate an effort figure for these other stages and hence for the whole project. Each organisation will develop tables of ratios based on its own experience, and to illustrate the approach Table 9.1

Table 9.1 Part of a table of ratios for the analysis and programming effort methods

F	C	Analysis %	Design %	CUT %	Testing %
1	1	2	14	59	25
1	2	2	14	55	29
1	3	5	14	47	34
1	4	7	16	43	34
2	1	2	15	63	20
2	2	2	14	59	25
2	3	5	15	51	29
2	4	7	16	47	29
3	1	5	16	59	20
3	2	5	16	55	24

shows an example. The table relates to projects where the S factor is 3, that is to medium-sized projects with up to 12 people involved.

If we assume that our F factor is 2 and our C factor 3, we can read off stage ratios for our project as follows:

Analysis	5 per cent
Design	15 per cent
CUT (code and unit test)	51 per cent
Testing	29 per cent

Since we have estimated the analysis effort, we can use these ratios to extrapolate the effort for the other project stages and for the project as a whole. The ratios must not be followed blindly, however, and the estimator must use judgement as to whether special factors apply. For example:

- If a very efficient code generator is being used, the coding effort may well be reduced somewhat compared with the analysis. But coding is only a part of CUT as defined here, and unit- and link-testing effort is unlikely to be reduced in proportion. So care should be taken if considering a revision of the analysis/CUT ratio.
- If part of the functionality is to be provided via packaged software, then the design and coding are likely to be reduced; but link testing and integration testing (included, respectively, in CUT and testing) may actually be increased.
- If there are no interfaces planned with other systems – rare but possible – then no integration testing will be needed. In this case, the estimator may decide that some of the testing figure should be removed from the final estimate. However, if many interfaces are required, or if the system itself is complex with lots of test 'threads' to explore, then it may be sensible to increase the test figure.

The estimator therefore needs to examine the particular features of the current project and make any adjustments required to the ratios. If this is done, the nature of the adjustment and its justification should be fully documented so that someone else can review, and comment upon, the estimates.

Testing itself can generally be further subdivided as follows:

Planning test	10 per cent
Test preparation	25 per cent
Running tests	65 per cent

The estimates arrived at using the analysis effort method cover the main project activities. However, they do not encompass the range of supporting activities – such as project management, team leading, quality control and so on – which are needed on every project. These activities should be estimated explicitly, and some guidance on this is given later in the chapter.

9.3.3 Programming method

The programming method starts at a different point from the analysis effort method, namely that of examining the programming effort required and deriving values for the rest of the project tasks. The same project lifecycle definition is used as for the analysis effort method, with the project being broken down into analysis, design, CUT (code and unit test) and testing. The programming method generally requires that some preliminary design work has been carried out, but it could be used early in the project if it is possible to obtain, perhaps from the user requirements specification, some idea of the number and types of program that will ultimately be required. The programs will be related to the functions used in the analysis effort method in the sense that each function may consist of one or more programs.

The simplest way of assessing the programs is to decide if each is likely to be small, medium or large. The estimator then uses metrics from other projects or their own experience to establish an average effort figure for CUT in each of these categories. For a COBOL (or similar third-generation language, 3GL) environment, suitable figures might be:

Small program	5 days
Medium program	10 days
Large program	15 days

A slightly more refined approach is to make another assessment, as well as of its size, of each program's likely complexity. If three categories 'simple', 'average' and 'complex' are used, a grid can be constructed. For COBOL, this might look like Table 9.2.

Table 9.2 COBOL grid

Size	Complexity		
	Simple	Average	Complex
Small	5	5	10
Medium	5	10	15
Large	10	15	20

In general, online programs are simpler than batch programs because they do not need the same error-handling – problems can simply be referred back to the users. Programs with involved rules and processing logic will be more complex than straightforward enquiries or reports. More complex systems of classification can be evolved, with programs broken down by language type, for example 3GL or 4GL, as well as by complexity. It may be that the source documentation, an invitation to tender for example, does not contain enough detail to permit such an analysis of the programs. In this case, the estimator may notionally decide that all programs will be assessed as medium/average for estimating purposes. As always, the basis on which the estimates have been prepared should be documented.

At this point, the programming method converges with the analysis effort method. An assessment is made of the size, familiarity and complexity of the system as discussed earlier and the project stage ratios are used to extrapolate effort figures for all stages from the CUT estimate. Where a 4GL is to be used on the project, special consideration must be given to how this will affect the project estimates. Generally, using a 4GL decreases coding effort (in CUT) but does not affect either design or testing. A revised procedure which suits this situation is:

- Estimate for programming as described above but using man-day figures for CUT that have been adjusted for the appropriate 4GL.
- Estimate the programming again, this time using the figures for the COBOL environment.
- Use the COBOL programming estimates when looking up the ratios for other project stages.
- Obtain the total project estimate by using the 4GL CUT effort added to the COBOL estimates for the other stages.

As with the analysis effort method, the estimates arrived at here cover the main project activities. However, they do not cover the range of supporting activities such as project management, team leading, quality control and so on which are needed on every project. These activities should be estimated explicitly and added to the estimates for mainstream tasks. Some guidance on this is given later in the chapter.

9.3.4 Direct estimation based on project breakdown

This is the most detailed estimating technique and depends upon having a breakdown of the work to be performed. The two principal methods for breaking down the work – using a work breakdown structure or a product breakdown structure – are discussed in Chapter 8. Once a detailed list of the project tasks is available, the estimator, or preferably several estimators so their results can be cross-checked, review the tasks and assess the effort to perform each. The effort required for each project stage and for the project as a whole is then arrived at through summation. Provided the estimators have sufficient knowledge and experience, this method probably produces the most reliable results but, for a variety of reasons, it is not always possible to use it:

- At the start of a project, there is probably insufficient information to enable the full set of products or tasks to be identified.
- The method takes a great deal of time and effort, neither of which – and especially the former – may be available in, say, a bid situation.
- Even if time is available, the costs of direct estimation may not be justified if an acceptable result can be obtained by other means – through analogy, for example.

Direct estimating is therefore generally used in developing plans for the immediate stage or sub-stage of a project, with other, more approximate, methods being used for the later stages until sufficiently detailed information comes to hand.

9.3.5 The Delphi technique

The Delphi technique is based on the idea of obtaining estimates from suitably qualified people and then synthesising them to produce the final estimate.

Since people have differing levels of experience of estimating, and of the underlying hardware and software to be used, the approach has a number of stages:

- Each estimator is given a specification of the work – activity, task or whatever – and asked to provide their estimate for it. These are filled in anonymously.
- The estimates are then summarised anonymously and the summary is circulated to each estimator.
- Estimators reconsider their own estimates in the light of the summary and provide a revised estimate if they wish.

The above processes are repeated as many times as necessary to achieve a reasonable consensus.

The principle involved here is that, by keeping the estimates anonymous, personal disagreements are kept out of the process. In addition, the technique avoids a possible outcome of a round-table discussion which is that the person who shouts loudest, rather than the person with the best estimate, will win the day. Individual estimators can reconsider and revise their ideas in the light of other people's estimates without public loss of face.

9.3.6 CoCoMo

The constructive cost model (whose acronym is CoCoMo) was developed by Barry W Boehm and is described in detail in his seminal book *Software Engineering Economics*. The model, which exists in three versions, presents formulae for calculating the effort and elapsed time needed to develop software based on an assessment of the amount of program code to be developed expressed in thousands of delivered source instructions, or KDSI. For the purposes of the model, delivered source instructions are program instructions developed on the project which are turned into machine code by compilers, assemblers, preprocessors or some combination of the three. The *Basic CoCoMo* formula for development effort is:

$$MM = 2.4(KDSI)^{1.05}$$

where MM = effort in man-months. So, if we estimate that our project will result in 10,000 delivered source instructions, we can calculate that the development effort will be:

$$2.4 \times (10,000)^{1.05} = 26.92, \text{ or about 27 man-months}$$

In the CoCoMo formulae, a man-month equates to 152 working hours or 19 working days, so effort figures can also be expressed in man-hours, man-days or man-years.

The elapsed time is calculated using the formula:

$$TDEV = 2.5(MM)^{0.33}$$

where TDEV is total development time. So, for our example, the elapsed time would be calculated as:

$$2.5 \times (26.92)^{0.33} = 8.94, \text{ or about 9 months}$$

These basic formulae are concerned with the total development effort for a whole project and produce estimates which should lie within a factor of two of the actual outcome about 60 per cent of the time. As such, the formulae are useful mainly in the early stages in planning a project or to provide a cross-check on estimates made using other methods.

Intermediate CoCoMo takes the process a stage further and takes into account many more of the variable factors which can influence project outcomes. These include such things as the attributes of the product (reliability, complexity, etc.), of the target computer (execution time, main storage, etc.), of the personnel (capability, general experience, language experience, etc.) and of the project (use of modern tools, etc.). This version of the method takes much more time to use but should produce results within 20 per cent of the actual outcome 68 per cent of the time.

Finally, *Detailed CoCoMo* considers the different factors which apply during the different stages of a system development and produces more detailed estimates on a phase-by-phase basis.

The problem with the CoCoMo formulae, however, is that they rest upon an assessment of the number of delivered source instructions to be written. These equate very roughly with the number of lines of code but, of course, until the programs are written, no one can be sure how much code will be created. Experienced developers can usually make educated guesses based on the specification of requirements but, even so, it can be seen that what is happening here is that one estimate – for development effort – is being based on another, for the amount of code to be written.

In recent years, Barry Boehm and his associates have been developing a new set of models, which they have called CoCoMo II. These models have been designed to take into account the wider range of development approaches that are used today compared with the 1970s, when the waterfall model (see Chapter 6) was the norm. With CoCoMo II, estimates are produced at different stages of the development lifecycle, namely:

- *Application composition*. This takes place where the system has been designed from the user perspective, using techniques such as prototyping. For a small-scale project using evolutionary prototyping (see Chapter 6), this approach may result in a finished system.
- *Early design*. For a larger or more complex system, it is necessary to produce an overall design before proceeding to designing the individual modules. A revised estimate can therefore be produced at this stage.
- *Post-architecture*. This is the point where, for a larger project, actual construction of the software starts.

CoCoMo II uses different approaches to producing the three types of estimate, including function points (see next section). As a result, it does get away from the 'lines of code' approach but it then becomes subject to the vagaries of the function point methods. The method also takes account of some of the key drivers of differences between projects, including innovation, flexibility (or not) of approach in meeting requirements, the degree to which the scope of the requirements has been fixed, whether the team is tight-knit or 'virtual' (see Chapter 22) and where the organisation is on the Capability Maturity Model (see Chapter 14).

Whilst the full original CoCoMo approach is not always followed, one of the major formulae – that relating effort to elapsed time – is quite widely used. To reiterate, this stated that the elapsed time for a project was defined as:

$$2.5 \times \text{(Estimated effort in man-months)}^{0.33}$$

Boehm's formula was derived from close analysis of a large number of projects and can therefore be claimed to be based firmly on reality. What Boehm's work and that of other researchers shows is that it is very unlikely that the schedule for a project can be compressed below about 75 per cent of the nominal elapsed time calculated as above. In turn, this suggests that adding staff to a project to try to shorten its timescale will probably not work – and may even have the opposite result from the one intended.

The main disadvantage of the CoCoMo equations is that they depend upon an assessment of the number of delivered source instructions – more or less lines of code. The obvious snag with this is that it is not possible to estimate accurately the likely number of lines of code until quite late in a project. In addition, it is not entirely clear how the CoCoMo formulae should be interpreted for projects using more advanced programming tools and fourth-generation programming languages. The elapsed time formula, however, is extremely valuable and seems to work pretty well whatever the environment.

Despite these reservations, all serious students of software development should study Boehm's book because of the insight it provides into the dynamics of the software development process.

9.3.7 Function point analysis

The technique of function point analysis was developed in the USA by A J Albrecht and J E Gaffney. Its objective is to be able to estimate for the size of a software system – or, to be more accurate, the amount of effort required to develop it – based on some observable features of the product to be developed. To use a metaphor for this, consider asking a builder for an estimate to build a house based on the number of floors, the total floor area and the number of rooms. Although this is not much information, if we said 'two floors, 65 square metres, 12 rooms', it is obvious that we are talking about neither a garden shed nor Buckingham Palace and the builder might be able to give a 'ballpark' estimate. The equivalent parameters in function point estimating are inputs, outputs and files accessed.

The original function point method has three stages:

- Analysing the system in terms of its information processing requirements at a logical level, independent of implementation considerations. Components of the system – inputs, outputs, logical files, interfaces and enquiries – are counted and each is assigned a number of *function points*. These are then totalled and the result is a score for 'unadjusted function points' (UFPs).
- A processing complexity adjustment (PCA) is calculated to allow for technical considerations such as ease of use, distributed processing, maintainability and so on.
- The UFPs are factored by the PCA to derive the final function point score for the project.

These ideas were further developed by Charles Symons in the UK to produce Mk II Function Point Analysis (FPA). This version considers three aspects of a system:

- Its information processing logic size, derived from the system's inputs, processing and outputs.
- Its technical complexity, whether batch or online, if it involves demanding criteria for performance or ease of use.
- Performance-influencing factors, such as the general development environment, available staffing and so on.

The method provides formulae which can be used to estimate both the effort and elapsed time for a project. It is recommended that organisations calibrate the formulae to match their own experience based on collected metrics, but there are some default metrics, derived from cross-industry research, which can be used until organisation-specific metrics are available.

FPA is suitable for use on transaction-oriented business application systems, online or batch, which manipulate data stored in files and databases. It is not applicable to other types of application, for example operating systems or command and control systems. FPA depends upon an understanding of the information processing, derived from the entities and data attributes involved in the processing, and on knowledge of the proposed system's balance of online and batch transactions. It is clear therefore that, for the method to work properly, a completed requirements specification is needed. However, FPA can be used earlier in the development process if certain assumptions can be made about system functionality; as always in estimating, the basis of such assumptions should be documented for future reference. FPA is particularly suitable when the project is to be developed using the structured systems analysis and design method (SSADM) as the project stages used within FPA are the same as those in SSADM's default structural model.

The basic procedure in FPA is described below but this is, necessarily, a great simplification of the complete process. For a detailed description of the method and the rules for function counting, you should read one of the books listed at the end of the chapter.

1 Determine the size of the system. This should be performed by calculation based on facts about the number and types of transaction etc. In the absence of that, properly documented assumptions may be used. Input attribute types, output attribute types and entity types referenced during processing are counted or assessed and a number of function points assigned to each. These are known as *unadjusted function points*.

2 Adjust the unadjusted function points for technical complexity. A *technical complexity adjustment* is calculated based upon an assessment of nineteen factors, including:

- Data communication
- Distributed functionality
- Performance
- Operating restrictions (for example, use of a shared processor)
- Transaction rates
- Percentage of online data entry
- Ease of processing required
- Percentage of online updates
- Complexity of processing.

The unadjusted function points are then multiplied by the technical complexity adjustment to get the overall system size in function points.

3 Calculate normative effort and elapsed time. The system size in function points is converted into an effort figure by using tables showing productivity rates (3GL or 4GL) in terms of function points per work-hour. Other tables, of function points delivered per elapsed week, are used to determine the elapsed time for the project.

4 Distribute effort and elapsed time by project stage. More tables are used to distribute the total calculated effort and elapsed time over the various stages of a project.

5 Consider estimates and adjust for risk factors. Various risk factors are considered which could influence the calculated effort and elapsed times. These include such things as whether the project is larger than the organisation has handled before; the degree of technical innovation involved; and also 'political' issues within the user organisation.

6 Consider the effects of time or manpower constraints. Finally, the calculated elapsed time is compared with the available time for the project. If the available time is less than the calculated elapsed time, then an assessment is made of the likelihood of being able to compress the project into the shortened timeframe.

The product of FPA is a set of estimates covering:

- The effort needed to complete the project.
- The elapsed time needed to complete the project.
- The likelihood of being able to deliver the project in the time available.

As we have indicated, FPA is most suitable when there is a requirements specification available to the estimators. If FPA is used earlier in the project, then the recommended procedure is to revisit the estimates whenever more detail is available, to re-evaluate if the original assumptions are still valid.

The criticisms of FPA revolve around the following issues:

- The methods of counting the inputs, outputs and data entities accessed (stage 1 above). These are, to some extent, subjective, although there are rules available to ensure that, whoever is doing the counting, the results should be the same.
- The subjectivity of the technical complexity adjustment (stage 2 above). The problem here can partly be overcome by getting several people to perform the assessment (perhaps using the Delphi approach described earlier) but, it has to be admitted, a degree of subjectivity will remain.
- Subjectivity, again, in the weighting of risk factors (stage 5 above). This can be improved by basing the weighting on a rigorous and agreed risk assessment (see Chapter 15).

Nevertheless, work continues to refine and improve the method and there is an International Function Point User Group, a member-governed organisation, which is dedicated to this end (www.ifpug.org).

9.4   Estimating for supporting activities

Whilst one reason that some projects go over time or budget is because activities were underestimated, the more usual reason is because activities were missed out altogether. It is relatively easy to identify the main tasks of the project such as conducting interviews, writing code and performing system tests, but there are scores of other activities which seem insignificant by themselves but which can amount to a lot of time over the length of a project. For example, an activity may have been defined for 'review program specification X', but what about dealing with the results of that review, like:

- Revise program specification X after review?
- Re-review program specification X?
- Rework program specification X after second review?

It is very important that all these supporting activities are catered for in the estimates. An aid to this is a standard work breakdown structure or product breakdown structure as described in Chapter 8 but, as with everything concerned with estimating, this should not be followed blindly. The project manager needs to consider carefully if there are any specific tasks which apply to *this* project and which should be taken into account.

There are two basic ways of accounting for these supporting activities:

- By estimating for them explicitly such as by adding a task called quality review and allowing a number of days to carry it out.
- By adding a percentage on top of one of the basic activities – say 10 per cent on top of program specification for quality reviews.

As long as the allowances are feasible, it does not matter too much which approach is adopted. However, it is important that the method used is documented properly so that, for example, a programmer with 15 days available for a program does not believe that quality review is additional when it is included as a percentage in the task estimate.

The supporting activities which should be taken into account are discussed below. Some of these activities can be calculated as a proportion of other, specifically estimated, tasks; for example, one might add 5–10 per cent on top of a design task to allow for quality reviews. Other activities, such as project management, are related more to the elapsed duration of the project.

9.4.1 Proportional activities

Team leading/ supervision There is a long-established, and generally quite reliable, rule of thumb that a team leader should be capable of running a team of up to five people. This means, in effect, that team leading should represent 20 per cent of the programming effort during coding, unit testing and system testing. However, this ratio only works for 3GLs such as COBOL. With the increased programmer productivity of 4GLs, a lower ratio of team leading to programming should be used – say 1:4 or 25 per cent. Team leading during other phases of a project is less easy to estimate. During analysis and design, a lot will depend on the experience of the individual analysts and designers. A figure of 10–20 per cent of the effort for functional specification, system design and program specification is a useful starting point.

Documentation Documentation refers here not to design documentation, the production of which is the specific purpose of the analysis and design activities, but to documentation such as the user manual and operations manual, which result from the programming work. Seven per cent of CUT is a good approximation to use here.

Quality control The project manager has to decide what form the quality control should take: for example, will it be supervisor reviews, peer reviews, structured walk-throughs, Fagan inspections or something else? Then, some allowance needs to be made on top of the analysis or CUT figure for the work involved.

Quality assurance Projects are also likely to get involved in some sort of external quality assurance (QA) review, either from the developers' own QA specialists or as part of a regular ISO 9001 surveillance and reaccreditation process. The project manager should discuss this question with the quality department when the project starts and schedule QA reviews as explicit activities in the project plan.

Staff technical training Staff technical training does not refer to generalised training, which may affect the elapsed time on the project but should not impact on the project's budget. What this involves is training designed specifically to enable team members to undertake their project work – perhaps training in a new language or version of the language. There can be no reliable yardstick for this and project managers will have to assess the requirements of the project in each case and allow for attendance at training courses as necessary. It should be remembered that not only is there a staff cost associated with this, but there also has to be some budget to pay for the training provided.

Familiarisation Team members may need familiarisation in any or all of:

- The customer's business.
- The customer's rules and regulations, especially if working on restricted or safety-critical sites.
- The standards and methods to be used on the project.
- The technical environment – operating system, programming language, CASE tools and so on.

The effort to be devoted to familiarisation differs considerably from project to project. The project manager must make some assessment of how much familiarisation, and of what sort, is required given the skills, experience and background of the staff assigned. There may also need to be some allowance for the development of team briefing materials.

Customer reviews Once again, the requirement here varies from project to project. At the very least, customers will be asked to review major documents such as the functional specification, and some allowance must also be made for:

- Possible presentations of the documents to customer representatives.
- Discussions with customers to amplify or explain points of detail.
- Revisions to the documentation arising from the reviews.

In some cases, it may be necessary to provide training to customer representatives to enable them to play their full part in the development work – in reading SSADM documentation, for example.

Some customers will take a detailed interest in the development and, particularly in safety-critical or mission-critical situations, may want to examine even technical documentation such as program specifications. It is important that the project manager discusses these requirements with the customer at the start of the project and makes sufficient allowance for the review work.

Data conversion and system migration The difficulty of converting data from an old system and managing the migration of data to the new one is often either forgotten or underestimated. This can be a time-consuming activity and may involve the use of additional personnel such as data preparation staff if direct data conversion is not possible.

Reviewing third-party work If subcontractors are being used to perform some of the work, some allowance must be made for applying quality control to their work. Ten per cent of the estimated effort of the third-party is a good general guideline.

Post-implementation review Some effort should be allowed for performing a post-implementation review at the end of the project. This enables the lessons of the project, good and bad, and also the ever-valuable metrics, to be captured for the benefit of later projects.

9.4.2 Elapsed-time activities

The problem with elapsed-time activities is that the duration of the project becomes apparent only once some detailed project planning has taken place. In this sense, therefore, estimating and scheduling can be seen to be iterative processes. However, Boehm's formula for working out the likely duration of a project can be used to give an initial idea of the extent and this, in turn, can be used in calculating the elapsed-time activities.

In the sections that follow, we use a figure of 18 days per month for a full-time person. This is based on the following calculation:

Total working days per year (52 × 5)	260
Less Bank holidays	8
Less Holiday (say)	25
Less Other non-working time (training, sickness etc.)	15
	212
Divide by 12 to give average days per month	17.66
Or, divide by 52 to give average days per week	4.07

Where there is, on average, more or less annual leave and/or sickness and training, then some other figure may be more appropriate.

These calculations show why, for long-term planning, project managers usually work on an average availability of four days per week for each person.

Project management A major decision needs to be made whether:

- A full-time project manager is to be used on the project.
- If a part-time project manager is to be used, do they perform some other activity, perhaps as a business analyst, on this project or fill in the remaining time with work on another project?

In general, it is preferable to have a full-time project manager where the overall volume of work supports this. The main problem with part-time project management is that other commitments, on the current project or another project, always seem to clash with some vital management task, and the project suffers accordingly.

For a full-time project manager, the allowance should be 18 days per month during the length of the project. The duration, as we have seen, can be derived from Boehm's formula, thus:

$$\text{Elapsed time (months)} = 2.5 \times (\text{Estimated effort in man-months})^{0.33}$$

Part-time involvement can be calculated in a similar way so that, for a half-time project manager, 9 days per elapsed month would be allowed.

Systems management/ technical support A systems management/technical support role may be needed from design onwards. If it is, full-time involvement can be calculated at 18 days per month, with lesser involvement reduced accordingly.

Configuration management An allowance must be made for setting up the configuration management procedures at the start of the project and operating them thereafter. On a large project, there may be a full-time configuration management role, in which case 18 days per month should be allowed. A less than full-time involvement should be factored proportionately.

Implementation management If a full-time implementation manager is needed, then they will need several weeks for preparation plus the usual 18 days per month during implementation itself.

Data administration Another non-trivial activity, particularly on a large project where a full-time role may be identified.

Project office Having a project office, or at any rate some sort of project support, is very valuable and cost-effective. It frees the project manager from some routine work, such as recording timesheets, and enables him or her to get on with actually managing the project. In addition, it is useful for analysts and designers to have support staff who can copy and distribute documents, arrange meetings and so on. If a full-time person is used, then the estimate should be for 18 days' effort per month over the duration of the project. If the project shares the use of project office support, then a suitable pro-rata allowance needs to be made.

Subcontractor management If subcontractors are involved, effort must be devoted to managing them. Quality control of subcontractors has already been mentioned but, depending on the size of the subcontract, there may also be a need for:

- Regular meetings to review progress.
- More meetings to agree and later review the contractual arrangements.
- Checking and authorisation of invoices.
- Interviewing subcontractors' staff.

9.4.3 Other factors influencing estimates

So far, in discussing estimating, we have tended to assume that all analysts are interchangeable, that programmers have equal levels of skill and ability and that all projects have similarities. However, it is obvious that none of these things is true in the real world and estimates must be adjusted to take account of the variations which can occur between people and from project to project. Some of the estimating methods we have reviewed – detailed CoCoMo and function point analysis – contain adjustment factors which enable the circumstances of particular projects to be taken into account. However, in using other methods, the project manager will have to make their own adjustments to the raw estimates obtained by those methods. In this section, we consider some of the factors to be considered in making those adjustments, but the list is not exhaustive and project managers will develop their own checklist as they gain experience of estimating and planning.

Use of inexperienced staff The productivity difference between experienced and inexperienced staff can be very marked. The first two or three programs written by an inexperienced programmer can take twice as long as the standard metrics suggest. An experienced programmer, using a new language for the first time, is also slower at first, although the difference is less marked. New analysts or designers, too, are more hesitant and hence slower than experienced people, particularly if they are working in a business or technical area with which they are unfamiliar. Familiarisation has already been discussed, but the prudent project manager will also allow some additional time to complete the analysis and design work with inexperienced staff. It should be remembered, too, that if the analysis or programming work takes longer, the amount of supervision has to increase proportionately.

Use of contract staff Increasingly, companies are making use of contract programmers. In theory, a contract programmer should possess good technical skills and so productivity should not suffer. However, outsiders are always an unknown quantity, unless they have worked for the company before, and there may, in any case, be some initial slowness as they get used to the local methods and standards.

User involvement and availability The project manager needs to form a view, before work starts, on how available and committed the users will be to the project. If users are enthusiastic and interested in a development, then getting access to them for fact-finding and reviews is fairly easy. If they are suspicious, antagonistic or just uninterested, access is more difficult and things will inevitably take longer.

Although a lack of user access initially affects elapsed time, it does also impinge on the effort estimates since, unless they can juggle their work around, staff may end up sitting around doing nothing useful but booking to the project nevertheless.

User support during acceptance Again, users can adopt varying approaches to this. Some happily conduct the acceptance tests themselves; others simply want to watch tests, perhaps the system tests, conducted by the developers. The responsibilities for testing should have been spelled out in the contract but some allowance should be made in the estimates for supporting the users during acceptance testing.

Installation and commissioning Depending on the number of locations at which the system is to be implemented, this could be quite a sizeable activity and should be allowed for in the estimates.

Warranty The type and duration of warranty will have been discussed and agreed during the contract negotiations. However, some allowance needs to be made for possible warranty work and this is most easily assessed as a proportion of the total development effort. Some guideline figures are:

3-month warranty	5 per cent
6-month warranty	9.5 per cent
12-month warranty	10 per cent

9.5   Human factors affecting estimating

One of the main reasons that estimates often turn out to be hopelessly wrong is that they are not real estimates at all: they are numbers contrived to meet a political situation such as being low enough to make a bid competitive. It is clearly important for IS companies to win business, and to do this they have to offer competitive pricing. But the price at which some work is offered is a very different thing from the cost. The price is determined by what the market will bear, the profit margin that the company wants to obtain, the strategic reasons for wanting the business and a host of other factors. The cost, on the other hand, is, or should be, some scientifically quantifiable measure of the resources required to perform the work and not influenced by market factors.

The typical problem that arises, however, is that the estimators on the bid team look at the requirement and come up with what they believe to be a realistic estimate. The salespeople then say, 'Oh, come off it, it can't cost that much', and there follows a period of haggling until the final 'estimate' is arrived at. It is of course quite legitimate for salespeople to question estimates especially if, as does happen, the estimators are conservative and try to build in some contingency against disaster. But the estimators must stick to their guns if they believe their figures are correct. This can be unpleasant for the estimators, and it is one of the reasons why project managers require considerable self-confidence in order to withstand the resultant pressure; but it must be done if the project, once won, is not to be compromised.

If cost – and hence, once profit is added, price too – really is an issue, then perhaps the bid team should consider a more innovative way of doing the work. They might try rapid application development (RAD), or phasing the project, or delivering a cut-down core system, or using cheaper resources, or a quicker programming language. What they should *not* do, however, is fool themselves that they can reduce the estimates arbitrarily across the board and still have a chance of delivering the project within time and budget.

It is quite legitimate for project managers to be asked to recheck and justify their estimates, to prove that they are not building in excess padding to give themselves an easy life. They may, too, be asked to agree to a challenging target that requires tight project control and considerable drive to push the project forward. But this is not the same as signing up to do the impossible, and sometimes project managers just have to fight their corner and keep on insisting, patiently but firmly, on the quality of their estimates and the inadvisability of committing to an unachievable target.

This is not easy and the pressures on the project manager can become intense and unnerving. There is no simple remedy for this, and obviously a fairly strong ego will be a help. The following can help too:

- Ensuring that the estimates have been thoroughly researched and based on realistic metrics.
- Making sure that more than one person has contributed to the estimates and that a high degree of consensus has been obtained.

- Using several different estimating methods and formulae and cross-checking the results.
- Insisting on a proper risk assessment on the probability of achieving the planned targets.

If it is then decided for commercial reasons to go with a price or timescale that is not supported by the estimates, the project manager can insist that the responsibility for the resultant disaster is shared by those making the commercial decision.

9.6 Practical experiences with estimating

In this section we present some practical tips on improving the quality of the estimating process.

Building up metrics

Systems developers are not usually very good at building up metrics, but a reliable body of metrics is the best way to take the uncertainty out of estimating. The objections raised here are that collecting metrics takes time and effort and that metrics from one project cannot necessarily be applied to another.

Whilst there is no doubt that metrics collection does take time and effort, statistics on effort expended are probably collected anyway as part of the project monitoring process or to support billing the customer. So the basic figures are there: all that is needed is to collect also some definition of where the effort went. Thus, we may know that J Soap spent 12 days coding program XY123B; if we can define that program in some way – for example, as batch or online; simple, medium or complex; written in Ingres – then we have the start of a collection of metrics. Ideally, metrics would be collected across an organisation. Even if there is no organisation-wide metrics initiative, however, individual project managers can still collect metrics for themselves, to use on their own projects later or, perhaps, to use when they get dragged in to work in a bid team.

The second objection was that metrics from one project cannot necessarily be applied to another, so what is the use of collecting them at all? Although this is true to some extent, metrics can be applied more widely than may be apparent at first sight. For example, although Ingres and ORACLE are very different environments, experience shows that the approach to using them both is similar, that staff can cross-train quickly and that productivity rates are similar. So, if no ORACLE metrics are available, you might try using some metrics from an Ingres project instead. Or, again, if you have estimated for a COBOL development, you might like to cross-check against the Ingres estimate; if the Ingres estimate does not come out somewhat smaller, then there is something wrong somewhere.

Using standard project structures

Although each IS project has its distinctive features, there are also areas of commonality between projects which can be used to the project manager's advantage. One of these features is that projects seem to follow a fairly common lifecycle from analysis, through design to coding and testing (we are ignoring the so-called rapid application development for the moment). Because of this, and making allowance for certain variables, ratios from one project may well be applicable to another. So, if you are using, say, SSADM, it is reasonable to assume that the ratios of one stage to another should be similar to those in previous SSADM projects. This is one of the great advantages of using a method like SSADM, since the work content is clearly defined and experience from previous projects is readily applicable. It also assists in the collection of useful metrics.

Getting more than one view

Estimating is one area in which two heads, or better still several heads, really are better than one. Different people will approach an estimating problem in different ways and each is likely to spot something the others have missed. So it is worth getting several people to contribute to the estimating process and comparing their answers. The Delphi technique that we have already described (section 9.3.5) provides a structured way of doing this. An extension of this is to use more than one method to produce the estimate. You may, for example, use function point analysis as your primary method and then perform a cross-check using the analysis effort. Where the different methods produce different results – as they are almost bound to do – the worst thing you can do is to 'split the difference': there may be good reasons why, in the particular circumstances, one of the methods is more likely to be right than the other. Therefore, the only solution is to sit down and consider carefully the two estimates, the data available as input to each and their underlying logic, and to reason out where the probable answer lies. Having done this, it is important to document the reasons for arriving at the final estimate.

Qualifying estimates

However good the estimates are, they are going to be based on some assumptions – that you will need to conduct 20 interviews during the analysis work, that customers will turn round review products in 10 days, that you have adequate access to a development machine, and so on. The estimates must, therefore, be qualified by stating these assumptions. Although it is sadly true that a customer will remember your estimate long after they have forgotten the assumptions around it, stating any qualifications or assumptions clearly and unambiguously helps in two ways. First, it reminds you of the basis on which you prepared your estimates – how you were going to tackle the work for instance. And, second, if the assumptions have been carried forward properly into the contract, it gives the project manager some bargaining chips if, say, the customer falls down on their part of the development.

Documenting the estimates

It is extremely important that the estimators document their work as they go along and that this documentation is kept somewhere safe and accessible. The reasons are three-fold:

- There may be a need to compare the results of different estimating processes and, if so, a record of the assumptions and thought processes, as well as the actual calculations, of the estimators, will form part of the arbitration process.

- During the project, if slippage occurs, the project manager can examine the basis on which the estimates were prepared to see if similar slippage is likely in tasks yet to come.
- After the project is over, the estimates can be compared with the actual time spent and the results used to calibrate and fine-tune the estimating process for future projects.

Unfortunately, documenting estimates is tedious and time-consuming and, in the pressure to get the estimates out, is often left to tomorrow – which never comes. Although it does require some extra work, the effort is repaid with interest later in the project and on future projects.

Estimating and risk analysis Chapter 15 discusses the important issue of risk management in IS projects. The initial risk analysis on a project should include an examination of the estimating methods used and an assessment of their reliability and likely accuracy. So, the estimates should be revisited after the initial risk assessment, to take the results of that assessment into account and to make any necessary adjustments.

9.7 Summary

Estimating for IS projects has a bad reputation, generally attributable to the number of cost and time overruns on such projects. Although there are some specific problems that arise on IS projects, most of the estimating difficulties can be put down to the lack of a proper approach to the process, as practised in more mature engineering disciplines. No single estimating method will produce the 'right' result for a particular project. The project manager must use several different methods and compare the results critically before settling on the estimates to underpin the project plans. In the longer term, the careful collection of metrics should lead to an improvement in the accuracy of IS estimating.

Finally, remember that, however difficult IS estimating is, project managers can help themselves to a great extent by using the approaches described here and by not allowing themselves to be bullied into producing or accepting estimates that are commercially or politically acceptable. In the end, the project will come out as it will and the only result of starting with overoptimistic estimates will be to increase the chances of its appearing to be a project management, rather than a commercial, failure.

Questions

1 Give three reasons why estimating for IS projects has a poor reputation and a bad track record. What can be done about these problems?

2 The analogy method of estimating is often used to produce broad-brush estimates at the start of a project. Why is this method particularly suited to this application?

3 The analysis effort and programming methods both rest on the principle of extrapolating the total development effort from detailed estimates of one phase of the project. Describe the approach taken in each of these methods and show in what circumstances each might best be employed.

4 The Delphi technique aims to achieve a consensus estimate from the efforts of a number of estimators. How is this achieved and what is the advantage of the Delphi technique over, for example, a round-table discussion?

5 Describe how you would go about estimating for the following supporting project activities and why you would take your chosen approach to each.
(a) Project management
(b) Team leading/supervision
(c) Quality control
(d) Familiarisation.

6 State three factors that could influence the estimates for an IS project and how you would attempt to adjust the estimates for these factors.

Case study

To develop the estimates for the project, Richard Vaughan, the E-Con project manager, has held a workshop with key members of the development team including the two team managers. They have produced estimates for the deliverables as shown in Figure 9.1.

The work has been costed at a rate of €950 per day for E-Con's consultants and €400 per day for the internal France Vacances staff.

It will be noticed that three activities – not identified via our product breakdown structure – have been added to the estimates to cover project management, team management and configuration management. These have been calculated as follows:

■ Duration of project: 3 months or 13 weeks.
■ Project manager's involvement full-time: 4 days per week = 52 days overall.
■ Two team managers, also full-time: 104 days overall.
■ Configuration management: one day per week = 13 days overall.

Case study continued

Deliverable		Effort	E-Con work		FV work		Total
No.	Name	(days)	(days)	(€)	(days)	(€)	(€)
1	Project Initiation Document	1	1	950			950
2	Project/Quality Plan	2	2	1900			1900
3	Checkpoint Reports	10	7	6650	3	1200	7850
4	Work Package Authorisations	5	3	2850	2	800	3650
5	Interview Notes	10	7	6650	3	1200	7850
6	Requirements Specification	15	10	9500	5	2000	11500
7	Hardware Specification	5	5	4750			4750
8	Website	40	40	38000			38000
9	Interface to Customer Databases	10	10	9500			9500
10	Interface to Booking System	10	10	9500			9500
11	Management Information System	20			20	8000	8000
12	Communications Links	12	12	11400			11400
13	Trained Booking Personnel	6	6	5700			5700
14	Trained IT Personnel	6	4	3800	2	800	4600
15	Tested System	4	3	2850	1	400	3250
16	Implemented System	3	2	1900	1	400	2300
17	Product Descriptions	2	1	950	1	400	1350
18	Quality Log	1	1	950			950
19	Quality Review Results	5	3	2850	2	800	3650
20	Test Plans	4	3	2850	1	400	3250
21	Test Results	4	3	2850	1	400	3250
22	Project Management	52	52	49400			49400
23	Team Management	104	52	49400	52	20800	70200
24	Configuration Management	13	13	12350			12350
Total effort/cost		175		237500		37600	275100

Figure 9.1 **Estimate for France Vacances internet project**

Further reading

Boehm, Barry W (1981), *Software Engineering Economics*, Prentice Hall

Boehm, Barry W and others (2000), *Software Cost Estimation with COCOMO II*, Prentice Hall

Brooks, Frederick P Jr (1982), *The Mythical Man-month: Essays on Software Engineering*, Addison-Wesley

De Marco, Tom (1982), *Controlling Software Projects*, Yourdon Press

Drummond, Ian (1992), *Estimating with Mk II Function Point Analysis*, CCTA/HMSO

Gilb, Tom and Finzi, Susannah (1988), *Principles of Software Engineering Management*, Addison-Wesley

Hughes, Bob (2000), *Practical Software Measurement*, McGraw-Hill

Treble, Stephen and Douglas, Neil (1995), *Sizing and Estimating Software in Practice: Making Mk II Function Points Work*, McGraw-Hill

10 Project planning: scheduling and resourcing

10.1 Introduction

In Chapter 8, we saw how a project is broken down into elements of work that are small enough to estimate with some accuracy and which can act as 'work packages' for individual team members. We also showed why it is important to understand the dependencies between activities and the permissible sequences in which activities can be carried out. In Chapter 9, we reviewed various approaches to estimating for IS projects. In this chapter, we show how the dependency information and the estimates are brought together to produce a workable schedule for the project. We also present a format for documenting the completed plan and examine the plans used in the PRINCE2® project management method.

10.2 Scheduling

10.2.1 Effort and elapsed time

The project schedule, which usually takes the form of a bar chart, shows two things:

- The sequence in which the work will be carried out.
- The dates at which we plan activities to start and finish.

Bar charts can also be made to show who will be responsible for each activity. Development of a workable schedule is invariably an iterative process. We make some initial assumptions, develop a first-cut schedule, compare the results with our desired outcome – particularly in terms of the project end-date – and reschedule as many times as are needed to achieve an acceptable plan.

Before turning to the scheduling process, however, we need to explain the difference between effort and elapsed time, since this difference is crucial to an understanding of the scheduling process. Let us suppose that we have estimated a task as requiring 20 days' effort. Assuming that we have only one person available to do the work, then – if our person has no absence during the period – this 20 days' work will take 20 elapsed days to perform. If we have two people available, and the work can be partitioned, then the 20 days' work can be accomplished in 10 elapsed days. With four people, it would take 5 elapsed days. In practice, for reasons we discuss in this chapter, partitioning of activities is not usually as straightforward as this but it does illustrate the point. In producing our project schedule, it is vital that we keep the distinction between effort and elapsed time in mind. Usually, the project manager cannot do much about the effort required to perform an activity, since the amount of work is inherent in the task itself. But the project manager can and must seek to influence the elapsed time by committing the right amount of resources to each task.

10.2.2 Developing the schedule

To illustrate the approach, we shall use the simple feasibility study that we described in Chapter 8. The dependency network shown there, with estimated effort figures for each activity, is shown in Figure 10.1.

To develop our initial schedule, we might decide to see how long the project would take with one analyst assigned to the work. Since, in this case, the activities have to be carried out in sequence, we would get the schedule that is shown in Figure 10.2.

Figure 10.2 shows that the elapsed time for the project would be the sum of all of the activities – 33 days. We know, however, that our customer wants the feasibility study more quickly than that, so we have to examine our network to see if any activities can be performed in parallel. We find that:

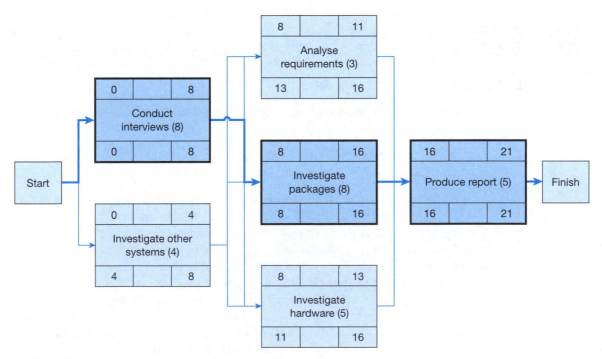

Figure 10.1 Dependency network with activity durations

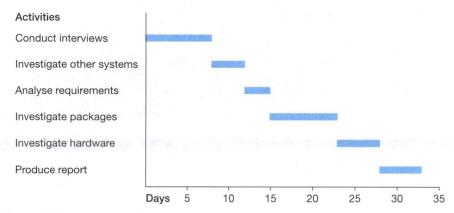

Figure 10.2 Schedule for one-person team

- *Conduct interviews* can be progressed in parallel with *Investigate other systems*.
- *Analyse requirements* can be done in parallel with both *Investigate packages* and *Investigate hardware*.

If we have a second analyst available, then we can take advantage of this parallelism, as shown in Figure 10.3.

In this plan, we have used one analyst on *Conduct interviews* and the other on *Investigate other systems*. Then, while one analyst is engaged on *Investigate packages*, the other first performs *Analyse requirements* and then *Investigate hardware*. By doing this, we have shortened the elapsed time of the project to 21 days. If our customer were very demanding, however, and if we had a third analyst available, we could partition the work again and shorten the timescale still further. Figure 10.4 illustrates how we could do this.

We have used two people on *Conduct interviews*, so the 8 days' effort now takes only 4 elapsed days. Similarly, we have used a different analyst on each of *Analyse requirements*, *Investigate packages* and *Investigate hardware* but in this case we do not gain anything since the elapsed time becomes the 8 days' effort of the longest of these activities, *Investigate hardware*. As a result we can now offer the customer the report in 17 elapsed days.

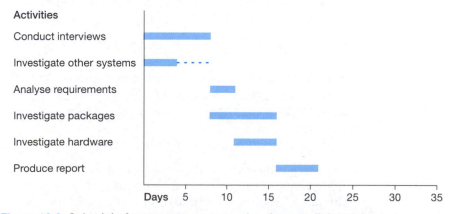

Figure 10.3 Schedule for two-person team showing parallel activities

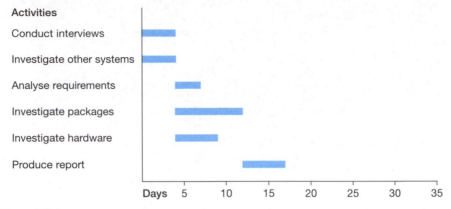

Figure 10.4 Schedule for three-person team

Although the feasibility study is a simple example, it does illustrate the approach that is used whatever the size of the project. An initial schedule is created and then it is adjusted and revised until the project manager is sure that it is realistic and provides a reasonable balance between the effective use of resources and the achievement of an acceptable end-date. There are, however, some other factors to consider in developing the project schedule.

10.2.3 Scheduling considerations

In our example we have assumed that each of the tasks on our schedule can be partitioned and that, if we share an activity between two people, each will carry out exactly half of the work. Whilst mathematically neat, neither of these assumptions is usually correct in practice. If we take an activity like digging a hole, then it is probably true that we can keep on partitioning it as many times as we have people available, the only constraint being the size of the hole and whether the people can all get down there without hitting each other with their shovels. Tasks on IS projects are more complex, however, and different considerations apply.

Let us suppose we have an activity for an analyst to produce a report comparing eight different relational databases. To do this, the analyst will:

- Study some background material and decide what evaluation criteria will be used.
- Read the technical literature about each of the eight databases and note how each performs against the evaluation criteria.
- Place the results of all the evaluations side by side on a table and compare them.
- Write a report documenting the findings.

If we partition this work between two analysts, then we find that not all of these subtasks can be divided neatly in half. Both analysts will have to study the same background material and it will probably take them longer to devise the evaluation criteria since there will inevitably be some discussion or argument about them. Each analyst can review four databases, so this subtask can be partitioned, but documenting the evaluations may involve further discussion and even, if there is only one PC available, delays while one analyst waits for the other to finish. Finally, the report will be a shared effort and there will be additional work involved in ensuring that the style of the document is consistent. So if in this case we had estimated that it would take one analyst six days to do this job, two analysts would be more likely to take, say, four elapsed days than the three we might initially imagine.

In addition, there is another subtle feature of projects like IS development that involve considerable complexity. This is that the members of the team need to communicate with each other, to share information and to coordinate their efforts. The volume of this communication obviously increases with the size of the team. If a person spends, say, only one hour per week communicating with each team member, then, in a two-person team, one hour will be spent thus by each person each week; but, in an eight-person team, more than a day a week for each person will be taken up with intra-team communication.

There is also the question of the learning curve to consider. However familiar someone is with a particular business or technical environment, there are unique features of each project that must be assimilated by each person involved in it. So, each person has to climb the learning curve before they become fully effective, and the more people there are on a team, the more learning curves there are to climb.

The conclusion we may draw from all this is that in developing our schedule we cannot necessarily take an activity of n days effort and divide it between two people to produce an elapsed time of $n/2$. Be warned, too, that many project-planning packages do not seem to be aware of this fact and will happily divide a task simply by the number of resources declared for it – so you will have to assess carefully if the plan produced by your software has actually taken these complexities into account.

Another issue to consider is whether the activities we have identified in our product or work breakdown structure are all that need to go on the schedule. In our feasibility study, we have assumed that *Investigate packages* and *Investigate hardware* can both start as soon as the analysts are ready, when they have finished *Conduct interviews* and *Analyse other systems*. But actually, we would probably have had to write away for information on packages and hardware and we may well not have received the replies by the time we want to start our investigations. Similarly, on many projects, there is 'dead' time for the project team while the users review and comment on various products. Unless we allow for these things, our schedule will be impossibly tight and allow no margin for accommodating slight delays.

There is also the important question of resource availability. Our feasibility study project is quite short – two to six weeks – and so we might expect to know our staff's leave and training commitments and build them into our plan. But what about unplanned absence like sickness? In developing overall project plans, it is necessary to plan on less than 100 per cent availability for the staff. In Chapter 9, we showed how a 'full-time' person was available for around 18 days per month, calculated as follows:

Total working days per year (52 × 5)   260
Less Bank holidays (normal, UK)   8
Less Holiday (say)   25
Less Other non-working time (training, sickness etc.)   <u>15</u>
     212

Divided by 12 to give average days per month   17.66
Or, divided by 52 to give average days per week   4.07

This represents an average availability of about 85 per cent overall or 4.25 days per five-day week. Allowing for other time-stealers like company meetings, appraisals and so forth, a good rule of thumb for long-term scheduling is to assume that each person will be available four days per week. If we adjust the schedule in Figure 10.4 on this basis, we would get the more realistic plan shown in Figure 10.5.

Here, we have multiplied each of our effort figures by 5/4 to give the elapsed time. Thus, for example, *Investigate other systems* – effort 4 days – gives an elapsed time of 5 days. Overall, we are now offering to complete the work in 21 elapsed days.

10.2.4 Project milestones

The schedule we have produced so far shows the sequence of activities that we shall need to carry out in order to complete our project. Completion will therefore mark an important *milestone* – the point at which our product is accepted by the customer or at which they will sign off our invoice for payment. However, we shall probably need to establish other milestones during the project, since:

- They provide useful control points at which we can evaluate progress and adjust our plans for the rest of the project as necessary.
- They can be used to illustrate progress to the customer.
- There may be intermediate sign-offs or stage payments linked to the achievement of milestones.

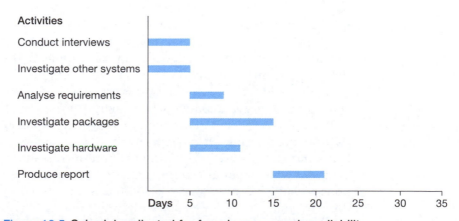

Figure 10.5 Schedule adjusted for four days per week availability

Figure 10.6 Bar chart showing project milestones

Milestones should be chosen carefully. If there are too many, they become rather meaningless and lose their significance as major points in the project. If there are too few, then control is lost. Usually, it is best to establish milestones that coincide with a significant deliverable, for example on completion of the specification or at the end of acceptance testing. Our example feasibility study project is probably too small to warrant intermediate milestones but, to illustrate the approach, we have modified our bar chart in Figure 10.6 to show milestones at the completion of the fact-finding, at the conclusion of the hardware and package investigation and at the delivery of the final report.

10.2.5 Showing 'overhead' tasks on schedules

So far, the tasks we have shown on our schedule are reasonably discrete, that is they have definable start- and end-dates which we can model easily. But how do we show 'overhead tasks' like project management, administration – completing timesheets and the like – and things like regular team meetings? We *could* try to model each team meeting individually and show a small task every Friday afternoon for doing the timesheets, but the schedule would become impossibly crowded. A better idea is to work out the average time that will be spent on each activity per week and then to spread this effort figure over the duration of the project as a continuous bar. Figure 10.7 shows the feasibility study with an extra line for project management added.

10.3 Developing resource plans

The resource plan is developed from, or alongside, the schedule and shows:

- How many of each type of resource will be required.
- When each resource will start and finish on the project.

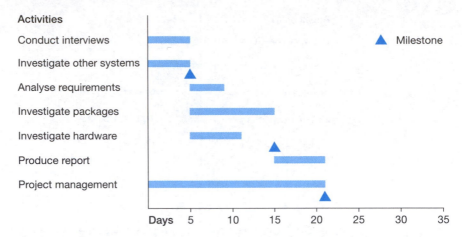

Figure 10.7 Bar chart showing project management as continuous activity over project

'Resources' in an IS project usually refers to people but it could equally include hardware, special software and bought-in services such as data preparation. We need to know exactly what resources are required and when they are required so that we can put in motion the processes for obtaining them and work out what costs they will bring to bear on the project.

Figure 10.8 shows the bar chart for the feasibility study project and, underneath it, a *resource histogram* which shows the deployment of project resources, in this case the analysts who will work on the study. It shows that, for the first nine elapsed days of the project, we need three analysts. The requirement then drops down to two analysts for two days and, finally, we need one analyst only for the last ten days.

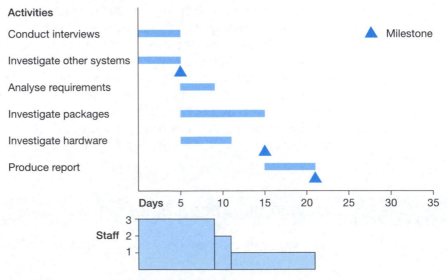

Figure 10.8 Bar chart with resource histogram

This gives us a total of 41 analyst-days, worked out as follows:

$$\text{Total number of analyst-days} = (9 \times 3) + (2 \times 2) + (10 \times 1) = 41$$

But we have to remember that this is elapsed days, not effort days which is 4/5 of the elapsed figure, or 33 days. We can double-check this by comparing this figure with the sum of all activities shown on our network diagram in Figure 10.1.

If our analysts are costed at £200 per day, we can now work out the staff costs of the project as $33 \times £200 = £6,600$.

We might also decide that, as the team is working on site, we shall need to hire a laptop PC for them to use at a further cost of £50 per day. We shall need this for all 21 days of the project, so that will cost £1,050. Thus, we can assess the total cost of the project as £7,650.

It will be noticed in Figure 10.8 that the use of resources over the duration of our project is not very even: 3 analysts for 9 days, 2 for 2 days and 1 for 10 days at the end. It may be possible to pick up people for the project and drop them again as indicated here, but it is more likely that you would want a more stable team structure for the duration of the project. This would be the case if, for example, you were using contract staff who would probably have to be hired for complete weeks rather than odd days here and there. In this case, you will need to attempt some 'resource smoothing' to try to get a more even allocation of staff over the life of the project. Some software packages have automated facilities for resource smoothing but without them you will have to adjust the schedule manually to achieve a better resource utilisation.

At the moment, we have produced our resource plans at a project level. On a small project like our feasibility study, the overall project plan would also be suitable for individual team members to see their tasks and when they are scheduled to take place. On a larger project, perhaps with hundreds of activities and dozens of team members, such an overall plan would be less useful at an individual level. We would want to extract parts of the overall plan to produce individual schedules and it is here that project planning software really comes into its own as most packages have the facility to produce selective reports in a variety of formats. Figure 10.9 represents a schedule for one of our analysts on the feasibility study project.

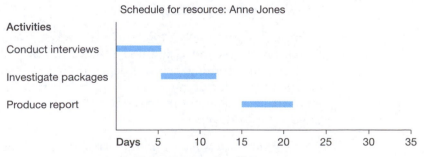

Figure 10.9 Bar chart for individual team member

There is, though, a danger in giving individuals copies of 'their' parts of the schedule. Remember that the schedule now shows elapsed time, rather than effort, and the team member may not appreciate this. In our example, Anne Jones might think she has five days' effort allocated for *Conduct interviews*, whereas in fact she has four days' effort spread over five elapsed days. Since, to some extent, estimates can become self-fulfilling prophecies, Ms Jones would then, in all likelihood, take five days over her four-day task. For this reason, many project managers prefer to give team members task specifications or work instructions showing the effort figure only, keeping the elapsed time plan under their own control. Quite a good incentive, though, is to share the dependency diagram with the team, so that everyone knows how their work will impact on that of their colleagues.

10.4 Contingency

So far, the plans we have developed have been *success based*, that is they are founded on an assumption that things will go according to plan, with activities starting and finishing when they are supposed to and taking no longer than the estimates allow. We have allowed some margin in our elapsed time plan for foreseeable staff absence, but otherwise we have not explicitly made any provision for things going wrong. Even in the best run project, things will inevitably go wrong and the prudent project manager will allow some additional margin, or *contingency*, in both the budget and schedule to deal with the effects of problems. The question, then, is how much contingency should we allow? There will be a different answer for every project based on a variety of factors, just some of which are:

- How tightly the requirement is defined and how much opportunity there is for growth in the scope of the work.
- The confidence we have in our estimates.
- The degree of innovation involved in the project.
- How confident we are of getting the resources we want, when we want them.
- Our knowledge of the customer and their likely commitment to the project.
- Our overall assessment of the risks involved in the project (these are discussed more fully in Chapter 15).

Contingency is usually expressed in two ways: as additional funds built into the project budget and as additional time built into the project schedule. The amount of the contingency will depend upon the project manager's assessment of the risk factors and, usually, upon a certain amount of haggling with senior management and the customer. There are two opposing dangers associated with contingency:

- No contingency is built into the plans, so there will be nothing in hand to deal with problems when they inevitably arise.

- Everyone concerned builds in contingency at each point – when assessing the tasks, producing the estimates and developing the schedules – so that contingency is piled upon contingency until the project becomes overblown and uncompetitive.

It is important, then, that reasonable contingency is allowed and also that it is allowed only once, preferably at project level. Contingency should be kept under the project manager's control and only the project manager should be able to authorise its use.

10.5 Documenting the plan

We have now completed the actual work of planning the project. We have broken the project down into individual activities, analysed the dependencies between them, estimated the durations for the activities and developed realistic schedules. To put the plan into effect, however, the plan must be documented in a way that is clear and accessible to all concerned in the project: to the team members, to the users, to senior customer staff and IT management. Development organisations will usually have standard formats for project plans but in this section we consider the subjects that should be included in a comprehensive plan. One issue to be decided in advance is whether the project plan should include the quality and risk management plans or whether these should be documents in their own right:

- Having one single document can avoid a lot of duplication – for example, all the plans mentioned would need some description of the project and this would be needed only once in a consolidated plan. In addition, having only one plan avoids a configuration management problem arising whereby one plan is revised but the others are not and thereby get out of step.
- On the other hand, on a big project a consolidated document may be unwieldy and the different sections may be the responsibility of different people – the project manager, risk manager and quality manager for instance. If this is so, or if the circulation of the various plans is likely to be very different, then separate plans may be the best idea.

Needless to say, the plan should not be produced once at the start of the project and then forgotten. There are few things more useless than a project plan that no longer reflects what is actually going on in the project. So the plan must be revised whenever any significant changes are planned in the project and copies must be issued to all the interested parties highlighting the changes. This is a good reason for restricting the circulation as far as possible so that there is not a massive distribution task involved. In the list of headings that follows, we have generally assumed the use of a consolidated plan. A comprehensive project plan should, at the minimum, contain the following.

1 Introduction. A description of the document and of the items covered by it.

2 Authorisation and amendment record. A description of the status of the document, information on its authorship and who has approved it, and a history of its amendments.

3 Distribution. A list of the people who will receive the document.

4 Related documents. Cross-references to other documents, for example to the risk management and quality plans if these are separate or to other relevant papers such as departmental standards to which the project must conform.

5 Overview of project. A brief description of the project and its objectives. If the plan relates only to one stage in a project, this section should also explain where and how the stage fits into the overall programme of work.

6 Products and deliverables. The overall product breakdown structure, which was discussed in Chapter 8, should be described, perhaps using the PRINCE2® subdivision of management products, quality products and technical products. The products should be listed with a cross-reference to the place where they are defined more fully – either in an appendix to the project plan, in a separate product description document or to an external document of some sort; if SSADM is being used, the SSADM manuals provide descriptions of the default SSADM products.

7 Milestones. A statement of the principal milestones of the project, what they represent and when they occur.

8 Organisation and responsibilities. A description of the main roles and responsibilities in the project, including, if useful, an organisation chart showing the relationships of the roles involved.

9 Monitoring and control. A description and explanation of the methods that will be used to monitor progress on the project, together with the mechanism – for example, a weekly progress meeting – that will be used to exercise control over the work.

10 Quality control. This defines where quality control will be exercised and the form that it will take, for example management reviews, formal inspections, walkthroughs and so on. The method to be used for categorising review comments and ensuring that they are cleared is also covered here. Quality control may be addressed in a separate quality plan.

11 Reporting. A description of the reporting mechanism: who will write the management reports, what they will cover, how often they will be produced and who will receive them.

12 Review and approvals. This is related to quality control and sets out, probably in tabular form, who is responsible for producing, reviewing and authorising the various project products.

13 Risks to the project. This may be covered by a separate risk management plan and risk register; there is more about this in Chapter 15. Otherwise, this section will include a description of the principal risks, an assessment of their likelihood and possible impact and an outline of the envisaged avoidance and mitigation actions.

14 Project schedule. The network diagram and bar charts for the project.

15 Task descriptions. These are probably best placed in an appendix. For each task on the network and bar chart, there should be a description of:

- The objective of the task.
- The work to be carried out.
- The methods to be used.
- The standards to be followed.
- The effort allocated.
- The products, both deliverable and intermediate.
- The completion criteria: in other words, how we will know when the task has been finished satisfactorily.

These task descriptions can therefore serve as work instructions to individual team members, defining for them exactly what they are required to do and how.

10.6 PRINCE2® plans

The PRINCE2® structured project management method defines a set of plans that seems at first sight slightly different from the project plan we have described so far. However, on closer examination, the PRINCE2® plans are seen to be quite compatible with our approach. The basic hierarchy of PRINCE2® plans is shown in Figure 10.10.

The diagram shows that the project may form part of a programme of projects (see Chapter 4) and, if so, the overall *programme plan* will probably dictate some general parameters of the way individual projects are planned. The *project plan* is produced at the start of the project and shows the main technical

Figure 10.10 PRINCE2® plans

activities and the resources involved. Probably, the information will be shown at summary level here, to be broken down into more detail on lower-level plans. The project plan is one of the main inputs to the project initiation process. PRINCE2® projects are divided into one or more stages and, as each of these is reached, a *stage plan* is produced. This is more elaborate than the project plan and shows the detailed activities involved in carrying out the stage. If required, *team plans* may be produced to focus even more closely on individual aspects of a stage and this is particularly so when a number of different teams (for example, package software vendors and in-house development staff) are involved. The dotted lines around *team plans* in Figure 10.10 indicate that these are considered optional products in PRINCE2®.

The **exception plan** is a novel PRINCE2® concept. The idea is that, if it becomes apparent that a project is going to exceed its tolerances (see Chapter 8), then the project manager must report this to the project board and get consent to a variation in the project's time, cost or quality/product constraints. To support this, the project manager must produce exception plans showing how the stage, or the whole project, will be completed in the changed situation. If the project board agrees to the variation, then the exception plan replaces the relevant project or team plan.

The project plan and stage plan are each made up of a number of components, as shown in Figure 10.11.

Figure 10.11 Contents of PRINCE2® project and stage plans

- The *product breakdown structure* and *product flow diagram* as described in Chapter 8.
- The **activity network** shows the interdependency between the tasks needed to develop the products and the critical path through the project.
- The *financial budget* shows how and when funds will be required to support the project.
- The *resource requirements* is a tabular summary of the resources and their costs required at each point in the project.
- The *risk assessment* summarises the main risks to the project or stage and the planned counter-measures (see also Chapter 15).
- *Quality plan* documenting the methods and standards to be used.
- We have met *Gantt charts* and *product descriptions* in this and the preceding chapters.

The resource requirements can be represented graphically, as illustrated in Figure 10.12.

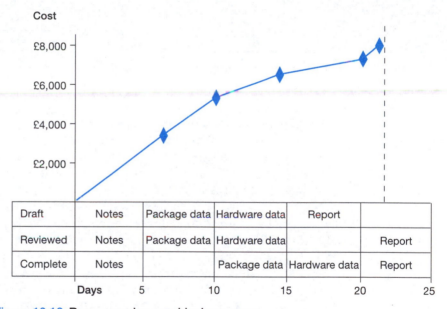

Figure 10.12 Resource plan graphical summary

10.7 Budgets

One last aspect of planning to consider is the preparation of an overall budget for the project. To a large extent, this is created by pulling together all the information the project manager has gathered in preparing the plans and expressing it in financial terms.

BUDGET FOR: NEW CUSTOMER CONTACT SYSTEM									
Expenditure code and heading		Monthly figures							Totals
		Mar	Apr	May	Jun	Jul	Aug	Sep	
A	Direct labour	50	50	70	90	120	70	30	480
B	Subcontract work		30	30	60	60	30		210
C	Hardware	100				200			300
D	Software	30				60			90
E	Telecommunications	10				60			70
F	Travel	3	3	1	1	3	2	1	14
G	Accommodation and subsistence	2	2	1	1	2	2	1	11
H	Project-specific training	10							10
I	Support services					2	6	5	13
J	Consultancy support	2	2	2	2	6	2	1	17
Contingency (10%) – items B–J only		16	4	3	6	39	4	1	74
Monthly totals:		207	87	104	154	513	112	38	1289

Figure 10.13 Example budget for an IT project

Budgets should present two pieces of information: what inflows and outflows of cash will result from the project and when they will occur. Figure 10.13 shows an example budget for an IT project.

In this example, the most significant cost is that of labour – direct and subcontracted – and this is very typical of an IT project. Hardware is the next largest cost followed by package software, telecommunications equipment and so on. The budget also includes some items that are often forgotten but can add considerably to the cost of a project, such as travel, accommodation and project-specific training.

Finally, it will be noticed that contingency has been added to most of the items in the budget but not to item A, which is the cost of employed labour. The reason for this in this case is that the effort estimates already include contingency, so to add financial contingency on top would be to include it twice.

The reason why the month-by-month figures are needed as well as the overall one is so that the cash-flow of the project can be managed to the best advantage. For example, if the project needs to buy in products or services from other organisations (like subcontractors), it is important to time the purchases so that, if possible, the project does not go into deficit (paying out money before the project gets paid). In addition, the organisation's accounts and treasury managers can plan the overall cash flow of the organisation by considering the cash flows of the various projects and, perhaps, by balancing them against each other.

10.8 | Summary

It is important to distinguish between the effort on a project and the elapsed time the project will take. The schedule is developed iteratively from the network diagram by trying various combinations of resources until a satisfactory balance is achieved between the effective and economical use of resources and meeting the required end-dates. Care must be taken in partitioning tasks so that adequate allowance is made for such things as start-up activities, and the learning curve for individuals. Milestones should be added to the schedule to indicate significant points in the project.

Once the schedule is developed, resource plans can be derived from it and project costs calculated. Adequate contingency must be allowed in the plan to cover any problems that may arise, and use of the contingency should be kept under the project manager's control. The plan must be fully documented and kept up to date to reflect changes as the project proceeds. PRINCE2® contains a standard set of planning products.

Questions

1 Explain the difference between 'effort' and 'elapsed time'. What is the significance of this difference for project planning purposes?

2 Scheduling a project involves understanding the degree to which project tasks can be 'partitioned'. What is meant by this term and what effect does partitioning have on the scheduling process?

3 In long-term project planning, it is wise to assume that staff will be available for project work for less than 100 per cent of the total available time. What factors will reduce staff availability and what adjustments should be made for them?

4 What do you understand by the term 'project milestone'? How would you decide how many milestones to show on your project plan?

5 The PRINCE2® project management method envisages a hierarchy of plans. Describe this hierarchy.

Case study

Using the network structure (see Chapter 8) and the estimated effort to produce each deliverable (see this chapter), Richard Vaughan has produced an enhanced network diagram to show the critical path. This is shown in Figure 10.14, with a supporting table in Figure 10.15 that shows the earliest and latest start and finish times for each activity.

Richard Vaughan's problem is the overall duration of the project revealed by this analysis: 101 days. If the project started on 1 April and is to be complete by the end of June, then there are only 61 working days in that period. The question is, how to shorten the project duration?

This is where knowledge of the critical path becomes invaluable to the project manager. Deliverable 6 is the requirements specification and is estimated to require 15 days' effort, and deliverable 8 is the actual website and is estimated to require 40 days' effort. Both of these durations assume one person working on each but they are, of course, amenable to sharing among more than one person.

For reasons that we discussed in the chapter, one cannot simply divide a 40-day task among two people and say that it will now take only 20 days – but it would be reasonable to think that we could get it down to 25 days. Similarly, by splitting deliverable 6 between two analysts we might reduce the elapsed time to, say, 8 days. So, Richard Vaughan revises the network diagram as shown in Figure 10.16, with the supporting data table in Figure 10.17.

Figure 10.14 Initial critical path network for France Vacances internet project

Case study continued

Deliverable No.	Name	Duration (days)	EST	EFT	LST	LFT	Float
1	Project Initiation Document	1	0	1	0	1	0
2	Project/Quality Plan	2	1	3	1	3	0
3	Checkpoint Reports	10	–	–	–	–	–
4	Work Package Authorisations	5	5	10	5	10	0
5	Interview Notes	10	10	20	10	20	0
6	Requirements Specification	15	20	35	20	35	0
7	Hardware Specification	5	20	25	47	52	27
8	Website	40	35	75	35	75	0
9	Interface to Customer Databases	10	35	45	54	64	19
10	Interface to Booking System	10	35	45	54	64	19
11	Management Information System	20	35	55	44	64	9
12	Communications Links	12	25	37	52	64	27
13	Trained Booking Personnel	6	55	61	64	70	9
14	Trained IT Personnel	6	75	81	75	81	0
15	Tested System	4	61	65	70	74	9
16	Implemented System	3	69	72	78	81	9
17	Product Descriptions	2	3	5	3	5	0
18	Quality Log	1	–	–	–	–	–
19	Quality Review Results	5	–	–	–	–	–
20	Test Plans	4	35	39	70	74	35
21	Test Results	4	65	69	74	78	9

Minimum project duration: 81 days

Figure 10.15 Network analysis results for France Vacances internet project

The minimum duration of the project is now 65 days – better than before but it still will not fit into the April–June timeframe. Richard's attention is now focused on deliverable 11, the management information system, with its duration of 20 days. He decides that the work on this can be split between two people and reduces the duration to 12 days. This results in another reconfiguration of the critical path and the durations as shown in Figures 10.18 and 10.19.

Now – at last – the project duration at 59 days is within the available time of 61 days. Even so, there is little margin for error here and, in practice, Richard would probably want to refine his model further to give himself some more latitude.

The process involved here illustrates very well why the use of project planning software has become so popular, since it enables the different scenarios to be modelled with relative ease.

Case study continued

Figure 10.16 Revised critical path network for France Vacances internet project

Deliverable No.	Name	Duration (days)	EST	EFT	LST	LFT	Float
1	Project Initiation Document	1	0	1	0	1	0
2	Project/Quality Plan	2	1	3	1	3	0
3	Checkpoint Reports	10	–	–	–	–	–
4	Work Package Authorisations	5	5	10	5	10	0
5	Interview Notes	10	10	20	10	20	0
6	Requirements Specification	8	20	28	20	28	0
7	Hardware Specification	5	20	25	31	36	11
8	Website	25	28	53	34	59	6
9	Interface to Customer Databases	10	28	38	38	48	10
10	Interface to Booking System	10	28	38	38	48	10
11	Management Information System	20	28	48	28	48	0
12	Communications Links	12	25	37	36	48	11
13	Trained Booking Personnel	6	48	54	48	54	0
14	Trained IT Personnel	6	53	59	59	65	6
15	Tested System	4	54	58	54	58	0
16	Implemented System	3	62	65	62	65	0
17	Product Descriptions	2	3	5	3	5	0
18	Quality Log	1	–	–	–	–	–
19	Quality Review Results	5	–	–	–	–	–
20	Test Plans	4	28	32	54	58	26
21	Test Results	4	58	62	58	62	0
Minimum project duration:		65 days					

Figure 10.17 Network analysis results for France Vacances internet project

Case study continued

Figure 10.18 Second revision critical path network for France Vacances internet project

Deliverable No.	Name	Duration (days)	EST	EFT	LST	LFT	Float
1	Project Initiation Document	1	0	1	0	1	0
2	Project/Quality Plan	2	1	3	1	3	0
3	Checkpoint Reports	10	–	–	–	–	–
4	Work Package Authorisations	5	5	10	5	10	0
5	Interview Notes	10	10	20	10	20	0
6	Requirements Specification	8	20	28	20	28	0
7	Hardware Specification	5	20	25	25	30	5
8	Website	25	28	53	28	53	0
9	Interface to Customer Databases	10	28	38	32	42	4
10	Interface to Booking System	10	28	38	32	42	4
11	Management Information System	20	28	40	30	42	2
12	Communications Links	12	25	37	30	42	5
13	Trained Booking Personnel	6	40	46	42	48	2
14	Trained IT Personnel	6	53	59	53	59	0
15	Tested System	4	46	50	48	52	2
16	Implemented System	3	54	57	56	59	2
17	Product Descriptions	2	3	5	3	5	0
18	Quality Log	1	–	–	–	–	–
19	Quality Review Results	5	–	–	–	–	–
20	Test Plans	4	28	32	48	52	20
21	Test Results	4	50	54	52	56	2

Minimum project duration: 59 days

Figure 10.19 Second revision of durations for France Vacances internet project

Case study continued

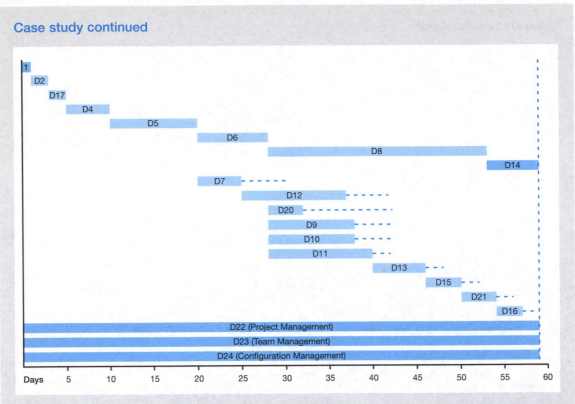

Figure 10.20 Bar chart for France Vacances internet project

Now that a workable network has been established, Richard is able to develop a bar chart to illustrate the sequence of the work against a timeline (Figure 10.20).

On this bar chart, the critical path deliverables have been shown first, followed by the non-critical deliverables with their 'float' indicated with dotted lines.

Finally, Richard can confirm the budget for the project. This is based, in essence, on the effort estimates discussed in Chapter 9 but, because more than one person is being used for deliverables 6, 10 and 11, the actual effort associated with these has increased somewhat, as shown in Figure 10.21.

It will be remembered from the project initiation document (Chapter 7) that E-Con had quoted a fixed price of €300,000 for their part of the work. So, it looks like the E-Con total of €286,050 will come within this budget and the project will be profitable – but only if tight control is exercised over effort and costs.

Similarly, France Vacances was advised to budget €50,000 for its involvement. Since its IT department's work will cost €40,000 this leaves €10,000 for other user involvement which looks just about right.

Case study continued

Deliverable No.	Name	Effort (days)	E-Con work (days)	(€)	FV work (days)	(€)	Total (€)
1	Project Initiation Document	1	1	950			950
2	Project/Quality Plan	2	2	1900			1900
3	Checkpoint Reports	10	7	6650	3	1200	7850
4	Work Package Authorisations	5	3	2850	2	800	3650
5	Interview Notes	10	7	6650	3	1200	7850
6	Requirements Specification	16	9	8550	7	2800	11350
7	Hardware Specification	5	5	4750			4750
8	Website	50	50	47500			47500
9	Interface to Customer Databases	10	10	9500			9500
10	Interface to Booking System	10	10	9500			9500
11	Management Information System	24			24	9600	9600
12	Communications Links	12	12	11400			11400
13	Trained Booking Personnel	6	6	5700			5700
14	Trained IT Personnel	6	4	3800	2	800	4600
15	Tested System	4	3	2850	1	400	3250
16	Implemented System	3	2	1900	1	400	2300
17	Product Descriptions	2	1	950	1	400	1350
18	Quality Log	1	1	950			950
19	Quality Review Results	5	3	2850	2	800	3650
20	Test Plans	4	3	2850	1	400	3250
21	Test Results	4	3	2850	1	400	3250
22	Project Management	52	52	49400			49400
23	Team Management	104	52	49400	52	20800	70200
24	Configuration Management	13	13	12350			12350
25	Hardware			40000			
	Total effort/cost	190		286050		40000	286050

Figure 10.21 Revised effort estimates for France Vacances internet project

Further reading

Cleland, David I (1998), *Project Management Handbook*, Wiley

Maylor, Harvey (2003), *Project Management*, 3rd edn, FT/Prentice Hall

Office of Government Commerce (2002), *Managing Successful Projects with PRINCE2*, 3rd edn, The Stationery Office

Rosenau, Milton D Jr (1998), *Successful Project Management*, 3rd edn, Wiley

11 Monitoring progress

11.1 Introduction

We have now covered planning the project – establishing what is to be done, by whom, by when, to what standards – and we have analysed the risks we face and devised measures to counter them. However, this is actually the easier part of project management. Much more difficult is the actual running of the project on a day-to-day basis, monitoring progress and making changes as necessary to ensure that it keeps on track for delivering its final objectives. We examine the continuing management of projects in the next two chapters. In this chapter, we discuss the mechanisms that the project manager will need in order to monitor progress, to see what is really going on; and in Chapter 12 we shall look at what can be done to exercise control when we spot that our project is not going quite as we planned it.

The project needs to be managed from three perspectives, those of the triple constraint of time, cost and quality. Sometimes, the management decisions we make will involve a trade-off between these three elements – we might be able to deliver on time if we sacrifice some of the performance of the system or guarantee the quality if the costs can be allowed to rise. These decisions may be outside the project manager's control and the project manager may have to get involved with some hard bargaining with the project board or the customer, or their own senior management, before a revised approach can be agreed.

In this chapter, we consider monitoring techniques for each element of the triple constraint.

11.2 Monitoring effort

To monitor progress, we need first some mechanism for collecting figures on the resources used. On IS projects, the major resource element is staff time but there are also costs to be considered for resources such as machine usage and bought-in hardware and services.

To gather information on the effort expended, there really is no alternative but to get the team members to complete timesheets of some sort. Although this is pretty obvious, there can be political difficulties in the way. Staff, and sometimes trade unions, may see the completion of timesheets as 'Big Brother' spying on them, and others, perhaps the more senior or experienced people, may resent having their work examined minutely in this way. In consultancy companies, the use of timesheets is quite usual as they support the billing process, and the same is also true for in-house IT departments that operate as profit or cost centres. If you are working somewhere where timesheets are not the norm, then you will have to practise your diplomacy in explaining to your team why timesheets are so important and how vital they are to proper control of the project. If there are problems in getting timesheets accepted, one possibility is to use a design that records only time spent on project work – in other words, you are not interested in time spent on non-project activities.

Figure 11.1 gives an idea of the sort of information that is needed on a timesheet:

- Identifiers for the team member, the project and the week being reported on.
- A code and title – taken from the project plan or bar chart – for each activity.
- The time spent on each activity each day and a total for the week.
- Very important, an estimate of the effort to go. (We say some more about this important item shortly.)

Strictly speaking, we are probably not very interested in the daily effort figure for each task, but experience shows that we get a much more accurate record if people fill in their timesheets daily. We might want to add to this minimal data some additional features, for example:

- Somewhere for the person to qualify their 'to go' figure and comment upon any problems or delays encountered.
- A column to record the predicted end-date as well as the effort to go – remember, the former is related to elapsed time and the latter to effort.

Name: DAVE SIMS		Project: PERSONNEL				Week ending: 19 May				
Code		Mon	Tue	Wed	Thu	Fri	Sat	Sun	Total	To go
A/01	CODE PROGRAM CV004	6.5	5.0	7.5					19.0	NIL
A/02	TEST PROGRAM CV004				7.5	3.0			10.5	NIL
A/07	CODE PROGRAM EN025					4.0			4.0	15.0
M/03	TEAM MEETING	1.0							1.0	
M/02	COMPLETE TIMESHEET					0.5			0.5	

Figure 11.1 Effort-monitoring timesheet

■ A place to record non-productive, but project-related, activities such as appraisals or progress meetings – though we may have assigned activity codes for this.

One of the most important pieces of information on the timesheet is the 'effort to go' figure. There is very little that can be done about the effort already expended, which is now so much water under the bridge, and the project manager's efforts need to be focused on the future and the work yet to be done. Because of this, it is essential that the 'effort to go' figure is properly estimated. It is not unknown for the figure to be arrived at by the following calculation:

$$(\text{Original estimate}) - (\text{Effort expended to date}) = \text{Estimate to go}$$

Now this is not an honest estimate at all but an expression of wishful thinking. Using this approach, activities will seem to be proceeding to schedule until they lurch disastrously into overrun. Team members must be encouraged to estimate their 'to go' figures as accurately as they can and the project manager can help here by the way in which he or she receives the bad news of a possible overrun. If the project manager always explodes, or otherwise reacts negatively, then team members will want to keep the bad news to themselves until the last minute – when it is probably too late to take any remedial action. Of course, the project manager has to look into the reasons for the predicted overrun, but this must be done in a neutral way, simply finding out the facts, not as a 'witch hunt' to apportion blame.

The reasons for any departure from the planned timescale must be examined thoroughly since the remedial action to be taken will depend upon the results of the analysis. We have more to say on this in the next chapter but, for now, let us consider the situation where a programmer is expecting an estimated ten-day coding task to overrun by two days. There could be various causes of this including:

■ The programmer's inexperience. In this case, the program may have been too difficult and the project manager could consider reassigning work so that this programmer has simpler programs in future.

■ Lack of clarity in the program specification. If this is so, the question to be asked is, 'does the same apply to the other specifications?' In other words, is this an isolated situation or is it likely to be reflected throughout the project so that all the programming estimates will be too low?

■ Lack of access to the development machine. Here, the project manager can ease things for the team by obtaining greater access.

■ The programmer is experienced and competent, the specification clear and there are no problems with access to the development machine. If this is so, then it suggests that the original estimate was too low and this might apply to other estimates also.

If the project manager is to take the right action to deal with the matter, it is necessary to know which of these problems – or any others – is at the root of the trouble.

Having collected information at an individual level, the next step is to summarise it at a project level to see the overall situation. Project planning packages usually have facilities to do this, although sometimes they are rather cumbersome to use. Alternatively, the project manager can set up a spreadsheet to do the same thing. For each activity, we need to know:

- Its current status – not started, in progress or completed.
- The original effort estimate.
- The original cost estimate (effort × daily rate).
- The original start-date.
- The original end-date.
- The actual start-date.
- The effort booked to date.
- The cost booked to date (effort × daily rate).
- The effort estimated still to go.
- The cost estimated still to go (effort × daily rate).
- The current predicted total effort.
- The current predicted total cost (effort × daily rate).
- The current estimated end date.

Some of this information can be expressed graphically on a bar chart. Figure 11.2 is a development of the bar chart for the feasibility study project featured in Chapter 10.

Figure 11.2 shows the situation at the end of the second week – shown by the vertical double line. *Conduct interviews* has taken two days longer than planned, due to the unavailability of some of the interviewees; this is shown by extending the time bar. As a result of this, the three activities that are dependent on *Conduct interviews* have started two days late. In addition, the analyst who will carry out *Investigate packages* has reported that the task will take three days longer than estimated owing to some difficulties in getting to see the package vendors; this will not delay the project as a whole since the report cannot be started in any case until *Investigate hardware* has been completed. It

Figure 11.2 Bar chart used to illustrate project progress

will be noticed, too, that the first of our milestones has been missed – we show when it did actually occur, together with its originally planned position. Similarly, we are predicting slippage in the second and third milestones.

This does, however, illustrate one of the deficiencies of a bar chart as a monitoring tool. We may *know* that *Analyse requirements*, *Investigate packages* and *Investigate hardware* can only start when *Conduct interviews* and *Investigate other systems* have both finished, but this is not necessarily evident from the chart itself. To find out the effects on other activities – and on the project as a whole – it is necessary to consult the network chart and to recalculate the critical path to take account of the slippage.

Returning to the bar chart for the moment though, the slippage of *Analyse requirements* has also had other effects on the project, not immediately obvious. Originally, it was intended that the second analyst would start work on *Investigate packages* as soon as they had finished *Investigate other systems*. However, a two-day delay has now been introduced, during which, presumably, the analyst will continue to book time to the project – so we have incurred an extra two days' costs as well. Similarly, the project manager's assignment will have to be extended for another two days, with further additional costs. This goes to show that an apparently small slippage can have more severe knock-on effects and that working out all the effects of a slippage involves careful examination of the plans.

11.3 Monitoring other costs

Labour costs are usually the main cost component of an IS project but there are other costs as well and all have to be kept under review. In this section, we consider how best to do this.

To start with, it is important to distinguish between the cost and the price of something. The *cost* is what we have to pay for the resource, be it staff salaries or a piece of hardware. The *price* is what we charge for the same thing, and the difference between the two represents our profit, if we are out to make a profit. If you are working within an in-house IT department, you may not be intending to make a profit but you may still wish to add a mark-up to bought-in items to cover your administrative overheads.

Staff costs are best dealt with by establishing some sort of daily rate for each team member, probably based on their grade or classification. Staff costs do not just include the person's salary; on top of that, there will be costs such as contributions to the pension fund, the employer's National Insurance contributions, perhaps a private medical scheme or company car. And on top of *that*, there will be overheads to cover things like office space, heating, lighting and the provision of furniture and equipment. Different firms calculate these things in different ways and the advice of the finance or accounts department should be sought.

Where contract staff are being used, they will probably submit a weekly timesheet. Once signed off by the project manager, this will be used by their agency as the basis for an invoice. That will then be submitted for approval, after which it will be paid and posted to the project's accounts. The trouble with this arrangement is that there might be quite a time lag between the work being done and the costs appearing on the accounts. So our advice to project managers is to capture the information at the timesheet stage and to keep your own records of contractor costs, perhaps on a spreadsheet.

The same applies to the costs for other bought-in items. If you are buying a piece of hardware, or perhaps hiring some for the duration of the project, the suppliers' invoices will probably trail behind the actual goods by quite a period. This can be useful if you want to take advantage of a favourable cash flow, since you can probably bill your customer before you have been charged yourself and enjoy the use of the money until the supplier's invoice arrives.

There are other expenses that could, depending on your organisation's accounting practices, get chalked up to your project, for example:

- *Project-specific training.* Sometimes, costs for general developmental training are borne centrally, though reflected in the staff costs or charge-out rates, but training for a project task – like learning a specialised programming language – may fall on the project.
- *Specially arranged accommodation.* If, for instance, your team is big enough to require a self-contained office, the rental of this space may be charged to the project.
- *Lodging and subsistence costs.* If project staff have to work away from base for any length of time, the project might have to pay for hotels, meals or perhaps the rental of apartments.
- *Travel costs.* Whether or not they have to stay away from home, staff may be entitled to reimbursement of travel costs over and above their normal journey to work. They may be entitled to travel *time* as well, usually at something like half the normal rate.
- *Consumables.* Such as stationery, diskettes, laser toner cartridges and other items that can add a surprising amount of cost to a project.
- *Insurance.* If special safety or other considerations apply, the organisation's normal public liability and similar insurance may not be adequate and special arrangements may have to be made and charged to the project.

As with other expenses, there will probably be some delay between the costs being incurred, being signed off and appearing in the accounts, so the prudent project manager will keep his or her own record of them.

11.4 Monitoring quality

11.4.1 Establishing the climate for successful quality control

Chapter 14 discusses the basic approaches to monitoring quality – inspection versus testing for example. Here, we review some techniques that may be employed to check the quality of deliverables as they are produced.

It is important, first of all, for the project manager to create the right climate for quality control to work properly. It is often difficult for people to divorce themselves from their work, so that criticism of the work becomes criticism of them personally. It is probably a good thing that people do feel personally involved in what they are doing – otherwise why should they care whether it is done well or not? But this does mean that reviews and criticism must be handled sensitively. Some do's and don'ts are:

- Do ensure that all criticism is impersonal – not 'you're doing this wrong', but 'this is wrong'.
- Do not be judgemental. Simply state the factual error or concern without appearing to cast doubt on the author's competence, commitment or intelligence.
- Do avoid comparisons with how you would have tackled the same task; other approaches, though different, may be equally valid and, as long as standards are followed, ought to be accommodated.
- Do not try to resolve problems during reviews. Identify the problem and leave it to the author or someone else to find a solution.
- Do use quality control reviews as an opportunity to coach junior staff. If it is clear that an error has arisen because of inexperience or a lack of knowledge, grasp the chance to improve the team member's skill or knowledge in that area.
- Do not aim for perfection. Excellence and conformance to requirement are not the same thing, and if the customer only wants, or can only afford, a basic product you will not get any thanks for delivering a gold-plated one.

11.4.2 Timing of quality control checks

There are two major phases in the quality control process: checking or reviewing work as it is in progress and testing the finished product. Taking the review process first, it is important to apply checks at sensible points in the project's lifecycle. In general, it is not sensible to apply quality control to each item as it is produced, for example to each module of code – although in the 'total quality' climate we would expect the originators of work to be applying their own checks on a continuous basis. On the other hand, it is no use waiting until, say, a whole suite of programs has been developed before checking them and finding that there is some fundamental problem with all of them. Where there is a clearly defined project lifecycle, there should be checks at the end of each stage and before the project moves on to the next stage. Thus, one would review the analysis work before moving on to design and check the design before starting development.

However, there can sometimes be a case for checking smaller units of work. If, for example, a new design method is being used or the person doing the work is unfamiliar with the techniques or standards to be used, it would be wise to carry out a check as the first unit emerges from production. As with many other aspects of project management, there are no hard-and-fast rules here, but a checklist of decision points at which to apply quality control would include:

- Having checks at the project milestones defined in the project plan.
- Applying checks when moving from one development phase to the next.
- Checking the operation of new standards after their first application.
- Checking on work involving new techniques or methods.
- Checking the work of inexperienced staff or those newly recruited who may have worked to different standards elsewhere.

With regard to the testing of finished products, there is a fairly self-evident hierarchy of tests to be followed:

- Individual components, programs or modules, for example, are tested to ensure that they meet their individual specifications.
- Components are linked together and integration tests check that they work satisfactorily in combination.
- The complete system is tested to ensure that all the components function together to deliver what the customer specified.
- The customer conducts an acceptance test to satisfy themselves that the product meets their requirements.

In addition to the above, there may be a need for other checks to ensure that the product can handle large volumes, or operate in adverse conditions or work reliably over a long period of time.

11.4.3 Methods for monitoring quality

Various methods exist for conducting quality control reviews, some rather informal and others highly structured. In choosing one, the guiding idea should be the usual touchstone of appropriateness. Whatever approach is taken, the review process must be planned. The reviewers must be clear about:

- The criteria to be applied.
- The definitions of pass or fail for the items reviewed.

Among the approaches you might consider are the following.

Self-checking This really supports the total quality management (TQM) theme and relies on the author of the work having a good understanding of the requirement and also of the skills and techniques needed to meet it. The approach is best suited to more experienced team members who should, as with any other check, formally record their reviews. The big disadvantage with self-checking is that, if someone has misunderstood something in, say, a design document, they will continue to labour under the same misapprehension during the checking process and the defect will not be discovered. For this reason, one of the other forms of check should be used in areas of known criticality and occasionally elsewhere to verify the self-checking procedure.

Team leader reviews Here, a team member's supervisor is responsible for checking that work meets its specification and conforms to any requisite standards. If defects are identified, corrective work is undertaken and the work is then reinspected. This method is useful when reviews of work are to be linked to coaching – as will often be the case for junior staff. The problem is that it is only as effective as the supervisor's ability to spot problems and, of course, the team leader may not in fact be as skilled as the author in the particular discipline or technique involved. In addition, bottlenecks can occur with this method, as all checking has to be undertaken by one person; this is particularly the case with projects that are using fast programming methods where programmer productivity can outstrip the ability of the team leader to review the work.

Peer reviews This is similar in principle to a team leader review in that one person is checking the work of another. Team leader review and peer review can be used in tandem, with the team leader in effect sharing the review work with one of the more experienced team members. Peer review does, of course, rely on the ability of the reviewer to spot defects, and some people are better at this than others. There is a special danger for the project manager to watch for with peer reviews: that of rivalry or one-upmanship between the author and reviewer. They may need reminding that the objective is not to score points off each other but to produce a high-quality product. In a multidisciplinary team, where the team leader does not have expertise in the area to be reviewed, peer review may be the only practical way of conducting quality control.

Walkthroughs Conducting a walkthrough, which involves a review by a group of people, can prove very effective, as the skills, knowledge and eyesight (for spotting errors) of a number of people are brought to bear. Walkthroughs do, however, require good organisation so that everyone concerned is clear about their objectives and has the necessary documentation available early enough for proper study. In addition, to keep review meetings moving forward and to stop them straying from the point, good chairmanship is essential. It is particularly important in walkthroughs to stick to the identification of problems and to avoid trying to find solutions. Obviously, if a solution does emerge immediately it would be silly to discard it; but since, in meetings, the length of time spent in discussion tends to rise exponentially with the number present, too many ideas for solutions will soon get the meeting completely bogged down. Finally, since reviewing is an intensive activity, meetings should be time-limited – say to a maximum of one or two hours. If the review cannot be completed in that time, it will be much more productive to adjourn and reconvene than to continue with the current meeting.

Fagan inspections Fagan inspections are a formalised form of walkthrough, named after Michael Fagan who devised the technique for IBM. With this method, the author of a piece of work reports to the project manager that it is complete and ready for checking. This triggers a six-stage review process:

- *Planning.* A trained Fagan 'moderator' organises the inspection, nominating people for the roles of inspector, reader and scribe and defining the date, duration and purpose of the meeting.

- *Overview*. This optional meeting can be used to provide background information on the work or on the Fagan process or to assign particular inspection tasks to individuals.
- *Preparation*. Individuals prepare for the inspection by examining the material and developing their understanding prior to the review.
- *Meeting*. This is very structured and chaired by the moderator. The reader paraphrases the item; each inspector, including the author and moderator, reports defects in the item and these are recorded by the scribe.
- *Rework*. The author takes the list of defects and, having corrected them, categorises them by severity and type.
- *Follow-up*. A reviewer, nominated by the moderator, checks that the rework is complete and that the defects have been categorised correctly. The data resulting from the inspection is recorded on a database and the moderator signs off the inspection.

The compilation of statistics is an important part of the Fagan process, since they can be used to:

- Measure the cost of the inspection.
- Produce defect rates for the project.
- Identify 'hot spots' in a project for more intensive management.
- Predict the effort required for quality management.

Disadvantages cited of the Fagan technique are that training is required in the various roles – especially those of moderator and inspector – and that inspections are time-consuming and expensive. Whilst there is some truth in both of these claims, it must be remembered that the costs of not discovering problems early enough usually outweigh the costs of thorough checking.

External review It may sometimes be a good idea to request a review of work from a body or individual outside the project team. This could be by a quality assurance department or simply from an expert in the work being undertaken. External reviews may be a requirement of the contract or they may be imposed as part of an ISO 11001 conformance procedure (see Chapter 14 for more on this). The principal disadvantage of an external review is probably cost, but, on a large project at least, the plans should allow some margin for it. There is an additional problem in that the reviewer will not have the same familiarity with the material as will members of the project team, so an external review is likely to take longer. The obverse of this is that the external person approaches the review without any preconceptions and the resultant objectivity should improve the effectiveness of the review.

11.4.4 Documenting quality control

Whatever methods are employed for the quality control exercises, it is important that the process be properly documented. Standards such as ISO 9001 require that it be possible to trace the quality control process from the discovery of a problem to its resolution. Even without this external discipline, how else can you be sure that everything has been covered and that you do not inadvertently go over the same ground more than once?

There are various ways of documenting the process and the precise documentation will depend to some extent on the method used – Fagan inspections, for instance, will generate reports in a particular format. However, a simple two-layer process which has proved effective is:

- A log is maintained of all checks carried out. For each review, the log shows the date, a brief description of the subject and a reference to the papers which detail the results of the check.
- For each check, a report sheet is compiled. This contains: the date of the review; details to identify the material reviewed; the identity of the reviewer; a description of each error or omission discovered; an assessment of the severity of the defect and space to record a satisfactory recheck of the material.

Figure 11.3 provides an example of a form used to document quality control reviews.

For each error found, there should be some assessment of its severity and of the remedial action required. The assessment will depend to some extent on the nature of the project; for example, the design of some life-critical software

QUALITY CONTROL REVIEW FORM				
Object of review:				
Version:	*Reviewer:*			
Date:	*Signed:*		*Date:*	
Author:	*Approved:*		*Date:*	
Location *Page Para*		*Class*	*Fixed* *Initials*	*Recheck* *Initials Date*

Figure 11.3 Quality control review form

for an aircraft command system may require the complete recheck of every defect found, no matter how trivial.

Two systems of classification that have been used in various types of project are:

A three-stage system
1 Severe defect, requiring considerable rework and reinspection.
2 Less severe defect, requiring some rework and reinspection.
3 Minor defect, requiring rework but no reinspection by the reviewer.

A four-stage system
1 Minor non-conformance to requirement; can be approved by project manager.
2 More serious non-conformance which must be approved by the customer.
3 Major non-conformance, requiring rework and reinspection.
4 Very severe non-conformance. Work must be scrapped and performed again.

11.5 Milestone slip chart

Before leaving the subject of monitoring progress, there are two other tools that can be used to illustrate and measure progress on a project. The first of these is the milestone slip chart, illustrated in Figure 11.4.

Figure 11.4 Milestone slip chart

In the milestone slip chart, the planned progress is shown on the *x*-axis and the actual progress on the *y*-axis. The diagonal line shows where the project should be if it proceeds according to plan and four project milestones are superimposed. The first milestone was achieved on time and at that point it was predicted that the other milestones would be achieved also; these are shown by the vertical lines. At milestone 2, some slippage has occurred but we are predicting that there will be no further delays so the remaining milestones are displaced to the right by an equal amount. But further delay does occur at milestone 3, and yet more before the final milestone is achieved. The milestone slip chart is a highly visual way of showing where in a project slippage has occurred and, more importantly, of illustrating what its final effects should be.

11.6 Earned value analysis

The other tool for monitoring progress is known as **earned value analysis** (EVA). This is increasingly popular, as it measures not only how much has been spent but also how much has been achieved, in other words, how much value has been earned.

One of the problems with EVA is that the terminology traditionally used is rather cumbersome and off-putting. For this reason, we shall use the traditional terms but also some modern ones that are becoming increasingly common and that make the concept rather more clear. To illustrate how EVA works, consider the simple software development project illustrated in Figure 11.5.

In the figure we have a project that requires the creation of five programs, A–E. Each is estimated to take two weeks to write and to cost £2,000, so the total project budget is £10,000. We decide to have progress checks every two weeks.

Now let us consider the position at the time of the second progress check, at week 4. This is shown in Figure 11.6.

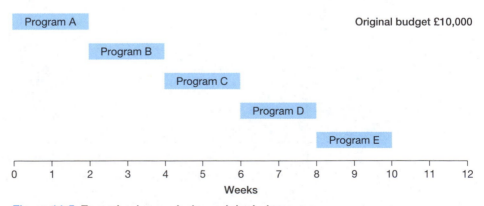

Figure 11.5 Earned value analysis – original plan

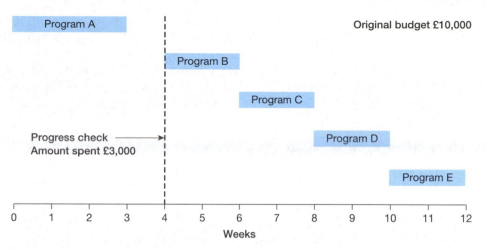

Figure 11.6 Earned value analysis – situation at second progress check

At the week 4 progress check, we discover that program A has been completed, but a week late at the end of week 3. The programmer has then gone off sick, so no work has been started on program B, which is now expected to begin next week. In summary, the situation is this:

■ The actual cost of work performed (ACWP), or actual spend, is £3,000. ACWP is the expenditure to date on the project which may have been spent on scheduled or unscheduled activities and may (in this case, does) include overruns on activities.
■ The budgeted cost of work scheduled (BCWS), or planned spend, is £4,000. BCWS is the amount the plans say should have been spent at this point on scheduled activities.
■ The budgeted cost of work performed (BCWP), or earned value, is £2,000 (for the completed program A). BCWP is an analysis of the work actually done, scheduled or not, priced on the same basis as the scheduled work.

By subtracting the actual cost of work performed from the budgeted cost of work performed (BCWP – ACWP), we get the *cost variance* for the project. By subtracting the budgeted cost of work scheduled from the budgeted cost of work performed (BCWP – BCWS), we arrive at the *schedule variance*. These two variance figures provide a good measure of where the project is in terms of meeting its requirements against the planned cost and effort budgets. In addition, we can make predictions about the final outturn of the project, in both time and cost terms.

So, applying this to the situation in Figure 11.6, we get the following results:

■ Cost variance = (Earned value – Actual spend) or (BCWP – ACWP), or £2,000 – £3,000 = –£1,000. The negative figure indicates that we have an overrun on costs in getting to this point.
■ Cost performance index (CPI) = (Earned value)/(Actual spend) or (BCWP)/(ACWP), which is £2,000/£3000 = 0.67. This means we are getting 67 per cent of the value we expect for our expenditure.

- Schedule variance = (Earned value) – (Planned spend) or (BCWP) – (BCWS), which is £2,000 – £4,000 = –£2,000. The negative figure shows that we have an overrun on time in getting to this point.
- Schedule performance index (SPI) = (Earned value)/(Planned spend) or (BCWP)/(BCWS), which is £2,000/£4,000 = 0.50. This means we are getting only 50 per cent of the work done each week we work.

We can use the two ratios to predict the final outturn of the project, as follows:

- Predicted budget outturn = (Original budget)/CPI = (£10,000)/0.67 = £14,925.
- Predicted timescale = (Original timescale)/SPI = (10 weeks)/0.50 = 20 weeks.

So, unless we take some corrective action, our project will come in 10 weeks late and £4,925 over budget.

Although the theory of EVA is simple enough, in practice there are some difficulties in using it, including:

- Getting accurate information about the current amount of work completed (the earned value), especially when tasks are part-done.
- The problem of measuring many of the intangible tasks associated with IT projects.
- The fact that delays and problems encountered thus far in a project may not be typical of the rest of the project and this makes prediction of overruns likely to be inaccurate. For this reason, EVA experts recommend that each stage or phase of a project be evaluated separately.

Nevertheless, EVA does provide valuable additional insights into the real situation on a project and helps to uncover the situation where, for example, a project appears to be operating under budget but where this is because less value is being earned than should have been.

11.7 Summary

To monitor effort on a project, it is essential to have some sort of time recording system. For each activity, team members should record the time spent so far and a fresh estimate of the effort left to go. With this information, the project manager can assess the likely outturn of the project and identify where corrective actions may be needed on the project. Other costs need to be monitored as well and, in view of the delay that often occurs between authorisation of an invoice and its appearance on the accounts, project managers will probably have to devise their own system to track costs.

There are various techniques available for monitoring quality, and methods must be chosen that are appropriate to the project. The results of quality control measures should be properly documented.

Milestone slip charts provide a visual way of illustrating project progress, and schedule and cost variances can be calculated to show the current status of a project against its planned progress.

Questions

1 How is effort monitored on a project? It is important that the effort to be spent on activities is reassessed on a regular basis. Why is this so vital?

2 Staff time is usually the principal cost component of an IS project. Describe five other areas where project costs could arise.

3 Describe three methods than could be used to exercise quality control and explain the advantages and disadvantages of each.

4 In what circumstances might you consider increasing the volume and/or frequency of quality control checks? When might you decrease their volume or frequency?

5 What does the term 'earned value analysis' mean? What additional insights into the dynamics of a project are afforded by the use of EVA.

6 Explain these terms: actual cost of work performed (ACWP); budgeted cost of work performed (BCWP); budgeted cost of work scheduled (BCWS).

Case study

Since the issues of monitoring progress, exercising control and reporting are intimately connected, their application to the case study is discussed at the end of Chapter 13.

Further reading

Association for Project Management (2002), *Earned Value Management* (CD), Association for Project Management, High Wycombe, UK

Maylor, Harvey (2003), *Project Management*, 3rd edn, FT/Prentice Hall

Turner, J Rodney (1999), *The Handbook of Project-based Management*, 2nd edn, McGraw-Hill

12 Exercising control

12.1 Introduction

In Chapter 11, we considered the various methods that can be used to monitor the progress of the project in terms of the triple constraint of time, cost and quality. But monitoring is by itself not management, and finding out how things are going is quite useless unless you are prepared to do something to apply corrective action where it is needed. This may sound obvious but it is surprising how many project managers are happy to sit at their computers all day, lovingly capturing in immense detail the timesheet, financial and quality review data, whilst the project is careering crazily out of control. This has been described as 'management by spreadsheet' but, in reality, it represents the antithesis of management; it is merely book-keeping.

Exercising control really has four elements, illustrated in Figure 12.1.

The first stage is to evaluate the current situation – in other words what will happen if things continue as they are? The second is to consider various corrective measures that could be applied and to assess the pros and cons of

Figure 12.1 Monitoring and control cycle

adopting each alternative course of action. The third stage is to select and implement one of the courses of action. And the fourth stage links back into the monitoring process since you need to check that the control action has had the desired corrective action on the project. We shall examine the first three stages in this chapter and, for stage four, you are recommended to reread Chapter 11.

12.2 Evaluating the current situation

The starting point for this is the information you have gathered through your monitoring processes, for example:

- Timesheet information showing the effort booked to date on a task, the effort still to go and the predicted end-date.
- The results of quality reviews showing whether the deliverables are meeting their defined quality criteria.
- Financial information showing costs accrued so far and expected in the future.

This information is compared with the various plans to find out if there is a problem and, if so, how big it is likely to be. For effort and timescale information, the important plan to examine is the network diagram. If a task is – or is expected to get – behind schedule, is it on the critical path? If it is not, is there sufficient float or slack to accommodate it? Even if there is, this does not deal with the effort overrun, so can we afford the extra work that now seems to be involved? If the task *is* on the critical path, what will be the knock-on effects? For information on quality, will the defects discovered affect our ability to deliver a conformant product at the end? Do we need to rework the deliverables and, if so, have we the time and resources available to do so? Is the quality failure a one-off or does it indicate some deeper problem, such as an overall lack of the necessary skills, or a too-tight timescale, or an imprecise specification? For cost information, is the project likely to come in over budget at the end? Can we compensate for some increased costs now by using cheaper or alternative materials or suppliers later?

In carrying out these evaluations, you need to consider what the balance is on this particular project between the triple constraints of time, cost and quality. Each project will be different and Figure 12.2 illustrates three extreme-case possibilities.

If the project's aim is to get a system in very quickly so that the customer can secure some competitive advantage, then time will tend to be the dominant factor. If, on the other hand, the project has safety-critical implications – an airliner's control system or a system to run a nuclear power station, for example – then quality will be most important. And if the customer wants something done as cheaply as possible, perhaps because of the pressure of legislation, then cost will predominate. This does not mean that the other constraints do not matter, just that one or two of them may be dominant in a

Figure 12.2 Time/cost/quality triangle for projects

particular situation. A knowledge of this balance is vital in developing corrective actions since, for example, one response to a time problem is sometimes to throw resources – that is, money – at it; and quality can often be improved by taking more time over the work.

So, the question is, what will happen if I do nothing about this situation, and does it matter? If it does, what will be the impact in terms of time, cost and quality? And, very importantly, what are the risks associated with the current course of action? It may be at this point that the project manager alone cannot decide how to act. It could well be appropriate to bring the customer into the discussion, to say quite frankly that this is the situation, these are the possible results and how do you view these outcomes? This is discussed further in Chapter 18 where customer management issues are covered in more detail. Before getting the customer involved, however, it is necessary to identify and evaluate the alternative courses of action that may be available.

12.3 Possible corrective actions

It is impossible within the scope of this or any other book to identify all of the possible corrective actions that might be considered during an IS project, not least because typically we end up with some sort of composite solution. However, we present here some of the most common project management responses to problems encountered on IS projects. Incidentally, in trying to identify control actions, do not forget one of your most valuable sources of ideas: the project team members.

Doing nothing This option should always be considered first as it provides the benchmark against which to evaluate the other possibilities and it may even be the right answer. By doing nothing, we do not mean failing to act. We mean considering the alternatives and then deciding that allowing things to continue as they are is the best – or perhaps the least bad – option.

There are two major dangers associated with the 'do nothing' option:

- An indecisive project manager may wish to disguise inactivity as a constructive act, thereby claiming that doing nothing is the best answer when, in fact, some more vigorous action is needed.
- The desire to be seen to be 'doing something' may cause the project manager to take an action which makes the situation worse, whereas letting things continue on course for the time being might have been the correct response.

Avoiding these pitfalls requires that the project manager be rigorously honest with themselves and it also needs considerable strength of character to withstand the pressure to be seen to be taking some action. It can be helpful if a proper risk assessment is made of the various options, including doing nothing, so that the decision not to act can be seen to be based on a full analysis of the situation.

Adding more staff If the problem is that an activity is getting behind schedule, then one possibility is to assign more staff to it. However, as we discussed in Chapter 10, this will work only if the task can be partitioned since otherwise we shall get a situation of 'too many cooks spoil the broth'. Even if the task can be partitioned, the need for the additional staff to get up to speed on the work, the need for the existing staff to brief and guide the newcomers and the need for communication between the staff will all mean that the overall productivity will be lowered to some extent. At the limit, adding more staff may actually make the task take *longer* than if we had soldiered on with the original people.

Adding different skills As an alternative to adding more staff, we could consider adding people with different, or greater skills. For example, if we are using an unfamiliar programming language and creating programs is taking an inordinate time, one possibility might be to recruit an expert in the language – perhaps an external consultant – and let them act as a technical adviser and guide the rest of the team. Alternatively, if the problem is that the staff lack experience in the general sense, adding a few 'old hands' to the team could make all the difference. There is a noticeable difference in productivity between experienced staff and new trainees, so a sprinkling of experience could yield great improvements in overall team efficiency and effectiveness.

Using overtime Overtime is often the cheapest way of buying additional effort. It is cheap since, although we pay an enhanced hourly rate for it, we do not have to pay additional overheads for National Insurance, pension, office space and so on. So, to meet a short-term crisis, overtime is a good answer. However, long-term or consistent use of overtime is a different proposition. If people are regularly working long hours, their overall productivity gradually reduces. Also, people come to rely on the income from overtime and therefore – whether consciously or not – may begin to spin out their tasks in order to guarantee the overtime payments. Finally, if a team is already working permanent overtime, what contingency is there left to deal with a real crisis when it develops? There is a cultural issue at work here too since, in the UK, performance is often judged by the hours one puts in rather than on the output produced; in Scandinavian countries, people who work regularly over their contracted hours are assumed to be inefficient.

Reassigning tasks

Without adding anyone new to the team, you can sometimes get better productivity, or better quality work, by switching the tasks around. For example, if you have someone who is extremely pedantic and thorough, they may be very slow in producing anything worthwhile – though it will be of good quality once it appears. If this slowness is a problem, then why not use this person in a quality control or reviewer role? Some people are good at creative work, developing ideas from a blank sheet of paper, but not so good at following through into detailed designs. So use them for the up-front analysis tasks. You can use your knowledge of the characteristics of your team members to make sure that they are assigned to tasks that will exploit their strengths. There is more on this in Chapter 22.

Increasing individual supervision

A member of the team may be having productivity or quality problems with their work and this may be coming to light only when they deliver products. If so, consider partitioning the tasks and creating some smaller deliverables, so that quality control can be exercised more frequently. If you have an inexperienced or nervous person on the team, they will welcome the opportunity to share their difficulties and obtain guidance on a more regular basis.

Decreasing individual supervision

An opposite situation can arise with experienced personnel. They may resent being checked up on every five minutes and may, in the end, give up any personal interest in producing good quality work as it will only be combed through by someone else. You can increase job interest, motivation and productivity by giving experienced people greater individual responsibility for larger deliverables. There is another gain from this too, in that the work of the supervisor is reduced, thereby allowing more concentration of management effort on the less experienced team members.

Finding improved methods of working

As well as the work itself, you need to consider whether the methods adopted are the most suitable for the tasks in hand. For example, you may be involved in the analysis phase of the project and you find yourselves shuttling back and forth between different users trying to reconcile what seem to be mutually exclusive requirements. The answer here might be to abandon the conventional analysis techniques and to adopt some sort of Joint Application Development (© IBM) approach, staging workshops where all the users can come together with the analysts and thrash out their requirements. Or you may be trying to make a fourth-generation language handle some complex algorithmic manipulation of data when you could more effectively commission a small amount of assembler code to do the job instead.

Streamlining the procedures

The procedures you have defined for tasks such as quality control may prove to be bureaucratic and time-consuming. If, for instance, you have decided to use Fagan inspections and are finding a very low rate of errors, you might consider a less rigorous approach such as peer review for most work, with the Fagan technique used only for the most critical areas.

Changing resource priorities It is possible that access to a development machine may be restricted. More likely, you will have only occasional access to a production environment – at weekends, say – for important testing. If this sort of thing is creating a bottleneck for your team, then you will have to negotiate increased access or perhaps find an alternative environment in which your team can work. If this is not possible, examine the critical path for the project and use it to decide who should have first call on the time that is available.

Replanning the project Your evaluation of the problems may reveal some fundamental flaws in the way the project has been planned. This is irritating, as planning is an intensive process and it is galling to find that the plan is not working out. However, there is no point in pretending that a plan is still viable if some of its assumptions have been proved invalid, and the only recourse is to go back to square one – or at any rate, back far enough – to see whether a more realistic plan can be devised for the rest of the project. In particular, once the work has started, you may become aware of dependencies between tasks that were unsuspected at the beginning. If so, you need to take them into account now in producing a new plan.

In developing your new plan, remember that the old one gave rise to certain risks; the new plan may remove or mitigate these risks but it will almost certainly introduce new ones, so a reappraisal of the risks should form part of the replanning process. And in case you think it looks silly to go along to your management and the customer with a new plan, remember that you will look even sillier if you are later seen to have clung to the old plan long after it had been proved inadequate.

Changing the phasing of deliverables Short of a complete revision of the plan, it may be possible to achieve a big improvement in effectiveness by changing the phasing of the deliverables. For example, the original plan may have shown the requirements specification as being delivered as one document but the initial analysis may show that the system can be partitioned into several discrete elements. If so, some of these may have higher priority with the customer than others and it could be possible to consider phased delivery, with effort initially concentrated on the most urgent requirements. You may also decide to adopt parallel working, for example with the design work overlapping the requirements analysis. There is always an element of risk in this approach, in that some design work may have to be repeated if the analysis turns up something unexpected, but accepting the risk may be justified if there is a pressing timescale for delivery. Again, proper risk analysis of the options will provide the best factual basis on which to make your decisions.

Decreasing the number of inspections Decreasing the number of inspections could be considered as a response to falling behind the schedule but only if you are convinced that the inspections are uncovering an acceptably low number of defects. If the defect rate is high, then reducing inspections may improve delivery rates in the short term but the problems will come back to haunt you later during system or acceptance testing or as an excessive volume of warranty or maintenance work.

Increasing the number of inspections

If, on the other hand, you are getting a very high level of defects on completed large deliverables, a response could be to increase the number of inspections. This should ensure that errors are caught earlier when they are more easily rectified.

Encouraging the team

Over a long project, project fatigue often sets in. This manifests itself in various ways: lowered productivity, increased absenteeism, resignations, complaints about management and the users, and so on. If unchecked, this can have an increasingly corrosive effect, and methods you might try to counteract it include:

- Refocusing on the team's achievements to date, to rekindle enthusiasm.
- Some sort of social event, ideally in company time, to bring the whole team together and engender a sense of team spirit.
- Redistribution of work, to increase interest and give people opportunities for development.
- A team-building exercise of some sort.
- Reducing the size of deliverables. This is subtle as, in the later stages of a project, deliverables tend to get bigger. The benefit of this ploy is that it creates a series of small successes which is, in itself, motivating.

Introducing incentives

Depending on your organisation, you may or may not be able to offer financial incentives for improved performance. However, you should be able to take someone out to lunch or give them an afternoon off for meeting or beating a deadline. Or you could introduce some form of recognition, such as a 'programmer of the month' award for exceptional achievement. If you have multiple teams working on a project, you could consider some sort of inter-team competition, always bearing in mind that you want all the teams still to be focused on the overall project and not just on beating each other.

Subcontracting parts of the work

You may find that, despite using all your tools and techniques of management, you are falling behind schedule or not producing work of the required quality. If so, you could consider subcontracting some of the work to companies specialising in the skills or materials required. For example, small software houses that specialise in particular environments often have greater expertise per person than a larger, general-purpose organisation. If you do subcontract the work, remember that you cannot subcontract the responsibility and you will have to make sure that the subcontractors work to the required standards. Chapter 19 has more on supplier management issues.

Negotiating changes in the specification

If all else fails, you may have to go back to the customer and negotiate some change in the specification. It could be that the original objectives have proved too ambitious for the time or money available but it may still be possible to deliver something that would achieve a large proportion of the hoped-for benefits. Alternatively, you could agree phased delivery, with the majority of important functions being delivered as originally planned, followed by incremental improvements until the full functionality is achieved. It has to be admitted that these sorts of proposal are not usually well received by customers but, on the other hand, you will probably get more credit for delivering something by the due date than you would for a complete system six months late.

12.4 Implementing corrective actions

Whatever control actions you decide to take, there are two important things you must do:

- Make sure that everyone knows about the changes you are making and how they impact on the project as a whole. There is nothing more infuriating for team members, or wasteful of scarce resources, than for someone to be left working on a deliverable that is no longer wanted, or is wanted in a different form, because of a change of plan.
- Evaluate, through your normal monitoring system, whether the changes have had the desired effect.

With regard to the first, copies of the revised plans and work instructions must be circulated to everyone affected. If the changes are extensive, it is probably best to hold a meeting to present the revisions and discuss their implications.

The effects of the changes should be monitored closely to see whether they are working or not and, in particular, to see if the risks associated with them are coming to pass. It is likely that you will have to make further adjustments, and it is a sign of strength, not weakness, to make these when necessary. However, resist the temptation to keep fiddling with the plan: if your control actions seem to be having broadly the desired results, leave things alone unless they are seen to be going adrift again.

12.5 Change control

During the lifecycle of anything but the smallest IS project, change is inevitable. Project changes can arise for many reasons, including:

- Change in the business environment in which the customer operates and to which they must respond – for example, the introduction of a new product or service by a competitor.
- New personnel coming into the customer organisation with different views from their predecessors, particularly if the sponsor of the project or leading users change.

■ Revised user ideas of what the project should be about, perhaps triggered by the discussions that have occurred during detailed requirements analysis.

■ Suggestions from the development team, based on an improved understanding of the users' requirements.

■ The availability of new technology, offering different possible system solutions.

■ New or revised legislation, imposing additional or different responsibilities on the customer.

■ A straightforward change of mind by the users as to what they want.

The chief problem with changes is that they are not always seen as such by all the parties involved. Quite often, the developers will classify something as a change which the users say is merely a clarification of a requirement that was always there. Disagreements of this sort have always bedevilled IS projects and seem to stem from the inability of users and developers to find a common means of communication. The use of structured analysis methods, for example SSADM, can help in this area by replacing a reliance on written specifications with the use of diagrammatic techniques – it is less easy to commit sins of omission or ambiguity with pictures than it is with text. Nevertheless, there are still likely to be areas where different interpretations of the requirement are possible and it is almost inevitable that the project manager will get drawn into discussion or even argument with the customer over whether something is a change or not. Chapter 18 offers some suggestions on how to handle this conflict.

One factor that often decides the intensity of the argument is the perceived cost of implementing the change. Generally speaking, the earlier the change is identified, the less will be the costs of incorporating it. If a change is noticed during analysis, then it is likely that the requirements specification will simply be written a little differently. If it is identified during the acceptance test, however, then the design will have to be changed, the programs rewritten and the various tests repeated. This is, incidentally, another argument for the use of structured analysis techniques, since their increased rigour reduces the likelihood of missing something out in the early stages of a project.

Before a decision can be made on whether to implement a change, a thorough investigation needs to be conducted to discover:

■ The total impact of the change on the development work – time, cost and quality.

■ The effect of the change on the users – on their training and implementation requirements, for example.

■ Any implications of the change on the proposed size or configuration of hardware or communications.

■ The consequences of not implementing the change.

■ The risks resulting from implementing, and from not implementing, the change.

All changes therefore need to be subjected to proper cost/benefit, impact and risk analysis. Once this information is available, the project manager and the customer can have an informed negotiation on the change and, hopefully, agree the way in which to handle it. This will almost certainly involve some change to the plan and quite possibly a variation to the contract as well.

A maxim that the project manager should bear in mind is that there is no such thing as an insignificant change – or at least there is not until you have investigated it thoroughly. A moment's reflection will reveal the truth in this assertion. A change that seems at first sight trivial may, in fact, have very significant consequences. Moreover, the investigation of a change in itself incurs effort and takes time, so that will have a small impact on the project if nothing else does. In view of this, the project manager should ensure that the mechanism for investigating and costing changes is explained to the customer at the start of the project and an early opportunity should be sought to put the mechanism into practice. If this can be done for a small change, for which it is decided ultimately not to charge the customer, then at least it establishes the principle of change control and the way changes will be handled.

One final thought on changes. It is not unknown for an external supplier to win a contract with a competitive price on the basis of a tight specification. Then, as soon as the customer makes the smallest change in the requirement, tough change management is employed to drive up the value, and the profitability, of the project. This sort of approach is perhaps understandable in a highly competitive marketplace but it seldom leads to a successful project in that the customer and developer spend much of their time in contractual wrangles and part bitter enemies at the end.

12.6   Change control and configuration management

Configuration management is discussed in Chapter 14 but it has been included here as well because there is often confusion between change control and configuration management. The basic distinction is this:

- Change control is the set of procedures that ensure that changes are made only after due consideration of their impact.
- Configuration management ensures that, if the changes are implemented, then amendments to each of the affected deliverables are properly controlled and recorded.

Configuration management is required in all projects, whether or not they ever have any changes imposed on them, and the evaluation of the effects of a change will be greatly facilitated if there is a good configuration management regime in place.

12.7 | Exercising control in PRINCE2®

PRINCE2® identifies a number of **control points** for a project:

- **Project initiation**. Here, the question for the project board to consider is whether the project should be undertaken at all. Agreement of the project initiation document signals the formal start of the project.
- **End-stage assessment**. At the end of each stage, progress is reviewed and the business case for the project re-examined. Only if progress is satisfactory should the project board authorise the project manager to proceed to the next stage.
- **Highlight reports**. These are provided to the project board by the project manager on a regular basis and give updates on how the project is proceeding.
- **Exception assessment/report**. If it looks as if a project will go outside its tolerances for time, cost and product/quality, the project manager has to seek specific authorisation from the project board to vary the tolerances.
- **Project closure**. Based on a formal report from the project manager, the project board decides whether or not the project should be declared completed and closed.
- **Work packages**. These are the main control mechanisms for a project manager. A work package consists of one or more products to be developed by an individual or team. Each work package will have defined effort, timescale and cost estimates associated with it and the project manager monitors progress by checking whether these estimates have been, or are likely to be, met.

Exercising control within a PRINCE2® project is similar to that for any other project and the range of options available to the project manager is much the same, except that changes to the basic time, cost, product/quality parameters have to be negotiated in the first instance with the project board. If the project board cannot agree to the changes, then the executive member of the board may have to take the issue back to corporate or programme management.

12.8 | Summary

Exercising control involves evaluating the current situation, considering the pros and cons of potential corrective measures, selecting and implementing one of the options and checking that the control action has had the desired corrective effect.

In evaluating the current and optional situations, the project manager needs to consider the project's constraints of time, cost and quality/performance.

There are various control actions that could be applied and these will generally involve a trade-off among the three constraints. Once a control action has been selected, it needs to be reflected in the plans and communicated to those involved and should then be monitored to check on its effectiveness.

Most projects involve changes and these should be properly evaluated and costed and agreed with the customer before implementation. A good configuration management regime will make it much easier to assess the effects of proposed changes.

PRINCE2® identifies a number of controls that should be applied to check whether the project is likely to deliver to specification within the defined timescale and budget.

Questions

1 What is meant by the term the 'triple constraint'? What are the three elements of the triple constraint and why is an understanding of their relative weights important in exercising control over a project?

2 Your project is behind schedule and you are considering adding extra staff to the team. What would be the potential advantages and disadvantages of this approach?

3 In what circumstances might you (a) increase or (b) decrease the amount of supervision given to a team member?

4 Changes often bedevil IS projects. What steps are required to ensure that proper change control is exercised on a project?

5 Explain the difference between *change control* and *configuration management* and the relationship between them.

Case study

Since the issues of monitoring progress, exercising control and reporting are intimately connected, their application to the case study is discussed at the end of Chapter 13.

Further reading

Brooks, Frederick P Jr (1982), *The Mythical Man-month: Essays on Software Engineering*, Addison-Wesley

De Marco, Tom (1982), *Controlling Software Projects*, Yourdon Press

Gilb, Tom (1988), *Principles of Software Engineering Management*, Addison-Wesley

Office of Government Commerce (2002), *Managing Successful Projects with PRINCE2*, 3rd edn, The Stationery Office

13 Reporting progress

13.1 Introduction

In this chapter we examine the ways in which progress is reported. Usually, when we talk of reporting progress, we are thinking about reporting upwards – to our immediate boss, to the board maybe, to the customer certainly. But for the project manager, there is another group of people who need to know how we are doing: the project team. You might imagine that team members would know how they are doing, but it is surprising how often people feel in the dark about the overall progress of the project, the significance of their contribution, and their own management's and the customer's perception of their work.

Reporting progress to the team can often be a very motivating experience, as team members can see the importance of their own contribution and the appreciation that others feel for their efforts. Even when the news is bad, explaining the situation to the team will help them understand why you may be putting more pressure on them and – who knows? – someone may just respond with a suggestion that will help you to put the project back on course.

13.2 Recipients of progress reports

Apart from the project team members, mentioned already, who is likely to want to receive reports on the progress of the project? The situation will differ from project to project, but recipients are likely to include:

- *The project manager's immediate superior*. In an in-house IT department, this may be a systems development manager or IT manager/director. In a systems company, this is likely to be a business manager or, for a very large project, perhaps a board member. There may also, or instead of these, be a project controller or project director – someone with overall responsibility for all project work.
- *The customer*. Where the work is being carried out under a contractual relationship, the customer will be the person who has commissioned and will pay for the project, sometimes known as the project sponsor.

■ *The users*. The users may well be different people from the sponsor. In some organisations, and on some projects, the users may be a large and disparate group, and generating the paperwork to keep them all informed may involve a regular assault on the world's trees!

■ *The quality assurance department*, if there is one.

Each of the above groups will have rather different reporting requirements. The users will be interested primarily in seeing when they are likely to get their system and when, perhaps, they will have to start preparing themselves for training or system implementation. The sponsor will also wish to know these things plus, if the work is being done on a time-and-materials basis, a summary of the costs to date and the likely overall cost. The IT manager will want to know when resources will be required for this project and when they will become available for other work. In the systems company, the business manager will require predictions on the current and forecast profitability of the project and will need to know when invoices should be raised for payment. Finally, the quality assurance people will want to arrange quality audits at appropriate points in the project. Consequently, depending on the organisation in which the project is taking place, the project manager may have to prepare a variety of reports, each with a slightly different slant. Clearly, the more open the organisational climate or the contractual arrangements, the easier this task will be for the project manager, since there will be less need to adjust the information that is provided to the various stakeholders.

13.3 Frequency of reporting

Some judgement needs to be exercised in deciding how often to produce the various reports. If they are too frequent, then their production can become a full-time occupation to the detriment of other project management work. On the other hand, if they are infrequent, you lose the opportunity to raise important issues and to get decisions made and clarified. Possibly, the major reporting cycles will have been established at project initiation or mandated in the contract. For internal reporting, a monthly cycle is common, usually tied to the end of accounting periods.

Reports should, at the least, be prepared at the end of project phases or stages, or perhaps keyed to project milestones. This gives everyone an opportunity to take stock, review the project and decide if any changes of direction are needed. If the project has a very long stage – requirements specification often falls into this category – some mid-stage report may be advisable.

13.4 | Report content and format

13.4.1 Written reports

The reporting requirements should be established at the start of the project, when the contract is being agreed or the project plans are being developed. That way, the project manager can include effort for report preparation in the plans. In addition, the format and structure of the reports should be agreed and documented.

The usual recommendation is to aim for a system of reporting 'by exception'. What this means is that, instead of trotting out a long list of things which have gone according to plan, we highlight only – or at any rate, mainly – those activities that for some reason or other are not going according to plan. Assuming the project is running reasonably smoothly, this form of reporting should lessen the work involved for the project manager and enable everyone to concentrate on those areas that are not going quite so well and hence require more management attention.

There is, however, quite a significant drawback to exception reporting, especially if the project manager is trying to sustain the enthusiasm and commitment of sponsor and users. The snag is that exception reporting, by its very nature, tends to concentrate on failure – missed deadlines, cost overruns, staffing problems and so on – and this can engender a negative view of how the project is going. As an example, when the Stock Exchange 'Big Bang' reorganisation took place in 1987, the national newspapers reported that some of the new computerised systems had not worked properly. Whilst this was true, Big Bang involved the coordination and interlinking of dozens of systems built for different clients by different developers. The wonder was not that a couple of systems did not work but that so many did; but the impression created by the press articles was overwhelmingly negative at the time. So, to create a more positive impression of project progress, the project manager needs to develop a formula that not only highlights problems but also emphasises the project's achievements.

Reports are normally provided in writing, as this enables them to be circulated easily and gives the recipients time to read and digest the information. Often, though, the report will be supplemented by a progress meeting where the project manager will present a summary of the report and deal with any comments or questions that arise from it.

The reports to the various parties will usually take the formats that follow.

Reports to the customer/sponsor

Reports to the customer will contain:

- A report identifier – project name, report sequence number, date of report.
- A short narrative review of progress since the last report.
- Milestones achieved, with dates and comparison with planned dates.
- Problems encountered – ideally with solutions used or proposed.
- Current predicted project end-date and dates for other significant events such as system implementation.
- Change requests – details of new ones, status of existing ones.

■ Costs to date and estimated outturn. However, if the project is being under-taken under a fixed-price contract, the internal costs of the project (though not the costs of agreed changes) are the business of the supplier only.

In addition to the above, the report may also contain an updated version of the project plan, perhaps at a high level – showing only the main phases of the project – and highlighting any variations from the previous version.

Reports to the users

The user reports will contain:

■ A report identifier – project name, report sequence number, date of report.
■ A short narrative review of progress since the last report.
■ Milestones achieved, with dates and comparison with planned dates.
■ A revised schedule of user interface activities – such as review meetings, pro-totyping demonstrations, training and implementation dates.

In writing this report, the project manager needs to remember that one responsibility is to sustain the interest and commitment of the users and to ensure that they are able to play their full part in the project. So, without disguising or ignoring difficulties, an effort must be made to frame the report in an upbeat way that emphasises the benefits that the users will ultimately derive from the system.

Reports to IT and business management

Reports to IT and business management should include:

■ A report identifier – project name, report sequence number, date of report.
■ A short narrative review of progress since the last report.
■ Milestones achieved, with dates and comparison with planned dates.
■ Problems encountered – ideally with solutions used or proposed.
■ Current predicted end-date and dates for other significant events such as system implementation.
■ Change requests – details of new ones, status of existing ones.
■ Costs to date and estimated outturn.
■ Significant customer interface issues encountered – for example, any dis-agreements over the scope or specification of the work.
■ Opportunities for additional work or follow-on business.

These reports should be completely frank and open and should be written to ensure that senior management is fully apprised of the true current state of the project. This frankness can sometimes create difficulties for project man-agers who work in closed cultures or where their managers do not want to hear about problems. Project managers have to tread a fine line between keeping information to themselves, in which case they will probably take all the blame for any subsequent disasters, or seeming to do nothing but report problems. The answer is to present not only the problems but also the possible solutions with a recommendation on the best course of action. It is possible, though sometimes difficult, to present bad news in a positive way.

It will be noticed that we have included opportunities for further work in this report. The project manager, unlike, say, a sales manager, will have the benefit of close day-to-day contact with all sorts of people in the customer/user organisation and so will be in a good position to identify opportunities. Whether the project manager personally follows these up will depend on his or her character and attitude – some people just do not like up-front selling – and on the organisation, which may want all sales opportunities handled by the salesforce. Nonetheless, the project manager's input is invaluable both in spotting the business in the first place and in helping to decide the best way in which to exploit it. For more on the project manager's role in selling, see Chapter 17.

Reports to the quality assurance function
The quality assurance (QA) personnel are generally regarded as either police to keep the project teams in order or valuable additional resources available to the project, depending on the attitude of the project manager and the way in which the QA people go about their business. Reports to QA should include:

- A report identifier – project name, report sequence number, date of report.
- A short narrative review of progress since the last report, focusing mainly on the project's quality control activities.
- Milestones achieved, with dates and comparison with planned dates.
- Quality problems encountered and solutions applied.
- Current predicted end-date and dates for significant quality events such as major reviews or stage-ends.

The objective of the report should be to enlist the help of the QA function in reviewing areas where quality problems have become evident and in suggesting better, more rigorous and perhaps less time-consuming methods of applying quality control.

Reports to the project team
Reports to the project team are usually less formal than those discussed already and it is probably better to hold a team meeting and deliver a verbal report, as discussed in the next section. However, on a large project, perhaps with the team dispersed over several sites, this may not be practical on a regular basis and a written communication will be necessary. A more discursive, chatty style may be appropriate for a team report and the aim should be to focus on the positive: the achievements to date, the quality of the work produced and the long-term benefits of the project both to the users and to the developers. If there have been, or still are, problems, mention them, but also stress the way in which they are being overcome. There is no harm, either, in singling out individuals for praise, but make sure you do commend the right person; nothing is more annoying than seeing someone rewarded for another's achievements.

13.4.2 Report presentations

Quite often, the written report will be followed by a presentation – to the project sponsor, to the project steering committee, to a user group, to senior IT management or to a team briefing. Although some people dislike speaking at such gatherings, presentations do provide an opportunity to inject some more animation into the reporting process and to rekindle the enthusiasm and commitment of the audience. So, the project manager needs to prepare carefully for the presentation.

The main thing *not* to do is to use the presentation to read through the written reports. This is a waste of an opportunity and an insult to the audience – after all, they can read for themselves. Instead, prepare a short, punchy presentation, ideally illustrated with slides or overheads, focusing on the main issues. These should include:

- The objectives of the project and its expected benefits. It is always worth restating these, especially when the project has been running for some time, everyone is up to their ears in its difficulties and interest is beginning to flag.
- The achievements to date. Starting here helps engender a positive view of the project, whatever comes next.
- The problems. Be frank but do not seek to apportion blame. Problems happen and they need to be dealt with, so identify the possible solutions and engage the audience's commitment to getting the problems out of the way.
- The vision of the future – where the project is going and when it will get there.

This book is not about giving presentations, and there are many excellent publications and training videos on the subject; a companion book to this one, *Systems Analysis and Design* by Yeates and Wakefield, has some useful things to say. All the experts agree that the presenter must concentrate on impact and on getting a few simple messages across. So, do not put up lots of overheads with complex charts and tables and long bulleted lists of achievements. Use a very few slides with one or two points on each – made pictorially if possible.

If the project is not going too well – and, at times, most projects are not going too well – the project manager can expect to suffer a fair amount of criticism at a meeting. Stoicism and an even temperament will help here, and the main thing is not to be drawn into argument and recrimination. However much 'getting it off your chest' may make you feel better at the time, you will probably have antagonised someone in the process and their enmity will come back to haunt you later. So, take a deep breath, respond calmly and try to focus the discussion on nice, neutral facts. You may even gain in stature and authority for your ability to ride out a storm. There are some helpful ideas in Chapter 18 about dealing with these situations.

13.5 Reporting in PRINCE2®

The PRINCE2® project management method includes a set of control mechanisms which include reports at various levels. Some of these controls take the form of meetings and some of written reports only. The basic **control points** are described below.

Project initiation   A project initiation meeting is held at which the plans for the project are presented and the objectives and scope of the project are agreed. This meeting gives approval for the first stage of the project to begin.

End-stage assessment   At the end of each project stage, the project manager prepares a report on the stage and the project assurance team provides a review of the project from the user, technical and quality perspectives. The plans for the next stage are presented and reviewed and, if acceptable, approval is given to move on to the next stage.

Mid-stage assessment   Mid-stage assessment is optional in PRINCE2® and will usually occur in the following circumstances:

- If an exception situation has arisen that will cause the stage to exceed the tolerances given to the project manager.
- If there are requests for change that need to be considered urgently and which cannot be accommodated within the tolerances of the current stage.
- If it is desired to start work on the next or another stage before this one is complete, thus overlapping the stages.
- At some point during a long stage, to review progress and to provide a confidence boost.

The format of the mid-stage assessment is similar to that of the end-stage assessment.

Highlight report   The highlight report is PRINCE2®'s main ongoing reporting mechanism, prepared regularly by the project manager and supplied to the project board, the project assurance team and the stage manager, if this is a separate role from the project manager. The report should be short and include:

- Project identifier and date.
- The period covered by the report.
- The current budget and schedule status of the project.
- Products completed during the period.
- Problems either encountered or anticipated.
- Products scheduled to be completed during the next period.
- Total of requests for change approved.
- Budget and schedule impacts of the changes.

The frequency of highlight reports is agreed at project initiation; a monthly cycle is common.

Checkpoint   The checkpoint is the main internal control mechanism of a PRINCE2® project. Checkpoint meetings are held frequently, usually weekly or fortnightly, and are attended by the team leaders and team members and, optionally, by the stage manager and project assurance team. Progress is reviewed against individual work plans and a report is produced showing:

- The date of the meeting and the period covered.
- The follow-up of activities from previous reports.
- Activities during the period and products completed.

- Quality reviews performed during the period, with results.
- Problems encountered or anticipated and deviations from the plan.
- Work planned for the next period.
- Products scheduled to be completed during the next period.

Project closure The project closure meeting is held at the end of the project and brings it to a formal conclusion. It is attended by the project board, project assurance team, project manager and stage manager of the final stage. The objectives of the meeting are:

- To bring the project to an orderly close.
- To confirm that all the planned work has been carried out.
- To check that all technical exceptions and quality review actions have been closed off.
- To agree that all the documentation needed to maintain the delivered system is available.
- To confirm that the various acceptance letters have been signed off.
- To review any lessons learned from the project for future reference.

A report summarising the meeting is submitted to the executive committee.

13.6 Summary

Various interested parties will wish to receive reports on the progress of the project. These include the customer, the users, senior IT management and members of the project team.

The reporting frequency needs to be set to ensure adequate control without imposing an undue bureaucratic overhead on the project manager.

The content and format of reports should be tailored to the needs of the recipients. Written reports may be supplemented by presentations.

The PRINCE2® method includes a series of reports at different levels and different stages in a project.

Questions

1 What factors would you consider when deciding on the frequency with which you would report progress to (a) senior IS management, and (b) customer management?

2 What is meant by the term 'exception reporting'? What are the benefits and the disadvantages of this type of reporting?

3 What are the benefits to the project manager of providing regular progress reports to the project team members?

Questions continued

> 4 Explain the following terms used in the PRINCE2® project management method:
>   (a) Project initiation
>   (b) End-stage assessment
>   (c) Highlight report
>   (d) Checkpoint.

Case study

It has been mentioned already that regular checkpoint meetings are held weekly between the project manager and the two team managers. This is the main forum used by Richard Vaughan, the project manager for the France Vacances project, to monitor progress. In addition to this, however, the E-Con consultants complete timesheets similar to those discussed in Chapter 11 – in part to monitor project progress but also so that E-Con can bill its customers for the work done to date.

The notes of the fifth checkpoint meeting are shown in Figure 13.1.

The report suggests that the project is generally going well. The only slippage reported is to the hardware specification but (see Chapter 10) there is some float on this product and so the managers are not too worried and agree that no corrective action is required at this point.

Notice that Richard Vaughan has decided to supply the project board with copies of this checkpoint (to avoid having to produce a separate highlight report) and that E-Con's project support office provides one of its staff, Jane Flett, to write and distribute the minutes of the meeting. Richard has also decided to circulate the checkpoint report to project team members so that they have a clear picture of where the project has got to and where 'their' parts fit into the whole programme of work.

In the checkpoint report, mention was made of the quality reviews carried out on the interview notes. The content was reviewed informally with the interview subjects and E-Con's quality manager also checked them over for format and style. An example of the quality control form is shown in Figure 13.2.

On 20 May, Helen Winter, a member of the project assurance team, approaches Richard Vaughan and asks him whether it would be possible to have an additional feature in the internet booking system whereby a report could be compiled of customers who do not proceed to a completed order. Her idea is that the sales team could then contact these customers to find out why they did not proceed and perhaps to secure the sale through direct contact. Richard says that, although this is clearly a good idea, the requirements specification was signed off some weeks ago and work is now

Case study continued

Meeting:	France Vacances Project Checkpoint No 5
Date and time:	Friday, 5 May, 10:00 hrs
Period of report:	1–5 May
Venue:	France Vacances Offices
Attendees:	Richard Vaughan (Chair) Peter Clay Siobhan Reid
Author:	Jane Flett
Distribution:	Attendees, Project Board Members, Project Team Members

Progress since last checkpoint and products completed

PC said that work had started on the MIS elements of the requirements specification. Work was proceeding according to plan.

SR reported that the internet aspects of the requirements specification were also under way and on schedule.

SR also said that work had started on the hardware specification.

Quality reviews completed

PC and SR reported that the interview notes had been reviewed for format by Norman Pierce and for content by the interview subjects. Minor errors had been discovered and these had been corrected.

Problems encountered

SR said that some information required for the hardware specification was unlikely to be received in time to deliver the document on the planned date; she envisaged a two (working) day delay (delivery on 9 May instead of 5 May as originally planned).

Plans for next period and products to be delivered

Continue with requirements specification (due to complete 12 May).

Continue with hardware specification (now rescheduled to complete 9 May).

Start work on development of communications links (due to complete 26 May allowing for slippage in hardware specification).

Risk assessment

Risk 013 (Inability to find enough internet-skilled resources) can now be retired as the teams are fully resourced. However, risk 014 (loss of internet-skilled resources) remains under review.

No change to other risks.

Figure 13.1 Checkpoint meeting report

▶

Case study continued

E-CON – Quality Review Form

Object of Review: Notes of interview with Sylvie Atelier

Version:	0.1a (draft)	**Reviewer:** Norman Pierce	
Date:	27 April	**Signed:** *N J Pierce*	**Date:** 3 May
Author:	RJS	**Approved:** *Siobhan Reid*	**Date:** 4 May

Location		Comments	Class	Fixed	Checked	
Page	Para		*	(Initials)	Initials	Date
1	2	Refers to 'booking'; should be 'bookings'	A	RJS	N/A	
1	3	Sudden change in font; should all be Arial	B	RJS	N/A	
1	6	Check number of bookings; seems high?	B	RJS	N/A	
1	6	Sentence not clear; rephrase	B	RJS	N/A	
1	8	Add cross-reference to example document	B	RJS	N/A	
2	1	'Courchavel' should be 'Courchevel'	B	RJS	N/A	
2	1	Needs organisation chart to clarify	B	RJS	N/A	
All		Check French spellings throughout	B	RJS	N/A	

* A – Trivial, B – Rework & issue, C – Rework & re-review

Figure 13.2 Quality control report

advanced on programming the system. But he agrees to raise a change request to see what would be the impact of introducing the change (Figure 13.3).

Having investigated the possible change, the team find that implementing it would cause a two-week delay to the project and incur costs of an additional €20,000. There is also the risk that the new feature, if operating in real time, might adversely affect the performance of the system. The change is considered by the project's authority, David Martin, who likes the concept but is not prepared to risk delay to the project at this stage. It is therefore deferred for further consideration after the system has gone live.

E-CON – Change Control Form	
Change no: *0005*	
Date: *10 May*	Form completed by: *Richard Vaughan*

Description of proposed change:

An additional feature has been requested whereby, if a customer abandons an internet transaction before completing a sale, that fact is advised to the sales team so that they can follow up and find out why the customer did not complete.

Reason/justification for change:

The proposed feature would enable the sales team to find out why customers had not completed the sale and, possibly, offer them different accommodations; this would increase the number of sales and also demonstrate interest in customers and their requirements.

Change requested by: Helen Winter

Impact assessment	**Time:** 2 weeks' delay to project while new feature is investigated, specified and programmed.
	Cost: Additional €20,000 due to additional work and also because of delays to project.
	Quality/product: May have to have real-time polling for aborted changes in addition to report to sales team.

Risk analysis:

If new feature operates in real-time (when aborted transaction ends), may impose additional loads on system and lead to poor performance.

Decision:	Approved	Rejected	Deferred until: After implementation

Signed:	(Project Manager): *Richard Vaughan*	(Project Sponsor): *David Martin*

Figure 13.3 Change control form

Further reading

Office of Government Commerce (2002), *Managing Successful Projects with PRINCE2*, 3rd edn, The Stationery Office

Yeates, Donald and Wakefield, Tony (2004), *Systems Analysis and Design*, 2nd edn, FT/Prentice Hall

14 Quality

14.1 Introduction

Wherever you look nowadays, companies and their products use the term 'quality' as a differentiator, real or perceived, from their competition. Advertising and other publicity material, even company names, include the word 'quality' for additional impact. Why is this necessary? There are three main reasons. The first is that the word carries with it implications of excellence, value for money, superiority over the competition. The second is that the buying public, both private and commercial, recognises the fact that products and services have often fallen short of – however we define it – an acceptable level of performance. The third reason is that the Japanese have demonstrated that, by concentrating on quality, you can become world beaters from a standing start over a relatively short period of time.

The information technology industry is relatively new and rapidly changing. Issues of quality are different in a software development project from those on an automobile production line. Customer expectations, however, are much the same and it is for this reason that the national and international quality management system standards, ISO 9000, have been adopted equally for the IT industry as for all others.

In this chapter we discuss some of the issues around quality in IT projects.

14.2 Quality concepts

First of all, what is quality? It is a word that has many definitions. 'I own a quality car'; 'I am pleased with the quality of my car'; 'My car has some interesting qualities' – all of these have different undertones with regard to the word 'quality'. It is essential therefore to ensure that everyone involved in a working 'quality' environment has the same understanding of the term.

Among the commonly used definitions of quality are the following:

- 'The degree of excellence of a thing' (*Oxford English Reference Dictionary*, 1996). This definition is fine as a general statement of intent but, when a product or service is being developed, it suffers from not being really testable; in other words, customer and supplier may well fall out over whether the product or service is truly 'excellent' or not.

■ 'Conformance to requirement'. This means that the product or service does exactly what the customer has specified for it and is the one usually adopted for work carried out under contract. It has been said that this is a supplier's definition, as it gets the supplier off the hook if the customer has failed to state something that should be obvious in the specification. For example, the specification for a hammer might state that it should have a metal head and a wooden handle and the supplier could then deliver one which has a soft lead head and a balsa wood handle – which would obviously be of no use for driving in nails but which would meet the literal demands of the specification.

■ 'Fitness for purpose'. This is better from the customer's point of view as, in the hammer example, it should be obvious to the supplier what the hammer will be used for; and the lead/balsa model would clearly not be fit for purpose. The problem here, though, is that what is obvious to the customer (and therefore perhaps not stated in the specification) may not be so obvious to the supplier and the fitness for purpose definition offers plentiful scope for misunderstandings and argument.

The international standard ISO 8402:1991 offers the following definition of quality: 'The totality of features and characteristics of a product or service that bear on its ability to satisfy stated or implied needs'. This seems to roll the 'conformance to requirement' and 'fitness for purpose' definitions into one neat phrase and the use of the words 'implied needs' would cover our hammer example. But, the definition is potentially dangerous for suppliers since all of the 'implied' needs might not be self-evident. As an example of this, one project that we encountered a few years ago called for the use of small hand-held terminals. The customer asked if the design chosen could survive being dropped into buckets of water or microwaved, because they expected their staff to do both these things to sabotage the project. It is doubtful if, had the customers not asked this question, the supplier would have spotted the 'implied' need for the terminals to survive these rather unusual uses.

So, in practice, it is the 'conformance to requirements' definition that is usually used and this explains why it is so vital to get a detailed specification of requirements before work starts. However, bear in mind that the customer could reasonably accuse the supplier of professional incompetence if the latter fails to spot an obvious 'implied' need – such as, for example, for a report to be printed in a typeface large enough to be read by someone with normal eyesight.

Many organisations, both in product and in services businesses, have evolved and nurture a reputation for quality. In many cases, this is confused with ultimate excellence such as with a Rolls-Royce car. In our terms, where quality means conformance to requirements, a Rolls-Royce is a quality car only for the person who has considerable funds, requires the capability to carry more than four passengers, has a large garage and so on. We can assume that someone who is prepared to consider buying a Rolls-Royce will do so largely on its reputation alone, but most car manufacturers (including Rolls-Royce) now go to considerable lengths to find out what their customers want before their engineers set to work on their designs. Similarly, successful supermarkets such as Tesco cultivate relationships with both their customers and their suppliers, so that the latter can understand the important quality issues surrounding the products they provide.

Furthermore, many organisations include the word 'quality' in their mission statements, their publicity material and their recruitment advertisements. In other words, they address the three key dimensions of any business: customers, shareholders and staff. A generic mission statement might say:

> *Our mission is to deliver competitive advantage to our customers through the use of our high-quality products and services, a challenging and rewarding career to our staff, and a fair return for our shareholders.*

Because the definition of quality is so imprecise and all-pervasive, techniques have emerged to formalise aspects of 'quality'. They are usually promoted by a highly persuasive champion, or 'guru'. Most of the quality gurus of the past fifty years have been concerned with the formalisation and improvement of the process:

- W Edwards Deming was trained as a statistician and based his ideas on statistical process control to separate 'special causes' of production variability from 'common causes'. He used this technique to promote a systematic and rigorous approach to quality improvement.
- Joseph Juran claimed that management is responsible for 85 per cent of failures within organisations. He emphasised that quality control should be an integral part of management control and that management should adopt a structured approach to company-wide quality planning.
- Philip Crosby promoted the 'four absolutes' of quality management:
  1 Quality is defined as 'conformance to customer requirements'.
  2 The system for implementing quality is prevention not inspection.
  3 The performance standard must be zero defects.
  4 The measurement of quality is the price of non-conformance.
- Michael Fagan developed inspection as the primary defect prevention tool. It involves a formal critique of one document against another that looks for and records inconsistencies, initiates rework as necessary, is led by an independent chairperson and makes use of checklists based on historical data.

The proliferation of techniques, initiatives and pilgrimages is gradually leading to a realisation that a holistic approach is the most likely solution to all the quality-related problems of an organisation. Thus total quality management (TQM) has begun to emerge as the most generally acceptable way forward.

14.3 Total quality management

Although a well-controlled process is important in the delivery of a 'quality' product, it is not a guarantee of success. When we look at the example of

Japanese industry, we see a culture in place which is far removed from the type of discipline engendered by the adherence to an international standard. This 'culture' has been established from early school days and is therefore ingrained into the attitudes and behaviour of the entire workforce. The visible effects of this are:

- The removal of hierarchical differentiators in the workplace – for example, the managing director of a manufacturing company wearing the same clothing as the person on the shop floor, or the provision of a single canteen for management and staff alike.
- The commitment of all staff to the organisation's mission – many companies are now publishing and issuing corporate vision and mission statements to their staff, often on small cards, so that they will be carried about, referred to and shown to customers.
- The application of appropriate resources – quality circles or quality improvement teams are being introduced to encourage staff to become involved in the identification and solution of problems at the point of issue.
- The continual striving for improvement – suggestion schemes and their associated rewards are becoming the norm rather than the exception.

All of these are parameters in what may be called a 'total quality' approach.

Gradually, industries in the USA and in Europe are evolving methods of describing their aspirations in terms of business excellence and, equally importantly, of measuring their progress towards that excellence. In the USA, the Baldrige award was introduced to measure that progress and to motivate management and their companies to improve the overall quality of their organisations in a demonstrable way. More recently, in Europe, the European Foundation for Quality Management (EFQM), formed by an informal consortium of major organisations, developed a model, similar in concept to Baldrige, which would provide a means for quantitative evaluation of the key criteria for a total quality business.

The model, illustrated in Figure 14.1, shows the interrelationship between people, processes and results. In other words, the processes are the means by which an organisation harnesses and releases the talents of its people to produce results.

In essence, this tells us that Customer Satisfaction, People (employee) Satisfaction and Impact on Society are achieved through Leadership driving Policy and Strategy, People Management, Resources and Processes, leading ultimately to excellence in Business Results.

The nine elements shown in the model correspond to the criteria which are used to assess an organisation's progress towards excellence. For the purposes of quantitative assessment against the model, a relative value is ascribed to each of the criteria. Enablers and Results each total 50 per cent. Within those totals, individual percentages, as shown in the diagram, reflect the relative importance attributed to each criterion.

The Enabler criteria are concerned with *how* the organisation approaches each of the criterion parts. Information is required on the excellence of the approach used and the extent of the deployment of the approach: vertically

Figure 14.1 **The business excellence model of EFQM**

through all levels of the organisation and horizontally to all areas and activities.

The Results criteria are concerned with *what* the organisation has achieved and is achieving. The organisation being assessed should present numerical data including perception or direct feedback and predictor or relevant performance measures. Graphs showing trends over a period of years should also be presented.

As an example, let us take a look at a 'typical' company, Quality Services plc. This company has always been proud of its staff recruitment, appraisal and training scheme, which it applies to all of its junior technical staff. The company has a five-year rolling business strategy, which it uses to determine both the numbers and the skills profiles of the staff it needs to recruit. It operates a regular appraisal process, which determines the training needs and promotion potential for each member of staff.

Under the heading People Management, Quality Services plc might score well for its approach to human resource planning and improvement, although not so well for the deployment, since senior technical staff and administrative staff are not part of the scheme. Under both this criterion and also the result criterion People Satisfaction, the company might be marked down for not positively canvassing the views of its staff as to the effectiveness, from their point of view, of the scheme; for not establishing a quantitative measure of their satisfaction or of the evolution of that measure over time; and for not implementing the results of the feedback in order to improve the process. Thus, out of the 18 per cent of the total quality measure assigned to the People criteria, Quality Services plc might achieve only 5 per cent. The comprehensive nature of the model, however, should enable Quality Services plc to address the areas in which it could make improvements, rather than feeling bad about a notional score.

The British Quality Foundation (BQF) has adopted this model as the basis for the UK Business Excellence Awards, whose first winners in 1994 were Rover Group and TNT Express. In 2003, the diverse group of winners were TNT Post

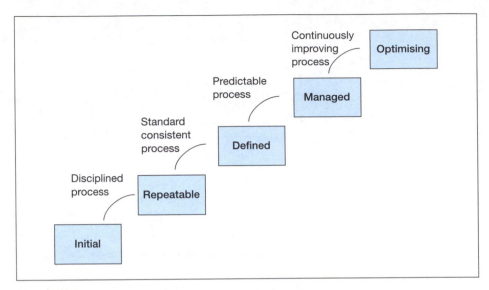

Figure 14.2 **The five levels of software process maturity**

Group Information Services, Eaton Aerospace Lakeside and AMS Operations Hillend.

Another approach to TQM is represented by the **Capability Maturity Model** for Software (CMM). This was developed by the Software Engineering Institute of Carnegie Mellon University and shows five stages that an organisation must pass through before its software development process is considered truly mature. The model is illustrated in Figure 14.2.

By its nature, TQM applies to the entirety of an organisation and, where that larger unit operates a TQM policy, then it is natural that IS projects should also subscribe to the same approach. TQM, however, implies a significant, long-term commitment to a specific culture. If that is not in place within an organisation then it is most unlikely, if not impossible, for a single project manager to implement it within the constraints of a project. Nevertheless, all the techniques discussed later in this chapter that form part of a TQM approach, and many of the ideas encapsulated within the model, are worth considering for implementation in individual projects. For example:

- Is it clear who is the customer, internal or external, and exactly what that customer expects of the project in terms of timescale, cost, function, benefits?
- Are there agreed ways of carrying out the project and its subtasks and is everyone on the lookout for ways of improving those methods?
- Will the appropriate resources be available to carry out the project:
  - Are appropriate budgets available?
  - Do we have the technical skills?
  - Do we have the necessary effort?
  - Is there an adequate information flow?
  - Is there an appropriate technological infrastructure?
- Are staff suitably motivated for the project to succeed?

14.4 Quality management and the quality plan

14.4.1 Quality management systems

The international standards for a quality management system (QMS), ISO 9000, are generic in nature and represent maximum agreement across all sectors of industry. As a result, the standards represent minimum, not maximum, best practice within any one sector. TickIT is an initiative, promoted by the UK Department of Trade and Industry, to establish the relevance of these standards to the production of software. Its objectives are:

- To harmonise QMS standards, through the common route of ISO 9000.
- To improve market confidence in third-party certification of QMSs.
- To provide authoritative guidance material to help QMS implementers.
- To improve professional practice among software QMS auditors.

In addition, it has the objective of stimulating software developers to think about what quality really is and how it may be achieved.

A quality system brings together all the functions, objectives and activities that contribute to the consistent quality of a product or service. Writing down these policies and procedures demonstrates how each aspect of the quality system interacts to ensure the system's success in improving the efficiency, performance and cost-effectiveness of the entire operation. The term 'quality management system' may be used, rather than the more limiting one of 'quality system', to reflect the additional management responsibilities. For example, where procedures from the conventional management system can affect quality, such as the recruitment programme, then they need to be part of the QMS.

The QMS is a snapshot of an organisation at an instant in time and is founded upon a statement of the organisation's objectives and policy for quality. These should correspond to the type and scope of product or service being offered. There must be a description of the responsibilities and the internal organisation for the QMS, to ensure that all quality practices are understood and are operated effectively. The structure of a typical QMS is shown in Figure 14.3.

14.4.2 The quality plan

Having established a QMS, the visible sign that the system is operational for a given project, product or service is the quality plan. The quality plan has a number of direct and indirect benefits:

- It is a formal definition of how the work is to be accomplished.
- It provides a key reference point for project team members.
- It acts as a bridge between the customer and the supplier.
- It provides a discipline for the project manager, offering a framework around which all the issues in prospect for the work can be considered and addressed before and during the project.

Of these, the last is probably the most important. Writing the quality plan, though often considered a chore, forces the project manager to sit down and

Figure 14.3 Quality management system structure

think out, in detail, exactly how the work is to be tackled on this project. What standards could and should apply to the work? What methods should we use to perform the work? Which techniques should we use to check that products are satisfactory? Who will be responsible for carrying out these checks? It has to be admitted that often, and particularly where compliance to an external standard such as ISO 9001 is required, quality plans are created just to satisfy the bureaucracy and sometimes even by just copying a plan prepared for another project; but this is the very antithesis of creative thinking and largely defeats the purpose of having a quality plan at all.

There is no generally accepted format for a quality plan, although there is an ISO standard – ISO 10005 – which provides guidelines for quality plans. Indeed, as was mentioned in Chapter 10, the distinction between a project plan and a quality plan is becoming increasingly blurred. However, the presentation of the document should be standardised wherever possible. It should be easy to use by project staff, easy to update and should clearly demonstrate that it fulfils contractual or external requirements. Topics that could be covered in a quality plan include:

- Project overview – to set the scene.
- Glossary of terms – any words that have a specific meaning within the context of the project.
- Product requirement – general outline of what is to be produced.
- Project organisation and responsibilities – organisation chart and main roles described.
- Availability, reliability and maintainability – requirements spelled out.
- Quality management responsibilities – who carries out reviews tests, etc.
- Quality control methods (see later in this section and also Chapter 11).
- Testing – when and how.
- Technical methods and standards – to be followed by the team.

- Configuration management – methods and tools to be used (see later in this chapter).
- Change control – if not covered in the project plan.
- Documentation and filing – systems to be used for computerised and manual files, including document naming standards.
- Purchasing – how it will be done: who is responsible.
- Subcontractor management – methods and responsibilities.
- Handling, storage and delivery of subcontracted work – quality control of subcontracted work.
- Support tools – what they are, how they are to be used.
- Non-conforming items – how to deal with incoming products from suppliers who follow a different quality management system (especially if they are not ISO 9001 accredited but the main contractor is).
- Project risks – if not the subject of a specific risk management plan.

Clearly, not all of these issues are relevant for all projects, and the way they are addressed will differ from project to project. One of the key tasks for the project manager is to consider exactly which topics are relevant to the project in hand, based on an assessment of its scale, scope and complexity.

In preparing a quality plan, or even in thinking about a standard for quality plans, it is important to place it in the context of the scope of work being carried out. For a large, complex, innovative project, it may be appropriate to address all the issues covered by the ISO 10005 standard, although many of these sections may just warrant a reference approach. For the supply of a standard product, or for a well-understood development, where the risk to customer and supplier is relatively small, a concise, report-by-exception type of plan would be more effective. The key issues, in either case, are:

- What are the lifecycle stages of the project?
- What standards are to be used throughout that lifecycle?
- What controls are to be exercised by the project manager to ensure quality?
- What checks, independent of the project, are to be imposed?

The supplier's quality plan should be a deliverable of the project at the earliest practicable time from its start. It must be produced by the project manager and the team, not imposed by the quality assurance function. Since an objective of producing a quality plan is to address likely problems before they arise, it should not merely be a copy of a previous plan. The use of electronic documentation makes it more and more tempting to do this.

14.5 Quality control methods

As we have seen, one of the key issues to be decided by the project manager is what quality control methods to use on the project. Methods range from the simple and informal (self-checking of products by their authors) to the detailed and rigorous (walkthroughs and Fagan inspection). The pros and

Figure 14.4 Quality control methods compared

cons of the various approaches are discussed under 'Monitoring Quality' in Chapter 11 and they are summarised in Figure 14.4. The general issue of 'inspection versus testing' is discussed in section 14.7.

14.6 The cost of poor quality

We are all aware of the costs of producing poor quality systems. We add to the work to be done to correct and retest programs. We have to make design changes late in the lifecycle because we did not identify or understand the user's needs. For this reason the cost of the additional work is often referred to as the 'cost of poor quality', or the 'price of non-conformance'. The objective for a project is to minimise this price of non-conformance. Its measurement can be broken down into four elements:

- Prevention
- Appraisal
- Internal failure
- External failure.

The cost of prevention is the amount spent to ensure that the work will be done correctly. It includes risk reduction and error prevention, for example ensuring the design is right before beginning production. Examples of prevention costs are supplier evaluation and the training and development of staff. Figure 14.5 shows that if we allocate resources early in the development lifecycle to prevent poor quality – by training people thoroughly, for example – the incidence of defects and the cost of rectifying them will fall.

Appraisal costs are those associated with inspection and testing of both the company's own products and the products received from suppliers. On software projects, we might have the appraisal costs of testing, walkthroughs, Fagan inspections and design reviews. As with prevention, we should make appraisal cost investments early in the development lifecycle. Figure 14.5 illustrates how, by dedicating more resources to appraisal, the number of defects in

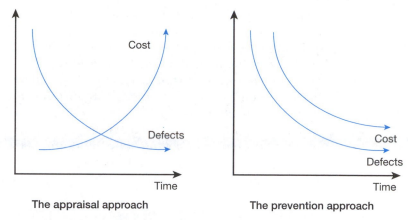

Figure 14.5 Cost of quality against time

the end-product is drastically reduced. For example, the more design reviews carried out during system design – an increased investment in appraisal – the greater the chance of spotting and correcting defects before resources are wasted programming those incorrect designs.

The cost of internal failure is the cost of rectifying everything that is discovered to be wrong while the product or service is still under our control and before it is delivered to a customer. An example of an internal failure would be part of a software system having to be scrapped and then designed and coded again as a result of a major problem being unearthed during integration testing. One of the key strengths of the Japanese quality approach is that Japanese companies have been able to reduce the costs of internal failure to almost zero, because they are orientated around defect prevention and process improvement – in other words, solve the problem, not the symptom.

External failure costs are incurred by a company because defects are detected only after delivery to customers. These costs are typically incurred under a warranty agreement or in handling customer complaints. In the latter category, however, are the unseen costs of lost repeat orders and a damaged reputation. On average, it costs five times as much to win new customers as it does to keep existing ones. According to one survey, if you buy a product and are happy about it, you tell, on average, 8 other people about it. If, on the other hand, you are unhappy about a product you have bought, you will make your dissatisfaction known to 22 other people. This puts into perspective both the indirect costs of quality and also the need to prevent errors occurring late in the cycle.

14.7 Inspection versus testing

The software quality problem may be defined to be the result of defects in code and documentation causing failure to satisfy user requirements. For the purposes of this discussion we shall define a defect to be an instance in which a requirement is not satisfied, and a requirement to be anything agreed on commitment – either a recognisable, external product requirement, or an internal development requirement.

Examples of such internal requirements are a test plan that completely verifies that the product meets the agreed needs of the user, or that the code of a program must be complete before it is submitted for testing. Although defects become manifest in the end-product documentation or code, most of them are actually present while the functional aspects of the product and its quality attributes are being created during the development of the requirements or the design or coding or by insertion of changes.

How can this software quality problem be eliminated? The attributes of software quality may be evaluated by two principal methods: testing and inspection. Both methods are aimed at the detection and elimination of defects during the lifecycle of a project. The principal difference, however, is the frame of reference for that detection process. Figure 14.6 shows the software development lifecycle model (a simplified version of the 'V' model encountered earlier in the book) and the scope of inspection and testing within the components of the model.

The solid lines show the progression through the stages in the lifecycle. Inspection takes place at each stage, using the information available at the tail of the line for verification of the information created at the head of that line. Testing uses the information at the tail of the dotted lines to verify the information at the head of those lines. For example, the unit test has to ensure that the program specification has been satisfied, whereas the system test is used to verify that the requirements specified in the analysis phase have been met.

Most, if not all, development environments require a combination of both types of defect detection. It can be seen from the diagram though that the later in the process detection occurs, the further back you will have to go and the more far-reaching will be the implications of correcting defects. For example, an error detected in unit testing will require recoding, whereas an error discovered as late as the acceptance test may require a rework of all the specification stages and all the testing phases.

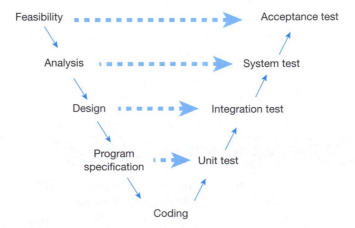

Figure 14.6 The software development lifecycle

Inspections are intended to minimise the number of issues, defects or errors propagated to the next level of the lifecycle. In this way they help to overcome the known cost escalation of finding and correcting errors. Inspections are document-based and people-intensive and consequently their use must be carefully controlled if they are to be cost-effective.

The objectives of each inspection in the software development environment are:

- To find and record issues – checking for discrepancies between the document under inspection and any source documents used to create it.
- To instigate rework as necessary and verify that corrective action is complete.

Additional objectives include the improvement of the software development process by identifying both recurring sources of defects and potential for the creation of defects, and the improvement of the inspection process itself.

Inspections, if they are to be used, are a normal part of the lifecycle of a project. Normally, this means that their use is identified within a specific project plan. When considering whether it is worthwhile conducting an inspection, the key decision criteria are:

- The importance of the document to be inspected, within the context of the project.
- The cost-effectiveness of the inspection process.
- The complexity of the document.
- The impact on other areas of the project.

Having decided that an inspection is worthwhile, the appropriate, trained resources must be committed to it. This means, they must be assigned, briefed, and available to give the necessary time and effort, both before and during the inspection.

Authors of documents may often feel threatened by the idea of an inspection, but enlightened authors are grateful for the defects found during an inspection, since it avoids a less friendly person finding them later.

14.8 The management of software testing

Software testing is an important part of any quality plan; in fact, the interpretation of ISO 9000 for software development stresses the significance of planning, reviewing and authorising a test environment in the quality planning process. In addition, the results of each test must be recorded and the problems identified must be tracked. Following the standard therefore ensures that at least some testing will be done in a well-documented fashion. The problem with software, though, is that it is virtually certain that you will never find all the errors. Projects often seem to be pouring time and resources into a black hole called 'testing' and, even after this has been done, the end-customer will always find too many errors themselves.

The project manager's problem is to optimise the return on the effort put into the testing exercise. Inspection, as discussed in the previous section, is part of that equation, the use of test techniques gives a more effective process, and the use of tools may make the test process more efficient. We have seen that in the software development lifecycle shown in Figure 14.6 several levels of testing are required and that the specification of those sets of tests is carried out in the reverse order of their execution, with unit tests being the first to run. A key factor in the optimisation process is to plan the tests early in the life-cycle, even though the execution will not take place until later on. Also, the recognition that each type of test is different in nature, in objective and in execution will help the members of the project team to clarify the different issues addressed by the testing process as a whole.

Testing can be performed manually or using software tools. The decision about whether to use tools depends upon the size and complexity of the project, the size and complexity of the task, the monotony of the manual task, the relevance of the tools and the quality of the tools – in every sense of the word 'quality'. For each of the types of test the number of individual tasks is significant and includes the following:

- Planning of the entire test – the identification and scheduling of tasks and assignment of resources.
- Designing the test conditions.
- Specifying test case.
- Preparing test data.
- The formal setting-out of the expected outcome of each of the tests planned.
- Running of the software with the chosen input data.
- Comparing the actual results against the expected results.
- Identifying and correcting errors in the software, the design, the analysis and the requirement.
- Monitoring the progress of the tests.
- Improving the testing process – a continuous search for enhancements to all aspects of the test process.
- Using volume tests and performance issues to ensure that the hardware and software configuration can cope with operational extremes.
- Evaluating the non-functional aspects, such as user-friendliness of the system, maintainability of the code.
- Finally, regression testing, to show that corrections to the software as a result of the detection of errors have not had knock-on effects elsewhere.
- A statistical assessment of the completeness of the testing undertaken.

It is easy to be misled into believing that in a world of sophisticated software there must be a software tool to carry out these tasks; but bear in mind that the errors have been put there by one or more human beings and the delivered system is to be used by human beings. Only through significant intervention by human beings will quality be delivered. For example, if a software tool were able to generate the expected results from a given set of input data, then that tool would be doing what the developed software is required to do – but correctly. Why not just use the tool instead of developing new software?

Nevertheless, there are several useful software tools under the CAST (computer-aided software testing) banner, which will be worth considering. Most of the market research organisations have produced reports, which are updated regularly, evaluating and comparing the available products and their suppliers.

14.9 Metrics and statistical quality control

It is tempting to measure 'everything that moves' on a project in the belief that by measuring you are in control. Part of the quality planning activity will be to identify those aspects of the project which are key to the control, evaluation and improvement of the software development process and to the quality of the service or product delivered to the customer in the context of the current project.

As the project manager, you need to have a feel for how the project is going. Where individual team members are falling behind with their work, you will need to recognise:

- Where external events are having an impact on the progress of the project.
- Where initial assumptions may have been optimistic, or wrong.
- Where risks were calculated at the start of the project.

Intuition, or experience, can count for a lot, but concrete, statistical evidence is easier to demonstrate to people outside the project and also makes remedial action easier to quantify and to justify.

The most apparent measures for project management control are time, effort and money. Before the start of any project, estimates will have been drawn up of the total elapsed time for the project, of the manpower effort required to deliver the work and of the cost of the various elements of the project. Often, the person drawing up the estimates is not the same as the person having to live with them. It is essential, therefore, that in conjunction with those estimates there is a clear statement setting out the reasoning behind the estimates, the assumptions upon which they were based and the commercial decisions taken. During the course of the project, the project manager should report the above measures in terms of spend-to-date and spend-to-go: budget and actual.

History – and collected data – tells us that for programs, or documents of a certain size, novelty and complexity, we can expect certain levels of error. The calibration of such measures for your own development environment provides an invaluable platform for estimating and controlling projects. The key issue is to determine which are to be the metrics on which to establish the statistical baseline.

If you decide to use inspections as a standard technique, then establish a database showing the size of document, number of defects per page, severity of those errors, and the time it takes to inspect each page. If you use function point analysis or lines of code (LOC), establish a measure of development effort per function point or thousands of lines of code (KLOC). Then, at the system test stage, measure the number of errors detected per unit of the system and their origin – whether from analysis, design or coding.

In this manner, you can quickly tell whether there are issues related to particular parts of a system, to particular programmers or teams, or to this project as a whole, which are causing it to be more or less defect-prone than normal. Once such an evaluation has been made, decisions can be taken as to whether to make fundamental changes to the estimates, or to the team, in order to achieve the project's objectives.

Project managers often have a view that they and their projects are unique: no one has ever done anything like them before and no one will ever do anything similar in the future. For those reasons it is not worth exploring historical data, nor is it beneficial to 'waste time' recording data for posterity. The prophecy is often self-fulfilling. It is usually the role of an installation quality manager to establish a culture of continuous improvement, often through the use of such statistics. On large projects, where project managers will see the benefits of statistics within the lifecycle of their own work, this is not difficult.

The key to the successful implementation of a useful, statistically based project management and quality improvement environment is to make the statistics easy to understand and, more importantly, easy to collect. To the latter end, the collection of statistics should be a part of the project management process and, if possible, should be automatic. Thus, for example, if project management is normally carried out using an electronic tool, whether a specific project management package or a word processing or spreadsheet package, templates should be built in which can prompt for, or calculate directly, the information required with the minimum of additional effort on the part of the project manager.

14.10 Supporting activities

ISO 9000 identifies a number of activities within the quality management system as being of a supportive nature – outside the software development lifecycle itself. This section addresses the key issues for project managers in these areas, which are not dealt with elsewhere.

'Documentation', said Dick Brandon, the pioneer of computing standards, 'is like sex. When it's good, it's very, very good; and when it's bad, it's better than nothing.'

As part of the quality planning process, the project manager is responsible for identifying the key documents which will form the framework for the project. These will include documents outside the manager's control – such as installation or customer standards – and project-specific documents – such as local standards, planning documents and project lifecycle documents, from phase inputs and outputs, to operational and user guides. For those latter documents, which are the responsibility of the project, there must be mechanisms in place to control their preparation, approval, release, change, access and removal. This will go a long way towards eliminating the errors which so often arise when information about documents is taken for granted. For paper documents such controls are relatively straightforward to envisage and to implement. Increasingly, however, technology is enabling project managers to introduce electronic documents as the norm. Similar disciplines are available and must be enforced, through password protection, electronic signature and time stamping.

The purpose of quality records is to demonstrate the achievement of the required quality and the effective operation of the quality system. This is another area for optimisation of effort in order to achieve the desired result. It is often tempting to flood the project with paperwork, just to impress an auditor. The quality plan should, however, have identified the key processes, responsibilities, communication mechanisms, and process improvement opportunities. Evidence is needed that these issues have been addressed, through minutes, action planning and follow-up, debriefs and, where appropriate, supporting statistical information.

In all aspects of project management there are software tools and well-tried techniques to support you. The ISO 9000 standard identifies the fact that project managers must be aware and make use of such tools and techniques *where they are appropriate*.

In this context, the tools will be used by the project manager for project management purposes; and also by the project team for product development in order to support and make more effective the quality management system. These are discussed under the separate subsections to which they apply.

Every issue that we have dealt with in this book requires some element of training, experiential self-study, or formal classroom work. Part of the planning activity will require the project manager to identify the skills required to address the tasks involved in the project and to match those against the resources available.

It is always tempting to try to gain time by assigning people to tasks as soon as they are available. This temptation must be resisted in favour of providing the necessary training for a task before its launch. ISO 9000 requires records to be maintained of training received, both for the benefit of an individual's career progression and also for the sake of future task assignment.

14.11 Configuration management

British Standard BS 8488:1984 defines configuration management as:

> The discipline of identifying the components of a continuously evolving system (taking into account relevant system interfaces) for the purposes of controlling changes to these components and maintaining integrity and traceability throughout the system lifecycle.

This definition means knowing where you are at any given time with regard to the components of a system – hardware, software and documentation – and being able to say with certainty what the status of each item is, both on its own and in relation to other items.

The importance of configuration management is best appreciated by considering what happens when it is not properly addressed:

■ No one can be certain which version of a component is the current one, so, for example, time and effort may be wasted by working from an obsolete version of the specification.

■ Individual items, such as program specifications, the completed code and the test specification, are mutually incompatible.

■ The release of products is not controlled, so that no one can be sure which version of a program is running; which version of system software is currently in use; or which combination of hardware items is relevant.

■ Changes to the environment – program, system software or hardware – are applied in an uncontrolled manner, without proper analysis of their impact.

■ If a catastrophe occurs, no one can be sure what the current state of the project should be, or how to regenerate it.

The larger and more complex the project, therefore, the more relevant will be a configuration management system to support it. Configuration management includes:

■ *Version and variant control*, recording the history of items and records during development.

■ *Configuration control*, the orchestration of processes for maintaining the visibility of the software parts of the system during the development lifecycle.

■ *Change control*, the management of changes through suitable evaluation and authorisation.

A configuration management environment should be established during the quality planning stage of a development project. Any later, and the system, by its nature, is liable to be 'chasing its own tail'. Procedures should be flexible enough to control all items, whatever their origin, within the same framework. An item will normally come under configuration control when it reaches a relatively stable state and has been reviewed and approved. Points of reference should be established for each item at each stage of the project, giving the reference, author and approver. Equally, there must be a readily available reference point for the whole system and provision for keeping a history of changes. In this manner, the system is traceable through its life, and the release of products, both internally and externally, can be easily controlled.

The project manager should consider whether to instigate regular audits, or spot checks, to ensure that the configuration management procedures are being followed properly.

14.12 Managing quality with PRINCE2®

In PRINCE2® a project is regarded as having a defined and unique set of products, a set of activities to construct the products, appropriate resources to undertake the activities and a finite lifespan. PRINCE2® also requires an organisational structure with defined responsibilities. Within the context of the software development lifecycle, PRINCE2® is typically used to control activities or the subactivities which make them up, from feasibility study through production and installation. PRINCE2® does not specify the activities that a project should embrace. Thus more than one activity, such as design through production, may be controlled as one PRINCE2® project.

Other activities within the lifecycle, such as operation, do not fall within the PRINCE2® definition of a project and are not controlled using PRINCE2®. However, many of the PRINCE2® procedures are relevant to the control of such activities but need to be supplemented by further documented procedures and standards. These further procedures and standards often already exist within an organisation and their introduction merely involves formally specifying and documenting them.

PRINCE2® was not designed to be a comprehensive quality system. However, three of its constituents contribute to a significant part of such a system. These are:

- Quality controls which are clearly defined technical and management procedures.
- Product-based planning and the product descriptions which define the product quality criteria.
- The PRINCE2® organisation.

Because PRINCE2® is not in itself a quality system, its use does not automatically produce conformance to ISO 9000. In fact, PRINCE2® itself may need tailoring to meet the specific needs of the organisation. Further procedures and standards which are required to satisfy ISO 9000 and which PRINCE2® does not cover, in the context of project management, include:

- The availability of procedures for verification and use of automated tools.
- Procedures must be defined and documented for the distribution of replicated systems, such as software products.
- Procedures should be defined and documented for reviewing and updating the quality system.
- Procedures must be defined and documented which provide records demonstrating the effectiveness of the quality system. These records should include:
  - internal and external quality audit documentation;
  - results of customer satisfaction surveys;
  - quality system change control documentation.
- Audit procedures and schedules must be defined and documented.
- All issues relevant to staff training and to measurement and statistics need to be addressed.

14.13 Summary

In this chapter we have discussed the use and misuse of the term 'quality'. We have noted the many new aspects and initiatives which have evolved in recent years and which are so important to project managers. We have described the benefits of the formal approach to quality and the cost of not adopting such an approach. We have also shown how project managers need to be aware of the areas closely related to quality management which form an integral part of the management task.

Questions

1 How could the quality culture behaviours described in section 14.3 be applied in a hospital?

2 Why do you suppose there is an increasing number of organisations concerned with the development of quality practices for IS development?

3 What is the purpose of a quality plan? Who should create it?

4 Do you agree with what Dick Brandon said about sex in section 14.10? Do not take this question too seriously!

Case study

In devising the quality plan for the France Vacances project (part of a combined project/quality plan), Richard Vaughan, the project manager, has decided to use a variety of quality control techniques:

■ All products will be reviewed by their authors.
■ Certain products will be reviewed internally for format and adherence to standards (by the relevant team managers) and will also be given to France Vacances personnel to check the correctness of the content. A good example of this is the set of interview notes.
■ The technical design will be checked by peer review within the development teams, since neither team manager is a designer and thus neither is able to review this product themselves.
■ Also, Norman Pierce, E-Con's quality manager and a member of the project assurance team, will review a sample of products to ensure that standards are being met; an example of this is Norman's review of the interview notes described in Chapter 13.
■ Software products will be reviewed through progressive testing (at module and then system level and finally through customer acceptance tests) against test specifications derived from the requirements specification.

Further reading

Crosby, Philip B (1978), *Quality is Free*, McGraw-Hill

Deming, W Edwards (1982), *Out of the Crisis*, MIT Press

Evans, M W and Marciniak, J (1987), *The Assurance and Management of Software Quality: A Practical Guide*, Wiley

Fagan, Michael (1976), 'Design and code inspections to reduce errors in program development', *IBM Systems Journal*, No. 3

Juran, J (1988), *Planning for Quality*, The Free Press

Various (1994), *The Capability Maturity Model: Guidelines for improving the Software Process*, Addison-Wesley-Longman

15 Risk management

Introduction

All projects involve risk of some sort. These risks may stem from the nature of the work (for example if there is a lot of innovation involved), from the type of resources available, from the contractual relationship which is in place or from political factors which influence the project. It is usually not practicable to eliminate risks altogether – indeed, this would not be desirable since it would inhibit innovation and stifle creativity. But it is possible to manage projects in a way that recognises the existence of the risks and prepares, in advance, methods of dealing with them if they occur.

In recent years, the subject of risk management has become increasingly important. This is partly because the use of project organisations, with associated project management techniques, is now often seen as a means of achieving some desired change in an organisation and is used more widely than in traditional areas such as the development of information systems. In addition, projects are assuming ever greater levels of complexity, with many different skills and technologies being employed and the resulting interdependencies leading to a higher degree of uncertainty in the project's outcome.

15.2 Outline of the risk management process

The **risk management** process is illustrated in Figure 15.1.
Reduced to its essentials, risk management requires:

- The establishment of mechanisms to keep risks under review and to make sure they are being addressed.
- A means of identifying the potential risks to the project.
- An assessment of the likelihood of each risk's materialising.
- An assessment of the probable impact of each risk.
- The formulation of measures to avoid each risk's occurring.
- The development of fallback measures to ameliorate the risks if avoidance actions fail.
- The determination of the urgency of the risk and of taking appropriate countermeasures.

Figure 15.1 The risk management process

Also vital to successful risk management is the issue of ownership – that someone should be responsible for each risk. Each of these issues is addressed in the sections that follow.

15.3 Risk identification

Clearly, the first step involved in managing risks is to discover what they are, but this is more easily said than done. To some extent, each project is unique and its risks will arise from the interdependencies between factors that may not have been seen in this combination before. Nevertheless, there are some broad areas in which to look for potential risks and some of these are considered below. It is clear that there are many areas in which risk could arise and it is difficult for the project manager to be sure that all of the possible risks have been identified. It is often valuable to get a second, or third, opinion from experienced project managers who may have encountered similar projects in the past. The most important thing, though, is for the project manager to be rigorously honest about the risks. All known risks *must* be highlighted, even if some of them are politically unpopular, as sweeping them under the carpet does not make them go away – it just makes it harder to manage them.

Once the risks have been identified, they need to be described succinctly so that it is clear exactly what each risk is about. For example, 'poor contractor

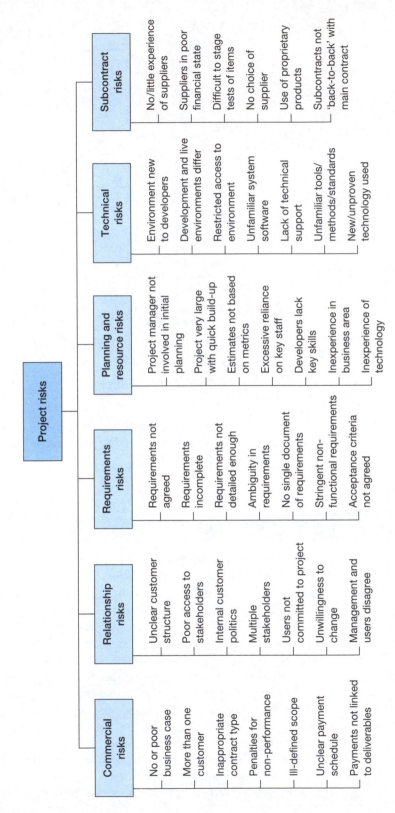

Figure 15.2 **Risk breakdown structure**

performance' is obviously risky but described thus it will be difficult to decide what can be done about it. This risk might be better broken down into three, more specific risks, thus:

■ Contract staff do not work at the pace assumed in preparing the estimates.
■ Contract staff do not grasp and conform to the developer's programming standards.
■ Contract staff are difficult to manage with inexperienced team leaders.

Once we have a fairly precise description of the risk, we are in a better position to describe its impacts and what needs to be done to counter it.

One way of identifying risks – or at least of prompting questions that will help to identify risks – is to use some form of risk breakdown structure. This, like the other breakdown structures encountered in this book, works on the principle of progressive decomposition to uncover more detail about an issue. An example of a simple risk breakdown structure is given in Figure 15.2.

In Figure 15.2, project risks are at the top of our structure. We then break these down into six subcategories, such as commercial risks and technical risks. At the next level, we have the risks themselves. A risk breakdown structure can have more levels of breakdown than this and it is a good idea for project managers, and the organisations they work for, to develop such structures that reflect the types of project they undertake and the types of risk that are commonly encountered.

The following list expands the risks given in the risk breakdown structure. Although by no means exhaustive, it provides a starting point for the identification of risk in an IS project. In each case, the nature of the risk is described and some approaches to avoiding the risk, or mitigating its impact, are outlined.

The commercial background
The business case for the project may be unsound or the funding may not have been approved. There may be more than one customer, or several suppliers, involved, and the commercial relationships between them may be unclear. The contract type may be inappropriate for the type of work – for example, a fixed-price contract for a research project. The business area may be one in which the supplier has little experience. There may be immovable end-dates or price ceilings.

The best way to avoid these risks is to have a pre-project review procedure where commercial issues are considered along with the technical problems that the project will face. If any commercial risks are identified, these should be reflected in the way that the project is set up, including the contract terms that are agreed.

The contract
The biggest risk where the contract is concerned is that the scope of work is ill-defined or not agreed between the parties. There may be onerous penalty clauses for delay or underperformance. The payment schedule may be unclear or not linked to tangible milestones. If there are prime contractor or subcontractor arrangements in place, the contracts may not be 'back to back', with similar terms reflected through all the levels of contract, leaving one of the

parties exposed. Finally, there may be no signed contract, with work proceeding on the basis of more informal arrangements.

If areas of the contract are ill-defined, then a wise policy is to document any assumptions and ask the customer to approve them. Even if they do not, the resultant discussion provides an opportunity to remove the uncertainties. An experienced commercial manager or a contract lawyer should be asked to review all of the contracts to check that the interests of the various parties are adequately protected.

The customer The customer management structure may be unclear. Access to important customer staff may be difficult and it could be hard to get decisions made. There may be internal political difficulties in the customer's organisation, with no mechanism for resolving them. There may, indeed, be not one customer but several, each with a different perspective on the project and with varying levels of commitment to it.

If problems with the customer are anticipated, then the project manager, and perhaps also the salesperson, should make early efforts to get to know the various parties and to gain their commitment to the project. If there are internal political squabbles, then the project manager must make sure that the most important players – those with the most influence in the organisation – are supportive of the project and willing to use their authority to see it progress.

The users The users may not be committed to the project or be able to devote sufficient time to it. They may be unfamiliar with the technology and require additional training. There may be an unwillingness to change working practices to fit in with the new system. The customer's senior management and the actual users may hold very different views of what the system is supposed to do. The new system may threaten the jobs of many users.

Every effort must be made to involve the users in the project and this may involve providing training or familiarisation to enable them to play their parts effectively. If senior customer management is unwilling to involve the users, the project manager must try to persuade them into a more constructive approach.

Acceptance The acceptance criteria, and the acceptance mechanisms, may not have been defined in the contract. The acceptance criteria may have been drawn very vaguely and not linked to specific, measurable demonstrations of performance. There may be other aspects of the project that could delay the customer's carrying out the acceptance tests. The customer may have discretion over the acceptability of some or all of the system.

Acceptance is best handled as an incremental process. First, the test plan is agreed, then the test specifications, then the individual tests and then the whole system. This way, a big dispute towards the end of the project is avoided and the customer can be gradually led towards acceptance of the total product. It is important, too, that the functional specification is tight enough to provide a conclusive yes/no answer as to whether the system meets a particular requirement.

The functional requirement The requirement may not have been formally signed off before development began. The requirement may not be complete or may suffer from varying levels of detail or internal inconsistency. It may have been defined at too high a level, making it difficult to implement and operate change control procedures. The requirement may have been defined in more than one document, with the risk of inconsistencies and ambiguity between them. There may be a mismatch between the developer's and the customer's understanding of the requirement.

The functional requirement should be reviewed independently by someone not involved in the project – it is too easy otherwise to read what is supposed to be there rather than what is actually documented. A rigorous configuration management system is needed to ensure that documentation is consistent. A formal review technique, such as a walkthrough, will help to identify differences between the customer's and the developer's expectations of the system.

The technical requirement The system may be complex technically or require a high degree of innovation. It may require the use of tools, techniques or hardware not familiar to the developer. The system design may make testing difficult, particularly if phased deliveries are involved. There may be a need to interface with other systems and to test these interfaces through simulation.

If the project team does not have sufficient technical expertise (and there is more about this later) then expertise must be obtained from elsewhere to at least define a suitable approach to the technical issues. A complete overall design should be in place before proceeding to the detailed design of the components.

Performance, reliability, availability and maintainability There may be stringent performance requirements for the system. A high degree of reliability or availability may be required. It may be difficult to test the system using realistic numbers of transactions or users. There may be no way to simulate performance in advance of system testing.

The contract should be examined closely for challenging performance requirements and the project manager must ensure that the precise conditions and manner of measurement are defined. It could be advisable to build prototypes of critical functions and to test them early in the project in order to identify areas where additional effort will be required.

The project plan The project manager may not have been involved in the bid phase and so may not have contributed to the initial plan. The project may have tight timescales. The project itself may be large and require a rapid build-up of staff. The plan may not take into account the need to revisit work from previous phases. The estimates may not be based on solid metrics. Sufficient contingency may not have been added, or it may have been bargained away during the bidding process. There may be excessive reliance on a few key staff. Milestones may be too far apart, deliverables may not have been defined tightly enough or work packages may be too large for effective control.

If the project manager was not involved in the bid phase, then he or she should revisit the plans as soon as possible and flag up any concerns, inconsistencies or possible risks. Project managers need to assume that, if anything can go wrong, it will – and allow contingency accordingly.

The developer's skills

Key staff, for example the project manager or team leaders, may be new to their role. The team as a whole may be inexperienced in the business area or technology, or both, and there may be a lot of training required. The analysis or design work may have been performed by people with little experience in this work. Senior technical staff may be pursuing interesting, but unproven, methods or technologies.

If any of these risks are thought to be present, then the project manager should re-examine the estimates and consider on what basis they were prepared. If necessary, the plans should be adjusted to model the effects of using less experienced staff. If the project manager considers there is a dangerous weakness in some area – perhaps a critical technical skill – then he or she must lobby hard for additional, perhaps consultancy, support.

Project staffing

Staff may not be available when required, or may have to join the project too early, when there is little for them to do. Staff may have other commitments that could divert them from the project. There may be too many junior or inexperienced staff, leading to effort overruns, or too many senior staff, leading to cost overruns. There may be unproven customer or contract staff involved. The project may coincide with a period of high staff turnover.

In general, the project manager should aim to take staff on board just when they are wanted. If they must join the team early, they should be kept away from the people already in place or they will distract them from their work. If staff must be shared with another project, the project manager must negotiate with the manager concerned the exact terms of the share and when they will be available to each team.

The development environment

The environment may be new to the developer. The development environment may not match the live environment closely enough and there may be restricted access to it. It may not be possible to get out-of-hours access in contingency situations. Access to the development environment may be via remote links and it may not be under the developer's control. The hardware may be unreliable or poorly documented.

If the environment is new to the developer, proper training must be provided. It is wasteful and inefficient to learn by trial and error, and the quality of software developed in this way will be poor. If necessary, arrange for access to a technical expert to resolve difficult problems. The project manager may have to negotiate hard with the operations people to get adequate access to the development environment.

System software

System software may be new or unproven or not yet available. It may be unfamiliar to the developer and technical support may not be readily available. There may be excessive performance overheads. The version may be unstable and likely to change during the project. There may be several different elements to the system software, perhaps provided by different suppliers and not used in this combination before.

Proper training should be provided so that the development team understand the advantages and limitations of the system software. Consultancy support – perhaps from the vendor of the software – can prove cost-beneficial in the long run in terms of time saved and the most efficient exploitation of the software.

Tools and methods
The programming languages may be unfamiliar to the developer. It may be unsuited to the particular project requirements. If using a fourth generation language, there may be the need for some lower-level code to meet performance pinch-points. The standards and methods may be new either to the development staff or to the customers who will review deliverables. There may not be adequate tools for matters such as configuration management, project planning, testing and so on.

Training and familiarisation must be provided as required. It may be advisable to use a small area of the project as a pilot to gain experience of the tools, and that experience can be passed on to the rest of the development team. If tools are not available for, for example, configuration management, the project manager will have to develop them; spreadsheet packages are found to be very useful in these areas.

The target architecture
The hardware may be new or unproven, or not used before for this purpose. Some of the hardware may be custom-built and perhaps not available until late in the development. There may be doubts about the capacity of the hardware, for storage or performance or both. There may be many different pieces of hardware, from various suppliers, to be integrated.

Testing on the target environment should be scheduled as early as possible, to allow time to highlight and rectify any problems. If the equipment selected is near the top of its range, then examine the sizing calculations closely and pessimistically as the cost of a mistake could be large if it became necessary to switch to a totally different platform.

Bought-in items
If third-party products – hardware or software – are required, there could be little experience of the suppliers, or poor previous experience. The suppliers may be in a poor financial condition and at risk of going out of business. There may be difficulty in establishing tests for bought-in items.

The technical and financial credibility of potential suppliers should be examined closely. In general, using open, as opposed to proprietary, solutions should make it possible to switch suppliers if things get difficult. The developers should make sure that they are protected contractually if a supplier goes out of business:

- By having a copy of the software placed in escrow – held with a third party to be released in certain specified events, including bankruptcy.
- By having a *force majeure* clause in their own contract with their customer whereby they are released from their obligations if they are hit by events outside their control.

15.4 Risk assessment

With the various risks identified and described, it is next necessary to make an **assessment** of their *impact* and *likelihood*. This is so that management attention can be focused on those risks with the greatest probability of occurring and those that will most damage the project if they do happen. For a given risk, there may be more than one possible impact. Continuing with one of our contract staff examples, the impacts of slowness could include:

- Failure to produce unit tested code by the planned date.
- Inability to begin system test on time.
- The need to reschedule system test to work around modules not yet available.
- A switch of effort to other staff.

The seriousness of these impacts will depend on what proportion of the programming work is being undertaken by contract staff. If, as is increasingly the case, a lot of contract staff are being used, then the impact will be severe. If contractors make up only a small proportion of the programming team, then the impact will be less. It is sometimes necessary to try to assess the impact scientifically, perhaps by calculating the likely delay as a proportion of project effort. Usually, though, an assessment that an impact is large, moderate or small will suffice. These could be related to the time/cost/quality criteria like this:

- Large impact: could extend project by more than 10 per cent
- Moderate impact: could extend project by 5–10 per cent
- Small impact: could extend project by less than 5 per cent

or using some other scale that is appropriate to the project concerned.

The other factor to consider is the likelihood, or probability, of the risk's materialising. To continue with our example, the risk might be high if it were known that contract staff with the required skills were rare, if the developers had no previous experience of the contractors concerned, and if there were no independent way of verifying the experience claimed on the contractors' CVs. If, on the other hand, the plan was to use people who had been hired before, and on whom there were favourable reports, then the likelihood of the risk's materialising could be assessed as low. As with impact, it is possible to estimate the probability mathematically but, for practical purposes, a simple scale of high, medium or low will be adequate. The likelihood could be given a rough numerical value like this:

- High probability: greater than 30 per cent
- Medium probability: 10–30 per cent
- Low probability: less than 10 per cent

We are now able to compare the risks to decide which ones need the closest management attention. Obviously, the most important ones are those with a large impact and a high probability of occurrence. At the other extreme,

Likelihood of occurrence

High Medium Low

Potential scale of impact

Large

Moderate

Small

Figure 15.3 Risk map

we need be less concerned about those with a low probability and small impact. In between, there are various graduations of severity we can consider.

A useful way of highlighting the important risks is to use a *risk map*, illustrated in Figure 15.3.

A risk map plots the impact of each risk on one axis and its likelihood along the other. The risks shown in the top left-hand corner are those with the highest impact and probability and therefore, probably, the ones that need the closest management attention.

One other factor to think about, however, is the *urgency* of the risk. This has two aspects:

■ The urgency with which the risk is likely to materialise.
■ The urgency with which we need to take avoidance or ameliorative actions.

It may be, for example, that in comparing two risks one is found to be more severe than the other overall. But, for the less severe risk, there may be an immediate need to take the identified avoidance action. In this case, this risk might be addressed with more urgency than its severity might indicate.

15.5 Risk actions

So far, we have identified the risks and quantified their effects. However, this is rather useless unless some actions are taken to deal with the risks. In essence, there are four main responses to risk:

■ **Acceptance.** It may be that there are no feasible countermeasures, or that these are more expensive than suffering risk to occur. In that case, the only rational response may be to let the risk happen but also, perhaps, to build in time or budget contingency to deal with the effects of the risk if it occurs.
■ **Avoidance.** This involves the things we can do to try to prevent the risks from occurring (in other words, dealing with the likelihood).

- **Mitigation.** This includes the steps we can take to reduce the impact of the risks if they occur (in other words, dealing with the impact).
- **Transfer.** This involves making the impact of the risk, if it occurs, fall on someone else. Taking out household insurance, for example, does not reduce the likelihood of your house being burgled but, if it is, the impact is felt by the insurance company.

In practice, we need to consider all types of action, and particularly avoidance and mitigation, since avoidance measures may fail and we may need to recover from the risk's occurrence.

If we go back to our example of the risk associated with employing contract staff, we might decide that an avoidance action is to use only full-time, employed staff. That might, however, not work if competition from other projects means that enough staff are not available. We could then identify various mitigation actions such as:

- Ensuring that we use only contractors of whom we have experience.
- Setting prospective contractors a short test to assess their speed of work.
- Conducting searching interviews to discover their attitude to standards.

None of these measures would eliminate the risk entirely but they should go some way to reducing its likelihood and effect.

In identifying the countermeasures, we need to be aware of the creation of *secondary risks*. For example, if we decided that we would under no circumstances use contract staff, then a secondary risk might be that we could not get enough people to work on the project, leading to delay in delivery. If the secondary risks are serious enough, they should be treated like other risks and subjected to the full risk assessment process.

Once we have identified the actions, we can determine the urgency of taking the actions and act accordingly.

15.6 Risk management planning and control

The initial identification of risks and their countermeasures is only part of risk management. As a project proceeds, the nature of risk changes:

- Some of the predicted risks materialise and have to be managed like other project issues – hopefully using the mitigation actions previously identified.
- Some of the predicted risks disappear, having been overtaken by events.
- New risks appear, not anticipated at the start of the project.

Risk management is therefore an ongoing process. There needs to be a procedure to revisit the risk register regularly and to reassess the status of each risk. There also needs to be a forum where the risk 'owners' (discussed later) can meet and discuss the steps they have taken to deal with their risks. On many projects, the review of risks is undertaken at regular progress meetings.

Probably, only the major risks are reviewed here, with others being dealt with individually outside the meeting. On very large projects, with a large number of complex risks, there might be a specific risk review meeting. Whatever the approach taken, it should be documented in a *risk management plan*. This, depending on the project, might form part of the project plan or it might be a document in its own right. The risk management plan should set out:

- A statement of the *scope and intensity* of the risk management to be applied to the project. Risk management, like other project management tasks, must be tailored to the size, value and complexity of the individual project.
- An explanation of the *risk management cycle* to be used on the project, showing how and when risk reviews will be carried out and whether they will be a separate process or part of the ongoing project monitoring work.
- *Roles and responsibilities* – who will be in charge of the risk management process and the mechanism by which risks will be reviewed and controlled.
- A description of the *products* of risk management – for example, a regular risk assessment report prepared for senior management.

15.7 The risk register

Another important document in the risk management process is the **risk register**. This could take various forms – loose-leaf register, word-processor file, spreadsheet or database – and will act as a central repository for the information gained on each risk. Specifically, you need to record:

- A *reference* – each risk needs a unique identifier, perhaps keyed to the phase, task or product on which it impacts.
- A *title and description* of the risk.
- The *current status* of the risk – for example, candidate (identified but not yet quantified), live, or closed.
- *Potential impacts* – there may be more than one of these and, for each, you need to record a description and assessment of its likelihood and scale of impact.
- *Risk owner* – the person who will be responsible for carrying out the identified risk actions (see below).
- *Actions* – the avoidance, mitigation and transfer actions that have been identified.
- *Action log* – a record of the progress made in discharging the risk actions.

The storage medium for the risk register will depend on the scale of the project and on the volatility of the risks identified. For a small project with a few fairly long-term risks, a paper-based system would be adequate; for a larger project, with many changeable risks, a computerised system would clearly be advantageous.

15.8   Risk ownership

Part of the process of risk identification is to decide who should be the **owner** of each risk. The owner should be someone who:

- has sufficient information concerning the risk,
- has the necessary resources, and
- possesses the authority to do something about the risk.

It is a common mistake to attribute the ownership of the risk to someone at too low a level in the organisation. Such a person might well have a very good understanding of the risk and its impacts but may lack the resources and authority to do much about it. Likewise, assigning ownership at too high a level can mean that the owner has the resources and authority but does not regard dealing with the risk as their main priority.

On some projects, risk ownership has been placed on the person who will suffer its impact. Whilst this undoubtedly gives the owner an incentive to do something about it, it does not follow that they have the necessary resources or authority and so they may not in fact be the best person to own a risk.

15.9   Other risk concepts

In this chapter we have considered risk management at a fairly simple level. However, on large projects, much more sophisticated techniques may be employed. For example, it is possible to use information in the risk register and elsewhere to construct a 'risk network'. This is rather similar to a dependency network (see Chapter 8) except that it is the interdependency of risks that is being modelled. The model is then used to address what-if questions such as: 'If the contract staff do prove to be too slow, and we apply the countermeasure of reassigning work to our own staff, what will be the impact on the project outcome?' Sampling and simulation techniques can be employed. These involve the use of probability theory to model various project outcomes depending on the likelihood, impact and interaction of the various risks. If more than simple risk management methods are to be used, it is advisable to involve specialists, with the right statistical background, to provide consultancy on the construction and interpretation of the various models.

15.10   Risk management in PRINCE2®

PRINCE2® has some guidance on the management of risk in projects. It makes a distinction between business risk and project risk. *Business risk*, which is the responsibility of the project board, relates to issues that could adversely affect the achievement of the project's business objectives: in other words, things that might damage the business case. *Project risk* is mainly what we have been discussing in this chapter: that is, those things which could prevent the achievement of the narrower project objectives.

PRINCE2® recommends that an assessment of risk should be made at the inception of a project (during preparation of the project brief or the project initiation document) and that risks should thereafter be reviewed at significant points in the lifecycle of the project, such as at the transition between stages. The project manager should comment on the pattern and status of risks as part of the regular highlight report to the project board.

Finally, PRINCE2® uses the term 'risk log' where in this chapter we have referred to a risk register, but the purpose and content of these products is much the same.

15.11 Summary

IS projects are becoming increasingly complex and are subject to various risks. Risks cannot be avoided altogether but they can be managed in such a way that they are recognised and their impacts either accepted, avoided, mitigated or transferred. There are a number of areas where project risk can arise, from business, commercial and contractual risks to technical risks.

The basic sequence for risk management is identification, assessment, and the formulation and implementation of risk-reduction actions. The approach to managing risk on a project should be documented in a formal risk management plan.

Questions

1 Why is the use of risk management techniques becoming increasingly important in IS projects?

2 Describe a five-stage process for project risk management.

3 Three factors that need to be assessed when considering risks are *likelihood*, *impact* and *urgency*. Explain what is meant by each of these terms and show how each might be assessed.

4 Two types of risk action are *avoidance actions* and *mitigation actions*. Describe the relationship between these types of risk action and where each might be employed.

5 Describe the characteristics needed in a risk owner.

Case study

During the planning stage, Richard Vaughan, the E-Con project manager, carries out a comprehensive review of the risks facing the France Vacances project. He decides to use a workshop format for this, inviting the following participants:

■ Peter Clay, France Vacances IT manager in charge of the MIS development.
■ Siobhan Reid, in charge of the internet development.

Project:	France Vacances Internet System	
Risk ID: R013	**Title:** Inability to find enough skilled internet resources	
Date raised: 2 April	**Date closed:** 5 May	
Description: The success of this project is critically dependent on quickly gaining access to sufficient skilled internet resources. Although E-Con is a specialist company in this area, recent successes in winning work have meant that its resource pool is stretched and there is a possibility that resort will have to be made to contract staff (of less known quality) to fill any gaps.		
Impact description:	Delay in developing internet aspects of the project; delay to overall timescale of project.	
Impact assessment:	Large/~~Moderate/Small~~	
Likelihood:	High/~~Medium/Low~~	
Urgency:	Very urgent as project has short timescale.	
Risk owner:	Siobhan Reid	
Action history:		
Date	Action	
2 April	Establish final resource requirement and negotiate with E-Con resources manager; ideally switch resources from other projects and replace with contractors.	
10 April	Experienced staff obtained from less urgent project; gaps to be back-filled by experienced contract staff.	
5 May	Risk reviewed at checkpoint meeting. RETIRED.	

Figure 15.4 Extract from France Vacances internet project risk register

Case study continued

- David George, an E-Con principal consultant and an expert on internet technologies (and their problems).
- The project assurance team consisting of Helen Winter, Mark Southam, Gail Hardie and Norman Pierce.

Using a brainstorming technique, the group identifies 65 potential risks to the project, some technical, some commercial and some to do with resources. They categorise these by scale of impact (large, moderate, small) and by likelihood of occurrence (high, medium, low) and conclude that six risks come into the dangerous large/high category. One of these is risk 15, which relates to E-Con's ability to find enough skilled internet resources quickly enough. The risk register (risk log in PRINCE2®) entry is shown in Figure 15.4.

It will be noticed that E-Con is being extremely candid in admitting to this risk and to its difficulties in finding resources. Richard Vaughan, however, believes in working openly with his clients and that the risk management process will not work properly without such openness. In return, France Vacances staff also admit to some risks about their own lack of clarity in being able to define what they want their new system to do, and this mutual candour helps to create a good working relationship.

Avoidance actions and fallback measures are identified for each risk and owners assigned to deal with them. In the case of the resourcing risk, Siobhan Reid is tasked with negotiating for staff from E-Con's resource manager and, as we have already seen in the checkpoint meeting, this proves successful and the risk is retired.

It is agreed that a review of risks will be a regular agenda item at the weekly checkpoint meetings and other interested parties are encouraged to notify potential risks to Richard Vaughan whenever they arise.

Further reading

Boyce, Tim (1995), *Commercial Risk Management*, Thorogood

Jones, Capers (1994), *Assessment and Control of Software Risks*, Yourdon Press

Kendrick, Tom (2003), *Identifying and Managing Project Risk*, Amacom

Raftery, John (1994), *Risk Analysis in Project Management*, E&FN Spon

Simon, Peter, Hillson, David and Newland, Ken (1997), *PRAM Guide*, Association for Project Management, High Wycombe, UK

16 Value engineering and value management

16.1 Introduction

This chapter presents a brief introduction to the topics of value engineering and value management. It is brief since these techniques have not, to date, been widely applied to the information systems field. Where they have been used, mainly in the building/construction and motor/engineering industries, they have been found to yield significant benefits in terms of projects meeting their objectives and producing viable returns on investment. The concept of stakeholders in a new systems project and the ideas of value management additionally offer some new opportunities for project managers to explore when dealing with cost/benefit issues.

Value engineering dates back to the 1940s and is concerned with the achievement of a project's functional objectives at minimum cost, whilst ensuring that the constraints of time, quality, performance and reliability are met. The basic concept is that, for a given problem or requirement, there are various possible solutions that can be evaluated and compared on the basis of their costs. With the achievement of the functional objectives being a constant requirement for all viable solutions, the one that is adopted will be the one that costs least – in other words, the one that offers the maximum value. Value engineering is a disciplined process that follows a definite lifecycle. This is shown in Figure 16.1.

The process starts with a definition of the problem, or a specification of the requirement that is to be met. Then, alternative design solutions are generated and these are evaluated on the basis of whether or not they will meet the requirement. Those that are most feasible are developed further, with the emphasis on finding approaches that meet the requirement at minimum cost. Finally, again on the basis of cost, one of the approaches is selected as the design solution.

Value engineering can be applied to the whole of a project – to the design of a complete motor car, for example – or to the design of individual components. In a sense, it is easier to apply at the component level, since the specification of the component in terms of its size, materials and performance will have been defined quite explicitly and the designers can concentrate on how to meet the specification at minimum cost.

Figure 16.1 The value engineering approach

As an example of value engineering, consider the case of motor vehicle heating systems where the hoses always used to be secured with screw-operated Jubilee clips. These are quite expensive, so some manufacturers decided that an acceptable performance could be achieved by using simpler spring-wire clips instead. Although this represents a small saving in itself, the application of the same regime throughout the design of the vehicle can produce a considerable reduction in the overall costs of manufacture.

Once the original design has been subjected to the value engineering discipline, the management of the project is constrained by the same regime with changes, for example, being evaluated on the basis of their cost compared with the value of altered objectives. Value engineering is also often used in trying to 'rescue' a project that is facing unacceptable cost overruns. Here, a rigorous examination is made of each aspect of the project to see if anything can be done more cheaply and still meet the project's objectives in terms of time, cost and quality. An underlying assumption of value engineering is therefore that there is agreement among the various stakeholders on the project's functional objectives.

Value management is a more recent development on the value engineering theme and recognises the common problem that, at least in its early stages, there may not be general agreement on the project's functional objectives. In this case, it is not possible to compare alternative solutions solely in terms of the cost of carrying them out; they also need to be evaluated in terms of the value of functionality that they each offer.

To appreciate the difference between these approaches, consider the following scenario. An organisation wishes to introduce a new payroll system. The stakeholders are the organisation's finance director, payrolls manager and IT manager, and they agree that the new system should offer the same facilities as the old one but require fewer staff to operate it. In this case, the functional objectives are clear enough and the possible solutions – for example, in-house development, contracting the work to a consultancy, buying a ready-made package – can readily be compared in terms of cost. Traditional value engineering would support this comparison. However, consider what would happen if the stakeholders actually had different objectives, for example:

- The finance director wishes to reduce the overall cost of payroll processing. With this objective, one option might be to outsource the whole payroll operation.
- The payrolls manager wishes to expand the scope of her operation and therefore wants a new system that will cover personnel and pension administration systems in addition to payroll.
- The IT manager is pursuing an open systems strategy and so is mainly interested in technical solutions that support this approach.

Unless these objectives can be reconciled, it will not be possible to define a set of functional objectives against which the various solutions can be compared in terms of cost. Value management techniques can be used to develop and agree a set of defined objectives – with, perhaps, different weights being given to the various requirements – as well as to carry out the necessary comparison of costs with benefits.

Value management can thus be seen to be most useful to the project manager at the start of a project, when the objectives may be ill-defined and where there are many possible solutions. However, it can also be used as the project develops to help refine and select among the various options that will arise.

16.2 An approach to value management in projects

The basic approach of value management is illustrated in Figure 16.2. It can be seen at once that this is a more complex model than that for value engineering and this reflects the fact that, because it is trying to deal with uncertainty, value management necessarily requires an iterative approach. Although we have shown iteration only between consecutive stages, there could well be other iterations; the evaluation of solutions may, for example, cause you to revisit the 'value tree' (Figure 16.3). In addition, value management is concerned with identifying the value, as well as the cost, of the different design approaches.

The starting point for value management is the identification of the stakeholders in the project. To continue with our payroll system scenario, we have already identified that the finance director, payrolls manager and IT manager will be stakeholders, but there might be others interested in the project as well.

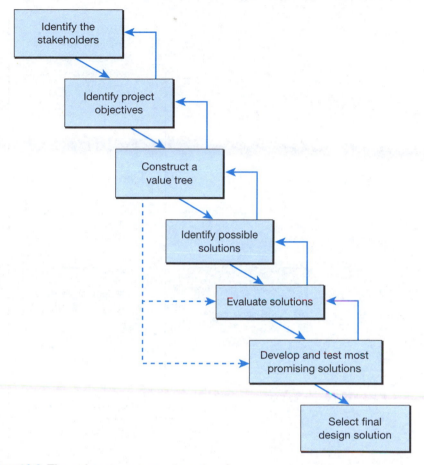

Figure 16.2 The value management approach

For example, there may be a personnel director who will want to ensure that no industrial relations problems will result from changes to the way the payroll is processed. There could be staff bodies, works councils or trade unions who will be concerned at the employment implications of the change. There could be a telecommunications manager interested in the infrastructures needed to support a different sort of system. The point is that, unless all of the stakeholders are identified and brought into the discussions at an early stage, the project's objectives will be incompletely defined and this is almost bound to invalidate to some extent the decisions made. This reinforces what we said earlier in the book about the importance of proper organisation for project management.

With the stakeholders identified, they are next asked to define and discuss their objectives for the project. The best environment for this is probably a workshop session, but this will have to be facilitated very skilfully to be effective. With the list of raw objectives on the table, agreement next needs to be reached on the overall objective of the entire project. Agreeing this will probably require a lot of discussion, even argument, but it is vital that this objective

273

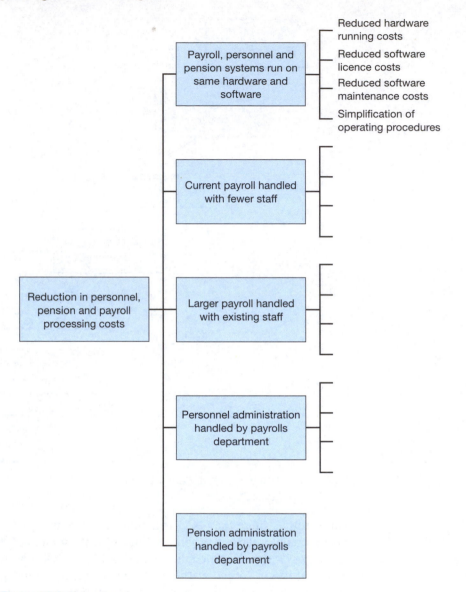

Figure 16.3 Value tree

is identified. Once it is, the overall objective can be broken down into sub-objectives which can be represented as a value tree. This is somewhat like a work breakdown structure or product breakdown structure, discussed in Chapter 8, and an example is shown in Figure 16.3.

We have assumed that the various stakeholders in our payrolls project example have agreed that the overall objective of the project should be reduced costs for running the payroll, personnel and pensions systems. Subsidiary objectives of this include the ability to handle the current payroll with fewer staff, or a larger payroll with the same staff, and the ability to run all of the systems on the same hardware and software. Each of these can be broken down further and we have identified sub-subobjectives for the IS elements.

Next, the list of objectives is reviewed and evaluated and each is subjected to the question: 'how can it be addressed?' Combining the solutions to each objective produces an initial list of possible overall designs; these are then evaluated to get an initial idea of the costs and benefits of each. Once the outline costs are available, the value tree is revisited to see how well each proposal meets each objective. To do this, we need to decide how the various objectives compare with each other in terms of priority; some will be essential, others useful and others just nice to have. The best way of dealing with this is to rate each objective on a scale of 1 to 10. Then, each proposal can be scored against each objective, perhaps in percentage terms. These two assessments, the relative weight of the objective and its percentage achievement, can then be used to rate the proposals against each other and decide which ones best meet the objectives set for the project. Finally, with the effectiveness of each option assessed on a comparable basis, the costs of each option are also compared to get a final cost/benefit comparison which can be used to make a shortlist of options to be developed in more detail.

The value management cycle is then repeated once the shortlisted designs have been developed further. The objectives will not have to be created all over again, but they should be revisited to check that they are still valid and that, for example, none of the stakeholders has changed their mind. The development of each design will produce a more defined view of its features so that it will now be possible to say with more certainty how well each of the original objectives is likely to be met. In addition, with the designs more clearly defined, a more accurate assessment can be made of the likely costs of proceeding with each. The costs and benefits of each solution are then compared and a final decision is made on which way to proceed.

There are two main benefits claimed for the use of value management. The first, and perhaps most important, is that the technique of involving all of the stakeholders in the definition and quantification of the project's objectives means that there is greater consensus about the goals of the project and greater 'buy-in' from the participants. This greatly improves the project's chances of meeting the stakeholders' expectations. The second benefit is that the selection of the solution has been based upon as rigorous an assessment as possible of the possibilities so that there is an improved likelihood that the right solution has been chosen.

Once the project is under way, value management offers other opportunities. The techniques used for the identification and quantification of objectives, and for the evaluation of alternative solutions, can also be applied to potential changes. Here, the aim would be to build consensus on whether the changes are really required and, if they are, what value should be placed on them. A clear advantage of this is that the project's original goals, in terms of producing value for the business, can be kept in mind and can provide a useful check on the possibility of uncontrolled – and perhaps unjustified – expansion of the project's scope.

Value management clearly has something to offer the IS practitioner. Most IS projects suffer from some initial uncertainty as to their precise objectives and the value management technique provides a vehicle for securing consensus on those objectives. It also provides a disciplined structure for evaluating and selecting among approaches. Once the objectives have been defined, the value engineering approach can be applied to rigorously scrutinise each component of the project to ensure that it meets its requirements most cost-effectively.

16.3 Summary

Both value management and value engineering are concerned with the achievement of the project's functional objectives – expressed in terms of time-scale, quality, performance and reliability – at the least cost. Traditional value engineering is predicated on the assumption that there is consensus on the project's objectives and that the only variable is the cost at which the objectives can be met. Value management recognises the greater complexity of projects and the fact that there will almost certainly be multiple stakeholders with differing perspectives on the project's objectives. Value management therefore offers an approach to the development of agreed objectives and the selection of project solutions that can meet those objectives most cost-effectively.

Questions

1 Explain the difference between value management and value engineering.

2 What is meant by the term 'value tree'?

3 How can value management be used to compare different possible design solutions?

4 Once a project is under way, how can value management be used to evaluate proposed changes?

Further reading

Crum, L W (1971), *Value Engineering: The Organised Search for Value*, Longman

Green, S D (1994), 'Beyond value engineering: SMART value management for building projects', *International Journal of Project Management*, Vol. 12, No. 1

Miles, L D (1972), *Techniques of Value Analysis and Engineering*, 2nd edn, McGraw-Hill

17

Selling the project

17.1 Introduction

This chapter is not intended to try to turn you into a salesperson. Its purpose and that of the one that follows is to give you some understanding about why people buy, about what made them decide to have you manage their system project, and, having begun the project, how you can manage the customers to create a helpful and profitable environment for your project. The three things we examine in this chapter are:

- Why people buy; how buyers make purchasing decisions; the different kinds of buyers.
- The selling process and how to make proposals that are persuasive.
- Negotiating and how to reach an agreement that works for both parties.

Why are these three things important for project managers? Let us look at some of the 'sales' situations you could find yourself in.

- At one extreme, you are a project manager working for a supplier of professional services of some kind, such as consultancy, project management, software development, outsourcing or software products. Your company is bidding to a prospect to supply its services. You are involved, as a project manager, for several reasons. Firstly, many bid teams find it useful to have the potential delivery project manager as part of the team. It helps to avoid an overenthusiastic sales approach resulting in the promise of unachievable goals in terms of cost, delivery dates or functionality if delivery people are involved in the sale. Secondly, if your company wins the bid, doing so will partly be the result of you and the prospect hitting it off on a personal basis. You do not have to like each other but you do need mutual respect. Also, your experience of running this kind of project will influence the offering: you know the pitfalls. The prospect will get something extra from your company, namely your experience of having been through it before. So, you are not leading the sale but you have an important part to play in it. You contribute to the achievement of winning the sale.
- Now the project is under way. You and your team are probably spending a lot of time with the client and meeting people at all levels throughout the organisation. Soon you know far more about what really happens in the

client's business than your sales team does. By luck or skilful exploration you uncover some new potential opportunities. Who is best placed to scope this potential new business? You are; knowing something about the sales process will be invaluable. This is true whether you are from an external services supplier or from the central, internal IS department. The ability to explore new opportunities and to firmly establish needs in the users' minds will be valuable to you as a project manager.

■ All projects are subject to changes in requirements. The common mistake is to regard these as problems rather than opportunities. Every change opens the door to an opportunity to be creative, technically and commercially, and to explore with the user how better to deliver to their real needs. Project managers face the danger of identifying too closely with the work that has already been done – and may now need to be changed; with the technical solutions already reached – that may now need to be discarded; with the efforts of their team – that may now be wasted. This is natural. The project manager is, after all, a team manager responsible for maintaining the spirit of the team; experiencing the team's hopes and frustrations is part of this team maintenance. This inward-looking approach needs to be balanced by an outward view that recognises the need to meet changing user requirements and to take advantage of them to win benefits, tangible and intangible, for the project and for the team.

Let us now see this sales process through the customer's or user's eyes. Effective selling begins with an understanding of how people buy.

17.2 Buying and buyers

It is easy to believe that every project is different and that the buying decisions that people make for your project are unique. This is a convenient excuse when things go wrong, but research shows that all buyers go through clearly identified stages when they buy. This buying cycle applies irrespective of what is being bought. Think about how you make important purchasing decisions yourself. Let us imagine that you are going to buy a car. What went through your mind before you decided to replace your existing car? Perhaps you had some problems with it. It let you down occasionally. Sometimes it caused you serious difficulties: you were late for meetings or social events, or you were stranded in dangerous areas. Eventually you decide that you need to do something. Your options include substantial repairs to the car, buying a newer used model, leasing a car or buying a new one. After you have determined which option to take, you still have some residual worries: can you trust the dealer's warranty, what will family and colleagues think of your choice? The stages you go through in buying a car are in essence the same as those made by buyers of professional services. As buying decisions become more complex and the cost of the service to be purchased rises, more time is taken before a final decision is reached. Let us look at these stages.

We begin with a recognition of needs. The customer recognises that there are problems and imperfections with the current situation. The existing systems do not work properly, they do not deliver what is needed, business needs have changed. During this stage, buyers assess their current problems and their severity. They begin to specify their new needs and a decision is taken to solve the problem. This is where you have the opportunity to help the customer to identify problems, clarify them and develop them into clearly stated and recognisably important needs. Now the buyer begins to evaluate what options there are to finding an acceptable solution. During this time, buyers measure different solutions, using formal and informal means, against the decision criteria they have established. They are looking for the best fit between their view of their requirements and the solutions they are offered. Eventually a choice is made. This follows a final resolution of concerns by the buyer: 'Now, can you be quite sure that the team will include project manager A and chief designer B?', and perhaps some final negotiation. So a decision is made and implementation begins. This is where the project manager plays the main part. The buyer is still worried about whether or not the right choice has been made and hopes never to have to say, 'Well, they were clearly the best choice when we had to decide. I can't understand why it's all going so wrong now.' The project manager is the key person in ensuring that the buyer's decision is always the right one. This activity is so important that the next chapter is devoted to it. Finally, no solution remains perfect for ever. New dissatisfactions arise, new needs are identified and the whole process begins again. This cycle is shown in Figure 17.1.

So far in this section we have talked about 'the customer' or 'the buyer' as if it were one person, but systems development projects are often substantial, expensive, risky and have far-reaching consequences. In these circumstances it is unlikely that the decision to buy will be made by one person. Many buying decisions are made by committees that do not march in step through the buying cycle. For example:

- Some may see no need for what you are offering.
- Some may think that the problems need a different solution.
- Some will be concerned at the expense involved.
- Some may be concerned about the implementation and the management of change.
- There may be internal politics between certain of the decision-makers.

Often there are four influences at work:

- Firstly, there will be one person who has the final responsibility for making the decision. We can call this person the economic decision-maker, since they have the authority to spend the budget, to commit finances to solving this problem. This individual will almost certainly take advice from others but in the end he or she eventually pays for the solution, for the new system that you will be managing into production. The economic buyer is concerned with costs and benefits.

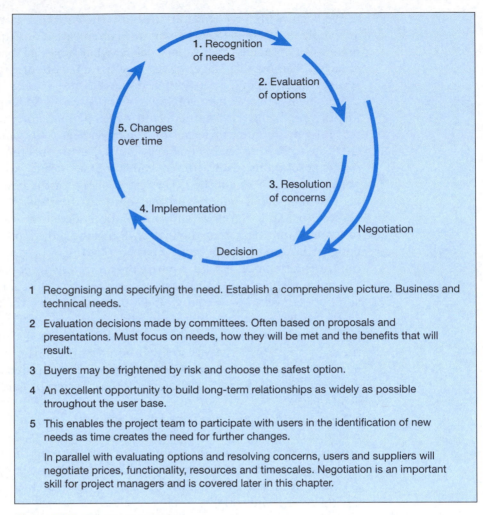

1 Recognising and specifying the need. Establish a comprehensive picture. Business and technical needs.

2 Evaluation decisions made by committees. Often based on proposals and presentations. Must focus on needs, how they will be met and the benefits that will result.

3 Buyers may be frightened by risk and choose the safest option.

4 An excellent opportunity to build long-term relationships as widely as possible throughout the user base.

5 This enables the project team to participate with users in the identification of new needs as time creates the need for further changes.

In parallel with evaluating options and resolving concerns, users and suppliers will negotiate prices, functionality, resources and timescales. Negotiation is an important skill for project managers and is covered later in this chapter.

Figure 17.1 The buying cycle

- Secondly, there are technical experts who explore the technical merits of your solution, the skills and experience that you bring. They may of course be IT specialists but could equally be application area specialists, personnel people or accountants. The technical buyer is concerned with functionality.
- Thirdly, there are the users of the system that you will deliver. They have an indirect influence on the decision to buy. Solutions proposed or ways of developing solutions should be presented in their terms and follow implementation plans that fit into their business cycle. The end-users are concerned about how it will affect them.
- Finally, there is a buyer who supports you and helps you to propose a winning solution. Often called the champion or coach, they are on your side and want your solution to be chosen. Perhaps your solution accords with theirs, perhaps you have worked together successfully before, perhaps your solution will result in greater status or influence for the coach. Few competitive bids are won without at least one inside coach or champion.

17.3 The selling process

In the lifetime of a project there will be many opportunities to sell. We are not talking here of big new investments in new projects, but of small additional features to the system or changes to the way that the project is being run so that it suits the customer better. The principles are the same for each kind of sale, small, large or in-between. It is tempting to think of selling as a 'telling process'. The seller tells the potential buyer about the wonderful features of the product or service. It is tempting, but wrong. Selling is an asking process. People who are most successful in selling systems development projects or consultancy assignments are those who ask lots of questions. They ask questions about:

- *The customer's situation.* What happens now and how it works. 'Could you describe for me how you record the orders when they come in and how these records generate the invoices at the end of the month?'
- *The customer's problems.* 'So, sometimes then, the invoices are wrong because there have been mistakes when the orders were taken.'
- *The implications of the problems.* 'If the invoices are wrong then you have to raise credit notes then re-invoice. There must be a cost in doing this. How badly does it affect the cash flow? Is there an impact on customer satisfaction? Does it also mean that you supply the wrong product? What is the impact of this on production and stocks?'
- *The payoff or benefit from meeting the needs.* 'Suppose, then, that the order-taking system were reliable, how would that benefit you?' 'If orders could be analysed by customer, how could that help to increase sales?' And so on.

In short, the seller seeks to explore all aspects of the problem and aims to encourage the buyer to identify all the problems of the present situation, the implications of those problems and their financial impact, in order to establish that there is a clear value in having a solution developed for the buyer. Steadily and progressively the seller seeks to build up in the mind of the buyer a greater and greater need for a solution. We mentioned earlier in this chapter that there is not just one single buyer: there are economic buyers, technical buyers and so on. Different needs must be built up for the different buyers, so the kinds of questions asked will also be different.

The whole approach behind 'selling by asking questions' is built on the realisation that, when we identify a problem ourselves, explore all its aspects, its implications and the consequences, we build up a powerful need for something, or someone, to solve the problem for us. Couple this with the fact that we have been taken through this process by a skilled diagnostician and it is easy to see how we are ready to accept ideas for a solution. Readers wishing to learn more about this approach should contact the Huthwaite Research Group whose address is listed in the Further Reading at the end of this chapter.

Eventually, the point is reached where the potential buyer says something like, 'That's very interesting. Could you send me a proposal along those lines? I'd like to take it further.' If your proposal is for a new television franchise then you will need a luggage trolley to deliver it; if it is to change the time of the weekly project team meeting you will need one sheet of A4. Let us use as our model a proposal from the project team that additional work needs to be done to more fully explore some aspect of the business and to re-examine the conclusions about it. At first sight, this will involve additional work and increase the cost, but it could lead to a reduction in rework later and to an improved solution that will better meet user needs. It is not a big additional task but it is significant enough to require authorisation from the user for the extra work. A proposal is required. The foundations of an effective proposal are:

- Appearance
- Content
- Structure

and we need to use each of these foundations to help us to secure our goal.

The appearance of the proposal can do a lot to make it look professional and interesting. Pictures, graphics and diagrams can break a lengthy text and emphasise points for the reader. Good presentation makes the proposal attractive to the eye, helps the reader to retain the content and helps to make the content accessible. It is, however, of much less importance than the content in helping to make the sale.

The content may be intended to inform or persuade. If we are concerned with the simple reporting of facts following an investigation then we are principally concerned with informing. In our example here, however, we are trying to persuade the customer to authorise some new work. In a 'persuading' document we will talk primarily about the interests of the customer and will show an understanding of their concerns and of the implications of those concerns. It will demonstrate how the adoption of the proposed solution will help to solve the difficulties or dangers identified and it will explore the benefits accruing from making the decision.

The key to a persuasive proposal is to relate it as much as possible to what the customer has already said. For our example we might structure our proposal into:

- *The customer situation*. Keep it brief. Describing in detail everything everyone already knows is tedious and turns the customer off. Something along the lines of: 'We studied the X department procedure relating to Y. We found that . . . and the conclusions were . . . On that basis it was agreed that . . . Changed business circumstances now seem to show . . . Consequently some of the agreed conclusions may be invalid.'
- *Potential problems*. Here is where you deal with the problems that will arise if the project continues as planned when we now know that earlier work may be invalid and need to be redone. What are the implications? What are the possible future costs if the changed business circumstances do show up new needs and we have to do rework later? Remember that you will have discussed all of this with key users so you will not be building up a fragile case. The situation and the problems will be understood and will have been articulated by the user.

- *The needs as stated by the customer.* This will state the needs for a solution and the resolution of the present uncertainty.
- *A proposed solution.* By this stage it should be clear that a solution is needed and the present circumstances cannot be allowed to continue. It is best to concentrate on those aspects of the solution that fit most closely to the users' needs. Summarise the solution by restating how the solution solves current problems and brings future benefits. State the cost of doing the work.

To assess your proposal, work with a colleague to determine whether your proposal:

■ Recaps more or less the terms of reference	*or*	Shows an understanding of customers' concerns and their implications
■ Emphasises the technical details of the solution	*or*	Emphasises how the proposed solution will resolve the customer's concerns
■ Emphasises advantage statements	*or*	Explores the benefits resulting from going ahead with the change
■ Addresses only one reader	*or*	Addresses all the different readers/buyers
■ Has few charts or diagrams	*or*	Has clear diagrams that show the solution clearly
■ Offers little or no navigation help to the reader	*or*	Provides clear cross-references and navigation aids
■ Gives a full and detailed breakdown of costs	*or*	Gives a clear summarised statement of costs and does not offer a range of options
■ Has no executive summary	*or*	Summarises the issues and the good news

Needless to say, your proposal should be close to the criteria in the right-hand column.

The content and structure of a persuasive proposal should follow the outline and be rated according to the list above. It will be a summary of work that has been done beforehand and should therefore contain no surprises. The content should be matched to the users' interests and concerns.

When advising professional staff about how their clients or users behave, David Maister wrote:

There is an old joke about doctors that they get fascinated with the disease, but couldn't care less about the patient. Unfortunately, this attitude and behaviour is all too prevalent in a wide array of professions. Too many professionals get overly focussed on technical matters, and lose sight of the essential relationship nature of professional transactions. This doesn't mean that technical skill is irrelevant – of course it is critical. But having technical skills is only a necessary condition for success, not a critical one. Above all else, what I, the client, am looking for, is that rare professional who has both technical skill and a *sincere desire to be helpful*, to work with both me and my problem. The key is empathy – the ability to enter my world and see it through my eyes.

17.4 Negotiation

Project managers negotiate all the time; with their team members; with their back-up people – accountants, technical experts, support people generally; and with their customers. The negotiation might be about money: more money to do more work or more money to do the originally specified work. The negotiation might be about time: more time before a deliverable can be ready, or for a delivery date that has not yet been agreed. The negotiation might be about who will do a piece of work, Fred or Jill – both project team members, the team or the user, the team or a contractor. In this section we describe a model for negotiations in general and review the use of power in negotiations.

A negotiation is a meeting between two sides, and the objective is to reach an agreement. The kind of agreement that interests us is one that is good for both parties. It is a win/win agreement where both sides win and neither side feels that it has lost. To reach this desirable outcome requires both sides to be creative about moving from their starting points to an agreed finishing point. There is a typical process that leads from start to finish, but before we examine it there are some preliminaries to consider.

There is always a climate to a negotiation. It may be a harsh climate that will create tough negotiations; a low-key climate may create long-winded negotiations that grind on and on; a creative and friendly environment may lead to new solutions and the establishment of good long-term relationships. Since the climate has such an influence on negotiation, how is it created and what can be done to build a helpful climate? Project managers will often be negotiating with people they know and with whom they have regular contact – the project team, user staff and so on. Sometimes, then, the climate will have been created by what has already happened, but there is still much that can be done in the opening moments to influence the climate. What happens now can be more powerful than what happened in the past. Other negotiations will be with people the project managers do not know – suppliers, customer or user staff they have not met before. In these circumstances, the first few minutes of the meeting can set the climate. We are concerned here about building **rapport**, and there are many things that contribute to this feeling of comfort between people. Negotiation is an interaction between people and can be affected not only by what we say and how we say it, but also by our non-verbal behaviour. The non-verbal behaviours are often grouped under the general heading of 'body language', and, whether or not we consciously recognise the different behaviours individually, we take in a lot of information in the opening moments, during the rapport-building time. We notice:

- *How the other person looks at us.* Do they look us in the eye? How long do they maintain eye contact? Do they avoid eye contact? What else is happening with their face, do they smile?
- *What kind of contact is made?* Here we really mean 'the handshake'. We are not trying to demonstrate that we have the grip of a body builder, but nor do we want to offer a 'limp fish' for the other person to grasp. How do I feel

if the other person grasps my hand with both of theirs, or holds my upper arm while shaking my hand?

■ *The overall appearance.* My overall appearance has an impact too. Is my posture confident and relaxed? Am I dressed appropriately? Am I neat and tidy?

We also need a few minutes for introductions and social chat, for ice-breaking. Just as fact-finding interviews need time for the interviewer and the interviewee to settle down together, a similar process is needed at the beginning of a negoti-ation. Through this opening behaviour, we are trying to create a 'CCBB' climate; a climate that Bill Scott in *The Skills of Constructive Negotiating* calls:

■ Cordial
■ Collaborative
■ Brisk
■ Business-like.

Eventually, with the preliminaries over, the negotiation begins. Face to face, we discuss, propose and bargain, and before any of this we will have prepared. Without thorough preparation it is easy, in the heat of the moment, to make decisions and arrive at agreements that are subsequently regretted. Personal preparation:

■ Establishes your objectives, what you want to achieve.
■ Identifies problems that may arise.
■ Identifies the advantages of your position.
■ Gives you a path to follow.
■ Helps you to feel confident.

It helps during this stage to separate out the essential objectives that you must achieve and the ones you would like to have as well but can manage without.

Fully prepared and having built a rapport with the other side we can begin the next stage in the negotiation process: discussion. Here both parties explore the other's position and create an agenda of what really needs to be negoti-ated. 'So Fred, you want to do this particular piece of work because it would be developmental for you and give you the opportunity to use the new software. On the other hand, I think that Jill should do it because she already knows the new software and she'd catch up some time for us.' For Fred then, the issue is about learning some new things and developing some new skill. It is not really that he wants to do *this* task. During the discussion stage it helps if we reduce tension, get the issues clearly stated and begin to think about how the two positions could be moved closer together. Perhaps there are other develop-ment opportunities for Fred, for example.

We now begin to propose some solutions, some offers, some claims. We get offers made to us and we make counter-offers. It should not be like a tennis match, however, with the ball of the offer and counter-offer being hit backwards and forwards over the net. It helps to explain, to refer back to the original objectives, to clarify and summarise and to reflect. Finally a bargain is reached and we agree what has been agreed.

So we have prepared, discussed, proposed and agreed and in a very simple negotiation perhaps we have gone through those stages in a linear fashion. It is more likely, however, that we have been negotiating a deal that has linked components and we have had to trade time against money, for example. In this case we would have prepared, discussed and proposed within a more complex framework and cycled through the stages of discuss, propose and bargain several times.

Where does power fit into all of this? Power means the capacity to dominate; it is what gives you competitive advantage; it is the ability to get things done your way. Power is either:

■ Personal, coming from your personal characteristics, what you know, your interpersonal skills, your mental agility and your skill in the use of power behaviours.
■ Positional, coming from your position, your authority, the organisation you work for or from some dominance in the situation.

Typically, people make assumptions about where power lies. Sellers are thought to have less power than buyers, and small companies to have less power than big ones. But this clearly is not always the case. If yours is the only supplier in the territory for a particular applications package, or if your staff are fully assigned for the next *n* months, then as a seller you will behave differently from how you would behave if your people were coming to the end of a big project without future work ready for them. Whatever your assumption about which side has the relative power in a negotiation, there are some power behaviours that you can use:

■ *Be prepared.* If you know you have a weakness or want to hide an area that the other side might probe, have your answers ready and make them powerful ones. 'Yes, I agree with you, this system change does need to be made. I'll look at people's work schedules and see when it can best be fitted in', is much more powerful than, 'All right, we'll do it straight away. Roy's not busy next week.'
■ *Have some creative option.* This is the other side of the 'be prepared' coin. By having ready some new, creative and perhaps unusual options to offer you give out a strong message of 'we've put a lot of thought into this'.
■ *Maintain control.* The person asking the questions is the one setting the agenda and moving the discussion in their preferred direction.
■ *Summarise.* People in charge summarise. Chairpersons of meetings do it; it is associated with power and status and is another aspect of maintaining control.

Developing your own negotiating style is something only you can do. You can adopt a massive power play and kill off the other party who will never do business with you again, or you can build up a long-term collaborative relationship. Whatever you do, being prepared is essential.

17.5 Summary

Project managers 'sell' all the time. They influence buyers to buy and they build the reputation of their project through their commercial skills. In this chapter we have considered the buying cycle, and the importance of 'selling by questions' has been emphasised, as has the importance of building up a clearly identified and urgent need with all of the different buyers.

We have examined the appearance, content and structure of proposals and suggested a framework for evaluating proposals.

Finally we considered negotiation and emphasised the need for preparation and the use of power behaviours, and described a simple negotiating process.

Questions

1 How would you assess the importance of sales skills for a project manager? Are they, in your view, increasing or decreasing in importance? Why do you think there is this change? Is it more important to understand selling or buying?

2 Persuading someone to buy is a complex process. Why is this? Is the process inherently complex or is it because so many people are involved?

3 If selling is an asking process, how could you use it to help you sell some extra functionality to a system under development?

Case study

As we already know, France Vacances has come to its own conclusion that it needs an effective website to retain its existing customers and to reach new ones. But how did it come to select E-Con as its preferred consultants for the internet development project?

To some extent, this was accidental. Jean-Pierre Massenet had read an article in *Accountancy Age* about web-smart companies and E-Con's marketing director had been widely quoted in the article. So, when he was discussing the internet idea with David Marsh, it seemed a natural first step to contact E-Con and ask if someone could be sent to talk to them.

This turned out to be Barbara Currie, one of E-Con's account managers, and she rapidly struck up a good working relationship with the two France Vacances directors. Instead of trying to 'sell' to them, she preferred to explore their ideas and concerns through skilful questioning, and it gradually became apparent that there was an opportunity for the two firms to work together to their mutual advantage: France Vacances would get its new website and E-Con would gain experience in the travel market where it had not hitherto operated.

Once the development project started to take shape, Barbara knew that its success would depend crucially on the ability of E-Con's project manager to get on well with the France Vacances personnel and to work with them. So, she introduced Richard Vaughan who proceeded to meet people at all levels within France Vacances and to establish working relationships with them. Mostly, this was quite straightforward but Richard had to devote special attention to Peter Clay, the IT manager. Richard realised that Peter's somewhat negative attitude was caused by his fears about his own job and the future of his small department: would they be abolished or taken over by E-Con? Richard gradually brought him to see that, far from weakening the position of IT, the introduction of the new website would place IT at the centre of France Vacances's business and Peter began to see the skills transfer possibilities of working with the specialists from E-Con.

Eventually, France Vacances asked E-Con to make a formal proposal for the development of the new website. France Vacances decided not to go out to competitive tender since its staff had by now developed a high degree of confidence in E-Con and wanted to work with them, thus vindicating Barbara Currie's relationship-building strategy. Although E-Con had the 'inside track', the company was careful not to ruin the good work done so far and submitted a very competitive proposal, which was accepted. Because of E-Con's painstaking background research into its client's requirements, E-Con was confident enough to offer a fixed-price for their parts of the development and to leave some parts for France Vacances's own IT department.

Further reading

Fisher, R and Ury, W (2003), *Getting To Yes*, Random House

Freemantle, David (1998), *What Customers Like About You*, Nicholas Brealey

Huthwaite Research Group, Hoober House, Wentworth, Rotherham S62 7SA, UK

Miller, Robert and Heiman, Stephen E (1988), *Strategic Selling: Secrets of the Complex Sale*, Kogan Page

Rackham, Neil (1989), *Major Account Sales Strategy*, McGraw-Hill

Rackham, Neil (1995), *SPIN Selling*, Gower

Scott, Bill (1996), *The Skills of Constructive Negotiating*, Gower

18 Managing stakeholders

18.1 Introduction

Throughout this book we have explored the full extent of the project manager's job, from the need to understand something about business strategy to the need to select and develop the project team. In this chapter we deal with stakeholder management issues: how one best manages all of the stakeholders so that everyone has realistic expectations, feels successful at the end of the project and maintains enough sanity and goodwill to see the benefit in working together again.

We begin by exploring the concept of business stakeholders and project stakeholders and examine some strategies for managing project stakeholders. Particular attention is paid to the customer stakeholder as the customer is often seen as the main stakeholder. In this context it is possible to deal with managing customer expectations, how to deal with customer relations issues around changes and variations to a project, the need to manage conflict and the importance of networking. All of this becomes theoretical, however, unless you have the skills you need, so we also consider some practical interpersonal skills such as managing conflict, establishing rapport, active listening, and networking.

18.2 Stakeholders

Stakeholders are individuals and groups who are affected by the activities of an organisation. This organisation can be a global company, a local government body, a project team or a football club. Stakeholders are people who have an interest in the activities of some other organised group of people because they expect to be affected by them. Let us look at this first from an organisation's point of view.

A profit-making enterprise has internal and external stakeholders. The internal stakeholders are the people who work for it. They may not all be seen as having the same kind of stake as there may be differences between old and young employees, male and female, ethnic minorities, disabled employees, managers as opposed to employees generally, employees who are shareholders or who have share options, board members and so on. So, employees in general certainly have a stake in the business and could be said to have the most to lose from the firm's actions. This does not mean that they have the most power, however. There are external stakeholders who have an interest or stake in the enterprise. They could be individual shareholders, although they have to own a significant part of the shareholding to make much difference. Managers of institutional shareholdings make a difference, however, and investor relations activities seek to manage these pension fund or investment trust stakeholders. Suppliers also have a stake in the business, as do governments, local communities, pressure groups, industry regulators and the general public. As we see in Figure 18.1, stakeholders and the organisation have an exchange relationship where stakeholders provide resources of one kind or another in exchange for a return from the organisation.

Typical stakeholders are:

- *Customers* for whom our organisation provides products or services. They are stakeholders because every change we make has a potential positive or negative impact on them. We manage the customer stakeholders by advertising, publicity, loyalty schemes, discount cards, websites, seeking feedback and providing regular communication about what we are doing.

Figure 18.1 Stakeholders and the exchange relationship
(Adapted from C W L Hill and G R Jones, *Strategic Management*, Houghton Mifflin, 2001)

- *Suppliers* who provide us with the goods and services that we use. Suppliers are stakeholders because we are important to their business and our business health impacts on theirs. Also, they have an interest in the way we interact with them in the procurement and payment processes. Changes here have a direct impact on our relationship with suppliers. Expecting suppliers not only to receive all of our orders but also to change from paper-based systems to electronic ones needs to be managed carefully.

- *Competitors* have a keen interest in the changes we make to our business and may adopt tactics to reduce or to negate the benefits that we had planned to gain.

- *Regulators*. There is an increasing trend in the UK for business to be regulated. This applies to professions, the media, privatised utilities, the financial services sector and in other areas. In October 2003, the Better Regulation Task Force study found that there were 108 existing regulators in the UK and called for rationalisation, citing examples of poor and ineffective regulation in the ever-growing number of regulators across industry sectors (reported in the *Financial Times*, 15 October 2003).

- *Shareholders*, whether individuals or the proxy shareholders who manage financial funds, have a stake in the financial future of the company.

- *Employees* clearly have an interest in the way the business is run and in the changes it makes. Their livelihoods are at stake in many cases and sometimes their health and their pensions too.

- *Managers* too have a stake. Firstly, they are employees and so have the same stake as other employees; but, secondly, as the people charged with the direction of the company they stake their reputation on the decisions they make.

This same process of stakeholder identification and assessment applies to projects.

Agreeing success criteria with all of the stakeholders is an important determinant of project success. In the mid 1990s, research published in the *International Journal of Project Management* about IS projects asked sponsors, users, designers and project managers to recall recent projects they had worked on and to say whether, in their opinion, these projects were successful or not and which criteria they had used to make their judgements. On successful projects, all groups identified the same success criterion: that the project should provide value to the sponsor. On unsuccessful projects, these different groups of stakeholders wanted to achieve different things. It should therefore be an early objective for a project manager to get from the project stakeholders a clear set of success criteria for the project. This does not mean that all the stakeholders will have the same objectives; they are unlikely to have the same 'stake' in the project. It does mean, however, that some stakeholder analysis can be done and linked to the risk analysis for the project.

The first step is to assess the importance or weight to be given to each stakeholder. This is usually plotted on a matrix showing the power of the stakeholders and their interest in the organisation, project or activity. The idea of plotting the power and interest of stakeholders in this way was first introduced

Figure 18.2 Mapping stakeholders' power and interests

(Adapted from G Johnson and K Scholes, *Exploring Corporate Strategy: Text and Cases*, 6th edn, FT/Prentice Hall, 2002)

as a tool for examining organisational strategy by Gerry Johnson and Kevan Scholes in 1999. We show in Figure 18.2 how this power and interest can be mapped so that practical steps can be taken to manage each category of share-holder. We might ask a few questions to help us decide on appropriate courses of action:

- How can we influence this group of stakeholders to support the project?
- What kind of support do we want from them?
- What will the project deliver to meet their concerns?
- How could they demonstrate their lack of support? What recourse do we have if this occurs?

The matrix allows stakeholders to be grouped into four categories shown as A, B, C and D. Each of these categories should be treated differently.

A *High power but low interest.* Stakeholders in this quadrant can have a signific-ant impact on the project should they choose to use their power. They could be senior managers on the fringe of the project whose departments are not really affected and who are not really concerned about the direction the project is taking. Project changes that take it in their direction can change this level of interest. The usual stakeholder management approach here is to keep them informed and up to date about the project, emphasising the minimal impact on their activities. In some circumstances, however, just the opposite approach may be best. Getting a powerful but neutral stake-holder to support the project can be a force for success if it means that new resources become available or others take notice of that person's support. In general, though, this group of stakeholders does not occupy the project manager too much, so it is a 'minimal effort' approach that is followed.

B *High power and high interest.* These are the key stakeholders for the project. They are directly interested and usually involved in the project and have the power to move it on or hold it back, declare it a success or a failure. They are often the managers of the departments involved, the technical authorities for the project, or important corporate functions such as audit or finance. Some assessment needs to be made to determine whether these stakeholders are positive about the project or negative. Those with a positive view should be nursed so that this view continues, and those who are negative need to be convinced to change by having their concerns addressed as far as possible. The support of a low interest/high power supporter may help here.

C *High interest but low power*. Many people fall into this category. They are directly affected by the project but are unable to exert much influence on its shape or direction. This can result in frustration with the project and subsequently in passive resistance to its implementation. In this case these people act like a drag anchor, always pulling the project down. It is well worth doing something about it. It is also worth remembering that people with low power can do things to increase their power by banding together or by publicising their concerns or objections. This group of stakeholders needs to be kept informed, but not in a passive way. An active campaign must be devised to address their concerns and to sell the project to them. Line management has an important role here, helping the project manager by being honest about the need for the change – and the negative consequences of not making it. Frequent and focused communication is required.

D *Low interest and low power*. These people have neither a direct interest in the project not any real power to affect it. It is tempting to ignore this group, but remembering that stakeholders can change positions on the map, occasional briefings about what is happening will be welcomed and prove useful.

It is clear then that the client or customer is not the only stakeholder in an IS/IT project, but he or she is the one whom the project manager is expected to manage on a day-to-day basis. For this reason, then, we now examine the relationship with the customer in more detail and ask, who is the customer? We subsequently look at managing expectations, managing changes to the requirement and managing conflict, and suggest some stakeholder management skills.

18.3 Who is the customer?

This could appear to be an obvious question. However, in many projects it becomes clear that there will be a variety of customers you need to manage. For example:

- You may be working on a project where the customer is another organisation – an external customer. They agree a contract with your company that defines the scope of work and how they will pay the bills. You may personally have some contact with them or it may be through other people in your organisation.
- You may work for an 'internal customer'. This might be your own IS manager who has given you a part of a contract to complete. In turn your IS manager may have a contract, or service-level agreement, to supply services

to the rest or other parts of the organisation. You will be part of that delivery team. Therefore, there may be several layers of 'customers'. Another type of internal customer may be another department or division or team in your organisation that needs your support. For example, a sales or marketing team may rely on your support in order to make a bid for some work. They will depend on your expertise and advice in order to win new business.

■ Your customer may be the end-user. You need to be sensitive to all of the trials and tribulations, concerns and gripes that come from using systems in a practical, everyday way. Think of yourself and your demands when you buy a new piece of software or an appliance for your home. You want the product to work with a minimum of effort and you want the maximum amount of support should the thing go wrong. End-users often feel that senior managers are insensitive to their needs and the problems they face. They believe that managers are divorced from the 'coal face'. Those with direct customer contact often need to be handled with extra sensitivity and given practical, but realistic, solutions. They can feel like neglected step-children, but neglect them at your peril – they are usually the key in implementing a successful project.

It is important to establish for customers, just as we have done for stakeholders:

■ Who are the customers?
■ What does each stand to gain?
■ What does each stand to lose?
■ Where can you get this information?
■ Do you have a plan for each of them?

Establishing the correct organisational structure, as discussed in Chapter 4, can help in this initial customer identification stage.

18.4 Managing expectations

Each customer is different in his or her expectations of you, the project manager. Those expectations are based on rational or irrational notions. For example, the customer may have worked with you before, had a good or bad experience and will expect more of the same this time. You or the company you work for may have a certain reputation in your field that might be based on word of mouth, personal experience or facts and figures that support your place in the market. You may be the only show in town and have a monopoly on what the customer needs – they may resent you for your price and their lack of choice. Customers approach you and you approach the customer with many unspoken expectations that colour the ways in which you deal with one another. Assumptions may be perilous. There are many examples of assumptions and expectations that have not been discussed and clarified early in a project that have come back to haunt it later on. If they are not dealt with openly, unrealistic expectations may break down what could otherwise have been a highly successful project.

Expectations are created by things that can be controlled and things that are less controllable. Together they equal customer expectations. We can divide controllable expectations into short-term and long-term expectations. Short-term controllable expectations can include such things as:

- *Sales promises* – the salesperson or your IS manager has agreed that the system will be able to do this function and that function and the customer expects that it will.
- *Marketing* – perhaps there has been an advertising campaign and your product or service has been portrayed as all-singing, all-dancing and one that can be installed overnight.
- *The nature of your products and services* – are they cutting-edge or relatively conservative?
- *First impressions* – you look professional, have good references and say that you can deliver.

Long-term controllable expectations include:

- *Innovation in products and services* – stick with us and we will give you the benefit of our research and development, our ability to keep up to date with new developments in technology and the fact that we intend to stay one step ahead.
- *Marketing efforts* – that promote a growing involvement in your customer's sector.
- *Long-term quality standards* – these demonstrate a commitment to quality. They must not only have a proven track record but also support the need for good procedures which give the customer confidence.

In truth, it may be difficult for a customer to change suppliers because of a high level of sophistication and past commitment from the supplier. Initial agreements were seen as long term and significant investment was made with that in mind. That long-term view will colour the customer's expectations. As project manager, you will need to be doubly sure that the relationship is not jeopardised over petty issues that might cloud these longer-term objectives.

The less controllable expectations are driven more by the market and might be created by competitors who are interested in taking the customer away from you. If you are the internal IS department you may find yourself competing with external suppliers keen to sell a different solution. They may go to great lengths to do that by marketing, advertising and positioning themselves with the customer in a more advantageous relationship. By word of mouth, individuals may say positive or negative things about you: they may be other satisfied customers who will sing your praises; they may be ex-employees who were made redundant, found incompetent, missed out on a bonus and hence wish to run you down; or a friend of a friend who thinks you are terrific, and so on.

The customer may lie behind most of the fundamental problems that develop in many projects. Expectations should be clearly defined at the start of a project and should be revisited at regular formal and informal points throughout the project. The risk of misunderstanding, confusion and conflict runs high if this is not done.

Managing directors also have preferences and think that the system should 'just work a certain way'. They have it in their head that it will be done in a certain manner and have not checked whether this is reasonable. This can be a problem if there is a gap between the customer's expectation and the reality that you will deliver. This gap ultimately reflects the level of customer (dis)satisfaction. So, how do you go about managing the customer's expectations so that these expectations and the reality that you will deliver are the same? Customer satisfaction is often measured through:

- Meeting frequently with the customer to discuss what is working well and what could be better. The project plan should have established a mechanism for these meetings.
- Customer satisfaction surveys. Although it is unusual to use these during a development project, they can nevertheless prove useful. An outsourcing project should regularly survey the customers to determine their level of satisfaction with the service.
- The number of escalations up through the management chain before issues are resolved.
- The number of disputes or complaints.

In essence, there are four steps in managing customer expectations:

1 Define what customer satisfaction means in this case.
2 Discover the source of the expectation. Why is this the expectation?
3 Calibrate where you are – find out how well or poorly you are doing.
4 Create an action plan.

Define customer satisfaction The project will have been defined in terms of time, cost and quality. These definitions need to be specific and measurable. Customer satisfaction should also be defined: what does the project need to look like at the end in order for the customer to be satisfied? Are there named individuals in the organisation whose statements of satisfaction you need? What will ensure that the customer returns to you for future business? Lastly, what are the customer's business goals and how far are you going to meet them? By the same token, what are *your* business goals and how will a satisfactory outcome look to you and how will it meet your objectives? Be certain that you are clear what your organisation stands to gain from this project and what your role will be in making that happen.

Discover the source of the expectations What is the source of your customer's expectations? Perhaps they have decided to outsource the entire computer department as a result of government legislation or in a drive to save overheads. Do they expect this to save *x* million pounds over five years? Do you think that is realistic? Have you a certain reputation in the marketplace? Are you on the leading edge? Has this customer worked with you or with individuals in your organisation before? If so, what do others in your organisation have to say about your relationship with the customer and what might you expect? What are the implications for you in doing this project? Do you have the resources, the time, the staffing, and the power to make this happen? What if you do not? Who do you need to talk to in your company to get what you need? What is the customer's position – in their own market, in terms of the pressures on them to deliver to others and to keep up with competition? Where do they stand now and how will your help manage to change or maintain that position? What is your position in relation to these same questions and how will this impact on your business objectives? Your customer needs to know where you stand in order to be realistic about what you can deliver and how you will have to go about it.

Calibrate where you are
To calibrate where you are, you must judge where you each stand in relation to one another and how matched or mismatched your expectations may be. You do this by each establishing what you:

- Need
- Want
- View as a 'wish list'
- See as a political agenda
- See as a personal agenda.

The last two are not aired publicly. You will wish to discover as much as possible and factor these in for yourself when determining what is realistic within the context and what the motivators may be for each party – yourself included. Promotions, bonuses, perception and personal achievements within the organisation may play a far greater role than any of the issues that are discussed openly.

Create action plan
Now you are ready to plan what needs to happen to make your project successful. The action plan is where you record how you will manage the customer's expectations along the way. You cannot afford to get lazy or sloppy, as things eventually catch up with you and are invariably more difficult to deal with the longer they are ignored. Creating an action plan is in itself the first step in managing expectations since it leads the customer to be specific about how their expectations are defined. The first thing to do is to establish realistic boundaries that you both find acceptable. Then set out the mechanisms that will be used to keep the customer satisfied. Some can be stated explicitly and agreed with the customer but others will be part of your plan for managing the customer, which they need to experience but not necessarily know about beforehand.

Managing the customer's expectations is at the heart of customer management. Failure to manage expectations lies behind most of the fundamental problems that develop in many projects. Expectations should be clearly defined at the start of a project and should be revisited at regular formal and informal points throughout the project. The risk of misunderstanding, confusion and conflict run high if this is not done.

18.5 | Managing changes

One of the key expectations that should be managed with the customer is the inevitability of changed requirements or changes to plan. No project is without them and part of your success as a project manager will be your ability to handle these changes swiftly and effectively. Ignoring them or procrastinating may have an impact on the overall project and could affect how the customer views you in the long run. The sources of change are almost as great as the number of individuals involved in a project and are probably as unpredictable. However, they can usually be broken down into the following broad categories:

- *Failure to manage expectations* (you have already been warned!).
- *The learning process.* As the project develops, the customer will think of ways in which the original requirement could have been better expressed and will learn more about the technologies involved. Similarly, the project team will come up with new and improved ideas which they may wish to offer to the customer.
- *Internal forces* – suddenly your customer has other priorities which may come from real business pressures or be the result of internal politics.
- *External forces* – from your competitors closing in on your market or your customer and your need to keep ahead of the game. Or there may be changes in the customer's marketplace, or to legislation, to which the customer must respond.

A six-stage process you can use to help you to manage changes is:

1 Identify the initiator.
2 Define the desired outcome.
3 Initiate the change control process.
4 Discover the extent of the change.
5 Assess the impact of the change.
6 Develop an action plan.

Identify the initiator What – or who – has initiated the change or variation? Who has decided that the change or variation should happen? It tends to be either the customer or you. However, it might be the result of government legislation or competitive forces in the marketplace or perhaps a bank loan that needs to be repaid. It is important to be clear where the change is coming from so that you know who needs to be happy with the outcome. Otherwise, you could be wasting your time trying to satisfy the wrong person and could end up with an expectation that has gone all wrong.

Define the desired outcome Whatever the benefits of the change, you still need to remember to bring the project in to time, cost and quality. The customer's satisfaction in meeting their business goals is, of course, important, but you need to attain your own business goals too. These should be spelled out so that you will recognise whether or not you have achieved them. Often, you need to consider minor variations. It might seem to be a waste to spend time being specific about what you expect to see at the end, but it is important to consider doing this for every change as it can help you to avoid potential conflict – these things have a tendency to build up and grow in significance. It is hard to know which change will generate a critical incident, so for each one you must document what you hope to see as an outcome, no matter how small.

Initiate the change control process

There are three steps to this phase. First, you and the customer must both agree that you are actually initiating a change. Until you do, one of you will resist tackling the problem and its implications and someone will end up being frustrated. Acknowledging this initiation process happens by sitting down and saying, 'We've hit a point that was not in the original brief and we need to sort it out'. You must both recognise that it was not spelled out originally but is important now. Quite often, it is difficult to get agreement that you are in a change situation. The customer may insist that the 'change' was in the specification all along; you just failed to notice the requirement or appreciate its significance. Having a clear and detailed specification will help here but, even then, you are likely to have to use all your patience and negotiating skills to secure agreement.

The second step is to initiate a change evaluation process. This means that you both accept that this is a variation to the original agreement and that it will need to be handled separately from your other ongoing work on the project. This may have resource and time implications.

Thirdly, you need to decide who will pay for the change. No variation is without a cost. It does not always mean that the customer – whether internal or external – needs to pay, but you must not ignore that there is a cost attached, even if only for investigating the change. This cost should be acknowledged, even if it is just in the form of goodwill and an understanding of flexibility on your part. Make sure that it is stated and noted.

Discover the extent of the change

Often the first reaction to a change requirement is resistance, anger and making excuses. That is why finding out why the change is being requested is so important. If you have the chance to explain why the change occurred, you stand a much better chance of getting what you need – goodwill on a delay, an extension on the deadline – and still stay on good terms with one another. It works just the same when you have a change to a project. Allow the customer to give the background to the change, to define the problem, propose some solutions and describe the implications to the rest of the project. By allowing the customer to do this first, you have taken some of the anger out of the situation. Otherwise you run a risk of taking on that responsibility yourself, which also means you will get the blame if something goes wrong. Of course, as project manager you need to be there to offer advice and to help solve the problem, but the best rule of thumb is: let the person who brings the change be the one to start out by defining it and looking for possible solutions. Remember that you may be the one initiating the change, so having a neutral process will help you as well.

Assess the impact of the change When changes occur they have different impacts on different groups. It is useful to consider each group when planning how to respond. It is more than likely that each group has its own agenda and you may need to involve technical people, systems people, managers, users of the system who need it in their day-to-day work, and business or commercial people. Personal agendas with each of these parties may also come into play. A change to the project could be an effective and simple way for someone to put a spanner in the works, or could be someone else's path to glory, especially if the proposed timescale were cut in half.

Develop an action plan Whatever you decide to do, you still need a plan. Your options are:

- Initiate the change or variation within the project without any charge.
- Initiate the sales process. It may be that the change or variation that is proposed sends you back to people within your organisation who need to draw up further plans for work for this client. It may not be as simple as agreeing to do the work, and instead needs to include a wider group to help with a longer-range solution.
- Abandon the change. It may not be appropriate; you may find another way round the problem; logistics or cost may make it impossible.
- The change escalates into a conflict. This is not the desired outcome, but it does happen sometimes. If you cannot agree on how to handle the change, who will pay for it, who is responsible, etc., it may escalate and you will need to call in your procedures for handling a conflict. A lot can be done, however, before it gets to this point.

Change and variations come from a variety of sources. They are inevitable when working on any project. If you fear them, you will get caught out and caught up by them. Confront them directly, deal with them quickly and with honesty and they should become a natural part of the project rather than an unnecessary interruption. Change is part of learning. Change in a project shows that there is growth and adaptation, not failure. In addition, changes do have benefits. They enable the customer to improve the original requirement to take advantage of new markets or improved technologies. They give the developers the opportunity to add value for their customer by suggesting and implementing additional facilities. And, in a commercial context, they enable the suppliers to grow the value of the project as a piece of business.

18.6 Managing conflict

Why is it that handling conflict is sometimes part of a project manager's job? You thought you had done everything possible to avoid it, and suddenly you are in the midst of a situation that feels out of control and irretrievable. It generally is not, but there are times when it feels hopeless and endlessly frustrating. One of the main reasons that conflicts occur is that the smaller issues have not been confronted earlier. It often feels easier at the time to let them slide, assuming that time will sort things out, or perhaps you are too busy to put in the effort to sort out 'that minor issue'. Sometimes, though, life is just too messy and the conflict occurs. We have to accept this fact, so let us look at where conflicts come from and suggest some ways of dealing with them.

18.6.1 Why conflicts arise

Conflicts can come from anywhere, at any point in the life of a project. Sometimes they arise from practical matters, sometimes they are a result of personalities and personal agendas. Some you can avoid, others you cannot. Some of the more recognisable sources of conflict are:

- Different expectations – usually centred around timescales, costs or the range of facilities to be provided.
- Interruptions and the inability to keep to the original timescale.
- Lack of understanding of each other's position – this may be for technical, commercial or personal reasons.
- Issues that have been left unresolved or avoided come back at a critical point and can no longer be ignored.
- Physical distances, proximity and culture. These may play a role, particularly if you need to be working on the customer's site. You may feel alienated from your own company and get caught in some crossfire between your company and the customer.

Generally, conflict is about differences in perspective and the confusion that results from seeing a situation from different angles with differing motivations. The way out of this is to remove yourself from your entrenched position and to try to see the circumstances from a neutral viewpoint. This is easier said than done and demands a considerable degree of self-awareness. Try role-playing the situation with a colleague to bring out the different perspectives.

18.6.2 Resolving conflict

Having recognised how conflict can arise, what about resolving it? A process that has been found effective is:

1 Know your desired outcome.
2 Triage the conflict.
3 Agree a process.
4 Confirm the positions.
5 Take action.

Know your desired outcome You need to know what you will accept as your bottom line. Resolving a conflict involves negotiating, and you need to know where you can no longer compromise. It is best to have this objective clearly in your mind; discuss it with others, write it down. If the client is saying that the project must now be completed in six months rather than the twelve months that was originally agreed, you need to be clear whether or not that is possible. If it is, what are the implications in terms of cost and quality? If it is not possible, could you do it in nine months, and what are the implications of that? Do not consider a discussion with the client without this outcome very clear in your mind and be sure that everyone in your team sings the same song!

Triage the conflict To triage is to sort according to quality. Hospital casualty departments triage incoming patients into those that need immediate treatment to survive, those who will survive without treatment and those who will die whatever the treatment. In our context, it is important to sort through the issues surrounding a conflict to decide which are critical and which may be peripheral. The idea is to find the root cause of the conflict. Here, it is a good idea to look at the different groups that may have a stake in the outcome of the project. Decide what each has to gain and to lose and where the power may lie. The idea is to determine, in order of priority, which are the most important issues to deal with – which are the conflicts that are essential to resolve – and in which order you will do that. Who are the people you need to involve and are they aware of the parts they will play?

Agree a process You and the customer need first to agree that there is a conflict. With any luck, you will have established at the start of the project what might happen in the event of a conflict and it is now time to invoke that procedure. Even if only one side thinks that there is a conflict, then there is one. A good idea is to form a team that will work to sort out the conflict, because by doing so you broaden the discussion, dilute any personal disagreements and help to take some of the heat out of the situation. The process itself creates the need to behave correctly with one another. Instead of having just you and the customer it might make sense to have an independent third party involved as well. Finally, agree how you will resolve any impasse so that you have at least contemplated what happens if you reach the point of no return. Doing so often helps you both to put this conflict into perspective. People rarely want to forfeit a whole project for the sake of an individual conflict. Too much has already been invested, egos and reputations are at stake, not to mention time, money and resources.

Confirm the positions When the different sides in a conflict meet, they first need to establish their positions. In addition, the implications for each position should be put on the table and there should be an openness to resolve the situation. Naturally, this is the ideal situation, but anything less will probably result in the conflict taking longer to resolve.

Take action Once both sides have agreed that they want to get through this conflict, there can be some progress. It is important that you and the customer share the same objectives, for example that the project has to be completed in a shorter timescale, that you both know there may be consequences in doing that, but you will achieve the overall project goals.

Together you can:

- Generate alternatives to what you are doing at present.
- Evaluate the alternatives.

- Rate the alternatives.
- Agree a plan of action.
- Escalate it outside the team if that is appropriate.
- Make it happen.

There can be a great deal of creativity coming into the process at this point and the structure should not inhibit that at all. In fact it may be that better working relationships result from resolving a conflict.

Conflicts will arise in a project. There should always be a provision for them, if nothing else, to act as an insurance policy. Should they occur, try to deal with them clinically, with detachment and swiftly. Letting them linger can only make them worse. As the issues are rarely just about machines and procedures, the delicate business of dealing with people and their feelings make handling conflicts thorny at best. When through to the other side, you will probably have learned a great many lessons for the next time you work on a project – the same types of conflict keep on appearing.

18.7 Stakeholder management skills

Managing your stakeholders will stay highly theoretical unless you also think about, practise and incorporate the skills needed to make you successful at it. These may well take far longer to feel comfortable with than many of the technical skills but they are applicable in many other situations, in or out of work. Knowing how to listen and communicate, as well as not becoming overly emotional, is helpful in most relationships. Perhaps one of the hardest things for people who are new to work or who have had to move away from purely technical jobs is the unpredictable and messy business of dealing with people. People do not behave consistently, they do very odd things for seemingly illogical reasons – if any reasons at all – and do not always do what you think is best. Unlike machines, they talk back, they sulk and they can make your life amazingly difficult. Having a few techniques or skills in dealing with them may make it a bit easier. Some of these issues have been addressed elsewhere in this book – in the chapter on leadership, for example, and in the chapters dealing with team issues – but, as you will appreciate by now, the relationship with stakeholders brings added dimensions of complexity. Stakeholders need to be handled carefully, with respect but also with confidence and assertion. You do not have too many chances to get it right and it is worthwhile practising the skills in a situation where not too much is at stake, such as with friends, family and colleagues you can trust before you test it out where it counts.

Social and professional relationships Let us look first of all at how we develop relationships with people in general. There is a distinction between social and professional relationships. Each has its own rules of behaviour. Life can become very tricky and unnecessarily complicated if the two are confused, particularly when it comes to dealing with a customer.

Our social relationships are developed very early in life. We acquire the rules when we are children, initially at home. We learn to say 'please' and 'thank you', not to interrupt, to accept our place in a group of other children or adults and so on. Many of the rules that we learn at home are then reinforced at school, where knowing how to listen and pay attention, as well as accepting authority, is stressed. Most of these rules are then reinforced by our peer group, which can often be a powerful shaper of behaviour. For example, just think of the conformity of teenagers and the ways that they modify each other's behaviour. They can be very direct and very effective in their remarks to one another. As we get older, there are rules for behaving in social situations, such as at dinner parties, football matches and with boy- or girlfriends. These are, for the most part, unspoken ways in which we know how to and how not to behave with one another. We know what is acceptable and what is out of bounds.

Professional relationships are different from social ones. They may at times overlap when you socialise with people you work with, but for the most part they exist on a slightly different plane from your out-of-work friendships. Often we never acquire the rules for dealing with these relationships. We have to pick them up along the way. They are based on a different ethic. Whereas you may have social relationships with people who are similar to you in background and values and you have chosen one another, it may be the complete opposite with a professional relationship. The only thing you may have in common is the work you both need to do. The ground-rules for dealing with one another are often quite pragmatic in nature, might appear to be inconsistent with social rules and may last only for as long as the project or your time on a particular job. It can feel quite hurtful when you return to an office where you had worked for years to realise that 'your best friends' no longer know what to say to you – or you to them – and what seemed to be such close friendships were really much more fleeting and based on what was going on in the office when you worked there, and it was no deeper than that.

The confusion between social and professional relationships can sometimes make it difficult for you as a project manager to do your job. For example, when you are managing the customer, or trying to utilise a sales opportunity, there will inevitably be some manipulation involved on your part. Our 'social' ethics tell us that it is wrong to manipulate people, so we feel uncomfortable when we are being a little manipulative in a business situation. Similarly, when we consciously employ techniques for building rapport (covered in the next section) we may feel somewhat devious in doing so. There is no simple way to come to terms with this, but an idea which may help is to think of yourself as an actor in a professional situation, acting out the part of project manager or salesperson. In this way you can put a mental barrier between your social and professional self, which may help you to adopt different behaviours in each situation.

Establishing rapport

It is important to establish rapport with people you work with, and specifically with your stakeholders and especially with your customer. Rapport is when there are high levels of trust and confidence between two people. You have probably observed people who have personal rapport with one another. Sometimes in a pub or at a restaurant you may see a couple, deep in conversation, oblivious to the outside world. They will be leaning towards one another and, unconsciously, when one moves forward, so does the other – the same when they lean back. Also, they may 'mirror' one another's speech, using similar words or phrases. This all helps to establish or maintain rapport.

When you feel confident with someone and you are 'tuned in' to what is being said, your body and your words help you to have rapport. You can try to do this, in small ways, when you are first meeting with a customer or someone in your organisation. Listen, nod, do not obviously mimic their body language but try not to contradict what they are doing. If someone is leaning forward, looking you in the eyes and being open with their gestures, do not sit back with folded arms and look like you have closed the shutters to anything that is being said. Look them in the eyes, smile, nod when you agree and you will start to create some common ground. Discuss topics, inside or outside work, where you might have had similar experiences. Slowly, you will develop rapport. It does not happen overnight, just as friendships take a while, but with rapport you are looking to establish trust and confidence that will grow as you create the situations where you can prove to one another that you can be trusted.

Active listening Few of us are ever taught how to listen. It is actually very hard to do it well. Listening well to your customers and your colleagues will go far in helping you to understand their needs. Unfortunately, it takes a lot of concentration, can be extremely tiring and there are not obvious and immediate rewards. Active listening means that you are really hearing what someone else has to say, questioning, reflecting back and checking that you understand what is being said. Do not assume anything. Even when you look as if you are listening, your mind may be somewhere else. You may be framing your response, worried about if you know the answer, or playing amateur psychologist. We have listed below some of the ways in which we all block effective listening. Tick those things you do and then try your best to overcome them. It takes a lot of practice to break a bad habit. Highlight any listening barriers where you think you have a problem and concentrate on them.

- *Advising.* You are listening, but only to be able to offer advice afterwards. 'I know what that's like. Here's what I would do . . .'.
- *Being right.* You listen to the information, but only so that you can win a point. Instead of listening well, you twist the facts, start raising your voice, making excuses or accusations and revisit past sins. At all costs, you do not want to be wrong.
- *Comparing.* You focus on who suffered more or who is the bigger victim. You might look for evidence as to why you are better than the speaker. For example, someone tells you about an awful plane journey they have had. Rather than ask them more, you come back with your own even longer story which, of course, is far worse.

- *Derailing*. In order to eliminate discomfort or anxiety, you completely change the subject mid-stream or 'joke it off'.
- *Dreaming*. 'The lights are on, but nobody's home.' You have drifted away somewhere else, perhaps because you are uncomfortable, uncertain or just bored.
- *Filtering*. You are looking for specific pieces of information that support the plan that you already have in mind. When you are satisfied that you have the information you need, you stop listening.
- *Identifying*. You keep yourself as the focal point rather than the speaker. You refer most things back to your experience and not theirs, and cut in whenever possible about how what they are saying relates to you or something you know.
- *Judging*. In order to maintain your feelings of superiority, you hear only what fits into what you have already judged to be correct. You might be filled with preconceptions.
- *Mind-reading*. You are working out 'what the other person really means is . . .'. You pay less attention to the words and more attention to the way they are being said. This can be a self-defence mechanism. Why are you not concentrating on the message?
- *Rehearsing*. When you are rehearsing your reply, you are not able to listen much beyond the first thing someone says. You look interested, but your mind is busy elsewhere.
- *Placating*. In order to be perceived as nice, pleasant, supportive or whatever, you agree with everything. This can feel quite patronising if overdone.
- *Sparring*. Conversation is viewed as a glove sport because you enjoy an argument and will seek one out. This allows you to maintain control at all costs, but can feel like a put-down to someone else. They did not engage you in conversation because they wanted a fight.

Neutral emotion Managing stakeholders demands that you can take a step back and view a situation with an open mind. This can be very hard to do. You too often have a lot at stake – personally, professionally and politically. There are times when the best option for you is to be dispassionate and divorce yourself from the heat of the moment. That means that you put yourself into a 'neutral emotional state'. By dissociating yourself from the situation you are able to deal with the real issues, deal with criticism and deal with objections.

A neutral emotional state allows you to approach problems productively and to reach better solutions. If you are dealing with someone who is angry, then wait and, eventually, they will calm down. By removing yourself from the situation and taking on much more of the role of an observer, you eliminate for the moment your personal investment and therefore move things along positively rather than being part of the problem yourself. It might help if you think of a time when you have felt very sure of yourself, very confident and in control. Summon up this state of mind in helping you to feel the confidence you will need in order to put yourself in a neutral state. Try it out first when you are not in a high-risk situation – become an 'observer' at a party, a family gathering or a meeting. See how it feels and begin to learn how you can pull yourself back if you need to.

Communication   Ideas need to be communicated from one person to another, from the customer to you and from you to the customer. This is simple enough, but we all know that there are a myriad of ways in which messages can become confused, misunderstood and misinterpreted along the way. We are lucky if someone understands what we say or write in the way in which we intended. Understanding where and how things can go wrong may help you to avoid poor communication. For example, consider the process shown in Figure 18.3:

- Person A wishes to communicate with Person B. A then takes that thought and turns it into written or spoken language, so A has then *encoded* the message. Before it is encoded it passes through A's *filter* which will put A's own perspective on the message. This filter will include such things as A's cultural background, experience, education and values. It will colour the language that is used as well as the assumptions made about the listener. In addition, there might be words that denote urgency or importance which may have different meanings in different cultures. 'As soon as possible' may mean 'within the next day' in one setting and may mean 'when I get to it' somewhere else.
- The message then reaches *transmission*. This can be clear and easy to listen to or read, or there may be considerable *noise* such as in a meeting that is held in a busy hotel reception area where there are many distractions, an office where the telephone keeps ringing or even a crackly telephone line.
- B (the receiver) now has a chance to *decode* the message. In addition to all of the difficulties listed above that can interfere with understanding a message in the spirit in which it is sent, there are the problems already identified in being a good active listener. Poor listening habits can easily distort and edit a message.

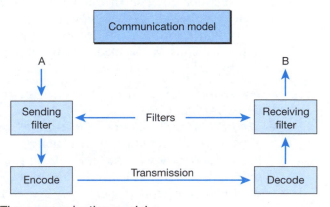

Figure 18.3 The communication model

■ Finally, with some luck, B has received A's communication. It is hard to believe with so many opportunities for things to go wrong that we ever manage to understand one another.

Knowing the high potential for things to go wrong when communicating means that you need to take extra care when dealing with your customers. You will need to check and recheck your understanding, ask the client to state what, in their opinion, has been agreed, and never lose your vigilance or patience for communicating well. It is a good policy, at the end of a meeting or discussion, to summarise what has been said and your understanding of the conclusions that have been reached, so that everyone leaves the meeting clear about the outcome.

Considerable skills are required when dealing with your customers. They are not different from the skills that you need in other aspects of your life. Watching those people who you think handle customers well is a good place to start. Notice what they do, and when. If you develop the art of being a good listener, you will have mastered the hardest part, because the other skills can follow on. Without hearing what is being said, questioning and probing so that you are sure what your client needs, expects and desires, you might be second-guessing and making assumptions at every turn. Start by observing and questioning those you can trust. In order to be successful you will need to develop these skills, but, most importantly, do not be impatient. Learning new skills and breaking bad habits can take a long time.

Networking

Networking is a very useful technique in managing customer relations. It is a complex business to find your way around not only the customer organisation but those of the other stakeholders as well. Networking is the skill of knowing which people inside and outside an organisation can help you. Because traditional lines of management hierarchies are fast disappearing, it helps to know people at different levels and in different departments. Networking is the system for reaching those people and tapping into their expertise when you need it. In addition, there are those people in the organisation who have powerful roles within a network. Their power may have little to do with their status in the organisation and may instead rest with them for many other reasons, such as their expertise, whom they know, their political influence, their out-of-work social activities and so on. When first assigned to a project, try to determine how the decisions will be made and by whom. The people you typically need to identify are:

■ *The decision-maker.* An individual or the most influential member of the decision-making group.
■ *The gatekeeper.* The person who controls your access to higher authority. Sometimes this could be the managing director's secretary or the decision-maker's secretary who can make it difficult to meet the person with the influence. Be wise and cultivate the gatekeepers. Also, get to know the receptionist and the support staff – they are often the ones who know the most and can be your best allies.

- *The influencer*. Someone who advises the decision-maker. Influencers are not always easy to find and you may only become aware of their existence when your perfectly argued proposition is turned down for some obscure reason. For this reason, it pays to do the research needed to find out who the influencers are and how they are likely to act.
- *The end-user*. The person or people who will use or are directly affected by your product or service. These people are critical in your success. They will help to make the system or project work and will give you powerful feedback for future improvements. Once over the initial resistance they may put up, you will find that it is in their interest to have the project succeed, because they will have to use your product or service.
- *The champion*. This is someone within the customer's organisation who is sympathetic to what you are trying to achieve and may be prepared to argue your case for you.

Effective managers have always established informal networks within organisations. As a project manager, you will want to create both informal and formal networks for getting things done. You should consider doing this both within your organisation and within the customer organisation. The wider and deeper your contacts, the more effective you will be. You will be perceived as knowing your way around, as being independent and productive. It demands a certain amount of getting out and about, chatting to people, handling the small-talk side of conversations as well as getting down to business and delivering at the right times and for the right people. It is hard to imagine a successful project manager who has not established a wide and effective network.

18.8 Summary

With today's unquestioning focus on stakeholder management and especially on the customer, it has become essential to feel comfortable with the different aspects of managing the customer relationship and the associated issues. Models can help in looking at managing the processes of expectations, change and conflict, but they will not be directly applicable to all of the variables you will encounter. That is because both you and the customer are complex human beings with your own sets of values, preconceptions, expectations and desires. They may at times be matched, but they will also clash. The skill is in handling these moments as they arise, keeping your cool and maintaining the focus of the project. No two projects and no two customers will ever be the same. Rather than bemoaning that fact, it is both realistic and productive to embrace the differences.

Questions

1 Stakeholders have different interests or 'stakes' in a project. How can you determine where to put your management effort?

2 What is meant by the term 'managing expectations'? Why is expectation management an important part of the project manager's job? What influences a customer's expectations?

3 Why is it important for the project manager to establish a network of contacts within the IS organisation and also within the user organisation? In what circumstances can these networks be useful?

Case study

France Vacances is obviously a company going places, and the owners have some ideas about how to expand their business. They also have a view about the timing of the introduction of the new system and the capabilities of their in-house team. France Vacances will be a demanding client. To begin with, you will have to decide some very specific things about France Vacances.

Who is the customer? Is it Massenet? He is the director responsible for finance and administration. Is it Mary Appleby? She is the administration manager and the IT section reports to her. Is it Martin? The new system is for sales and bookings and he is responsible for sales. Will the new system change his areas of responsibility?

There are some other people involved too. Peter Clay, the IT manager, may see a different future in France Vacances when the new system is up and running. Will the IT function become more important? Also, what about Richard Thornton; what are the implications for him of people booking online? Perhaps all of these people can become what Kotter (see Chapter 1) would call the 'guiding coalition' to ensure that the proposed changes do get implemented.

To a large extent, these issues have been addressed by setting up the PRINCE2®-style project board (see Chapter 4) but the tensions that will inevitably result from a project such as this will cause friction among the various stakeholders that E-Con must manage if it is to deliver successfully.

Think about the expectations that each person may have from the new system. Look through section 18.3 again and, for each of the main stakeholders, identify their possible expectations. Without actually meeting the people involved you cannot identify their expectations, but it is possible to begin to see what might lie behind the decision to implement a web-based booking system.

Case study continued

Did you spot the deliberate mistake? Which important customers have been ignored? – It is the high street travel agents and the paying customers who book the holidays. How will their expectations be managed?

Further reading

Hill, C W L and Jones, G R (2001), *Strategic Management*, Houghton Mifflin

Johnson, G and Scholes, K (2003), *Exploring Corporate Strategy*, 6th edn, FT/Prentice Hall

Turner, J Rodney (1999), *The Handbook of Project Based Management*, McGraw-Hill

Turner, J R and Simister, S J (2000), *The Gower Handbook of Project Management*, 3rd edn, Gower

19 Managing suppliers

19.1 Introduction

Often, a project team will have to call upon the services of outside people or organisations to supply specialist services or equipment or to cover a temporary shortfall in the organisation's own resources. Outside suppliers can be used in two situations:

- Where the project team retains direct day-to-day control over the supplier's work. This is the normal situation when, for example, contract programmers are used; aside from the fact that they are paid via invoices rather than through the payroll, they are managed just like any other members of the project team.
- Where a portion of the work is undertaken on a subcontract basis by the supplier, with the project manager exercising control on an 'arm's length' basis.

This chapter is concerned with the second scenario.

The use of subcontractors in a project is very often inevitable. If a software company has offered a 'turnkey' solution to its customer, it will have to deliver a system complete in all its components – hardware, software, communications, training and so on – and will have to buy in the non-software elements from subcontractors. This situation is likely to become more common as projects become more complex and call for the integration of an increasingly diverse blend of skills and resources. Customers, too, are seeking to simplify their own lives by appointing a 'prime contractor' who will take overall responsibility for the project and relieve them of the task of trying to manage a number of disparate suppliers. In turn, this arrangement transfers the risks associated with subcontractors on to the prime contractor. It is important, therefore, that the subcontract arrangements are set up properly, that the risks associated with the subcontracts are addressed and that adequate control is exercised over the work of the subcontractors.

19.2 | Setting up the contract

19.2.1 Subcontractor assessment and selection

It is important to ensure that the right subcontractor is chosen and that the 'scope of supply' is clear and properly understood by both parties. The process model shown in Figure 19.1 provides a framework for achieving this.

In general, the approach to subcontracting work follows a number of stages. Although the project manager should have a key role here, it is sensible to enlist the support of procurement specialists who will understand how to research the marketplace and who are trained in vendor assessment and contract negotiation techniques. The main stages in the subcontracting process are described next.

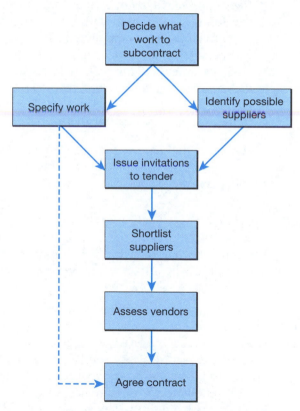

Figure 19.1 Supplier identification and selection process

Decide what work to subcontract

There are many reasons why an organisation may decide to subcontract some of the project, including:

- *Lack of skills or resources required.* This may be a temporary situation, resulting from a number of projects all requiring similar resources at the same time, or more permanent, because the organisation has decided that certain skills are not within its core competences.
- *Pressures to reduce headcount.* Many organisations face pressures from market analysts, regulators or the government to 'do more with less', and one way of achieving this may be to deliberately run down the level of employed staff. In this case, it will be necessary to subcontract work because the in-house resources no longer exist to carry out part or all of the project.
- *Relative costs.* Although an organisation may possess the competences in-house, it may be cheaper to subcontract the work to a firm that can offer economies of scale or perhaps lower labour costs through operating, for example, in the Far East.
- *Highly specialised skills.* It may not be worth the organisation's while to develop very specialised skills for a particular project and it may make sense to go to a specialist supplier instead. Also, it is probable that the specialists will be able to develop a high-quality product in a shorter timescale, precisely because they are working in an area in which they have expertise.
- *Risk transfer.* It may be desired to transfer the risks – technological, commercial and financial – to someone else; but see later about the contractual framework for some caveats here.

Whatever the reasons for subcontracting work, it is important to be clear what they are as this will influence the choice of supplier and also the way the supplier is managed.

Specify work

Next, a clear specification of the work to be done should be drawn up. If there is a specification from the end-customer, this should form the basis for the subcontract scope of work. It is important that the boundaries of the work between the subcontractor and prime contractor are made entirely clear.

Identify possible suppliers

Identifying possible suppliers is where the procurement specialists come into their own, as they should have experience of the marketplace and know who is worth approaching. The project manager may also have extensive experience of the technical marketplace and be able to suggest suppliers that are known to have relevant products or capabilities.

With public sector procurements within the European Union, competitive tendering is required by law. This process starts by asking for expressions of interest through the *Official Journal of the European Communities*.

As the dotted line in Figure 19.1 suggests, however, in some cases there may be no need to identify suppliers, or no point in doing so. It may be that there is only one possible supplier of a particular product or service or that the organisation always uses a particular supplier. In that case, the next three stages can be skipped and the process would move straight to contract negotiations.

Issue invitations to tender Having identified suitable suppliers, the next step is to ask them to make formal proposals for the supply of the products or services required. Again, the procurement specialists have a key role to play in drawing up the invitations to tender (ITTs). The format of the ITT will vary from organisation to organisation but it should include a clear scope of work and also, ideally, a pro-forma contract which the buyer wishes to use.

At the same time that the ITT is drawn up, it is sensible to establish the evaluation criteria against which tenders will be assessed. This makes the later shortlisting process easier through having predefined criteria to work with.

Shortlist suppliers If many suppliers respond to the ITT, it is not feasible to evaluate them all in detail. Therefore, it is necessary to get the original 'longlist' down to a more manageable shortlist. This can be done by using the evaluation criteria previously established and which are discussed more fully in the next section. Necessarily, some of the assessments made at this stage will be somewhat superficial, but that cannot be helped; using a panel of assessors whose views will complement each other can be of benefit here.

Assess vendors Once a shortlist has been drawn up, more detailed assessments can be made of those few suppliers left. The basic issue is whether the suppliers can provide the products or services required at the right time, cost and quality. However, other factors should come into the assessment, including:

- The size, reputation and financial status of the subcontractor. Where the subcontractor is part of a larger grouping, the assessment should include that too.
- The customers and markets served by the subcontractor.
- The size of the subcontractor in relation to the prime contractor organisation. The issue here is whether the prime contractor will have the 'clout' – in other words, the experience, resources and influence – to manage the subcontractor effectively, and this may not be the case if the business proposed is only an insignificant part of the subcontractor's turnover.
- Reference sites. Particularly where this subcontractor has not been used before, the project manager will want to investigate its track record with other customers.
- A possible inspection at the subcontractor's premises, to check on its methods and standards and possibly on the operation of its quality control procedures.

During the reference visits, an effort should be made to find out what it is like doing business with the subcontractor. Are the staff cooperative and open or are they secretive and liable to want to argue over everything in strictly contractual terms? There is nothing wrong with being clear about what is included in the contract, but some firms play a form of contractual hard-ball which can make them very hard work and unpleasant to work with.

Agree contract Finally, the contract can be agreed. This is an important issue and so it is discussed in more detail in the next section.

19.2.2 The contractual framework

The starting point for a successful subcontract is an adequate definition of the scope of the supply. There must be a complete and unambiguous specification of the equipment and services that are to be provided by the supplier and this specification should cover:

- The functional and technical requirements of the supply.
- The performance specifications, in absolute terms or expressed as a range of acceptable values.
- The budget available.
- A complete and precise list of the deliverables from the supplier.
- The dates on which materials and services must be supplied, and the locations at which they are wanted.
- The method of installation that is required.
- The criteria against which the products and services are to be accepted.
- The project management controls that the purchaser will wish to impose.
- The quality control regimes that will apply to the products and services, including the purchaser's rights to impose their own quality assurance mechanisms.

As purchaser, the project manager needs to ensure that both the developer's and the customer's interests are protected. In particular, it is important to ensure that the contract terms are 'back-to-back'. This means that, if the customer has imposed any terms on the prime contractor/developer, these should be reflected in the terms imposed on the subcontractor. If this does not happen, then the developer will be at risk because of the overlap between the contracts. This situation is represented in Figure 19.2, where the developer has signed up to contract terms that have not been imposed on the subcontractor.

Another important issue to address in the contract is the question of ownership of the developed materials. Where the work is being done wholly for and at the expense of the prime contractor it is reasonable to expect that the intellectual property rights (IPR) will pass to the prime contractor on payment.

Figure 19.2 The importance of back-to-back contracts

Where the subcontractor is providing something already owned, perhaps in a modified form, there will have to be discussion on the ownership of the IPR and the terms on which they will be sold, or licensed, to the end-customer. If the subcontractor will only grant a licence for the use of the product, then the contract must include arrangements for the situation that arises if the subcontractor goes out of business. With software, the usual response is to place a copy of the source code in escrow, that is lodged with a reliable third party who will release it to the purchaser in certain specified circumstances, including the bankruptcy of the supplier.

The contract should also cover the arrangements for warranty, support and maintenance of the deliverables after they are handed over to the prime contractor or customer. If the subcontractor cannot or does not want to offer continuing support, the project manager must ensure that alternative arrangements can be made.

Quite often, the prime contractor will insert penalty clauses into the subcontract for late delivery, or 'liquidated damages' clauses to cover various other forms of non-performance; these last set out the amounts that will be paid over in specified circumstances. Although these do give the prime contractor a measure of protection, and may help to offset the operation of similar clauses imposed by the customer, they should be treated with caution. First, even if the prime contractor is covered financially by penalty clauses and the like, that person/company is still responsible for the delivery of the overall system and it will probably prove both difficult and expensive to find a suitable replacement subcontractor. Second, the prime contractor could incur all sorts of additional costs arising from delays – such as staff sitting around with nothing to do – that may not be covered by the liquidated damages. Third, the failure of a subcontractor necessarily reflects badly on the reputation and judgement of the prime contractor in using them in the first place. Last, and not least, getting redress through the courts is a lengthy and expensive process with no automatic guarantee of success. The lesson of all this is that it is much better to select the right subcontractor at the outset.

19.3 | Monitoring supplier performance

The subcontractors should be required to produce project and quality plans and to report progress regularly against them. The best idea is to have these plans in a similar format to those used by the prime contractor's team, but larger subcontractors will have their own standards and procedures and will wish to follow them. The project manager should, at the least, ensure that these standards and procedures are adequate to give confidence that the work is being properly planned and controlled. The degree to which the project manager will be interested in the detail of the subcontractor's work will depend on its criticality and, for this reason, it is usually desirable to keep subcontracted tasks off the project's critical path. If this cannot be avoided, the amount of project management attention on the subcontractor must be intensified. Once work begins, various methods can be used to keep the progress of the sub-contractor's work under review. These are described below.

Approval of designs, drawings and specifications
The project manager should ensure that the project team can inspect and approve the subcontractor's designs as they emerge, and time should be built into the project plans to allow for this. Similarly, the subcontractor's plans should be checked to ensure that they have allowed for adequate review time in their own schedule. The subcontractor's documentation should be managed under a proper configuration control regime, ideally the same one as is used by the prime contractor.

Progress meetings
Progress meetings should be held regularly and should be aligned with the main supplier's reports to the customer, so that a complete picture of the whole project can be presented. The subcontractor's progress against the agreed plans should be reviewed and any departures investigated. The project manager needs to create an open and cooperative climate so that the subcontractor feels able to raise any problems or concerns and does not hide difficulties until they have turned into real crises.

Witnessing tests
The project manager should reserve the right to send observers to witness important tests conducted by the subcontractor. On a large project, with a lot of work being done by a subcontractor, it may well be worth stationing project staff permanently on the subcontractor's premises for this purpose.

Receipt of goods and services from the subcontractor
When the subcontractor delivers goods or services, a proper procedure should be followed for checking and receiving them. There should be a check that the acceptance tests have been carried out and signed off and that the items received are of the approved build standard.

Checking invoices
All invoices submitted by the subcontractor should be checked to ensure that the work charged for has in fact been performed. Particular care should be taken with stage payments that the agreed payment criteria have been met. In general, the prime contractor's intention will be to maintain a positive cash flow, that is to pay the subcontractor after payment has been received from the suppliers. With small subcontractors, though, care must be taken that this process does not force them into financial difficulties that could compromise their ability to complete the contract.

Risk management
Risk management is discussed in detail in Chapter 15, but the project manager needs to decide how subcontractor risk is to be handled. One approach is to regard the subcontractor's work as a black box: within it, the subcontractor has complete responsibility for all management issues, including risk manage-ment. Another method is to make the operation of risk management processes a contractual requirement, like the operation of quality control, and to carry out audits periodically to ensure that it is being followed. Where there is a high degree of risk associated with the subcontract, however, the best policy is prob-ably to bring the subcontractor within the scope of the prime contractor's risk management programme. This will have to be covered in the contract terms.

Managing the customer interfaces Quite often, where a subcontractor is working on a discrete or highly specialised part of the overall project, a difficult situation can arise concerning the way in which the subcontractor interacts with the customer. Two undesirable circumstances can develop:

- The prime contractor insists that all communication between subcontractor and customer be channelled through them, even though they have no direct interest in much of the detail being discussed. The result is delay and confusion, with the prime contractor being regarded as a nuisance by both the other parties.
- The subcontractor and customer cut out the prime contractor and communicate directly, so that the prime contractor has no real control over what is going on.

There is no simple answer to this, but the project manager needs to agree with the other parties the circumstances in which he or she will become involved in their discussions. Certainly, the prime contractor should be involved in anything to do with the specification, and perhaps the customer and subcontractor can be asked to copy all correspondence to the prime contractor, for review and comment if necessary.

Subcontractor evaluation At the conclusion of the project, an evaluation should be made of the overall performance of the subcontractor. This should include: the quality of the work performed and of the staff assigned to the project; the subcontractor's ability to meet timescales and deadlines; and an assessment of how easy – or difficult – the working relationship has been. The objective here is to build up data on subcontractors that can be used by later projects when considering using the same suppliers again.

19.4 Quality control and subcontractors

A major question to be addressed at the outset is whether or not the subcontractor will work within the prime contractor's quality system. Ideally, the prime contractor's system should apply but this may not be feasible where the subcontractor has a well-developed quality system. Some degree of reassurance will be provided if both prime and subcontractor's systems have been approved to an external standard such as ISO 9001.

If the subcontractor does not work to an externally approved standard, but this standard has been either offered by or imposed on the prime contractor, then the prime contractor will have to seek a 'concession' that the prime contractor's standards will not apply to the subcontracted work. This is not the same as saying that poor quality work will be accepted, just that the subcontractor's system does not have to conform to the same quality system. The project manager should ensure that the subcontractor's quality plan sets out an adequate quality control regime for the subcontracted work.

At each point where the subcontractor hands over completed deliverables to the prime contractor, a set of predefined acceptance tests should be performed. The acceptance criteria must be defined and agreed in advance and should cover:

- The test environment.
- The test schedule.
- The responsibility for performing the test – this could either be the prime contractor's or the subcontractor's, with the prime contractor's staff acting as observers.
- The expected results – as defined in the original specification.
- Any tolerances that are permissible in the results.

In general, the project manager should not authorise acceptance of the deliverables unless they have met the acceptance criteria in full. However, a tight schedule will sometimes dictate that deliverables be accepted subject to certain post-acceptance remedial actions being carried out. Where this happens, an element of risk is clearly involved and the issue should be monitored through the risk management process until the rectification work has been performed and accepted.

19.5 Summary

The use of subcontractors is becoming more widespread as an increasingly diverse range of skills is needed on IS projects and as customers seek to limit their own risk by the appointment of a prime contractor to manage and co-ordinate entire IS projects. The prime contractor needs to take great care in selecting the subcontractors and in devising contracts that offer back-to-back coverage of the customer's requirements. The work of the subcontractor must be monitored closely, from technical, quality and financial perspectives. At the end of each project, the performance of each subcontractor should be evaluated and the experience documented for the guidance of later projects.

Questions

1 Describe three situations in which an IS project may need or wish to use subcontractors.

2 It is important that the contracts between the main contractor and the customer and between the main contractor and subcontractors are *back-to-back*; what is meant by this term?

3 Subcontracts often include penalty clauses to give the main contractor protection in the case of the supplier's poor performance. Why are penalty

Questions continued

clauses not the complete answer to safeguarding the main contractor's position?

4 Describe four methods that can be used to monitor supplier performance.

5 Explain how quality control can be applied to a subcontractor's work.

Case study

E-Con is responsible for the overall management of the project and is itself developing the web software. But it usually subcontracts the provision of hardware and the network infrastructure to one of its preferred suppliers.

Over the years, E-Con has built up a list of these preferred suppliers and there are five at the start of the France Vacances project. E-Con's approach to each new project is in essence the same:

- A specification of the requirements is developed.
- All of the preferred suppliers are invited to bid for the work.
- The supplier is chosen who, in E-Con's opinion, offers the most attractive response. In assessing attractiveness, E-Con not only looks at the price offered but also considers the bidder's track record in this type of installation and how heavily loaded the company is at the moment (to avoid the E-Con project being harmed by diversion of skilled resources to other projects).

In this case, because of the tightness of the timescale, E-Con has adopted a slightly different approach. It has selected its supplier – Network Infrastructures (NI) – in advance of project start-up and has asked NI to work with the E-Con team in developing the hardware specification. Although this loses the potential ability to seek competitive tenders, E-Con feels that this is outweighed by getting NI's experience aboard earlier in the project.

Once the hardware specification is agreed, management of the subcontractors will be undertaken by Siobhan Reid who will hold a weekly meeting with NI's team leader prior to the main checkpoint meeting.

Further reading

Elliott, Catherine and Quinn, Frances (2002), *Contract Law*, 4th edn, Longman

Maylor, Harvey (2003), *Project Management*, 3rd edn, FT/Prentice Hall

Turner, J Rodney and Simister, Stephen J (2000), *Gower Handbook of Project Management*, 3rd edn, Gower

20 Leadership

20.1 Introduction

There are almost as many definitions of leadership as there are people who have attempted to define it. Some years ago, Keith Grint of Templeton College, Oxford, wrote that, between January 1990 and January 1994, 5,341 articles about leadership were published across the world in around 800 different English-language management journals. He calculated that the rate of publication was almost five articles every working day and publication continues apace today. To this total should be added all of the various books dealing with sociology, politics, management, psychology and business that include chapters dealing with leadership. Why do so many people write about leadership, and why is it included here in a book about project management?

There are two kinds of project manager. Let us not categorise them as successes or failures, those who get the job done and those who do not. Any project team member will separate them out; there are those for whom people want to work again and those for whom no one wants to work again. In our lives we work for both and sometimes we have to work on projects for the second kind of project manager, but we do not do it out of choice. Given the choice we would prefer to work again for the first kind. It is leadership that divides project managers into these two categories: the first have it and the second do not. But what is it that they do that turns them into leaders? If we think of the great leaders who have inspired us – Lord Nelson, Winston Churchill, Abraham Lincoln, Mahatma Gandhi, Martin Luther King, Nelson Mandela or even Margaret Thatcher or Lenin – we might think about the common behaviours or attitudes that bind them together, but their activities are all likely to have been fashioned by some great events that thrust them into history. This is unlikely to be the case for a project manager. What we are concerned with is what project managers can do to achieve better results through their people.

Ross Perot, the founder of EDS and a one-time candidate for the US presidency, said, 'People cannot be managed. Inventories are managed, but people must be led.' Straightaway this brings us to consider the relationship between management and leadership. Some people think that they are the same, some that they are different, some that leadership is part of management and some that management is part of leadership, but we want you to hold on to three important concepts:

- Management and leadership are not the same.
- You can be competent as a manager and nothing as a leader.
- Leadership is an observable, learnable set of practices.

We shall deal with the management versus leadership issue now, and at the end of the chapter you will find out how you might become a better leader.

Management is often described as 'getting things done through people' in order to achieve some business or organisational goal. This could be in the public or private sector, in a club, a charity or a church. The emphasis of management is a focus on tasks within a structured, hierarchical environment. Managers are concerned with setting objectives, forecasting, planning, organising, directing, coordinating, controlling and communicating. They perform these tasks with different emphasis according to their functional specialism and level in the hierarchy. The emphasis of leadership is more on interpersonal behaviour, on getting people to want to do things, on getting their enthusiastic support. People can operate as leaders without being the department manager or the hierarchical head. They work by influence. There is often considerable interest in this and the following differences have been suggested:

- Leaders take on a personal commitment and are very active about their goals. Managers, on the other hand, are rather impersonal about goals: for them, goals are organisational and not personal.
- Managers coordinate and balance activities so as to meet conflicting schedules. Leaders create excitement and change and enjoy the uncertainty.
- Leaders are emotionally involved with their people; managers maintain a greater distance.
- Managers belong to the organisation and see themselves as conservators, bringing certainty into a disordered environment. Leaders get their identity from their beliefs and ideas and are always looking to change things.

Someone looking out of our office window in Covent Garden in central London once summed up the difference between leadership and management in the following way:

> Imagine there's a sudden power failure on the tube. The system halts and all the lights go out. In the central control room someone is marshalling resources, implementing the standby facilities, rescheduling the trains, calling the emergency services. That's management. Someone else is walking along the darkened platform with a torch bringing a trainload of people to safety. That's leadership.

As a project manager, you are unlikely to find yourself in either of these circumstances, but you could try out the following example which is adapted from *The Leadership Challenge* by Kouzes and Posner. Assume that everyone working on your project is there because they want to be, not because they have been assigned to it. They are volunteers. What kind of project management would you need to be delivering to make them want to enlist?

A final point in this introduction: we are not saying that leadership is better than management, just that it is different. Projects and organisations in general need both. The opportunity is for project managers to be leaders as well.

20.2 | Motivation

Motivation is about what stimulates people to do things. Actors ask directors, 'What's my motivation here?' when rehearsing a scene; football teams are 'psyched up' or 'motivated' by their coach before going on to the pitch; individuals may describe their project tasks as 'pretty boring really', meaning that they are not very motivated by their work. In the context of this book, motivation is about stimulating people to do their job and releasing their energy into their work so that they deliver above-average performance.

What determines an individual's motivation? At first sight, it is a simple process. We have needs or expectations in life that we want to achieve through work. So we bring our needs to a job, and we hope to have them met by what we find when we get there. What might we find? Firstly, there will be economic rewards, such as pay, pension schemes, health insurance, a company car. These economic rewards might also include the security of having a permanent long-term job. There will also be aspects of the job itself – the job satisfaction – that give us a personal impetus to do the job. Finally there are the social aspects of the job, such as working together – or, conversely, working alone – belonging to a team or a well-known organisation. The combination of these incentives to work that we choose is subjective: your selection is different from the next person's. We also change our preferred combination from time to time. Sometimes we need the money and forgo the social and intrinsic aspects of work; we take on an unpopular assignment because of the premium pay that is offered.

It is useful, then, for you to understand something about motivation since it will be a foundation for the way your project team works. The problem is that there is no general-purpose, useful-in-all-circumstances theory of motivation. Fifty years of research have shown that ideas about motivation have moved from very simple concepts – people work to earn as much as they possibly can, and nothing else matters – to more complex concepts where managers have to understand the different needs and motivations of each member of staff. It seems to us that this is particularly true of highly mobile, expensively recruited and trained specialised professional people who work in IT. There are, however, two general theories that you could apply when trying to understand 'what makes Frank behave like that?' The two models are those of Abraham Maslow and Frederick Herzberg. Maslow's was first published in the late 1940s and Herzberg's in the late 1950s, so both have been examined and criticised over many years, have withstood these examinations and still have something to tell us today.

Maslow's model is called the **hierarchy of needs**, and in it he suggested that similar needs are grouped together and that we first aim to satisfy our needs in one group before turning our attention to needs in another group. These groups are arranged in a hierarchy that we climb, shown in Figure 20.1.

Beginning at the bottom we aim to meet our physiological needs of hunger, thirst, sleep, exercise and basic sensory pleasures. Safety needs include safety and security, freedom from pain and physical attack and protection from

Figure 20.1 **Maslow's hierarchy of needs**

(Maslow A, A Theory of Human Motivation, *Psychological Review*, 1943, 50 pp. 370–396)

danger. Social needs include affection, the sense of belonging to a community and enjoying social activities. The need for esteem includes self-respect as well as the respect of others and can include many work-based issues such as the ability to plan and organise one's own work, status, reputation and recognition by peers and seniors. At the top of the pyramid are what Maslow called 'self-actualisation' needs or being the best you can be: 'becoming everything that one is capable of becoming', as he put it.

Maslow suggests that most people have these needs in roughly this order, but recognised that there would always be occasions when his model did not fit perfectly. The starving poet writing in his attic bedroom to become 'the best he can be' is dealing with self-actualisation but hardly addressing his physiological or safety needs. Fortunately such cases are rare in project teams and we can use the model with some confidence.

Herzberg's model is based around answers to two questions asked through a series of interviews:

- When you are satisfied at work, what is it that is making you happy?
- When you are dissatisfied at work, what is making you unhappy?

Responses in the interviews were consistent enough to fall into a pattern and to show two different factors affecting how people were motivated at work. Thus Herzberg's *two-factor theory* of motivation and job satisfaction came to be developed. He called the dissatisfiers *hygiene factors*, and the satisfiers were called *motivators*. Absence of the hygiene factors caused dissatisfaction and their presence meant that people would not be dissatisfied but would still not be really motivated. His hygiene factors were: company policy and administrative procedures; the level and quality of supervision, salary and benefits; interpersonal relations; physical working conditions. The motivators were: achievement; recognition; the nature of the work itself; responsibility; advancement.

You will notice a relationship between Maslow's model and Herzberg's: the first three needs in Maslow's hierarchy equate to Herzberg's hygiene factors and the top two are Herzberg's motivators. There are two important outcomes for project managers. Both models show clearly the value of structuring jobs to give emphasis to the motivating factors at work so as to make jobs more interesting and likely to satisfy higher-level needs. Also, the motivators of Herzberg's model are within the scope of typical project structures and within the authority of project managers.

20.3 Leadership

In this section we turn our attention to the development of ideas about leadership and examine it under the headings of:

- Leaders are born, not made.
- Leadership is the functions you perform.
- Leadership style.

Leaders are born, not made Turning first to the idea that leaders are born and not made, we find the view that leadership consists of inherited traits and characteristics and it is these qualities that distinguish the leaders from the led. World-famous authorities were writing as late as the mid 1950s that 'leadership cannot be created or promoted. It cannot be taught or learned' (Peter Drucker in *The Practice of Management*, first published in 1955). This 'traits' theory of leadership was popular in the early part of this century in western democracies and one can see how the great entrepreneurs like Henry Ford, and the officer class of the First World War, gave it some credence, but no empirical work has ever isolated these essential traits and characteristics that are passed down the generations. Also the idea that certain people were born to lead and that others were born to be led went contrary to the development of political thought and particularly against the development of democratic ideas in the later twentieth century.

Leadership is the functions you perform Attention then moved away from traits theory and focused more on what leaders did: not on the personality and characteristics of the leader but on the functions of leadership. Whilst it was recognised that different situations would call for different emphases and that the same leadership position could change with time, the following fourteen functions of leadership were identified:

- *Executive*. The ultimate decision-maker, the most senior coordinator of policy and its execution.
- *Planner*. Determining how the organisation, department, team or group achieves its goals.
- *Policy-maker*. Establishing – with others but in the senior role – the goals and policies for the group being led.
- *Expert*. Here the leader contributes from what they know that others do not. Although using expert advice from others, the leader also has an expert role.

- *Representative*. The leader speaks for the group to the outside world. They are the group's official voice and the collector and channel of inward communication.
- *Organiser*. Designer – the leader creates the organisational structure.
- *Reward-giver*. The leader controls the led through the power to give rewards and apply punishment.
- *Exemplar*. The leader sets an example of what is expected through personal actions.
- *Arbitrator*. The leader is the final court of appeal for the led and controls the interpersonal relationships within the group.
- *Symbol*. The leader is a focus for the group and gives it some unity, additionally helping to set the team apart from other teams.
- *Backstop*. Individual members of the group can use the leader to take difficult decisions for them.
- *Ideologist*. Groups need beliefs, values and standards of behaviour. The leader creates these.
- *Father figure*. The leader is a focus for the positive emotional feelings of the led.
- *Scapegoat*. The leader is a focus for the negative emotional feelings of the led.

This is a long list and tends to stereotype the project leader as a take-away food menu: 'I'll have a portion of planner, organiser and symbol please with some father figure on the side', and leading a team is not that simple.

A much more practical and useful model than this rather functional 'have I done this today' approach is the one associated with John Adair, one of the UK's most influential leadership gurus and the first person to occupy a university chair in leadership in the UK. He held that the effectiveness of a leader is determined by their ability to meet three areas of need: the needs of the team, of the task, and of the individual. He represented these by three overlapping circles as shown in Figure 20.2.

Figure 20.2 Adair's overlapping circles

(John Adair, *Great Leaders*, Talbot Adair Press; www.johnadair.co.uk; info@johnadair.co.uk)

The team tasks that an effective leader carries out are:

- Building the team and maintaining team spirit.
- Developing work methods so that the team functions cohesively.
- Setting standards and maintaining discipline.
- Setting up systems for communication within the team.
- Training the team.
- Appointing subordinate leaders.

The leader's task activities are:

- Achieving team objectives.
- Defining tasks.
- Planning work.
- Allocating resources.
- Assigning responsibilities.
- Monitoring progress and checking performance.
- Controlling quality.

Meeting people's individual needs includes:

- Developing the individual.
- Balancing group needs and individual needs.
- Rewarding good performance.
- Helping with personal problems.

This is a very useful model in a project management context. It connects management and leadership: the task activities and some of the team ones being traditionally regarded as management, whereas satisfying individual needs and building and maintaining the team are leadership activities. The model also works best when there is a clear team focus, as in project activities. It also shows that attention has to be given to each of the three groups of activities, although the emphasis will change as the work progresses.

In his book *Great Leaders*, Adair writes:

> There are three kinds of need discernible in any human enterprise. First, people need to know where they are going, literally or metaphorically, in terms of their common task. Secondly, they need to be held together as a team. Last but not least, each individual, by virtue of being human and personal, also brings a set of needs that require satisfaction.

Leadership style We turn our attention now to issues of leadership style; how the leader carries out their leadership functions and relates to the members of the project or group being led. It is increasingly clear that managers can no longer rely solely on using their hierarchical position to discharge their leadership functions. This is particularly true in knowledge-based businesses like computing where individuals develop high skills and where there are many opportunities to use those skills. The importance of considering leadership style is based on the assumption that we are all more likely to work willingly and enthusiastically for leaders who have one particular style of leadership as opposed to another.

This is a rather simple view since a project team will have many members not all of whom may want the leader to have the same style. No doubt we can all think of people or occasions when 'just tell me what you want and I'll get on with it' is strongly at odds with 'could we discuss this issue and work out together the best way forward?' Nonetheless, leaders do have a style. Generally it comes from their attitudes and assumptions about human nature and how they would like to see people behave. Their style of leading their people may often mirror how they themselves would like to be led.

We could no doubt list many different leadership styles and identify their main characteristics. People talk of autocratic leaders, charismatic leaders, benevolent leaders and so on, but here we can focus on three general categories that you will probably recognise. The first is the centralist, autocratic, authoritarian leader. Here the centre of power is with 'the boss', who alone makes the decisions, sets policy, allocates work, and controls rewards and punishments. No doubt many of the leaders who were 'born and not made' in the industrial revolution operated in this way. At the other end of the scale is the democratic style where more power rests with the group, where leadership functions are shared and where the leader participates more in the group. There is still a clearly identifiable leader, but group members have the opportunity to influence and inform the decision-making processes and have the authority to take decisions themselves. We can also identify the supportive or *laissez-faire* style where the leader consciously decides to let the group have maximum freedom of action and not to intervene. The leader is available to provide support if it is needed but relies on the group members knowing when they need it and feeling comfortable in asking for it. It is, therefore, a special style requiring considerable maturity and skill in the leader and in each individual member of the group. In our view it is unlikely to be useful in typical project management structures. There is no doubt, however, that there is a resistance to autocratic styles of leadership and this trend looks set to continue. There is even legislation from the European Parliament in areas of employment law which legislates for an increase in the amount of consultation and democracy in industry and commerce.

In the late 1950s, two Americans, Tannenbaum and Schmidt, pulled together much of the work on leadership styles when they suggested that leaders have a range of leadership styles open to them, from one extreme where the boss exercises maximum control – boss-centred leadership – to the other where subordinates have a great deal of freedom – subordinate-centred or democratic leadership. Their continuum of leadership behaviour that was first published in the *Harvard Business Review* in 1973 is shown in Figure 20.3.

From this model came an identification of four styles of leadership employed by the leader. The leader:

■ *Tells*. The leader makes the decision and tells everyone what it is and what they must do.
■ *Sells*. The leader still makes the decision but then sells it to the people so that they accept it willingly.

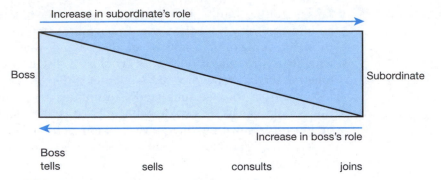

Figure 20.3 **The continuum of leadership behaviour**

(R. Tannenbaum and W. Schmidt, 'How to choose a leadership pattern', *Harvard Business Review*, May/June, 1973.)

- *Consults*. The leader presents ideas and gets feedback or makes proposals that can be changed. Perhaps at the extreme the leader presents the problem and takes the decision based on the information collected.
- *Joins*. The group makes the decision here within the scope of their authority that has previously been described to them. The leader then endorses their decision.

Tannenbaum and Schmidt also suggested that the particular style adopted by the leader depended on three forces: those in the leader, those in the subordinate and those in the situation. For example, a leader who found it difficult dealing with uncertainty, with a subordinate who was inexperienced, in a situation where there was some pressure of time, might well choose to operate at the 'boss-centred' end of the continuum. Conversely, in a relatively non-hierarchical organisation, with subordinates ready to assume some responsibility for decision-making and in whom the leader had confidence, then a more appropriate leadership style would be found towards the subordinate-centred end of the continuum. When revisiting this work in the early 1970s, Tannenbaum and Schmidt added a commentary emphasising the interdependence of the three forces and they recognised the growing importance of a fourth force: the environment or the context within which leadership is exercised.

In our experience, this is a useful model for project managers to consider since it links into the situational leadership ideas described in the next chapter dealing with project teams.

20.4 A leadership process

It will be clear that there is no one best style of leadership and that you could usefully use aspects of Maslow and Herzberg when thinking about motivation and – for leadership – aspects of Adair's three-circle model and the continuum of styles set out by Tannenbaum and Schmidt. With this in mind we want to conclude this chapter with some more recent and practical suggestions that result from the work of two American researchers, James Kouzes and Barry Posner. In the research a sample of leaders were asked what they did when they felt they were at their personal best as leaders, not managers. Over 1,300 middle and senior managers provided information based on their own experiences. A further 3,000 managers and their subordinates were involved in follow-up work. The findings were dramatic. In their book *The Leadership Challenge*, Kouzes and Posner say:

> Leaders do exhibit certain distinct practices when they are doing their best. And this behaviour varies little from industry to industry, profession to profession. Good leadership, it seems, is not only understandable but also a universal process.

To balance this view of leadership, they enquired about the expectations followers have of their leaders. Almost 4,000 people contributed to this study. According to this research the majority of us admire leaders who are:

- *Honest.* Followers observe the leader's behaviour and make an assessment about honesty. 'Practice what you preach', 'do what you say', 'let us see your values, where you stand' are what followers say about their leaders. Connected to honesty is trust. Good leaders trust their people and in so doing earn their people's trust.
- *Competent.* Whatever else you are, your people expect you to be competent, capable and effective. Competent at project management certainly – good at setting objectives, planning, scheduling, resourcing, monitoring and controlling. But there is something else. It is something special the leader brings that meets a key need and enables everything else to move forward.
- *Forward-looking.* Leaders are expected to have a sense of direction and some concern for the future of the organisation or the project or activity they are leading. At first sight this looks like a difficult expectation for a project team to have of their leader. By definition, project teams are formed, complete the project and then break up. There is, however, a future that project managers can describe. It is the future of the project completed and delivered to the overall satisfaction of the user. It is also a future where members of the project team have developed new skills and had this development recognised, signed off even, by the project manager.
- *Inspiring.* We all expect our leaders to be enthusiastic and positive about the future. Followers want to be inspired by their leader. This may be an uncomfortable concept for some people, coming too close to charismatic leadership and touching our emotions, but if our leader displays no commitment, no passion for our goal, why should we?

If this is what followers want, how does it translate into what the leader needs to do? The Kouzes and Posner research identified five leadership practices common to successful leaders. As project leaders you can implement them straightaway. They are:

- *Challenging the process.* Leaders are not content with what happens now and the way things work now. Leaders want things to be different, better. This is difficult for project managers who work hard to turn uncertainty into certainty. The challenge is to look for a better way of doing this and to be prepared to live with this uncertainty just that little bit longer.

■ *Inspiring a shared vision.* In our own research this was seen as a key characteristic of a leader. There is an urgency to make something happen and to create something that has not been created before. Describing this 'something' in a way that captures the hearts and minds of the team is inspiring a shared vision.

■ *Enabling others to act.* Leaders cannot achieve success by themselves. They enlist the support, help and commitment of their followers. A good leader empowers others to move the organisation towards the vision.

■ *Modelling the way.* This is all about behaving as you want your people to behave in achieving the shared vision. This vision cannot become a reality without hard work and the leader has to provide the resources to enable the vision to become reality. It is also about practising what you preach. Your people take more notice of what you do than of what you say.

■ *Encouraging the heart.* A timely and honestly meant 'well done' from our boss works wonders. Too often are people called to see the boss because of a failure or a complaint. Not often enough do managers look for opportunities to celebrate a success.

The Kouzes and Posner research shows that good leadership is 'an observable, learnable set of practices.' Like them, we commend to you the following behavioural commitments:

■ Challenge the process
  – Search out opportunities for improvement.
  – Experiment with new ideas and take some risks.
■ Inspire a shared vision
  – Describe the future for your people and help them to feel what it could mean.
  – Get others to help you to communicate this vision.
■ Enable others to act
  – Encourage people to work together to solve problems for the group.
  – Develop and coach your people so that they grow in confidence and skills.
■ Model the way
  – Be the example and behave as you want others to behave.
■ Encourage the heart
  – Recognise individual accomplishments.
  – Celebrate success.

You might like to look ahead here to the end of section 22.4 where the BT Global Challenge sailing race is mentioned. The highest-performing skippers all used components of this model at different times.

20.5 | Summary

As a project manager you can make a great difference to the success of your team by your leadership. It is not enough to be a good manager, even though that is a real achievement in itself.

We discussed the importance of motivating your team and described two useful models: Maslow's hierarchy of needs and Herzberg's two-factor model. We saw how they fitted together, how they could be used to give us a better understanding about motivation and how project managers could use them to help to motivate their teams.

Finally we looked at aspects of leadership and saw how ideas about it developed over time. We concluded by suggesting that you could make a real difference to the effectiveness of your project teams by adopting the leadership practices described by Kouzes and Posner.

Questions

1 Refer back to the introduction and consider again the leadership challenge at the end of the section. What kind of project management would you need to deliver to have people volunteer to work on your projects?

2 How can Maslow and Herzberg's theories of motivation help you to organise your project team and the way work is allocated?

3 Think of a situation at home, at work, at university or in a club to which you belong. It is a situation that involves you. You want to change the present circumstances and set a new basis for the future. Using the behavioural commitments at the end of section 20.4, what could you do to change things?

Case study

It will have become apparent by now that the leadership approach of Richard Vaughan, the E-Con project manager, is in essence inclusive and democratic. Although the tightness of the project timescale might suggest that a directive approach be used, Richard is aware that he is working with skilled individuals who need to be able to do things their own way as far as possible. In addition, of course, one of the development teams is managed by Peter Clay, France Vacances's IT manager, and Richard knows that Peter needs to be managed sensitively because of his residual worries about his own future once the project is over.

▶

Case study continued

Richard's approach is sensible in this type of project where, it can generally be assumed, staff do have the necessary technical skills and a desire to do a good job. The main danger on technical undertakings of this sort is over-engineering or perfectionism. The E-Con staff are less of a worry in this respect, as they are used to working within tight commercial constraints, than are France Vacances's own IT staff. For this reason, Richard makes special efforts to check progress informally on a regular basis with Peter Clay but, after the first few weeks, Richard is satisfied that Peter and his team are working as hard as the E-Con team to meet the project deadlines. In view of this, Richard scales back his visits and relies more on the regular checkpoint meetings.

At one point towards the start of the project, Siobhan Reid asks Richard to become involved in the issue of resourcing. This, it will be remembered, was one of the key risks and Siobhan was tasked with getting the resources tied down with E-Con's resources manager. However, she hits something of a 'brick wall' and asks Richard to use his greater authority (and to call in a few favours from the resources manager) to get the commitment she needs. Richard feels that this is an area where he should intervene and does so with good results, but thereafter he lets Siobhan get back to running her team in her own way.

Further reading

Adair, J (1989), *Great Leaders*, Talbot Adair Press

Kakabadse, A, Ludlow, R and Vinnicombe, S (1987), *Working in Organisations*, Cambridge University Press

Kouzes, J and Posner, B (1987), *The Leadership Challenge*, Jossey-Bass

Tannenbaum, R and Schmidt, W (1973), 'How to choose a leadership pattern', *Harvard Business Review*, May/June

21 Performance management

21.1 Introduction

In any project, it is the team members who do the work. Their performance is the project's performance; so it is important to be able to get a good performance from everyone. Each person in your team is more complex than all the computer systems you will ever work on. Each of us is an unpredictable mixture of rational and not-so-rational thought and emotion, ideas, feelings, ambitions, anxieties, good and bad. The challenge of managing such creatures as ourselves excites many project managers and makes them see this aspect of their job as the most rewarding. The same challenge makes other project managers fearful of this aspect of their job. Some of these managers avoid the more risky aspects of managing people by pretending that these aspects do not exist or are not important. This is a pity given that the effective management of people is almost always a distinguishing characteristic of a well-run project.

In days gone by, the purpose of a management was to control the workforce: to tell them what to do and keep them at it. Nowadays it is recognised that such an approach will not bring competitive advantage – quite the reverse. People in the IT industry are well educated and expect to be involved in the enterprise to which they commit their time. Therefore, whilst management still needs to coordinate the efforts of people and groups, an approach based on power and close control is no longer appropriate. The modern view of management is that it supports the workforce, enables it to do its work and, especially as IT skills change fast and are often in short supply, develops people through coaching and exposure to new skills in their jobs.

Most people carry around in their heads their own private theories of how to deal with people. These develop from personal experience and reflection. Most managers adapt these ideas into private theories of how to manage others and make a team perform. Unfortunately, no one person's experience can tell us the whole story as we are all so different. Some 'private theories' of management are actually harmful and none is good enough by itself. That is why it is important to read about and discuss management methods widely. However, many managers do not bother, and the training supplied for this most complex aspect of organisational activity is usually far less than that supplied for more measurable skills such as programming or accounting.

The project manager needs to motivate the team as a whole and to motivate each individual separately. Team motivation stems from the personal enthusiasm of the manager, how the work is allocated and structured, a clear vision of the goal and the agreed standards for getting there. The project manager sets an example with his or her own personal organisation and behaviour and creates a climate of progress and acceptance of change. Individual motivation is achieved through personal rapport and the 'unwritten contract' of what the individual and the project manager expect from each other. A crucial ingredient of this motivation is the design of the individual's job, which must have the right amount of challenge and variety and lead towards a visible and significant end-product. We all need agreed objectives that tie into goals we understand as well as personal and career development from challenging work, professional standards, feedback and coaching.

You probably already know a great deal about managing performance from your own experience and observations. Your learning will continue as long as you let it and as long as you are prepared to question your current ideas. This chapter will help you.

21.2 Setting objectives

An objective is a statement of something to be achieved. At the minimum, an objective will state the product or result of an activity and a time by when it is to be achieved. The level of challenge presented by an objective should be appropriate to the person who is to achieve it. If it is too low, the person has no opportunity for development and may get bored and frustrated. If it is too high, the objective may be seen as unachievable and the person will not wish to expend much energy on it. This also means that the achievement of the objective must be in the person's power and not dependent on chance or the actions of others. The objective must also specify a precise outcome so there is no doubt about whether it has been achieved or not. It is useful, too, if an objective has measurable milestones on the way to completion so you can, if it is appropriate, check on progress.

It is easy to get bogged down with long lists of criteria for 'what makes a good objective'. Such lists can be helpful if they remind you that your objectives have room for improvement; but they can be unhelpful: setting objectives is hard enough without feeling obliged to work at them until they meet a whole list of qualities. If you feel this is happening when you try to set objectives, step back and remember their purpose: we set objectives to coordinate effort across the team and to motivate team members by giving them clear tasks and development opportunities. Objectives lead us towards the overall aim of the project – and towards people's career aims as well; they provide the strategy for getting there by showing each of us the next step we have to take. The purpose is to write objectives which are useful, not necessarily to write objectives that meet any list of qualities.

Let us approach this subject instead, then, by looking at the process of developing objectives. We can imagine a cascade of objectives. At the top is the purpose of the organisation for which you work. Part of that purpose will be the successful completion of your project – that is your project's objective. Part of that will be objectives for particular pieces of work or functions of the system. Contributing to those will be the next level of objectives, those of particular teams. The cascade runs down to personal objectives for each individual on the project and finally to detailed work instructions for each task. This idea is appealing for its logical sense of smaller efforts all combining to achieve combined efforts which come together to meet an overall goal.

However, this neat picture conflicts with one more important attribute of an objective: it must be agreed between the manager and the person accepting it. Simply imposing a set of objectives on someone will often not work because that person will have no ownership of them and so have little commitment to meeting them. Team members will usually work towards imposed objectives but without much enthusiasm; they will not take much trouble to solve problems they encounter and their overall level of commitment to your project will be low. Also, the team members who do the work may have better ideas on how to do it than their managers – some would say they will almost always have better ideas because they are closer to the work. Thus the idea of a top-down cascade of objectives is complicated by the fact that the objectives must work from the bottom up as well.

This apparent paradox of having a downward cascade of objectives, which is agreed and accepted by everyone below, can be resolved in the following way:

1 Firstly, you must communicate a clear vision of what your project is there to achieve. This will enable your team members to appreciate that their objectives must contribute to that purpose.
2 Secondly, you will need to negotiate with subordinates and superiors to achieve a consistent hierarchy of objectives with which all parties are satisfied.
3 Thirdly, you must be prepared to reconsider the way you planned to go about things. For example, you may have planned to keep team members on work they are already familiar with in order to get the job done quickly. When you have heard your team members' concerns you may decide to give them work they are less familiar with so they can learn new skills and stay interested in their work.

The negotiations up and down to reach agreement on all sides, the changes in project needs and staffing supply that will happen and the improvements that can always be made to objectives – to make them more specific, measurable and so forth – mean that objectives, like a system design, are never done, finished and correct in one pass. The development of objectives is an iterative process. They will always be subject to change, even after they have been agreed. A set of objectives is a living document.

This means that setting objectives takes a fair, but not huge, amount of work on a more or less continuous basis. Balance that against the benefits: having people working with commitment towards objectives that are truly

Good objectives are **SMART** objectives because they are:

- **S**pecific. There is a specific or precise outcome or deliverable; some new behaviour or achievement.

- **M**easurable. Progress towards the achievement of the deliverable can be measured.

- **A**chievable. The objective is capable of being reached. It doesn't have to be easy or simple; it should be stretching and developmental.

- **R**elevant. The person or people given the objective must be able to have an impact on it. It needs to sensible for them and relevant to their work.

- **T**ime bound. When do we start, when must we finish, or when will the next review assess progress?

Figure 21.1 SMART objectives

relevant to the project will mean good productivity. As well as that, the very process of setting and amending objectives with a team member is a perfect opportunity to build your relationship and provide coaching and support.

Figure 21.1 uses the mnemonic SMART to describe good objectives.

21.3 Reviewing performance

Having set objectives, you will be able to review performance against them. Good project managers do not necessarily wait until formal appraisal to review performance: they are constantly alert for any sign that things are not going as they should and will investigate them quickly. They also check team members' work at a frequency which depends on:

- The level of skill or competence of the team member.
- The commitment of the team member.
- The importance of the team member's work to the project.

The frequency of these regular checks will be discussed and agreed with team members. Remember, the purpose of performance reviews, whether it is the annual appraisal or an informal chat in the corridor, is not simply to find instances of poor performance or mistakes and correct them. It is better to 'catch people doing something right' and use that as an opportunity to recognise and acknowledge positive contributions.

When you find an aspect of performance that is below the standards you expect or is not contributing to agreed objectives, you have a coaching opportunity. More is said about coaching later in this chapter but for now we shall look at one approach to closing the gap between actual and required performance. Your objective is not just to solve the immediately apparent problem but also to develop the team member so similar performance problems do not arise again. It is most important that poor performance is addressed as soon as it appears. Project managers cannot afford to tolerate it if they are to meet their objectives.

Preparation Gather all the information you can. Clear, indisputable facts are best, but feelings are also worth considering in the case of, for example, a team member who has upset another. Be warned that facts that you think are clear and indisputable may not be seen in that way by your team member. If your or the team member's feelings are high at the time, have a cooling-off period. Decide on your objective for the performance review. In general it will be to improve performance but you need to work out just what that means in each case.

Establish and agree the performance gap This involves establishing the standards you expect for your team member's performance and the actual level of performance, to demonstrate that there is a gap between them. Do not get into debates about the facts of the matter. If you have a fact wrong, acknowledge that. If you disagree over what is a fact, listen to the team member then assert the truth as you see it. It is acceptable to have differing points of view but in the end it is yours that counts. Stay calm and non-threatening and listen carefully to what your team member has to say. Show that you have heard and understood the team member's point of view without necessarily agreeing or disagreeing with it. Do not yet get into discussion of reasons for the gap or mitigating factors; that comes later. You are not trying to apportion blame, just to establish the facts.

Explore reasons for the performance gap As the manager, you are ultimately responsible for any shortfall in performance. Even if it is clearly the fault of the team member, it is no use blaming them; you have to find a way forward. So at this stage discuss how the shortfall came about. Some possible causes might be:

- Inadequate job description, work instruction or objectives.
- Lack of training or on-the-job coaching from you.
- Personal problems such as a medical condition or problems outside work.
- The team member did not understand or accept the performance standards.
- The team member has a grievance against the organisation and is taking private industrial action.

Focus on behaviour – what the team member did or did not do – rather than personality. This is the time to discuss mitigating factors but the key skill is listening. Ask open questions and concentrate on the responses without making judgements about them to make sure you get a good picture of the team member's point of view. You can give your point of view only when you have done this, so avoid questions like, 'Surely you must have thought that . . .', as these carry your judgements. You may find the performance problem is a result of a deeper problem such as dissatisfaction with career progress. Only patient listening will uncover such underlying issues. It takes time, so make sure you have allowed enough.

Agree steps to eliminate the gap The possible reasons for poor performance listed above could be overcome in many ways. It is better if the team member suggests solutions, as he or she will be more committed to personal ideas for eliminating the performance gap.

You may have to accept that the performance shortfall was a result of a shortfall in your own performance: perhaps you had not given enough time to coaching or support or objective-setting. You were never meant to be perfect and you can use cases like these for your personal development and as a means for building trust between you and the team. If the performance problem does turn out to be the result of a more personal problem, you must refer the team member to someone qualified to deal with it. You may also decide to lower the performance you expect of that team member until the problem is resolved. If so, you must explain this allowance to other team members without breaching confidence.

Summarise   Go over the main points of your discussion again to make sure you both have the same understanding. Make sure the steps for eliminating the performance gap are clear, with precise dates and actions to be taken. Inform the team member whether you are keeping a written record of the interview, and, if so, for how long. Inform the team member what will happen if the agreed steps are not taken. Finish with an assurance that there is nothing to worry about if the team member does what you have both agreed.

Follow up   You need to fix a follow-up date to review progress towards the agreed actions soon after the first interview. You will also need to agree other review dates to monitor progress all the way back to the required performance standard. Recognise progress but do not hesitate to take the matter further if progress is unacceptable.

This model can be applied to all sorts of performance problems. For most problems, in the first case it will be applied very informally – just a chat in a quiet corner which the team member will not think of as anything more than helpful concern on your part. For more serious problems, and lesser problems that are not resolved by the informal chat, you will need to increase the level of formality. This may make you feel uncomfortable. If so, talk it over with someone first. If you ever come close to invoking formal discipline procedures, always discuss it with a qualified person such as a personnel manager.

21.4 Performance appraisal systems

Most organisations have a formal performance appraisal system of some kind. These systems vary a great deal in purpose, depth, style and degree of bureaucracy. They also vary in the benefits they bring to an organisation and the degree of respect they attract from the workforce.

You need to ask: what is the purpose of my organisation's appraisal system? The answer may be: to assist the management in the determination of pay rises – and perhaps promotions within a grade or job title system. In this case the key feature of the appraisal must be fairness. Find out how the pay system works in your organisation so you can make it work for your people. No pay system is ever totally objective. You need to make sure your team members understand the subjective element. It helps if you have clear objectives against which you can measure performance. The situation you are aiming for is that everyone understands why they got the pay rise they did.

The answer may be: to develop staff. In this case the formal appraisal system is just one component of your continuing effort to develop a flexible workforce, able to work in a variety of situations, to contribute in many ways and with a range of skills that spans the whole of software development. Fairness is not really an issue in this case as the appraisal focuses on one person at a time.

Most likely, the answer to the question is: a bit of both. The appraisal system exists to develop staff and to assist with decisions about pay. Even if it is said to be only about pay or promotion, you will want to use it as an opportunity to develop your staff. Even if it is said to be only about development, your staff probably believe, rightly or wrongly, that what goes on at the formal appraisal will affect their pay levels in the future.

This leads to a problem. If your boss asks you which areas of your work you need to improve, then you will probably be prepared to discuss some if you think the purpose of the meeting is to help you develop. But if you think your boss is gathering information for the next pay review, you may be tempted to brush over your weaknesses.

The way around this problem is to tie good pay awards with proven development. After all, why should an employer give you more than a basic rise if you are no more skilled than you were last year? Now, when your boss asks you about your weaknesses, you are doubly keen to discuss them, both to have them resolved and to be rewarded for this development at the next pay review. The importance of setting objectives for a team member's development is now clear.

Preparation for an appraisal

The best way to prepare for an appraisal is to practise day-to-day developmental management: regularly revisit the objectives you agreed with a team member, review performance at appropriate times and provide coaching whenever an opportunity arises. You may find it helpful to keep a log of these ongoing interactions so that when the time comes for the formal appraisal, your preparation is mostly done. But you will still need to review all that has happened in the previous period and decide what you want to achieve in the appraisal. The team member also needs to prepare. Fix the meeting far enough ahead to allow sufficient time. Remind the member of the purpose of appraisal and the type of preparation you think they should do. If it is the first appraisal, you should sit down and talk the process through. Remember, people are often nervous about their appraisal.

During the appraisal meeting

You and your team member need to review performance, if only to set the scene for looking to the future. You will find many books which give you formulae for how many good points are needed for each bad point or which suggest rules such as starting and finishing with a good point and sandwiching the bad points between. These hints are useful, but what matters more is how you go about raising bad points – or improvement areas, or development opportunities, or whatever you wish to call them. One approach is not to raise them at all but to ask the team member to assess personal performance using a technique called drawing out. This means asking neutral, not loaded, questions about how they think they have performed, particularly strong points and areas in which they would like to improve. Most people are modest about their performance. You will find you have many opportunities to praise the team member for contributions they have overlooked or played down. They are likely to come up with more areas for improvement than you could identify and will be more keen to work on them than if you had pointed them out. Drawing out avoids the risks associated with criticising a colleague, and it usually leads to greater improvement than criticism would have done.

However, there are problems with drawing out. Firstly, you must make sure your questions are neutral. You will have your ideas about areas in which the team member should improve and, when the member does not identify them, it is tempting to turn neutral drawing out into a form of forced confession. This is a serious mistake as it will undermine your credibility as a genuine listener and therefore as a good manager. If your team member comes up with several valid areas for improvement but not a minor one which you had thought of, you may wish to abandon your minor point in favour of the ones identified by the team member. Do not abandon your idea if it is important or simply to avoid any awkwardness in bringing it up. If you decide not to abandon it, do not dress it up as drawing out. Say: 'I've thought of an area I think you should work on . . .'. It might seem a crucially important problem to you but the team member may not think so or may genuinely not have noticed it. A second problem with drawing out is that you can overdo it. Most team members will want to know what you think of their performance. So give them your views on what they have said even if it is a simple agreement.

The most important activity during the appraisal interview is listening. If you find you are doing most of the talking then you are doing it wrong. Second most important is a 'future orientation': however the areas for improvement have been identified, you and your team member need to devise a plan for making the improvement happen.

Recording the appraisal interview

You may have to complete a form summarising the discussion. An example of an appraisal form is included here (Figure 21.2). This is the appraisal form used at Henley Management College. You will see that it covers a review of past performance and the achievement of objectives, provides an opportunity to deal with general issues not covered under the review of objectives – such as the supervision you get from your boss – establishes objectives for the next appraisal period, and sets out a development plan and career objectives. It is used in practice with sets of guidance notes for the person being appraised and for the appraiser. Some of these notes have been incorporated into the form for this example to better show how it works. If the contents of the form are going to be used for decisions about pay or career development you need to get the form right. But very often the main benefit of appraisal is the private discussion between the two of you, building your relationship, reflecting and

PERFORMANCE & DEVELOPMENT REVIEW

Name: .... Department: ....

Job title: .... Date appointed
to current position: ....

Date of last review: .... Date of this review: ....

Reviewer: .... Second level Reviewer: ....

Section 1: REVIEW OF PAST PERFORMANCE/OBJECTIVES

SIGNIFICANT CHANGES IN WORK CONTENT DURING PERIOD UNDER REVIEW (if any)

Have there been any big changes in your job/role that were not originally planned, or things that you've done for the first time? Perhaps you've run some user workshops for the first time, or mastered some new technology or method.

Please ensure an updated job description is sent to Personnel

REVIEW OF OBJECTIVES

This assumes of course that you and your boss did agree some objectives for you! To what extent have they been achieved. What is the evidence for this achievement? If you haven't achieved them, what are the reasons and what do you propose should be done about it?

Figure 21.2 Appraisal form

(Reproduced with permission from Henley Management College)

REVIEW OF OVERALL PERFORMANCE

This is where you think about the way you do the job. What strengths do you want to highlight? What development areas do you want to discuss? You'll need to think about technical and non-technical issues, interpersonal skills, contributions to the team, problems that you've solved that were difficult or important. Have you been supervising others? What about relations with the client?

How much effort have you put in? What new things do you know (look ahead to what is said in the last chapter about keeping a learning log)? How much more valuable have you become to the project and to the organisation?

GENERAL COMMENTS/ISSUES DISCUSSED DURING REVIEW

Here you can note and comment on things not covered elsewhere. These might be the working environment, the support you get from your boss and any other general issues that you want to raise.

To what extent have the development plans made at the last appraisal been achieved?

Figure 21.2 *(continued)*

Section 2: PERSONAL OBJECTIVES FOR THE COMING YEAR

Objectives agreed	Date to be achieved by
What are the key targets for you over the next appraisal period? They can be project based or personal. They should support the project's goals and your long-term career development.	

Section 3: DEVELOPMENT PLAN

Areas for further development – identify skills, knowledge or attributes to be developed	Type of activity identified	Timing
This is your development plan. It can include things that will make you more useful to the project and things that give you transferable value, things that increase your employability. How will this training and development be achieved and assessed? Is there a budget for it?		

Figure 21.2 *(continued)*

How well does the current role meet the jobholder's aspirations for the next 12 months and in the longer term?

This section is about describing the match between the work challenges and demands, and your own personal goals.

Section 4: EMPLOYEE COMMENTS

Please indicate whether you have:

a. Fully discussed all aspects of your performance   Yes ☐   No ☐

b. Agreed the contents of this Review form   Yes ☐   No ☐

c. Agreed the objectives for next year   Yes ☐   No ☐

D. Fully discussed any training and development needs with your reviewer   Yes ☐   No ☐

Comment below if you wish to record any additional information or areas of disagreement.

Section 5: SIGNATURES

SIGNATURE OF EMPLOYEE

Signed_____ Date_____

SIGNATURE OF REVIEWER

Signed_____ Date_____

COMMENTS FROM NEXT LEVEL OF MANAGEMENT

Signed_____ Date_____

Figure 21.2 (*continued*)

learning from the past, planning developments in the future. In that case, do not let the form get in the way. It might be useful in setting an agenda for your discussion and recording the main points, or you may decide to set your own agenda and complete the form in the sequence that seems best. If the team member has any problems that you think might lead to disciplinary action it is essential you record these. It is also only fair to record other significant problems, otherwise you are giving the team member leave to ignore something that may slow their career progress for years to come. Opinion is divided over whether to complete the form during the interview, and so avoid any dispute over wording later, or write it up alone when the team member is back at work. Decide for yourself, but be consistent and do not be one of those people who writes it up the next day, the next week, never. Your team member should get a copy of the completed form.

The secret of successful appraisal is to make it an ongoing process, part of your regular contact with team members, just as you regularly review objectives and progress towards them. The formal appraisal then becomes just a summary of all that has happened, with no surprises on either side, and an opportunity to step back, reflect on it all and plan for the future.

21.5 Reprimands

The previous two sections dealt with the continuous process of developing staff. There are occasions, however, when a single event needs a quick response. For example, an outburst of anger or an excessive lunch break need an immediate reprimand or you will be seen to be condoning the action. Like some other aspects of management, giving a reprimand fills some managers with dread because they are fearful of the consequences. But there is nothing to fear if you approach the reprimand from the point of view that it is not a telling off, like parents give to naughty children, but another opportunity to build the relationship with your team member and provide coaching. The purpose of the reprimand is to improve performance. The process of delivering a reprimand described below is a tailored version of the general performance improvement process described in section 21.3.

Fact-finding and diagnosis If you have witnessed the event in question you need to make sure your feelings about it are controlled before taking action. If you have had the event reported to you, remember such reports are often interpretations of the facts. Keep an open mind until you have heard the other side of the story. This means the fact-finding continues into the interview with the individual concerned. You could start with a question like: 'I've heard there was an altercation of some kind in the tea room this morning. Can you talk me through events as you saw them?' Reflect back the content of what you are told as well as the feelings behind it, to get a clear understanding. Summarise this to make sure you have a correct understanding.

Communicating the reprimand If, having heard all sides of the story, you decide a reprimand is in order, here are a few guidelines for communicating it.

- Do it in private and keep the discussion confidential.
- Stick with the facts of what the person said or did at the specific instance or instances you are discussing. Do not make generalisations such as, 'You're always upsetting people' – this cannot be literally true and so is easily attacked. Also avoid comments about character such as, 'You're difficult to work with' – this may be your view but you need to justify it with examples.
- Do not get into an argument – as soon as you do, you have lost. When the team member responds, listen and reflect back what you have heard, to check and show you have understood. Be prepared to change your mind, but if not, stick with your view on the matter while also acknowledging the team member's view.
- Explain the consequences of a repetition of the behaviour, such as a formal warning.
- Disclose your personal disappointment over the incident.
- Finish with a statement like, 'Aside from this one aspect, your work is going really well and I'm especially impressed with the way you . . . so it's important that this present issue doesn't recur.'

Follow-up When you next have a chat about progress as part of your general supervision, bring up the issue that led to the reprimand. If appropriate, acknowledge any improvements and congratulate the team member over the way they took it. You could ask for feedback on how you handled it: the team member may have things to offload, and talking these through will help. Reaffirm the value you place on having that person in your team. All this will help commitment, performance and motivation. If feelings have calmed down you can use the event to progress your relationship. Discussing what led to the event and how the reprimand went may lead you both to agree a new coaching style or that more challenging work is needed. If things are no better, you will need to take it further using the performance improvement process described in section 21.3 or your organisation's formal disciplinary procedure.

21.6 Performance improvement through coaching

So far, much of this chapter has dealt with situations in which there is a performance problem. But if you wait until there is a problem before helping someone develop, you will soon earn a poor reputation. The development of team members is seen by many people as one of the main reasons for having managers at all, so you need to be doing it all of the time. One of the first questions to tackle is: who needs coaching? The simple answer is everyone, but it is possible to spread your coaching effort too thinly. It may be better to concentrate your efforts on just one or two team members for a few months, then review the situation. Do not forget you can sometimes delegate the coaching of more junior team members to senior team members. This will help them both, but you need to keep an eye on things.

There are three matters to consider when deciding where to focus your coaching effort:

- *Motivation.* How much does each team member want to develop at this stage in their career? What sort of skills or work are they interested in? Do they bring enthusiasm to their work? If not, then the new skills you help to develop may be put to little use.
- *Potential.* Is the team member capable of learning the new skills at the moment? Consider long- and short-term potential.
- *Benefits the coaching would bring.* If a person is already good at their job and happy in it, coaching will bring less benefit than if it were applied to someone with room to improve.

Having identified that a team member needs coaching, how do you go about it? There can be no doubt that the prime means of helping someone to develop a new skill is to give them a job that requires use of that skill. If you divide up your project's work so everyone works with just a narrow set of skills, not only will they become frustrated, but they will also develop only their narrow set of skills and so be a less flexible workforce.

Once the work has been divided in a way that exposes the team member to new skills, you can take them through a process of learning and development. The process outlined below is based on **situational leadership**, developed by Kenneth Blanchard and his colleagues.

Situational leadership uses two sets of management behaviours: direction, which is one-way communication consisting of giving specific instructions and close supervision; and support, which is two-way communication, consisting of listening, supporting, encouraging and talking around problems. This can be represented in Figure 21.3. This shows the leader's behaviour and how it matches the follower's needs. Let's take an example. A new person joins your team. You have to rush off to a meeting so you give them the standards manual to read, sit them in front of a pc with some interview notes and tell

Figure 21.3 Coaching styles

(Based on the Situational Leadership Model developed by Blanchard *et al.*)

them to draw up a current physical DFD. They are at development level four – they need some substantial direction about what they should be doing and how they should do it. And you're treating them as though they are fully familiar with what's needed and confident enough to get on with it and don't need any direction at all.

The model suggests:

1 That people new to a job or unfamiliar with a task tend to be very keen but not very competent. This is sometimes called 'unconscious incompetence' as they may not be aware of their lack of ability. They need some support and a great deal of direction.

2 As time moves on, they start to acquire skills but the initial enthusiasm wears off. They have had a few setbacks but, with your help, have learned from them. They still need direction as they have more to learn, but you must increase the level of support.

3 Later still, they reach a stage of competence at the job, but enthusiasm and commitment waver up and down from day to day. This is the stage most of us are at for much of the time. They need less direction now. More than a little direction will probably irritate as they know the job now. They still need a good level of support to keep them emotionally tied to the work.

4 If the three earlier stages have been done well, new team members will probably make it to the fourth stage. They are very skilled at the job and it has become part of them, so that they always tackle it with energy. They require only infrequent direction from you and the level of support can be cut down, though never removed entirely. Such a team member takes up very little of your time and is probably ready for a new challenge. What can you delegate next?

Thus your management style needs to change as the team member changes. That sounds obvious and it is, but managers do not always do it. The model is simple but there are some important things to remember when using it. Firstly, people do not move through the four stages at a constant rate. People move at different speeds depending on their ability and the work involved. People also move backwards through the stages: someone once very committed to the job becomes weary of it; someone once highly skilled gets sloppy. You need to adjust your coaching style appropriately (see Table 21.1).

It is not for you alone to decide on a team member's stage of development and the style it requires. This is best done in partnership. You need to agree

Table 21.1 Summary of appropriate coaching styles at changing stages of development

Stage	1	2	3	4
Level of skill	Low	Fairly low	High	Very high
Level of commitment	High	Moderate	Variable	High
Direction needed	High	High	Low	Low
Support needed	Low	High	High	Low

any changes in coaching style with the team member or they will wonder what is going on. Every change in style will feel like a risk to you because it is a risk to delegate important work to someone else. You may feel you want to be in control more, doing the most important work yourself, giving precise instructions for how to get a job done and supervising closely. This will not work. Your staff will become demoralised and you will overwork. Effective managers take risks – but they limit them by planning and managing the risk. They can design exposure to new skills into a team member's job and then coach that person – or have someone else do the coaching – even though the acquisition of those skills forms the main process by which technical skills are developed in your team and the industry as a whole. A well-thought-out appraisal system and appropriate monitoring of performance play their part.

There are other ways of developing skills that work well alongside these primary means. The first is training courses – often the first solution thought of when a skills deficit is noticed. Courses make a big difference when good ones are used at about the right time but are of limited use unless tied into coaching on the job. As well as traditional courses, consider other learning solutions. There are correspondence courses, videos and – often overlooked – books. You can also consider conferences, lending a team member to another team and promoting internally as an alternative to recruiting from outside. The IT industry often complains of skills shortages. You can help avoid this problem by developing your staff through coaching.

21.7 Performance management tools

This section presents an overview of methodical approaches to skill development and to the assessment of and reward for skill acquisition. The traditional approach most often taken in analysing an area of skill is to break it down into its component parts, often in great detail. This approach has had great success in the design of industrial processes. In recent years, however, the concept of the 'competence' has become accepted in the service industries and many professions. A competence is a detailed statement of what a skilled worker will do to achieve a task within the job and the standards by which the activity will be done. Two examples are shown in Tables 21.2 and 21.3.

A competence is a basic unit of skill. On the positive side, this approach to the analysis of skill enables jobs to be defined in great detail, training to target the identified skill elements, and the assessment of people against the required skills. Other potential benefits are the identification of best practice and accurate recruitment based on selecting candidates with a defined skill profile.

On the negative side, this approach can become bureaucratic and inflexible: large documents are written describing the identified skills that can be out of date before they are published. The focus sometimes shifts so far towards analysing a skill that the question of developing it is overlooked. If pay is linked to the acquisition of competences the issue becomes contentious and a great deal of resentment can be generated over what counts as a competence, what

Table 21.2 Example of a competence: from a systems company

OPERATION OF A SUPPORT SERVICE COMPETENCE		
Description: the participant must be able to provide a centrally supported service for a development project.		

Condition	Activity	Criteria
Given maintenance requirements	(a) Monitor performance against agreed service levels	Performance statistics, activity logs and fault logs are regularly collected and analysed
		Performance degradation of the system is recognised and possible solutions researched and actioned
		Unreliable or outdated components are replaced
		Need to enhance or upgrade the system is recognised and reported to management
Given agreed service levels	(b) Monitor customer satisfaction	Regular reviews of service performance are conducted with users
		Users are informed of problems and consulted about solutions
Given changes to required service	(c) Establish changes required	Changes in requirements are documented
		Plans for changes in capacity to meet changed requirements are researched fully
		Plans for changes in maintenance requirements are researched fully
		Alternative plans and costs are presented clearly and discussed with management and users
Given requirement to change configuration	(d) Initiate changes to configuration	Instructions to users are given clearly and checked to have been understood
		Changes initiated are in accordance with manufacturer's and organisation's procedures
		Documentation requirements are specified

Table 21.3 Example of a competence: from a civil service organisation

EQUAL OPPORTUNITIES COMPETENCE	

Performance criteria	Outcome
Is committed to equal treatment for all staff	People help and support each other and there is a good team spirit
Ensures equal opportunities and fairness for all staff so that no member of the team is unfairly discriminated against	Team readily cooperates to achieve team goals

it takes to be accredited as having one, and their relative value. Skilled engineers may resent the apparent reduction of their skill to small elements and may be right in thinking that this reductionist approach loses a great deal of what the job as a whole entails.

In the face of these potential advantages and dangerous pitfalls, many organisations and some professional bodies are devising their own system of methodical skill definition, designed to suit their own purpose and circumstances. Your organisation may well have such a system in place, perhaps as part of a professional development scheme. If so, it is important that you understand what it is trying to achieve – and what it is trying not to achieve – as well as how to operate it on behalf of the staff of your project.

The system will be documented. Like a quality system, it is there to help you, but it will not always help if you want instant answers. If the system has been devised thoroughly there will be a considerable volume of documents but structured in such a way that the section you need at any time can be found quickly. Like a quality system, it should have a means for you to challenge it if you find it unhelpful so that it can be continually improved. Such improvement processes will be built into the system so it can keep up with changes in technology and working practices. No job is the same as it was a year ago.

In the same way, no one job is the same as any other so it is usually not worth trying to define every aspect of a job and including them all in the job definition. There are certain skills that everyone needs. These are the core competences and include skills such as writing a progress report, making positive contributions in a meeting, telephone skills, and health and safety awareness. Then there are skills which are part of some jobs but not all and yet are still common enough for it to be worth analysing them. These are the job competences and could include skills such as writing a unit test plan, conducting an analysis interview and presenting a training event. Every job will also require its special skills which are not a part of the formal skills system – for example, the skill of determining which skill to use in a given situation or some technical skill related to a project application. Just because these skills are not listed in the list of competences, do not forget to coach people in them or recognise their effective use.

A job profile is a list of all the competences a person requires to perform a job. Ideally, the job holder will have enough of these competences to do the job but not have them all, and so can develop these competences through doing the job. A job holder who has all the required competences may or may not be able to do the job as a whole well but will probably become bored by the lack of new skill challenges.

Systems such as these can help you in your performance management activities by defining the standards of the job and identifying the learning needed by each member of your team. Acquisition of competences can by itself be a useful reward and motivator. If your organisation has such a system it should provide a useful framework for many of your performance management activities. Even if your organisation does not have such a system you can involve your team in their own management and development by discussing the core competences with them as a group and discussing job competences with them individually. But always remember, a framework such as this is meant to help and is not an end in itself.

21.8 Summary

Managers who are uncomfortable with the human side of projects sometimes dismiss it as 'soft stuff' of little relevance. This may help them feel better but they are underrating what many other managers see as the most challenging and rewarding part of their job. It is also the aspect that makes perhaps the biggest difference in the success or failure of a project.

The project manager can make an immense difference to productivity, morale and the quality of working life by paying attention to performance development, through designing the project so staff get to use a wide range of skills and seeing that they receive the necessary coaching and support to master these skills. This in turn can help the IT industry to overcome problems of skills shortage and damage to its reputation from the regular stories in the media of expensive, even catastrophic, project failures.

Effective performance management takes time, but the effort required from the project manager is spread out, so that it is rare that a long period needs to be spent on it. Performance management becomes a natural part of every day.

Questions

1 You are dissatisfied with the general level of performance of one of your team. The quality of work is below your expectations. How will you deal with this?

2 A member of your team exhibits disruptive behaviour. Her work is good but she is not a team player. The consequences are that she does not contribute to team effort and her colleagues find her difficult to work with; the project team secretary has refused to work with her at all. How could this serious problem have arisen? What can be done now?

3 Describe the process of setting objectives. What might be three objectives for a newly appointed junior programmer?

Case study

Soon after the development of the website begins, Siobhan Reid starts to notice that one of her developers, Greg Martin, seems unable to keep up with the timescale for his tasks, which are all delivered one or two days late. By juggling tasks around, Siobhan is able to avoid any slippage in the project but she is puzzled by Greg's performance. She does not know him very well but he came to the team highly recommended by other E-Con managers and she wonders what to do about his underperformance.

She discusses the matter with Richard Vaughan, the project manager, who has worked with Greg before and is similarly baffled by the situation since he rates Greg very highly. It is decided that Siobhan must tackle the problem as, although she has managed to contain the slippage to date, this may not be so easy later in the project.

Case study continued

Siobhan makes an arrangement to meet with Greg. She reserves France Vacances's meeting room and sets aside a morning for the discussion as she does not want it to be hurried and wants time to explore Greg's problem in depth.

The meeting begins with the usual courtesies and Siobhan asks Greg if everything is well with him; he says that it is. Siobhan now produces her project plan and describes, factually and non-critically, where Greg has delivered late and the effect this has had on the project. Greg responds that the tasks must have been underestimated – 'not the first time in this company'.

This is the first indication that Greg is not happy with E-Con and so Siobhan explores that: 'Where else have the estimates been a problem?' After a little coaxing, it emerges that, on his previous project, Greg had worked for a rather inexperienced project manager who had a habit of underestimating everything. When tasks were (inevitably) finished late, this project manager then blamed everyone but himself for the result and tried to recover the situation by bullying people to work harder. Greg had been on the point of resigning when he was transferred to the France Vacances project and, although that should have provided some relief, he was still smarting from his previous experience and lacking in motivation.

Siobhan told Greg that she had been very pleased to get him on to her team as she had heard good reports of his abilities (including from the project manager that he did not like) and reassured him that, if he really thought the estimates were unrealistic, she was happy to review them with him. It was not her approach to deliver projects by exploiting her team and nor was it Richard Vaughan's approach: a sentiment which Greg said accorded with his own experience of Richard. It was agreed that she and Greg would review each task before he started, in order to confirm the estimates (although, as it turns out, Greg accepts them all).

Greg went back to work and his productivity improved immediately. At the end of the project, Siobhan and Richard recommended him for a special award for exceptional performance.

Further reading

Blanchard, K, Zigarmi, P and Zigarmi, D (1985), *Leadership and the One Minute Manager*, Collins

Forsyth, Patrick (2000), *How to Motivate People*, Kogan Page

Markham, Ursula (1993), *How to Deal with Difficult People*, Thorsons

22 Project teams

22.1 Introduction

The previous chapter dealt with the management and development of your individual team members. This chapter deals with the selection, management and development of your team as a unit.

You will not usually be in a position to select all the members of your team from everyone available on the external labour market. More often you will find yourself taking on an intact team or that team members are supplied by an internal resourcing function. However, you are very likely to be involved in selecting team members at regular intervals, either from inside or outside your organisation, to cover a growing need for staff or to replace people who leave. That is why the recruitment process is covered in this chapter.

Whether you select, inherit or simply receive the members of your team, you will need to work at developing them from a group of individuals, each with their own interests, goals, style and ambitions, into a team that works together to achieve common goals, using each other's strengths to best advantage. You can make an enormous impact on the extent to which the people on your project build into a team. This chapter covers the induction of new team members, theories on team development and teamwork and practical advice on what you can do to encourage the people who work for you to work together. The sequence of this chapter is designed to take you through the recruitment process, the induction of new people into your project and the building of teams.

22.2 Job descriptions and person specifications

The recruitment process starts with the identification of a vacancy to be filled. Recruitment is an expensive and risky process so it is worth spending time on each stage, including this one. Unfortunately, this stage is sometimes done with little thought: when a person leaves a team, it is assumed a vacancy is left, and then that recruitment is the means of filling the vacancy. Let us examine these two assumptions and consider alternative actions.

Firstly, when someone leaves the team it does not always mean a vacancy results. Project teams grow and shrink: is a person's departure a timely opportunity to start reducing the number of people working on a project that is approaching its goal? If not, can the work be subcontracted to another team or organisation? Can it be automated? If the answer to all these questions is no, you can still consider whether the job that has been vacated could be spread between other members of your team who may appreciate an additional challenge, especially if the new work gives them opportunities to develop new skills.

If, after considering the questions above, you still decide that a person's departure leaves a vacancy to be filled, consider the second assumption: do you need to recruit someone to fill it? It might be a better option to promote a more junior member of your team into the vacated job and then consider recruiting to fill the more junior job. This has many advantages: the job is filled by someone you know, which takes much of the risk out of recruiting (you still have to recruit for the more junior position but a mistake here is likely to be less costly), your promoted team member knows much about your work already and the message to all your team members is that there are opportunities for promotion while they work for you, which is very likely to have a positive effect on their motivation and commitment. So do not assume that a departure always creates a vacancy. It may instead be an opportunity for you to do something creative with your team.

The other side of the coin is that vacancies arise not only from people leaving; they come about as projects grow and as the level of work expands beyond the capacity of a team. The generation of vacancies as a project grows will have been included in the planning of the project. As with other aspects of project planning, you need to monitor actual events against the plan and act accordingly. It may be that the project requires staff earlier or later, or more or fewer, than was estimated at the planning stage.

The generation of vacancies as the amount of work exceeds what your team can deal with requires attention. You can reach the stage where your team is overloaded, losing its commitment and starting to make mistakes without your even realising it, perhaps because you are working very hard yourself. So monitor the level of effort your team is having to provide and, if it gets high, take steps before they all resign. The steps could be the recruitment of more staff, a reduction in the amount of work your team has to do, a change in procedures to make the work flow faster, better equipment or any number of other possibilities.

Let us assume now, that having considered the present state of your project and the future demands expected, you have decided there is a vacancy to be filled. The next activity required is job analysis. This involves defining the tasks which comprise the job: what is to be done, what is provided to the job holder and what the job holder is expected to deliver. At this stage, the attention is on the job itself and not the person who will fill it. In other words, job analysis is an impersonal description of tasks, inputs and outputs with no consideration yet of what it will take to do the job. This separation is deliberate and is intended to avoid unconscious assumptions being made about the required job holder. Job analysis is done in a similar way to system analysis: you talk to the people who will need to work with the job holder and perhaps people who have held similar (or even the same) jobs in the past. As project manager you will have your own ideas about the design of the job. Find out what is required of the job holder and write this in a document which is called a job description.

The job description says nothing about qualifications or experience levels – these come at a later stage. Job descriptions are used to write job advertisements for the press and for specifying vacancies to recruitment agencies. Anyone can write a job advertisement if they have a complete job description, but to write them well requires the specialist skills of a personnel professional. An example of a job description is shown in Figure 22.1.

Job descriptions are also used in the next stage of the recruitment process: the derivation of the person specification. This uses the information in the job description and any general company standards to describe the characteristics of a person who could do the job satisfactorily. It is important to derive the person specification from the job description and general company standards, rather than write it independently, in order to avoid any unconscious assumptions about the type of person required to do the job. For example, if all previous holders of similar jobs have been university graduates it might be natural to assume that all future holders of such jobs must be graduates. This might not be necessary. Working from the job description makes it more likely that such assumptions will be avoided. It also helps avoid the unfair or even illegal elimination of some candidates from the job because of unfounded assumptions about age or sex.

Examination of each element of the job description identifies required characteristics for the person specification. General company requirements, which are also included, might include a willingness to work on defence projects or a preparedness to work away from home for extended periods. But take care: a requirement for mobility might unfairly put off or exclude a good candidate who has young children in school or a partner with a fixed job. So make sure all general requirements really do apply in the case of the job you are filling.

Person specifications usually list the required characteristics in two categories: essential characteristics and desirable characteristics. Essential characteristics are those that the job requires and which cannot easily be learned or acquired through training. Desirable characteristics are those which either are not essential for the job but would help or are essential but which the job holder can learn, either on the job or through training, without its causing serious delays or problems. A common and regrettable mistake is the selection of a person who already has all the skills and knowledge required. Searching for such a person is arduous and sometimes unfeasible. Even if such a perfect candidate is found, the job will be unchallenging because they know it already. It is often better, cheaper and easier to recruit someone who has most of the required skills and knowledge but has an opportunity to grow into the job through learning the remaining skills. It also demonstrates your commitment to training staff in the skills they need, which makes your organisation more attractive to potential recruits.

Person specifications usually list the required characteristics under a set of general headings such as those shown in Figure 22.2. Do not be too concerned

JOB DESCRIPTION

Job Title: Software Development Engineer

Job Grade: Professional Engineer/Manager

Reports to: Software Release Development Manager

Job Purpose: The Software Development Engineer is responsible for the development of the software which will provide an identified functional thread of an IT system. This responsibility starts with the analysis of the client requirement for the functional thread and concludes with the acceptance by the client authority of the delivered software.

Specific duties:

- Production of an analysis document which specifies the functionality of the system thread. This will be done using SSADM version 4 and must be formally accepted by the client authority and the release manager responsible for the overall software release.
- Production of a subsystem design document using SSADM version 4. This must be accepted by the system design coordinator.
- Leading a team of contractors who will write and test the software.
- Leading a team of contractors who will produce system test documentation.
- Ensuring the system tests are conducted and all remedial work done until all HP systems tests can be shown to work correctly.
- Taking all steps required to enable the client authority to accept the software for the functional thread.
- Managing the above work to ensure as far as possible that it is completed within budget and by the required deadline.
- Monitoring progress and reporting it accurately to management. This will be done using the 'Multiskill' project management toolset.

General duties:

- To work with colleagues to achieve overall success of the project and profitability.
- To respond to changing needs, changing jobs and new technical skills.

Available resources:

- The Software Release Development Manager will be 20% available to the Software Development Engineer for coaching, support, advice and other assistance.
- The contractors will be supplied by the Resourcing Department in accordance with their service-level agreement.
- The Software Development Engineer will have access to the internal consultants whose job is to assist production staff with their specialist advice. Currently the available internal consultants cover analysis, design, project toolsets, quality, training and testing.

Other details:

- Terms of employment are as specified in the company's Staff Handbook.
- Internal and client confidentiality must be maintained.
- The job is based at the company's Maidstone office.

Figure 22.1 Example of a job description

PERSON SPECIFICATION

Physical Attributes:
Essential: Good attendance record. Tidy appearance.
Desirable: Excellent health record. Smart appearance. Positive impact upon others.
Able to work extended hours under pressure.
Note: This job would suit someone with a mobility disability but is not suitable for job sharing.

Attainments:
Essential: Qualified practitioner in SSADM version 4. Knowledge of project management tools and techniques. Some supervision experience.
Desirable: Knowledge of 'Multiskill' project management toolset.
Experience of leading a team in a commercial environment.
Management qualification.

Intelligence:
Essential: Demonstrated ability to understand software, systems development and IT in general.
Desirable: Demonstrated understanding of commercial pressures in an organisation with clear financial targets.

Aptitudes:
Essential: Excellent written communication skills. Good use of spoken language.
Programming skills.
Able to learn new technical skills fast.
Desirable: C++ programming skills.

Interests:
Essential: Computing as an industry and a career.
Desirable: An interest in industrial applications of IT. Interests which involve interaction or communication with other people.

Evidence of Character:
Essential: Works well in a team, especially when the pressure is on. Able to listen to and accept others' points of view. Willing to accept customer changes.
Desirable: Influence skills. Has led a team to success when significant obstacles had to be overcome. Has experience of dealing with customers who show excessive concern for their own needs over supplier's needs.

Personal Circumstances:
Essential: Willing to work beyond contracted hours on occasion.
Willing to adapt to organisational changes.
Desirable: Already has all permits required for work in this country.

Figure 22.2 Example of a person specification

about which heading a characteristic should be under; the important question is whether the characteristics are derived from a genuine need of the job or not.

The job description has been used to identify potential candidates through the use of an agent or an advertisement. With the person specification complete you can begin the process of selection.

Recruiting the team

Your agent or advertisement should bring in a number of applications. If not, you need to reconsider: are you asking for too much or offering too little? Assuming you have a good number of applications you can now shortlist those you will invite for interview.

Shortlisting means working through the applications, removing those that clearly fail to meet the essential requirements for the job. Not all the characteristics on the person specification can be assessed from the written application alone – or no further selection would be necessary – but some important ones can. Using as an example the person specification in Figure 22.2, the application will tell whether the candidate is qualified in SSADM, has the particular experience mentioned and it demonstrates the candidate's level of written communication skills. By removing the applications that fail to meet the minimum standards you identified earlier, you produce your shortlist. If the process leaves you with too many candidates for interview, use the desirable characteristics on the person specification to eliminate more. If there are still too many, consider sending out a form which requires more detail or talking to candidates by telephone to gain more information. The important point is to stick with the characteristics you identified in advance of reading the applications, and not to be swayed by anything else. We all have our prejudices, and unless the process sticks closely to the identified characteristics it is easy to be influenced by factors such as similar background or interests to your own.

Invite the shortlisted candidates to visit your office to find out more about the job and attend an interview. The letter should contain a note of thanks for and interest in the candidate's application, more information about your organisation and the job on offer, a choice of dates, details of what will take place during the visit and information about how to find the office.

We are all influenced by first impressions. Sometimes, the ability to make a good first impression is an important job characteristic, for example when recruiting a salesperson. For many more jobs it is not. The other point about first impressions is to remember that the candidate is considering you and your firm just as much as you are considering the candidate. So make sure the first impressions your candidates get of your firm are positive. Many organisations make costly mistakes over simple matters like failing to inform Reception that the candidate is expected. Other 'obvious' requirements, such as refreshments being available, travel expenses being refunded, the opportunity to meet existing team members, and a quiet interview room being booked are sometimes overlooked. A smart presentation about your organisation and its work and a sociable lunch can make a positive impact as well.

You need to prepare yourself by being thoroughly familiar with the written application and the job documents and by shutting out of your mind all the other matters that require your attention, such as work, home and so on. You need to prepare the interview room with an appropriate layout: comfortable chairs around a coffee table, or two chairs at ninety degrees by the corner of a desk will relax you and the candidate more than if you face each other across a desk. Finally, you need to prepare your interview plan and interview notes form.

The interview plan consists of the sequence you intend for the interview. The main element of your plan will be to work through the key components of your candidate's history as outlined in the written application. The plan is a straightforward document. As explained later, you cannot plan all the questions you will ask because most questions are a response to things the candidate says. What you can do, in addition to the simple interview plan, is mark up the candidate's written job application with ideas for areas you may be able to probe. You can also plan how you will use each interview to develop your interviewing skills, as is shown at the bottom of the example in Figure 22.3.

The interview notes form (Figure 22.4) consists of a list of those characteristics, taken from the person specification, which you will assess in the interview, a column to indicate whether the candidate has demonstrated each of these characteristics and space for a few words to remind you what the evidence was. There is also space at the bottom for you to note key words to remind you of areas you wish to probe some more.

As suggested in the plan above, the interview begins with friendly chat to build rapport and put the candidate at ease. You will be able to make the most accurate judgements about a candidate if they are as relaxed as possible. Many amateur interviewers like to do the opposite: they put the candidate under deliberate pressure. This is unhelpful because few jobs require the ability to cope well with deliberate interview pressure and it is not a reliable predictor of how the candidate will cope with ordinary work pressure.

With the opening smalltalk done, you can begin with the main business of interviewing. Taking each of the candidate's main areas of experience in turn, including work experience, education and interests, begin with an introduction

---

Interview Plan

1 Welcome; introductions; agenda. Establish rapport.

2 Open questions on educational history.

3 Open questions on previous jobs.

4 Open questions on interests and circumstances.

5 The company: history, business, opportunities.

6 The job: requirements, good aspects, not so good aspects.

7 Anything you want to ask me? Anything else you want to say?

8 What happens next – you should hear from us in one week.

9 Thank you, goodbye – escort candidate back to Personnel Department.

Figure 22.3 Example of an interview plan

Interview Notes Form		
Characteristic	Y or N?	Evidence
Good appearance		
Adequate health		
Impact upon others		
Has worked under pressure		
SSADM version 4		
Project management tools and techniques		
Supervision experience		
Commercial environment		
Management qualification		
Ability to understand IT		
Financial targets		
Spoken communication skills		
Programming skills (C++?)		
Able to learn fast		
Computing as an industry and a career		
Interest in industrial applications of IT		
Interests with other people		
Works well in a team under pressure		
Listens to and accepts others' points of view		
Customer experience		
Influence skills		
Has overcome significant obstacles		
Willing to work beyond contracted hours		
Willing to adapt to organisational changes		
Has required permits		

Areas to probe ...

Figure 22.4 Example of an interview notes form

such as: 'I see from your application that you worked for Megacorp for two years.' This allows the candidate to focus on this aspect of the past before you move on to the first open question: 'Tell me about your time there.'

Open questions are questions that invite the candidate to talk at length. Closed questions invite a shorter answer. So begin discussing an area of experience with a question which is open but not so open that it leaves the candidate with no idea of where to start. For example, 'Tell me about your main achievements' gives the candidate little idea of what sort of answer is wanted. Perhaps the interviewer asking such a question has equally little idea.

As the candidate answers your open question, make a note of key words to remind you of areas which you want to probe further. When the candidate finishes talking you can start to probe these areas, first with an introductory question like: 'You mentioned you had to deal with clients. Did any of them ever cause you problems?' Then, if the candidate answers yes, follow this with, 'Tell me about one example.' This gives you information about the candidate's experience of dealing with customers, which is one of the characteristics wanted in the example above.

Other methods of probing an area for more information are:

- Requesting more information: 'Tell me more about the system testing you did.'
- Reflecting back key words from the previous answer. This encourages the candidate to say more about the words you picked on. For example, if the candidate said, 'We did the design using Merise', you could respond: 'Merise?' The candidate will then tell you about this method.
- Just staying quiet and waiting for the candidate to say more. Candidates often need time to think or to find the right words. Give them that time. Poor interviewers fill even tiny pauses with a rephrased question which may only confuse the candidate, or possible answers, which make the whole process simply a multiple choice test.

The most precise form of probe question is the closed question, which invites a short answer on the specific information you require: 'What design method did you use?', 'How much money were you responsible for?'

In order to be able to probe you need to spot things the candidate says which can be probed. *The key skill in selection interviewing is being alert for areas you can probe which will give you evidence that your candidate has or has not in the past demonstrated one of your required characteristics.* To an extent you can prepare for this in advance. For example, if your candidate has worked in a fast-food restaurant, they are likely to have had to deal with awkward customers. But you need to listen carefully to all that your candidate says in order to spot things to probe further for the evidence you require. If you are listening properly you will always have another question to hand.

When you have finished probing an area or period from the candidate's application, reflect back a summary of your understanding of what you have been told. Begin with, 'Let me just check that I have got all this right . . .'. Summaries are useful as they allow the candidate to correct misinterpretations, which are common, and to add more information that may help. They show that you have listened and they tie up the area you have been talking about, laying the ground for the introduction of the next area. Although they do so much, summaries are often omitted from interviews, perhaps because interviewers are not used to doing them as part of everyday conversation.

The 'funnel' diagram in Figure 22.5 illustrates the process you go through with each area of the application form or CV; in other words each previous job, education course and other sections from the form. You start with an introduction and an open question, then probe, staying alert for anything that gives you the evidence you need.

Figure 22.5 The 'funnel' questioning technique

The diagram shows how probing a candidate about a summer job at a ware-house can provide evidence of a candidate's experience of procedures. By asking what the candidate actually did at this job, the interviewer can determine how precisely the candidate stuck to procedures, and whether the candidate showed initiative in challenging them and was given responsibility for changing them. Probing for such evidence, on what the candidate has done in the past, is a much better determinant of what the candidate is likely to do in the future than any other interview technique. Having achieved this, the interviewer could lead on to other aspects of the warehouse job to find evidence of customer contact, team problems, reliability and many other characteristics. Then the interviewer can open a new 'funnel' by introducing the next period of the candidate's history.

Just as there are useful kinds of question to ask, there are some types to avoid. In particular, try to avoid:

- *Leading questions.* These indicate the answer you expect. For example, 'I imagine you had to go through a formal process to get the changes agreed?'
- *Hypothetical questions.* These ask how a candidate would respond in an imaginary situation, for example, 'How would you go about selecting a team member?' The reply is a best guess at what the candidate thinks you would like to hear. It is much better to stick with what the candidate actually has and has not done.
- *Multiple questions.* These are rambling questions, frequently asked by interviewers who are not sure what they want to ask or who find silence so awkward they fill the candidate's thinking time with rephrased versions of the question: 'How was the work organised? I mean, was there a formal procedure or did you have to respond as things arose – not that there's anything wrong with that? And did you work alone or with the others? As a team, I mean.'

- *Aimless questions*. Many interviewers have pet questions that they always ask without any real idea of what they are looking for. Questions like: 'Where do you see yourself in five years' time?' and 'What are your strengths and weaknesses?' may be designed to extract evidence for a job characteristic, but more often are used to fill time by interviewers who will make their selection decision on subjective feelings about the candidate.
- *Riddles*. Silly questions such as: 'How would you estimate the number of fish in a pond?' Candidates may have heard these before and, even if they have not, the replies to such questions can never be reliable as evidence of the candidate's behaviour in real situations.

By the end of the interview, you will have one or many pieces of evidence that the candidate has or lacks the characteristics, including technical skills and interpersonal abilities, you have listed on the person specification. If you have no evidence for a characteristic you could try to find it by some other means or you must highlight this as an uncertainty and therefore a risk. All candidates who lack essential characteristics can be eliminated. Those remaining can be ordered by the number of the desirable characteristics they have and the strength of the evidence. The candidate at the top of your list can be recommended for the job. If no candidates have the essential characteristics, you have to go back to the start and reconsider your vacancy.

As soon as you have said goodbye to the candidate, write up a formal report of the interview. Do not delay it for any reason. Your notes and jottings on the interview notes form are not sufficient, and writing them out will help clarify your thoughts. By sticking to evidence for or against the characteristics you have determined you need, you are far less likely to be influenced by subjective judgements and prejudices.

The interview is not your only means of assessing whether a candidate has the characteristics you require. Some of the others are described below, but only in outline; you need to consult a recruitment specialist for greater detail.

- Examination of the written application, as already mentioned.
- Get the candidate to do some technical work. This is particularly appropriate when recruiting contractors for a particular technical skill. For example, when recruiting C programmers, give them a short but typical specification of one of your programs. They then write the C code and you can assess its quality.
- Simulations, such as group exercises. For example, a group of candidates are given a problem which they have to solve together. Trained observers watch for evidence of particular interpersonal skills. One example is that the group of candidates is the board of a company and they have to elect one of their number as the new managing director. Observers look for evidence of listening, building on other people's ideas, asking opinions and other desirable behaviours.
- Selection tests. There are many of these on the market and they appeal to many recruiters because they make the selection decision less personal. This does not make the decisions better. Used with caution by trained professionals, selection tests have their place as part of the process. They are not

acceptable as a means of avoiding the responsibility of making a selection decision.

■ Bring potential recruits in on short-term contracts to begin with. Those who perform well over a period of a few weeks can be offered a permanent position.

Once a successful candidate has been identified, a contract and other formalities are needed, but this book assumes these matters are dealt with by a central personnel department. You may wish to contact the successful candidate to sell your job more and invite them to visit again.

When it has been confirmed that a new person is to join your team you need to devote some time to planning the new member's induction. Even a person transferring from another team in your organisation needs a planned induction as the impact the first days make on a team member has a profound and long-term effect.

Do not assume that you will think of all the things you need to cover with a new person on the first day. Matters which seem simple and obvious to you may get overlooked. The other danger is overloading the new person on day one. Spend time listing everything a new person needs and then planning it out over days or even weeks, as suggested in the sample from an induction plan in Figure 22.6 (see overleaf).

22.4 The lifecycle of teams

Thorough inductions help new team members to settle in quickly and begin adjusting to and developing within the team. But just as individuals mature and develop, given the right circumstances, so too groups move through stages of development. Tuckman suggests that four stages of a group's development can be identified. This model is particularly applicable to new teams.

1 *Forming.* At first the team is a group of individuals probably selected for their functional or technical skill or particular experience. On the surface, the group discusses its purpose, methods, problems to overcome and so forth. Beneath the surface, members are trying to decide the extent to which they are accepted by the group, the extent to which they accept the group and its members, who has power and will take charge, who will challenge this leadership, what roles others will take and what sorts of relationships are going to form.

2 *Storming.* The forming stage usually leads to the storming stage. The group gets down to the real work here and, under the pressure that this generates, individuals start expressing their own personal views about how work should be allocated and organised, the methods and techniques to be used and so on. There are different views about leadership too, some people perhaps wanting a firm directive style and others wanting a more consultative approach. So, this conflict can be about goals, leadership, work methods,

INDUCTION PLAN

Name:
Position being taken:
Start date:

Day One
Introductions to team colleagues
Overview of project:
• Customer
• Deliverables
• Technology
• Progress to date – planning & monitoring
• Organisational structure – where you fit in
Demonstration of system
Health & Safety – a legal requirement in many countries
• Fire drill, fire exits, fire extinguishers
• First aid
• Office hazards
• Dangers of working with computers (eye strain, muscle strain, etc.)
Senior team member to demonstrate development environment
Lunch with team
Company culture – level of formality; social scene; how things work here
New person's aspirations
Our expectations
Read top-level documentation

Day Two
Introductions to management
Detailed working of our part of the system:
• Purpose of subsystem
• Interfaces
• Database
• Algorithms
• Input and Output
Local environment:
• Shops
• Banks
• Post Office
• Transport
• Facilities
Read functional specification of our subsystem

Day Three

Figure 22.6 Part of an induction plan

relationships, hierarchy and so forth and can generate some heat. Agreements will be reached, and then broken. Sometimes these matters are dealt with peaceably. Often they are suppressed only to reveal themselves, perhaps in another form, later. If the group does not get these disagreements aired and resolved it will never become a team, so the project manager, or someone else from inside the team, or someone brought in from outside has to help the group to recognise these difficulties, resolve them and move on.

3 *Norming.* The resolution of conflict requires the agreement of group norms and practices. The storming process results in agreed approaches to decision-making, work-sharing, meetings and work processes as well as generally accepted styles of interpersonal relationships such as the level of trust and openness. It is essential that, when a team has decided on its norms and someone new joins, these norms are fully explained. Even doing this may not prevent the team from reprising their storming stage as the new person may well question the way things are done. Indeed, a poorly performing team may have someone added to it to do just this.

4 *Performing.* Once the norms have been agreed, the group can use them to achieve its task.

A fifth stage is sometimes apparent too. This is called 'adjourning' or 'mourning'. It is when the team has completed its task and is disbanded. Partly it is a wake for the team's demise, but it also needs to be a time for evaluation and for recording and dwelling on the lessons learned so that, in the future, team members can more quickly become effective members of new teams. In practice, these four stages overlap. A group may be at several stages with different aspects of its work at the same time. Teams revert from a later stage to an earlier one, especially when a new or suppressed conflict causes a team to revert from performing back to storming.

Whilst an interesting model, what matters is how a project manager can use it to help move teams to the 'performing' stage as quickly as possible. At the forming stage, you can assist by encouraging open communication. Do this by being open yourself about your personal goals and the concerns you have about the project. Spend time with your team members allowing and encouraging them to speak their minds. Team-building activities such as training and social events will help.

When your team is in storming mode, as it will be on occasions, you may feel disappointed or upset by what may appear to be childish, obstructive or counterproductive behaviour. Suspend these judgements, remembering that real people have a child-like component and personal and social needs. The behaviour you are observing is a natural part of the team development process. So do not clamp down on storming, although there will be times when 'enough is enough' – you can intervene if you judge that the storming is getting out of hand. Try to guide the energy liberated by storming into problem solving rather than personal antagonism. Finally, remember that people can feel hurt by the storming process, so give these people time to express their upset and help them forgive their colleagues. They may also have to forgive you: although you will have tried hard to be fair, people have different ideas of what fairness means.

The norming stage is an opportunity to demonstrate your management skills by acting as a chair or coordinator for the process. As norms and work styles emerge, you can explicitly identify them and get everyone's clear agreement. If you do not, your team may believe they are all agreeing to something but have differing ideas on what that something is.

The performing stage is what all managers strive for. Once reached, it requires effort to maintain. The agreed norms and procedures will need to be changed as circumstances change, and it will help if these agreements are done in an overt way. But whilst the 'impersonal' aspects of teamwork, such as agreed ground rules and work methods, do help a team to work together, they are not by themselves sufficient for teamworking. A person will only commit to the team as long as the team is meeting personal, social and career needs. So do what you can to stay aware of the more personal needs of your team members and then find ways of meeting those needs.

There is no doubt that some form of structured team development activity brings teams together faster and helps them to operate more effectively sooner. This is true for IS project teams, an administration team in an office, or any team that has a shared goal that can be achieved only through the individual assignment of tasks. Very special teams operating in dangerous or pressurised or exacting circumstances bring out vividly the lessons for teams in general and provide signposts for project teams. This was clearly evident in the BT Global Challenge yacht race of 2000/01 in which, in the words of Cranwell-Ward *et al.*, '12 identical yachts each with a professional skipper and a crew of 17 men and women of all ages and backgrounds set out to race around the globe against the prevailing winds and currents, one of the toughest feats of teamwork, leadership and human endurance in the modern world'. Based on the experiences of the 1996/97 race, all skippers in the 2000/01 race led their teams through some form of team development before the race, and some added to this during the race at the stopovers between legs of the race. Dramatic improvements took place following the stopover activities, clearly illustrating the lesson for project teams that team development of high-performing teams never stops.

22.5 Belbin on teams

One of the most original and still one of the most useful studies of team effectiveness is the work of Meredith Belbin and his colleagues. This section gives a brief summary of their findings. More detail can be found in Belbin's own books, two of which are listed at the end of this chapter.

Belbin made a study of teams of managers in business simulation games and compared a team's degree of success with the results of psychometric instruments (questionnaires which attempt to measure aspects of personality) completed by the team's members. The key finding was that there is no one type of person who makes an ideal team player; what matters is that the team contains a mix of various types. Even teams deliberately formed entirely of, for example, very intelligent people did not fare well. Further work enabled Belbin to identify eight 'team roles'. If all the team roles are filled, a team stands a very good chance of success. If key team roles are missing, then the team is weakened and may fail. The eight team roles are described below with their key strengths and allowable weaknesses. The roles are given current names; earlier names for some of the roles are in brackets.

- *Coordinator* (Chairman). Any member of the team, not necessarily the appointed leader, can take this role. The role provides consensual leadership, coordinating the team's efforts but somewhat lacking in originality.
- *Shaper*. An alternative form of leadership, the shaper leads 'from the front,' pushing activities forward and bringing 'shape' to the team. The Shaper is dynamic and can be inspiring but can also be abrasive.
- *Innovator* (Plant). A source of original, even inspired ideas, the Innovator is creative but sometimes forms a personal attachment to impractical ideas.
- *Resource Investigator*. The type of person who is never in the office except when on the telephone. The Resource Investigator is the team's link to the outside world, and as such is another source of ideas, though not particularly original ones. The Resource Investigator knows people who can help the team, but once a problem is solved can lose interest with the implementation of the solution.
- *Monitor/Evaluator*. This is the person who sifts the group's ideas and separates those that are practicable from those that are not, keeps the group on the right track but is often insensitive to people's feelings.
- *Team Worker*. This person is very concerned with feelings, is sensitive to personal needs and upsets, works hard to keep people happy and maintains a positive atmosphere within the team but is indecisive in a crisis.
- *Implementer* (Company Worker). This person is the practical organiser who takes an idea and produces a schedule. The Implementer works well with milestones and plans but can be inflexible when things have to change.
- *Completer* (Completer/Finisher). This is the progress chaser. This person worries about what can go wrong with a project, checks up on detail and focuses the team on its deadlines, but can be too fussy.

When a team is well equipped with the selection of roles it needs, the strengths of each role counterbalance the weaknesses of others. Most teams require this balance at all stages of a project. For example, Innovators and Resource Investigators may be especially useful at early stages but they are needed later too.

Most of us can identify one or two of these roles that we can fill easily, and perhaps a couple more secondary roles that we can take on if others are filling our primary roles.

Project managers are not advised to select their teams on the basis of Belbin's team roles but to use this knowledge to help avoid the common problem of recruiting or promoting only people like themselves, which leads to convivial but unproductive teams. Belbin's work is most useful for developing existing teams: helping people to understand the strengths their colleagues bring and helping a team to identify which roles they lack, so they can compensate or seek external assistance.

22.6 International and virtual teams

Working in an international or a **virtual team** is the same as working in an 'ordinary' team – and it is also very different. The increase in the number of these kinds of team and the fact that there are such differing views about them is the reason for including this section. A few baselines need to be established at the beginning. There are business trends driving the increased use of international teams. These include:

- Globalisation. The need for many companies to expand globally in order to grow and to survive as commercial and economic interdependence between countries grows. Sometimes this leads to national companies becoming international, but it also includes joint ventures and strategic alliances – particularly with previously 'closed' economies such as the component countries of the former USSR, and China – mergers and acquisitions.
- Offshore working especially in IT, IT services and call centres. For example, scores of British companies have call centre services based in Delhi, Hyderabad and Bangalore in India. This trend is expected to continue as the ageing demographic profile of western economies means that they need to import qualified young people or to export jobs. All of this is only possible through developments in IT and communications technology as work is shared across time zones. Where this involves development work then new team issues arise through the use of virtual teams. There's more about virtual teams later.
- Increased complexity in the problems to be solved. Partly this is the result of globalisation but it is also an attempt to harness all the talents that are available without bringing them all into one location. Sometimes, co-locating all team members is not possible; for an oil company drilling for oil in Kazakhstan or in hostile oceans, with R&D in Houston, technical support in Aberdeen, computer modelling people in California and geologists in Sydney, remote team working – in a virtual team – using different nationalities is essential to get urgent problems solved.
- The use of IT that enables scattered team members to operate in an 'information space' where time zones matter more than physical locations. Corporate problems are solved globally through the use of shared workspaces, web-based conferencing, tutorials and email. A draft report you put into the workspace before you leave the office in England comes back to you via colleagues in the USA, Singapore and the Middle East as a finished document by the time you log on the next morning.

What are the issues that arise from this explosion in the use of multicultural and virtual teams? Firstly and most importantly is the need for these new teams to take a practical and commonsense approach to working in this way. It is easy to assume that everything will be new, exciting and different. There will be new and different issues, but the excitement can easily give way to frustration with IT systems that fall over, people who do not respond in the agreed time, and cultural differences that generate different ways of working.

It is also worth remembering that multicultural teams may not be international. In our experience, the cultural differences that exist across different divisions of an organisation can be quite challenging, especially where these divisions operate in markets with different products or where the organisation has grown by acquisition.

With the need for practicality in mind, then, there are some important cultural aspects that impact on the performance of international teams. It is easy to see cultural differences as a problem, but using the undeniable differences that do exist can bring extra insights to a team and the way it works. Team development activities and using **Johari's window** (Figure 22.7) can stimulate awareness and enable everyone in the team to learn about the cultural richness available to them.

The Johari window was created by Joe Luft and Henry Ingram in the mid 1950s to help people understand the differences between our perception of ourselves and other people's perception of us.

- In the Open area are things about us that we know and others see. These are our attitudes, behaviours and beliefs about which there are no secrets.
- In the Blind area are things about us that others observe but of which we are unaware.
- In the Hidden area are things that we know but choose not to disclose.
- Finally, in the Unknown area are things of which we are unaware and which are not apparent to others. Nonetheless, they influence our behaviour and unless we develop our self-knowledge we will never understand why we do some things and why we get the reactions we do.

By putting as much as we can into the Open box we help others to know us quickly, and the more we tell them, the more we reduce the Hidden box and increase the Open box. Reducing the Blind box through feedback from others to us about what they see us do can further increase the Open box. If a team goes through this process, then everyone can become clearer about their role in the team and about their contribution to the team's performance. Of

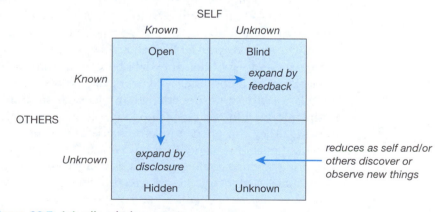

Figure 22.7 Johari's window

(Joseph Luft, *Of Human Interaction*, National Press, Palo Alto, CA, 1969)

course, we do not always hear what we would like to hear, so getting a skilled person to lead this activity will pay dividends.

There are many definitions of 'culture', and some models for examining organisational culture were suggested in Chapter 1. Here, though, we are looking at national cultures and the effect they have on behaviours. When we begin to explore our culture or examine another one, what do we see?

- At first glance we see physical things – little rituals and individual behaviours that characterise the way we do things or like to live and work. How are the offices laid out and organised, how do people like to greet each other and dress, what are the speech conventions that they use? If I am late for a work meeting in London, I try to slip quietly into the meeting room, I apologise in a low voice for being late and look for a seat around the table and sit down without making a disturbance. Not so in the Paris office. I am late but that is not too serious, as the meeting will not have started on time. I go into the meeting room normally, and then go around the table shaking hands and greeting everyone individually. Adapting to these superficial differences is the easiest way to fit in. This does not mean that you should be late, but at least you can greet the latecomer without embarrassment.

- At the next level down, we find the values and beliefs that explain the behaviours. At this level we see differences in the criteria for success, the team's purpose (is it all task oriented or are relationships important too?), the role of the manager and how people are selected for jobs.

- At the deepest level are the underlying basic assumptions that might be described as the foundations on which cultures are built.

A useful definition of culture to help us to work through this complex area has been developed by Ed Schein based on earlier work by Kluckholn and Strodbeck. According to Schein, 'Culture is a set of basic assumptions – shared solutions to universal problems of external adaptation (how to survive) and internal integration (how to stay together) – which have evolved over time and are handed down from one generation to the next'. The appeal of this definition is that it addresses the main challenges facing project managers and team leaders. It is about finding solutions to the problems of dealing with the environment – stakeholders and technology, for example – and of designing solutions to meet them by organising internal resources to deliver these solutions.

Whichever way you look at it, managing multicultural project teams is different – and very often they will be virtual teams as well. In the words of Lipnack and Stamps, they will work 'across space, time and organisation boundaries with links strengthened by webs of communication technologies'. In the information age, people no longer have to be in the same place to work together. They can operate in cyberspace. Let us look at the technology that enables the team to communicate. We can have synchronous media such as telephone or video-conferences and, in some cases, synchronous software that allow almost instantaneous, on-screen exchanges of data. Asynchronous communication includes email, the use of groupware and specially set up intranet project spaces. If the virtual team is a group of people in a global organisation then the technological issues are more likely to centre around making use of everything that is available and ensuring that all team members are competent with the technology. This technology might include:

- Video-conferencing, although desktop web conferences look more likely to be useful for IT teams.
- Groupware such as Lotus Notes so that different people can contribute to the same document.
- Newsgroups and bulletin boards for the posting of information that is available to everyone.
- Email for one-to-one or one-to-many communications.

More widely scattered teams with people working from home or from less well developed IT sites present different problems, involving incompatible software, slow communication lines and even poor power supplies. Good practice here is to keep the technological requirements simple and to avoid transmitting multicoloured presentation material, photographs and web designs.

As for the team, there are some additional challenges. The first concerns team-building. If the team cannot meet together at all, then sending personal information and audiotapes to each other is worth doing. If technology supports it, then uploading photos into emails and creating chatrooms or virtual offices can help to bind the team together. An 'e-coach' can help in the team-building process by offering feedback to the team as it works together remotely. This e-coach can also check that there is a shared and agreed understanding about the direction the team is taking and the conclusions it is reaching.

For the leader – the project manager – there are some additional factors to take into account. They are highlighted in research carried out by John Symons at Henley Management College and published in 2002. He says that:

- The contextual aspects of leadership change. 'Virtual working is fast and flexible. The concept of a single leader having a vision, aligning followers and then controlling the output is not appropriate to this form of working'. This means that rigid control by a project leader is unlikely to succeed and a more delegating style may be required.
- 'The leader has to recognise that he or she has little power at a distance.' Directive leadership behaviour is therefore inappropriate. The strength of a hierarchy is much less visible online.
- Bearing in mind the previous point, getting processes right and clarifying the issues at the beginning, preparing and getting agreement to a clear plan and well-defined deliverables become more important. The value of starting off slowly and securing a shared understanding of what has to be done pays dividends later. Project managers with a predisposition to 'rush to task' find this frustrating.
- The urgency and pace of face-to-face meetings where dominant personalities often assume a leadership role gives way to more thoughtful and reflective contributions. Roles in the team become more evenly distributed.

There is no new paradigm for the leadership of virtual teams. Being effective at it means that you recognise the situational differences that arise and create an environment that involves and rewards everyone.

22.7 The effective team

This chapter has shown that there is much the project manager can do to create and maintain an effective team. This is important because once a team has fallen apart and become disillusioned it is a very tough job to change things back. Prevention is much easier than cure. You can develop your team quickly by selecting people who can do their job to a large extent but find scope for challenge and personal development within it, then giving them a thorough induction; the team can then be allowed to develop through finding its own ways of doing things. You can encourage the process by providing a clear vision of the team's purpose and objectives, being open and engendering openness in others and taking steps to find ways of compensating for missing 'team roles' within your team.

It is natural for many people to see their team as an extension of themselves, just as many people see their work as part of themselves. In the latter case, this close identification with work can make people reluctant to see faults in their work. In the former case, managers can become reluctant to see problems in their team. So it is worth making an effort to identify potential problems before they develop. The points below describe some warning signs and give some suggestions on what to do about them. But every case is unique and there are no guaranteed formulae for dealing with people.

- *Productivity slips*. You may notice this from productivity figures or by less direct observations: people coming in late, more absenteeism, complaints from other teams which depend on yours, or a general atmosphere of going slow. Possible causes are a lack of identification with the work – you need to establish a clearer vision and purpose for your project; lack of a personal sense of direction – you need to spend time with team members on career and personal development planning; a belief that effort is unrewarded – ensure that your team members have the tools and support they need so that their effort results in better performance, and then reward that better performance, especially with personal recognition such as praise.

- *Discord within the team*. There are two sorts of discord to watch out for: that caused by cliques and that caused by bogeymen. Cliques differ from innocent friendships within your team in that cliques are more deliberately exclusive of those outside and they often have a political purpose, such as the monopolisation of high status or highly skilled aspects of the team's work. If you perceive a clique forming, explore its political purpose and find some better means of meeting this need for all your team. The bogeyman is a common feature of work units. What happens is that one individual becomes the focus for all the team's discontent – everything is seen to be their fault. If you believe the bogeyman to be an innocent victim, show your support and lead the team into finding the real causes of its problems.

- *Blame*. Cliques and bogeymen are forms of passing blame within your team. Your team may also start blaming another team for its problems; for example, a project team blames its problems on suppliers of hardware, desks or whatever. This can put you in an awkward position. Support your team in their fair and considerate demands on others, but if blame is becoming a habit it may be that your team is seeing its work as more important than the wider purpose of the organisation. Does your stated vision for the team ignore its context? Is your team becoming isolated? Are you empire-building?

Finally, when discussing the development and maintenance of your team, it is worth considering the matter of termination. It is right and natural that team members reach a stage when the best course of action is to leave the team. The first case is a team member who knows the job thoroughly and performs well. You will want to retain this person in your team as long as you can, but after a time the person will want more challenge. You will often be able to provide this challenge within your team, but if not, do not try to hold on to this person too long. It may breed resentment. The second case to consider is a team member who is not performing or who is behaving in some difficult manner. Other chapters in this book give advice for developing such people but there will be times when you wish to end their membership of your team. Do not shirk this uncomfortable aspect of your job, but do seek advice from a personnel professional first.

22.8 Summary

There is a great deal project managers can do to forge the members of their project into an effective team. There is much scope for managers to choose and express their own style; for example, you can choose the extent to which you share social activities and discuss out-of-work matters with your team. Any choice here can be effective, depending on your team and your circumstances. The only choice that is ineffective is to ignore this aspect of project management – some managers find it awkward or risky and so prefer to hide behind their terminals, focusing their attention on spreadsheets and planning tools. Although this option appears safe, it is the path of real risk. If your team wants your project to succeed, the chances are it will.

Questions

1 Prepare an interview plan for the post of Business Analyst in your team.

2 When you first assemble your project team, what can you do to build **team spirit**? What behaviours are the different individuals likely to exhibit during this team-building process? How do you demonstrate your leadership?

Case study

E-Con is in essence a team culture and the organisation has devoted considerable efforts to ensure that its teams work effectively together. For this reason, Belbin-type assessments are done on all new joiners and repeated occasionally thereafter so that the resource manager can take team roles into account when assembling project teams.

Of course, the primary determinant of team composition is the skills required, but E-Con has found that an understanding of the Belbin roles can help to predict how well teams will work together and assist project managers in ensuring their teams work effectively as a unit.

In the case of the France Vacances project, the team types of the internet development team turned out to be:

- Siobhan Reid, project manager: Coordinator/Resource Investigator
- Pam Stephanou, analyst: Implementer/Team Worker
- Don Short, analyst: Innovator
- Greg Martin, web developer: Monitor/Evaluator
- Janet Vine, web developer: Implementer.

This is not a badly balanced team, with most roles represented, but Siobhan realised that she was lacking a Completer. Looking at people's secondary roles, she noticed that Janet Vine also had some Completer tendencies so, in briefing the team and assigning responsibilities, Siobhan asked her to bring her Completer side to the fore.

To get the team working together as quickly as possible, Siobhan enlisted the aid of E-Con's training manager, Mark Taylor, and asked him to facilitate a half-day team-building event. A longer event would have been desirable but impractical in view of the tight timescale of the project, and Mark managed to devise an afternoon session with a combination of exercises and games followed by a meal. This enabled everyone to get to know each other and, Siobhan felt, greatly speeded the usual team-formation process.

Further reading

Belbin, M (1996), *Management Teams: Why They Succeed or Fail*, Butterworth-Heineman

Belbin, M (1999), *Team Roles at Work*, Butterworth-Heinemann

Cranwell-Ward, J, Bacon, A and Mackie, R (2002), *Inspiring Leadership – Staying Afloat in Turbulent Tmes*, Thomson Press

Davison, S and Ward, K (1999), *Leading International Teams*, McGraw-Hill

Kluckholn, F R and Stroderbeck, F L (1961), *Variations in Value Orientations*, Row Petersen

Lipnack, J and Stamps, J (1997), *Virtual Teams: Reaching across Space, Time and Organisations with Technology*, Wiley

Schein, E (1992), *Organisational Culture and Leadership*, 2nd edn, Jossey Bass

Schneider, S and Barsoux, J L (2000), *Managing Across Cultures*, Prentice Hall

Symons, J (2002), 'Critical success factors in leading virtual teams', paper given at the British Academy of Management Conference 2002

Symons, J (2003), 'Taking virtual team control', *Professional Manager*, March

Tuckman, B W (1965), 'Developmental sequences in small groups', *The Psychological Bulletin*, 384–99

23 Managing the project climate

23.1 Introduction

The French have a phrase for it, 'esprit de corps'; and Alexander Dumas in the 'Three Musketeers' used 'one for all and all for one'. In the UK we tend to talk about '**team spirit**'. However it is described, we mean that difference between a team that knows it is up for the challenge and one that grumbles around the coffee machine. The project manager is the person who makes the difference between these two kinds of team. We have already talked about team development and the lifecycle of teams, but it is more that. It is the climate or atmosphere of the team. The physical environment is important of course, but in this chapter we are mostly concerned with the emotional environment. In particular we look at stress, conflict and handling grievances. Skill in dealing with these issues means that the team's attention is not diverted on to internal matters of 'who said what to whom and why, and how it isn't fair'. The emotional environment is not a tangible thing and cannot be controlled in the way an electric heater can, but it can be controlled to an extent in more subtle ways.

The lack of direct control over the emotional environment makes some project managers uneasy, so they ignore it or hope it will fix itself. Some may believe that the team climate just happens and that there is nothing they can do to influence it. But there are actions you can take to influence the climate and ensure it does not just 'happen'. It is worth doing this, as a positive climate brings fulfilment and satisfaction for your team and productivity and quality results for your project. A poor climate means your project will always be struggling.

We know already that people do not work just for the money. People come to work to fulfil a need for achievement or advancement, or to occupy their time, or to have social interaction, or all of these and more. Work is now one of the main means of meeting new people and even partners for life. Whilst most of us can observe and relate to these other reasons for coming to work, few realise the extent to which people use work and the other people there to meet their personal, social and psychological needs. Larry Hirschhorn calls this other aspect of organisational life 'the workplace within', whereas Gerard Egan calls it 'the shadow side'. This chapter offers a short insight into this other aspect of the world of work and concentrates on the skills you need for dealing with some of its main manifestations: conflict, stress, grievances and problems that require counselling.

This 'shadow side' of work presents a new range of problems for you to deal with. It also offers you tremendous opportunities to tap and channel the fundamental motivations which different people have.

23.2 Creating the working environment

Although the working environment is more than just the physical environment, there is a relationship between them. If people are happy with the nature of their work and with factors such as recognition, responsibility and opportunities for development, they are likely to be committed to their jobs and not especially concerned about the physical environment. You may have come across teams that worked well and cheerfully in less than comfortable surroundings. You may remember the earlier example of the artist starving in a cold attic room, but content because he can do the work he loves. But when people are dissatisfied with their jobs, for whatever reason, they complain about the physical environment, the organisational environment – such as company policy and supervision style – and salary. You may have come across examples such as people who work in luxurious modern offices but complain because the subsidised canteen only offers two choices of hot meal.

This does not mean that you can ignore complaints about tangible issues such as the physical environment; dealing with such matters may not create satisfaction but it will reduce dissatisfaction, and taking such grievances seriously is a good opportunity to demonstrate that you care. But it does mean that, as well as doing what you can about the overt source of dissatisfaction, you should look for the deeper causes as well. A method for doing this is given later in this chapter. It also means that simply trying to brighten up the physical environment, for example with a new coat of paint or a few potted plants, will not improve the climate of your team if there are more fundamental problems to be resolved.

A physical feature of the workplace which does have a direct impact on the team climate is the layout of your building. First of all, where are you? A project manager who sits overlooking the team members gives an impression of very close supervision which will be interpreted as a lack of trust. On the other hand, a project manager who stays in a separate office with the door closed will be seen as out of touch, whose judgements of people and problems will not be given credibility. Secondly, where are the team members in relation to each other? If they sit facing away from each other they will feel isolated and will not communicate as effectively as they would if they were able to see each other easily. On the other hand, this may be desirable if too much communication is getting in the way of work.

Moving away from physical factors, there is much more that you can do to influence the working environment. Several have already been mentioned in this book: encouragement, praise, a clear vision or objectives and career development for all staff who want it. These factors seem obvious, and are, but it is often the obvious factors which get overlooked. Perhaps the most powerful means of influencing the working climate is to demonstrate the working style you want your team to adopt. This is more than simply setting a good example; it means modelling the style of interpersonal relationships you would like to see. You can model trust by delegating new work to people and giving your permission for people to try new ways of doing things, being willing to take the risk that they may not get it right at first. You can model openness and learning from mistakes by disclosing errors you have made in the past and how you have gained from them. Managers, like parents, do not have to be perfect. You will need to consider how close you want to get to your team: how well do you know them? On what do you base your assessments of them? Other small things you can try are the little social rituals such as doughnuts on Fridays, drinks after work on birthdays, tea and talk at eleven o'clock and monthly awards for the greatest achievement and the greatest foul-up – celebrating the opportunity to learn from it. You will be able to think of other factors influencing a positive climate which you have come across. Try them. Better still, get your team to come up with ideas.

23.3 Handling conflict

Earlier chapters have shown that conflict is a normal part of a team's development. Conflict often spawns creativity. Conflict shows that people care. But raw conflict can be destructive if it is uncontrolled. It can mutate into personal animosity, with grudges being held and sides being taken. If you take a back seat and let things take their natural course you may find it leads to intractable problems such as these. The solution is to channel the creative energy generated by conflict into joint problem-solving. This is especially true when the conflict is between you and someone else. Specific actions you can take are to give both parties an opportunity to present their case without interruption, ask probing questions and invite the other party to give full consideration. Stay neutral yourself and show neutrality in what you say and how you say it. At the very end of the discussion you may choose to abandon your neutral stance and make a decision yourself or you may leave it to your team. Very often you will find that, if you manage the process of debate well, the conflict will have evaporated and been replaced by mutually agreed progress. Do not imagine that you can keep out of conflict within your team – it is your business even if you would rather it were not.

The previous chapter also discussed the particular forms of conflict that arise when some members of your team collude to form an exclusive clique or to identify a bogeyman on to whom they project their dissatisfactions and anxieties. Both of these are really forms of psychological defence mechanisms: people form exclusive cliques when they feel threatened, as cliques give them a fantasy of being safe and special. People outside the clique can see it clearly, but those within invariably deny that a clique exists. People blame all their problems on a bogeyman to protect them from feeling responsible for any of their problems. The problem is that those excluded from the clique or picked out as a bogeyman suffer unfairly and the divisions in your team can have long-term negative consequences for your project. Negative consequences include direct obstruction of work and communication and less direct obstruction of career development opportunities, which has an impact on productivity and morale. A section in this chapter deals with counselling, and some counselling techniques can help people identify the real cause of their insecurity and so take responsibility for their problems. In particular, you should be prepared to challenge any statement or behaviour which appears to arise from one of these defence mechanisms.

One form of conflict that is often identified is the personality clash. There is such a thing as a personality clash: it occurs when two people have strong and opposite psychological traits and they are not sufficiently mature to recognise the strengths of the opposite type. Using Belbin's team roles identified in the previous chapter, we can say that Innovators and Monitor/Evaluators are likely to conflict over the value of an idea and Shapers and Implementers might argue over the pace of work. Two Shapers in a team may clash unless one is happy to take a secondary role. These conflicts reduce when all concerned can recognise that each brings a valuable contribution to the team. Education and training on team dynamics can therefore help, as will a focus on a shared objective. Separation is sometimes the only solution. If one individual frequently has clashes with several different people it implies that they are the source of the problem. Some people seek out conflict as they crave little victories over other people. Such behaviour needs to be confronted. If you can help a team member to realise why they are seeking out conflict, not only will you have removed a source of strife from your team, you will also have improved their quality of life.

However, many conflicts are blamed on a personality clash when this is not the real cause. Managers may prefer to dismiss conflict as a personality clash because that implies it is no one's fault and the manager could do nothing about it. In reality, the conflict may be one of the types already described or it may have structural origins. Some organisations have conflict designed into them, making destructive confrontation inevitable. A typical error is the splitting of dependent activities into separate functional groups. For example, analysis and programming are both parts of the software development process. Splitting the project into an analysis team and a programming team is a recipe for mutual antagonism. Look at your organisation chart and think about how you share out the work of your organisation: is conflict designed in? If so, consider restructuring your project so that teams are all focused on some ultimate deliverable.

23.4 Managing stress

The problem of stress at work is receiving more and more attention in the medical and management press. It has been related to the greater pressure exerted on enterprises from global competition and to the isolation we feel as a result of communicating by remote rather than intimate means. Because the issue of stress is receiving more attention you probably know a great deal about it already. You may be aware that stress has been linked to diet: a balanced diet without too many additives helps relieve stress. Stress has been linked to drugs: if you are used to more than a small intake of tobacco, alcohol or caffeine you will experience stress as a result. Stress has been linked to lifestyle: a moderate amount of exercise helps reduce stress and it is important to make time for activities outside work such as hobbies and meeting friends and family. This section is not intended to replace such commonly available advice on managing stress that can be obtained from health books and medical professionals; it aims instead to examine certain aspects of stress that relate to a project-based work environment.

We all need some level of stress. Without some pressure there would be less motivation to work and many of us would become bored. The amount of pressure which is comfortable varies from person to person. What this means is that some people take steps to avoid pressure: some look for less stressful jobs whereas others cope by planning their work in order to avoid crises. But many other people like crises and, subconsciously, create them. Work is left until the last minute and so has to be done in a rush; activities are invented which 'have to be done' although they may in fact be of little significance; items are left unorganised so a big show can be made of frantic searches; little problems are exaggerated; there are many sighs, groans and other indications of a person making heroic efforts for the good of the company. This style of hasty activity is sometimes given the noble title of 'fire-fighting' but it has been said that most 'fire-fighters' in this sense are also arsonists. By creating pressure, people get the excitement they want from work. It can also generate a feeling of importance: 'Look how hard I am working – this organisation really depends on me!' 'Look at all the papers on my desk – I have a really heavy workload!' This type of reasoning may be implied in the behaviour of an apparently very busy person with the hope that their 'hard work' will be noticed, leading to promotion or to the avoidance of redundancy. In many cases, it works. But an effective manager takes a cautious view of people who appear to be constantly busy and knows that effective people have occasional busy periods but most of the time are quietly efficient.

However effective a project team is and however well planned the project is, the approach of a deadline can nevertheless cause a period of high pressure if unforeseen events mean there is a great deal of work to do in a short time. If these circumstances are infrequent and not too long they will do no great harm, but you should ensure that your staff have time to relax and at least one day off work every week. Indeed, short bursts of pressure can build team spirit and generate loyalty, but only if they are short and not too frequent.

You need to look out for signs of stress in yourself and members of your team. Typical signs are working long hours, irritability, sickness, excess reliance on tobacco or alcohol, creating drama out of minor incidents, destructive criticism of colleagues, a change in behaviour, fatigue, and expressions of hopelessness, worthlessness or their opposite: extreme confidence or arrogance. Stress is not caused simply by too much work; too little work or work that is insufficiently challenging can be just as stressful. Stress can also be caused by conflict, especially if it becomes harassment or bullying, which must never be tolerated in your team. Lack of a clear job description or job goals can be stressful, as can problems outside work.

Most project managers are aware that life events such as marriage, divorce, bereavement and the arrival of a baby – especially the sleep deprivation which often comes with it – all bring stress, and allowance for members of their team in these situations must be made. Sensitive project managers are aware that smaller events away from work, such as an argument at home, a move and financial problems, all bring stress as well. You may be able to provide some help, refer your team member to someone who can give expert advice or simply provide some counselling as described later in this chapter. Even if you cannot help directly, you could temporarily adjust the standards you expect from a team member with problems at home by, for example, allowing some extra time off.

Finally, remember that one common source of stress at work is management. The types of problem you could be causing include an inappropriate leadership or coaching style, taking decisions too late or without the involvement of the people affected by them, restricting access to challenging or attractive work or simply demanding too much of your team.

When signs of undue stress have been detected you can select from the great many solutions that are available. A change of diet, more exercise, less exercise, some time off work, counselling, improved job design, training, greater or less delegation, help with planning finances or careers, or improved resources at work are all possible means of reducing stress, depending on what is causing it. Often, however, the cause, and so the solution, of stress problems relates to personal organisation and time management. Many people, especially managers, spend more time looking for things than they would imagine. They also waste time doing work that should be delegated, supervising too closely, switching between activities and being at formal meetings and informal encounters which they do not need to attend. So attention to the basic personal skills of time management and self-organisation, as well as a recognition that such problems are often a subconscious choice, is often a means for a less stressful life. Some things to do right now: schedule in some time, say one hour a week, to devote to your personal organisation. Clear out drawers, files and cupboards. Throw out old documents. Then devise a better filing system for organising what you have left. When this is done you can reduce the time spent on personal organisation to as little as twenty minutes every week. Next, schedule in some time, perhaps another hour once a week, to devote to planning. This does not mean project planning, which you are no doubt doing already, but personal planning. You might, for example, decide to fix regular slots for dealing with mail and administration. You could spend the time planning how working on your project could be made better for you and your team. You could reconsider your goals or think of new ways of approaching the problems which face you. It is perfectly acceptable to arrange regular slots when you tell everyone you are not available, giving you uninterrupted time to work on these tasks, provided that you agree an equal amount of time when you guarantee you will be available for them. Finally, do not forget to find time to relax. Just a few moments every now and then will help you get through the day without feeling so exhausted at the end.

23.5 Handling grievances

The handling of grievances is an excellent example of how espoused management practice frequently differs from actual management practice. Ask a manager how they deal with grievances and a typical answer might be: 'If someone came to me with a grievance, I'd listen carefully and make sure I had understood. We'd talk the matter over in order to get to the bottom of it. Then I'd consider carefully and, where I thought the grievance was fair and I could do something about it, I would. If there were any aspects of the grievance which I disagreed with, or which I felt I could do nothing about, I would explain my reasoning and hopefully we could come to some compromise.' All very sensible, but far removed from what happens in most cases. Many organisations have a code for the management of grievances but, except where there is a strong trade union presence, would be hard pressed to find a recent instance of its being followed.

First of all, most grievances are never raised with management because the managers are not trusted to deal with them fairly. Instead, grievances get expressed between employees in whispered conversations or out of work. This griping lowers morale and does nothing to resolve the grievance, but for the employee it often seems to be the only outlet for complaints. Secondly, this lack of trust is generally quite appropriate, for when grievances are expressed to management, most are ignored, trivialised or generate a defensive reaction. These are all means of avoiding having to recognise that a grievance exists. The grievance is ignored by putting it down as just some 'difficult' person moaning or by simply choosing not to notice it at all. It is trivialised by dismissing the complaint as being of no consequence and therefore requiring no management attention. The third approach, the defensive reaction, is worst. It occurs when a member of staff raises a grievance and subsequently receives some form of rebuke or disciplinary interview. These forms of response to a grievance happen because management often cannot bear to believe that anyone in their team might have cause to complain. Just as we often hold idealised images of ourselves, so managers, seeing their project or organisation as an extension of themselves, hold an idealised image of it. Grievances are then seen as a personal attack.

Because people feel their grievances are not being addressed, the problem tends to brew in their minds. It occupies more and more attention and, probably, discussion time at the coffee machine. Unless the grievance is dealt with effectively, people start to leave, protest in some silent way such as pilfering or arriving late, or the grievance may burst out of its containment in a dramatic row.

How should you handle grievances? Simply in the manner that everyone knows they should be handled, more or less as outlined at the start of this section. Listen, discuss, then plan. Grievances need not be confrontational; they can be an opportunity for you to improve conditions on your project and attract loyalty. The paragraphs below give some tips for achieving this.

Firstly, reflect on how you have handled grievances recently. If you manage more than a tiny number of people, it is likely that at least one of them will have had a grievance in the past year. If no grievances were raised, why not? It could be that you are not trusted to deal with them. Find an opportunity to show that you can be and, instead of showing outrage, show gratitude that the employee trusted you and gave you an opportunity to improve their conditions of work. If grievances were raised, how did you handle them? Did you take offence and show it, or has the problem been resolved to everyone's satisfaction?

Secondly, encourage people to raise their grievances so they can be addressed, in the same way that some businesses encourage complaints, as they are an opportunity for improvement. For example, you could regularly include an item in team or individual meetings on 'what's irritating me'. Everyone, including you, uses this as an opportunity to air and discuss grievances.

Thirdly, turn grievances into joint problem-solving sessions. To do this you need to see the grievance as separate from you, your team and your management style. Explore the problem. What does the person with the grievance want? If you can find out what the fundamental problem is you can often delegate its resolution to the person who raised it in the first place.

When people have a personal grievance, such as anxiety over career progress, they will often come to you with a less personal grievance, such as a complaint over a lack of car parking facilities. The reason for this is that problems with career progress are rarely simply other people's fault. The individual probably believes, or fears, that they are partially responsible for a slower rate of career progress than that desired. Rather than face this unpleasant possibility, the grievance is subconsciously transferred on to an issue over which the individual cannot possibly have any responsibility, such as some physical feature of the workplace. While the presented problem of car parking should be considered, you also need to explore such grievances to see if there is a deeper, more personal source of dissatisfaction. This requires the use of counselling skills.

23.6 Counselling

Counselling is traditionally seen as a specialist service provided by trained experts to people with some serious problem such as a marital crisis or a bereavement. Whilst these traditional domains of counselling are flourishing, the concept of workplace counselling has recently been receiving much attention. Workplace counselling is provided by people with a lower level of training than professional counsellors but with enough skills and a willingness to help people with everyday problems, such as those which commonly arise at work. This section introduces the concept of workplace counselling and the

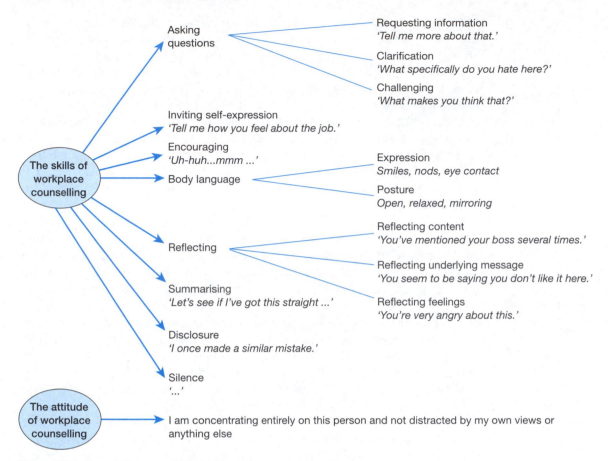

Figure 23.1 Key skills and attitude of workplace counselling

key skills and attitudes required to do it adequately. No book can substitute for effective training when it comes to interpersonal skills such as counselling. Fortunately, such training is readily available. Counselling is *not* giving advice, telling people what to do or indeed solving other people's problems. Counselling is helping other people to solve their own problems.

This sounds fine but it is not as easy as it sounds. Figure 23.1 shows the key skills, which are described in the paragraphs below. Most of us are better at some than others, perhaps because we use them in normal conversation. Other skills feel awkward and new. Therefore it may seem natural to help a person using the sorts of skills that you have always used, the ones that most people tend to use when talking to a person with a problem. Typically, the 'natural' approach is to give advice, as other people's problems always seem easy to solve. Advice-giving starts with a statement like: 'What you should do is . . .', or 'If I were you . . .'. Whilst giving advice is sometimes the right thing to do, for example when someone comes to you with a straightforward technical question, very often advice is not only unhelpful but also counterproductive. If you always solve your team members' technical problems they will grow dependent on you rather than willing to try their own solutions. When it comes to less technical problems, again advice is occasionally the answer, but you can never fully understand another person's problem and, even if you could, the solution which works for you might not work for them. Your advice might then show your lack of understanding, which can be interpreted as a lack of care. Your advice may simply not be workable in the situation the other person faces, which can lead to a state of helplessness: 'No one can solve my problems!' As the other person will have been thinking about the problem much more than you, it is almost certain that any solutions you offer as advice will have been thought of before. Your suggestion of obvious answers will then appear as an insult to their intelligence.

So cast aside your previous approaches to helping people with problems and consider the skills of workplace counselling presented here. The first one is asking questions. Questions can be used to encourage a person to talk about an aspect of their problem and to clarify some of the details. For example, if the person says, 'I hate it here,' you can probe by asking, 'What specifically do you hate?' The other person may not have thought about exactly what the source of their unhappiness is. Your probing with gentle questions like these can help identify the real source. Questions can also be used to challenge implied assumptions and personal perspectives presented as facts. For example, if someone expresses a worry such as, 'I don't know what I should do to help my cousin,' you could challenge the implied assumption with: 'Why do you feel you have to help your cousin?' If someone expresses a fixed perspective by saying: 'Noel is really difficult – he keeps interfering with my work,' you could challenge with: 'Are you sure the problem is entirely Noel's?' Complaints and criticisms about other people always need to be challenged, but that does not mean they are always unjustified – you need to probe to find out. Questions can also be used as a gentle way of suggesting possible solutions if you feel you really have to do this. For example, 'Have you thought of asking him to leave you alone?'

Inviting self-expression is a particularly useful form of question. You can use it to encourage people to consider their feelings about a situation instead of just the facts. Feelings are often at the root of problems and conflict, whilst 'facts' are not as objective as we might imagine.

Encouraging means all those little noises we make which encourage a person to continue. You can also say things like 'Yes . . . go on.' Take care in using words like 'Right' and 'OK' as the tone of voice you use can make these words sound like a request for the other person to stop talking rather than continue.

Body language is a big topic and one for which the saying 'A little knowledge is a dangerous thing' is apt. Be very cautious about interpreting another person's body language unless you have had considerable training. But *your* body language can be used to encourage a person to open up, which is what you are trying to achieve when counselling. A relaxed posture, a comfortable amount of eye contact and appropriate responses such as a smile or a raised eyebrow all encourage a person to continue. You may also have noticed that, when two people are in rapport, they tend to adopt similar body postures. This means that, by subtly following the other person's movements, without copying them directly, you can encourage a state of rapport to develop between you.

Reflecting means repeating a key word or phrase, commenting on what the other person has said or picking up on some unspoken message or feeling you suspect is there from 'reading between the lines'. Simply repeating a key word or two, as a question, from what the other person has just said will encourage them to say more about it. For example, if the person says, 'There seems to be some tension between him and me,' you could respond, 'Some tension?' and they will then expand on what is meant. Repeating is something we often do as part of everyday conversation without realising it. It is, however, one of the best ways to lead a person to disclose what is really on their mind.

Summarising what the other person has said shows that you have listened and gives the other person a chance to add to or correct what you have heard. In any work interview or meeting, summarising has a very positive effect. Unfortunately it is not used much, probably because we do not use it with our friends in ordinary conversation. If you want to pick just one new inter-personal skill to work on, you would probably improve your communications skills the most by working on doing more summaries. A summary is a statement like this: 'Right, can I just see if I'm with you so far? You are upset by what you see as Noel's interference; you have acknowledged that from his point of view he is probably just trying to help; but, all the same, it irritates you because it makes you feel he doesn't trust your competence. Is that right?'

Making a disclosure about yourself may seem risky, especially if you need to feel in control. But in fact it builds trust; it opens a door for the other person to come through. Making a disclosure does not mean saying, 'I had a similar problem once and this is what I did . . .', as that is the same as giving advice. It means disclosing that you too have problems and anxieties and have made mistakes. If you do need to feel in control, you could reflect on why that is. Such a feeling can be unhelpful in counselling and many other situations.

Perhaps the most powerful workplace counselling technique is silence. It can feel very awkward to sit in silence, even for just a few moments, but it gives the other person time to find the words or the courage to say them. Too many managers fill their employees' air time with what they want to say. So be prepared for a silence to hang for a fair while and fill it only when you are sure the other person needs you to break it. Finally, it can be helpful to have a box of tissues nearby. If the other person needs them, just hand them over and give time for recovery without saying anything.

But workplace counselling is more than just a matter of skills. If you simply act out these listening skills without genuinely being interested in the other person your insincerity will show. So forget that car repair bill, ignore your worry over the leaking radiator and suspend all judgements. You are fully available for the other person's problems, views and solutions. This is the attitude of workplace counselling, without which use of the skills is just a hollow sham. This attitude will also help you avoid some of those destructive behaviours that people do without realising it, such as interrupting and making judgements. Only attempt workplace counselling if you have the time and the will to help in this way. Assure the other person that everything they say will be kept confidential and then keep this promise.

The basic idea of counselling is that, if you can encourage people to talk their problem through with you, they will have to put vague thoughts into words, answer questions they may not have asked themselves and consider their problem from new points of view. This process helps them to reconsider their problem and come up with their own solutions, to which they will be more committed than any you might have suggested.

Your counselling skills will improve with practice, training and further reading on the subject. You will then be able to use workplace counselling for team-building, coaching, discipline, development and for helping people facing conflict, retirement, redundancy, change and personal problems.

The skills and attitude of workplace counselling are much more effective at helping people to develop than simply telling them how they should change. But it is not always the approach to take. There will be times when there is a problem with an employee's work or behaviour and all your counselling has not led to the person identifying and resolving it. In these cases, use the coaching or reprimand approaches described in Chapter 21. There are occasions when giving advice is appropriate, as described at the start of this section. There may also be occasions when you are out of your depth with basic workplace counselling skills. If a fellow employee has a serious problem, such as one involving drink or gambling, you have to refer them to a counsellor who is better qualified to deal with such issues. You can find such people through your personnel manager, medical professionals or the telephone directory.

23.7 Summary

The last three chapters have examined the human side of project management. People are far more complex and varied than money, yet the training and attention given to people who specialise in the human aspect of work is considerably less than that given to people who specialise in the financial aspect. The human side of project management is fraught with dangers and risks such as conflict, low morale and even sabotage. On the other hand, managing this aspect of your project presents you with your greatest opportunities for making a real difference and for bringing commitment, motivation, satisfaction and success.

You probably reached the position of project manager through your competence at technical skills, including skills such as planning and monitoring. It is likely that managing people is a new discipline for you. Many project managers choose to ignore the human side of management because deep down they lack confidence in dealing with people problems and even perhaps because they are afraid of getting hurt in the process. As well as being a key ingredient to the success of a project, the human side of management is a discipline that offers lifelong learning opportunities for you. Ignore it at your peril.

Questions

1 Consider a project manager with a team of 15 to 20 people: a mixture of analysts, designers, programmers and support staff. The project also uses some specialist staff on a part-time basis. How could the project manager influence the working environment of such a team so as to get the best out of them?

2 Conflict and stress arise naturally in IS project teams. Some people argue that a little of both is useful, but everyone agrees that too much is destructive. How could you organise your project team to minimise the destructive effect of conflict and stress?

Further reading

Egan, G (1994), *Working the Shadow Side*, Jossey Bass

Hirschhorn, L (1990), *The Workplace Within*, MIT Press

24 The project manager

24.1 Introduction

You should by now have a clear idea of the job of the project manager, and you may be asking yourself, 'What sort of person makes a good project manager?' This chapter considers just that question. We have looked at it in a number of ways and set out some ideas for you to consider. We have included:

- One company's vision of the role of the project manager.
- An outside perspective showing what the IS project manager can learn from management in other fields.
- A developmental approach used in one company we have studied.
- How psychometrics can help in the selection of the right person for the job and with the development of the right person once they are in post.
- One company's research into how psychometrics helped.

Taken together, these approaches to the topic should give you a clear outline of what it is like to be a project manager in an IS environment. And it should also help you to clarify your own idea about your development as a project manager.

24.2 The vision

One major international systems company has a vision statement that, for them, sums up what they want every one of their project managers to commit to. They accept that not all of it will be true for all of their project managers all of the time, but they have defined the feeling of the role in a way that everyone who starts managing projects for them knows what is expected of them in terms of attitude and final goal. As you read it, ask yourself if you would want to be seen like this by your manager, your peers, your customers and your team. If the answer is yes, then maybe it could be a vision for you as well as for others.

> As a project manager, you are determined to succeed and to bring your project to a successful conclusion – on time, within budget and to the customer's satisfaction. This isn't easy but it is rewarding.

It's not easy. You have to meet the client's requirements and bring together equipment, software and people to deliver a solution to a problem that hasn't been solved before. You know that equipment will be late, that software will give you problems and that you won't always get the people you need when you need them.

You accept this. It's no use crying over spilt milk, you have to get on with the job: replan, reorganise, reschedule, reallocate and remotivate. You said that you didn't want a boring job and that you wanted a challenge, an opportunity to shape events, the chance to build your reputation and your company's – well, you got it. Overcoming problems and winning through to the end is part of what turns you on. It feels good to manage a complex issue through to a successful conclusion.

But you don't have to do this on your own. You are the leader, but it's a team task and a team success. Team spirit, helping people grow and harnessing their skills and enthusiasm is important to you. You have a personal commitment to their development. You manage people well as individuals and as a team. They respond to you and trust your judgement. You enable them to perform.

Managing projects is what you do best. People know you and you are valued. Each project is different, each a new challenge. You welcome this challenge: it gives you new opportunities to learn. Your contribution is consistently above average, beyond the norm – even in a goal-orientated, customer service industry like ours. You wouldn't have it any other way.

For us this sums up the essence of being a project manager. Whilst all of the obstacles are perhaps not present in every project, the spirit of this vision statement is uplifting and motivational.

24.3 An outside perspective

Many project managers feel that their role is very different from that of the traditional manager and thus that they can learn very little from old-style management textbooks. Let us examine this belief. If we define a project as something with a clear start and finish, as something that brings about change and that has a clearly stated objective, then humanity has been managing projects since the dawn of time. Hunting a woolly mammoth or raising a crop are both projects that conform to this description. Given that, are there many differences between the relatively new discipline of project management and that of older, traditional management? Traditional management priorities often centre on control: controlling the team, the task and the individual. Classic texts tell us that the traditional manager has the functions of control, coordination, communication and the setting of performance standards. Are these so different from what today's project manager does?

There are some major differences. For example, there are differences in timing:

- Traditional management is continuous whereas a project is finite.
- Traditional managers expect to stay in post for a considerable length of time whereas project managers expect to manage a project for a finite length of time.

As well as this, the role of the IS project manager is to create a product – usually a new IS system incorporating hardware and software. The primary tool in this task is the brainpower of the project team. In this the project manager is different from traditional managers whose primary task is often to keep the status quo operational, whether this is to keep the assembly line moving or the office department functioning at full efficiency. In essence, traditional management is often seen as being repetitive whereas project management is mostly non-repetitive.

If project managers want to make best use of the skills and abilities of their highly able workforce, they must be willing to give them information so that they can develop a rational understanding of the tasks assigned to them. A skilled software engineer will function much better if he or she knows not just what is required but why it is required. In this way, the software engineer is not only doing the required job but is also quality checking the analysis and design work that was done previously. Again, this is different from traditional management.

Whereas traditional management often looks in great detail at how the workforce should be supervised – with close supervision often being recommended – many, if not all, professional engineers will look for an absence of detailed supervision, freedom from administrative routine where feasible and a working environment which sets them free to perform at their best. Naturally, in such an environment, the project manager has to trust the team to do a good job. The degree of control and supervision given so that they can do this good job will be different from many earlier management disciplines.

This shows that there is greater possibility for failure in project management than in traditional management. In traditional management, a manager will establish a closed loop in which staff performance is noted and measured, compared with performance standards and then any necessary corrective action is taken.

Particularly during the initial stages of an IS project, the analysis and design phases, the project manager is often flying blind. The degree of risk and uncertainty will vary from project to project, but all projects will contain some risk, and many are highly risky. Nothing exactly the same as this piece of work has been attempted before, so the project manager often faces real difficulty – in spite of all the tools and techniques – in predicting the outcomes of the work being done, and has the additional problem of knowing that any mistakes will have profound and perhaps costly consequences later in the project.

If there are differences between traditional management and IS project management, are there similarities between general project management, which has been a recognised discipline for over fifty years, and IS project management? Consider the following extract from an article published in the *Harvard Business Review* in 1960. It is by Paul Gaddis and is a classic early discussion of the emerging role of project management in hi-tech industries:

> Generally speaking, the project manager's business is to create a product – a piece of advanced-technology hardware. The primary tool available to him is the brainpower of men who are professional specialists in diverse fields. He uses this tool in all the phases of the creation of his product, from concept through the initial test operation and manufacturing stages.

The article then goes on to address many of the issues current today: what does the project manager do, what kind of person is he, what training is required? So, in over forty years of examination we are still puzzling over the same issues. Like leadership, perhaps project management is not the simplest job in the world. As an illustration of how the world keeps on reinventing the same old wheel, we came across a definition of project management and a list of the skills of a project manager produced quite recently by a well-respected international body.

A project was defined as 'a set of interrelated activities, with an agreed start and finish time, that is undertaken by an organisation in order to meet defined objectives within the constraints of time, cost and resources at specified quality requirements', and a project manager as 'the individual to whom authority, responsibility and accountability have been assigned for the overall management of resources – including the technical, time and cost aspects – of a project, and the motivation of all of those involved'.

When looking at the project manager in this context, those skills that will make a good project manager together with the attributes and skills which the project manager should develop to ensure the effectiveness of the team and the individuals in that team were described. There is much here that reflects the work of Gaddis all those years ago, much that reflects the engineering disciplines and the contractual nature of the project manager's role, and much that is currently occupying present-day thinking about the development of project managers. These skills are:

- *Leadership*. Project managers should be able to stimulate action, progress and change.
- *Technological understanding*. Project managers need to have an accurate perception of the technical requirements of the project so that business needs are addressed and satisfied.
- *Evaluation and decision making*. Project managers should have the ability to evaluate alternatives and to make informed decisions.
- *People management*. Project managers should be able to motivate and enthuse their teams and have a constant personal drive towards achieving the project's goals.
- *Systems design and maintenance*. Project managers should be able to demonstrate their individual competence and have a complete working knowledge of the internal administration of their project.
- *Planning and control*. Project managers should be constantly monitoring progress against the plan and taking any necessary corrective action using modern planning and monitoring methods.
- *Financial awareness*. Project managers should be proficient in risk management and have a broad financial knowledge.
- *Procurement*. Project managers should understand the basics of procurement and be able to develop the procurement strategy for their project.
- *Communication*. Project managers should be able to express themselves clearly and unambiguously in speaking and writing and be able to do this in a wide range of situations and with a wide range of people.

■ *Negotiating*. Project managers should be skilful in managing their clients and should be able to plan a negotiation strategy and then carry it out.

■ *Contractual skills*. Project managers must be able to understand the contract that defines their project and should be able to manage subcontractors to ensure that the contractual terms are met.

■ *Legal awareness*. The project manager should have an awareness of any legal issues that could affect the project.

24.4 A developmental approach

It is clear that in any project team the project manager is the key figure. However, as we have seen, although there is no such thing as a standard project in the IT industry, there are certain skills and qualities of project managers which can contribute materially to the success of any project with which they are associated. These skills and qualities are increasingly called competences, but they are often little more than the list above: groups of abilities and talents which shape the way the project manager does the job and so have an impact on the whole project. We can get a better grasp of these skills, abilities or competences if we break them down into four key areas. The skills and qualities that project managers use to manage:

■ Themselves, such as time management.
■ Their one-to-one interactions, such as negotiation skills.
■ Their one-to-many interactions, such as with their team.
■ The task, such as monitoring.

Let us look at them one by one, starting with self-management. Anyone setting out to manage the complexity of a project must be able to manage their own self. Many of the key qualities and skills for self-management are identified in Figure 24.1.

In addition, it is expected that a project manager provides the strength of character and the vision to keep the project on course. Along with this would go the ability to be seen as a respected and commanding figure within the team, the company and the customer's organisation. This will not come out of thin air, but it is often something that can be fostered in new project managers by their seniors. Without role models, it is unlikely that any aspiring project manager will ever learn what leadership looks like in their organisation. The project manager will set the tone for all of the interactions on the project. In every interaction, those who are involved learn the way the project manager does things, and this then becomes the project way of doing things.

Dealing with people on a one-to-one basis is a major part of the project manager's job. Sometimes these interactions will be with customers, sometimes with subcontractors, sometimes with project members; sometimes they will be with more senior staff, sometimes with junior staff. Regardless of whom they interact with, project managers must be seen to be professional and competent by all who watch them. Many of the key qualities and skills are shown in Figure 24.2.

Figure 24.1 Self-management

Figure 24.2 One-to-one interactions

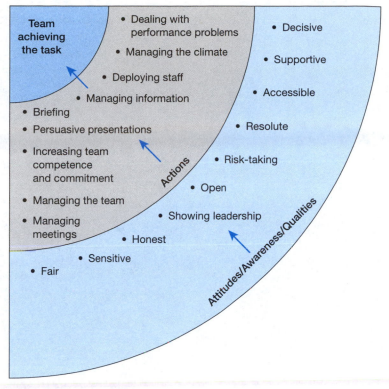

Figure 24.3 Managing others

Project managers frequently need to deal with large groups of people, for example in meetings or when giving presentations. Many feel anxious at the thought of presenting to a potentially critical audience, but the skills involved in doing so are an important part of the role. Also, the project manager will want to support the team wherever possible, but must be able to be authoritarian and critical when necessary. A judicious mixture of praise and control will be appreciated by all the team. As the leader of the project, it is the project manager who will drive, guide and motivate the team. Doing this well will enable the project manager to command the respect of the team. Figure 24.3 shows many of these key qualities and skills.

Everything described so far is of no use at all if the project manager does not manage the task adequately. Good communication and excellent self-organisation are no substitute for the planning, monitoring and control processes that the project manager will create. The effectiveness of these areas will be the key to the outcome of the project. So the project manager must be a capable planner, with the ability to identify the work to be done as well as the checks and balances needed to manage and control it. These key tasks are shown in Figure 24.4.

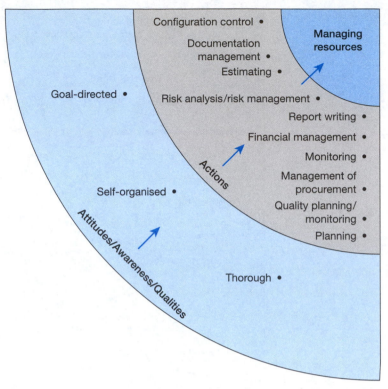

Figure 24.4 Managing resources

24.5 Using psychometric assessment

There is a truism: projects do not fail – people do. In companies that are project-led, nowhere is this more evident than in the selection and development of project managers. As will be obvious by now, a good project manager, well supported by more senior management, can mean the difference between the success and failure of the whole project. When people are most committed to the work they are doing and when they are most productive, there will be a number of factors at play. One of the most significant factors is that intangible one known as job satisfaction. For most of us this means a feeling of being challenged and of meeting the challenge; of working with others and helping them to give of their best as they help us to give of our best; of feeling positive about the work we are doing and the way we are doing that work.

The Institute of Personnel and Development published in early 1996 a study of staffing in UK companies. Its data gave turnover figures indicating that, on average, organisations can expect to replace the equivalent of their entire part-time staff every three to four years and to replace their full-time staff every six to seven years. If staff are unhappy, they will leave – if they can – more quickly than this. For each person who leaves, another has to be recruited, selected, trained and so on. The Institute's data demonstrated that the loss of just one professional – such as an experienced IS specialist – cost, on average, £23,000. And there are other, hidden costs too. The wrong person in the job will make mistakes while in post, is likely to miss opportunities, or perhaps commit the company to supplying something it cannot deliver. From this it is clear that:

- Companies need to ensure that they get the right people in the job as project manager.
- Companies must support, train and develop them on the job so that they perform well and have a satisfying job, ensuring that they want to stay with the company.

How can this be done easily and economically? Psychometrics can help, especially with selection and recruitment.

'Psychometrics' is often thought of as a buzzword, with many people using the results being unclear about what they really mean. However, with over 80 per cent of Britain's companies claiming to use psychometrics for recruitment, it is a good idea to outline their usefulness. Psychometrics are often called psychometric tests, as if somehow they could tell who were good candidates for a job and who were poor. It is more accurate to talk of psychometric measures or psychometric instruments, as many of them do not have passes or failures. They cannot distinguish between good and bad candidates – only a person can do that – but they can bring objectivity to the selection process. Correctly administered, there will be standardised conditions for carrying out the psychometric: standardised instructions, time, content, scoring and interpretation. This objectivity means that direct comparisons can be made, both with other candidates for a job and with an appropriate comparison group. And this means a greater likelihood of selecting the best candidate for the job.

There are three main types of psychometrics: measures of maximum performance or ability; measures of typical performance such as personality questionnaires; and interest inventories. Together these three can tell us a great deal about someone and provide information that it would be almost impossible to gain through interview. Let us now consider how they could be used to help in the selection and development of project managers.

Ability tests There are two main types of ability test (note that these are true tests, because it is possible to set a pass mark): attainment tests and aptitude tests. Attainment tests measure the results of formal training and are little used. Many employers simply check that a person has a particular educational qualification, and that can be done much more easily than by a test. Aptitude tests measure the ability of the person to acquire further knowledge or skills in a particular area. These are much more widely used. They are very good at measuring how good someone is in a particular skill area, such as verbal critical reasoning. If it is essential that the successful candidate is good at drawing inferences quickly and accurately from written text, then this is a good test to use.

Ability tests are not all paper-and-pencil tests. Simulations such as in-tray exercises are becoming increasingly popular, especially at senior management levels. Here the candidates are presented with a pile of letters, memos and items of background information. They are required to deal with this in a specified time and are awarded scores on abilities such as organising, forecasting, decision-making and written communication.

Interest inventories Interest inventories contain a wide sample of questions which might cover hobbies, school or university work, previous work experience or general life experiences and measure the direction in which an individual may want their career to go. Interest inventories are widely used in career counselling, and as such are particularly useful when someone is thinking of changing career – after all, that person may be able to do the job but would they enjoy doing it and would they stay in post? In both sales and management, for example, research evidence suggests that potentially effective managers may be identified by a specific pattern of likes and dislikes.

Personality questionnaires In many cases, the most important and useful type of psychometric measure is the personality questionnaire. Since personality is defined as 'a person's typical or preferred ways of behaving, thinking and feeling', you can see how important personality is in determining how well or badly someone might do their job. If you were drawing up a list of the characteristics you would want in a good project manager, you may well come up with something like the one below which is used by a major airline:

- *Influence/leadership*. Able to take charge and control a group towards an objective. Makes their presence felt in groups. Motivates subordinates, delegates effectively and monitors performance.
- *Communication skills*. Able to comprehend and express ideas accurately and persuasively both orally and in writing.
- *Organising/planning*. Able to think ahead, prioritise and organise work. Is able to structure activities and meet targets within appropriate budgets.
- *Motivation/energy*. Shows energy, drive and enthusiasm. Maintains a high output. Proactive and ambitious.
- *Creativity*. Generates and is receptive to new ideas. Seeks to innovate rather than necessarily accept the established solution.
- *Analytical*. Reasons objectively and critically with both verbal and numerical problems. Comprehends and processes information at a high level of complexity.
- *Empathy*. Able to understand the strengths, weaknesses, views and feelings of others. Supports others and is a good team member.
- *Emotional maturity*. Responds well to criticism. Frank and open. Able to take pressure.
- *Decision-making*. Has the confidence to take own decisions. Is prepared to take a balanced risk and be held accountable for the outcome.
- *Commercial awareness*. An interest in, and understanding of, the financial and profit implications of actions taken. A hard-headed concern for the bottom line.

Look closely at each characteristic described here. How many of the qualities asked for are aspects of personality? In fact, every characteristic asked for in this list could be measured accurately by psychometric measures, leaving it up to the skilled interviewer to determine who would be the best person for the job from a range of people who could all do it well.

Research conducted with companies has established that up to 70 per cent of attributes associated with success at work are dimensions of personality rather than ability. Looked at in this way, it becomes vitally important to be able to measure these attributes in an objective and accurate way. From the point of view of the would-be project manager, the same considerations apply. Few people would want to pin their hopes of a successful career on something which would be unsuitable, so the earlier a person can discover a career which best suits their strengths, the better.

One particular company has used psychometrics to profile its project managers. Firstly, those managing project managers were asked to list the qualities that they greatly valued in the most effective of their project managers. The project managers were then 'tested' to see whether they exhibited what was sought by their bosses. The qualities that were most important to their managers were:

- Political awareness
- Being a good people reader
- Being good at negotiations
- Giving persuasive presentations
- Being good at influence
- Having a positive presence and confidence.

Next in order of importance were:

- Responsible leadership
- Risk-taking
- Innovative, problem-solving
- Strategic thinking
- Self-organised
- Goal-directed thoroughness.

Least important, though still of above-average importance, were:

- Assimilation skills
- Good decision-making
- A win/win mentality
- Being supportive
- Being tough
- Being good at time management
- Being open-minded
- Sensitive.

The following list shows what was actually found. Each quality has a number beside it, between 1 and 10. An average score for a group of managers is 5, so we would expect all of the good project managers to be scoring 5 or more in each of the qualities their managers value. In the first group were:

- Political awareness 5
- Being a good people reader 5
- Being good at negotiations 5
- Giving persuasive presentations 5
- Being good at influence 5
- Having a positive presence and confidence 5

Interestingly, although these qualities were the most important to their managers, the project managers were no better than average.

Next on the list were:

- Responsible leadership 8
- Risk-taking 3
- Innovative, problem-solving 6
- Strategic thinking 7
- Self-organised 7
- Goal-directed thoroughness 7

In this group, our project managers were mostly above average. The exception is in risk-taking. Further research indicated that the group of managers actually wanted what they called 'a safe pair of hands', someone who could be trusted with a major project. When they were initially talking about risk, what they really wanted was intellectual risk – innovation, in other words.

The least important list showed:

- Assimilation skills 9
- Good decision-making 6
- A win/win mentality 6
- Being supportive 7
- Being tough 5
- Being good at time-management 4
- Being open-minded 6
- Sensitive 5

Here again we have almost the same picture. In many of these areas the project managers were above average. Two attributes are particularly worthy of mention. In assimilation skills, it was found that verbal skills were higher than mathematical skills, reflecting the fact that managing a project often involves having to read and understand long, complex documents.

In time-management, what came to light was that many of the project managers – enough to skew the average score considerably – were highly involved in the detail of their projects. This frequently meant that they were unable to carry out all of their own work in the allotted time. All those who were asked about this admitted that it was a failing, but felt that the project could be at risk if they did not devote their attention to this level of detail.

What does this research tell us? It validates the perceptions of those who select, train and manage project managers in the company where the research was done. There was a company feeling that they knew what a good project manager was, and this was upheld by the tests: looking at the twenty key competences, the project managers came out below average in only three. In addition, this tells us that psychometrics measure what good project managers actually do, and can give us a yardstick to help establish whether someone new to the job would find it a satisfying career.

24.6 Ethical considerations

This section is not about the big business scandals that make the headlines – they are far beyond the scope of project management. There are, however, ethical issues that affect project management and, whilst we do not suggest that they need to be at the forefront of your mind, they have a real impact when they do occur. One part of the problem is that different ideas of right and wrong arise at different times and reflect changes in society. Another is that different cultures – national and organisational – have different views. We see that, for example, in civil law cases about racial and sexual discrimination. Ethical issues now occupy a more visible position in organisations. The general public, the media and special interest groups all focus more on ethical issues even though they may be shrouded in the cloak of scandal.

Increasingly, organisations are establishing their own codes of ethical conduct. These may be called 'vision and value' statements or describe 'what we believe and how we work', but they are nonetheless sets of moral guidelines that govern behaviour. Often they are based on the beliefs of the organisation's founder – Cadbury is an example – or on the purpose for which the organisation was founded. The Protestant work ethic, based on the view that wealth is a sign of God's favour, strongly influences many western organisation cultures and hence their ethical stance.

But these complex issues, interesting though they are, lie outside the role of the project manager. There are, however, some ethical matters that lie within the scope of project management. There are two ethical frameworks that have an overriding influence. Put simply, they are

- *Fundamental principle.* There are basic and unquestionable rights and wrongs. For example, theft and deceit are always wrong.
- *Consequences.* This is the 'ends justifies the means' view.

Let us take an example. Our project does not have enough copies of a software product. It is not very expensive, a few hundred pounds perhaps, but we are up against cost pressure and we need the software for a couple of weeks so that some extra staff can be used to meet a deadline. Do we make some pirate copies or not? Fundamental principle would lead us not to make copies because it would be theft. Consequences might allow us to justify it for the good of the project. However, in a 1992 analysis of 1,100 software piracy investigations, the Federation Against Software Theft reported that 21 per cent were the result of illegal copying by budget-conscious MIS managers (see Robson in the Further Reading).

So, what can project managers do? Based on an article in *Computing* in January 1995 by McNevin, some steps to follow when dealing with stakeholders where there is a contractual relationship, with supplies and customers for example, include:

- Defining the outcomes with absolute clarity.
- Keeping projects short and simple.
- Ensuring that suppliers are properly qualified and resourced.
- Ensuring that the project team is properly staffed.
- Dealing with differences over expectations as soon as they arise.

Project managers can also demonstrate their ethical standpoint and establish one for the project team through the use of the British Computer Society Code of Conduct outlined in Figure 24.5. The full Code is on the Society's website at www.bcs.org.uk. In the USA, the Association for Computing Machinery (ACM) has a code of Ethics and Professional Conduct at www.acm.org.

The Public Interest
This section deals with members' responsibility for public health and safety issues, the protection of the environment and the safeguarding of basic human rights. Members are to ensure that they have knowledge and understanding of relevant legislation and that they comply with it.

Employers and Clients
Members are expected to work with due care and diligence and deliver work on time and to budget and to report on any likely overruns as soon as practicable. If their professional judgement is overruled they are to point out the likely consequences. Members are expected to observe the highest standards of financial probity and to respect client and employer confidentiality. There should be no misrepresentation of the capability of products or services.

The Profession
This section of the Code requires members to uphold the reputation of the profession, to work to professional standards and to avoid any action that will adversely affect the good standing of the Profession. There is a responsibility to represent the Profession in public in an honest and balanced way and to act with integrity towards fellow members and members of other professions. Members are expected to encourage and support fellow members in their professional development.

Professional Competence and Integrity
Members shall continue to develop their professional competence and seek to conform to good practice. They must offer to do only that work that is in their area of competence and to accept professional responsibility for it and for the work of their subordinates.

Figure 24.5 Outline of the British Computer Society Code of Conduct

24.7 | Summary

We have looked at the role of the project manager in a number of ways, and in each way the results have led to a similar conclusion. In one sense, we have gone full circle from the vision of the project manager at the start of this chapter to the list of qualities with numerical scales beside them which also describe a good project manager.

In each part of the chapter there is another important message: some things about the job can be learned – such as learning how to negotiate effectively, learning how to motivate the team or learning how to understand a contract – whereas other things are inbuilt. Anyone can learn the basic skills of managing a project; a few people, the right people, can go much further. And this is not just because they have the skills, it is also because they have the aptitude for career project management.

Questions

1 How does the 'vision of the project manager' in this chapter relate to the way you see the job? Are there aspects of the job that do not appear in the vision? Why might that be?

2 Consider the skills and qualities of project managers described in the 'developmental approach' (section 24.4). Can you add to these? How far do you see yourself being proficient in these skills? How could you develop further?

Further reading

Gaddis, P (1960), 'The project manager', *Harvard Business Review*, May/June

Robson, W (1997), *Strategic Management and Information Systems*, 2nd edn, Prentice Hall

25 Developing your career

25.1 Introduction

The way your career develops will depend on many things, and important among them are:

- You. There was quite a lot in the previous chapter about how you might see yourself as a project manager; but it is not just having the competences or having studied the bodies of knowledge (see below and the next chapter), it is about attitude and approach to the job. Whilst it might be a platitude to say that 'your attitude determines your altitude', it is worth remembering.
- The people you work for. Do you have good role models from whom you can learn? Are you learning good practices and behaviours from those above you? Do they demonstrate leadership, integrity, professionalism and sound ethical values? Do you and they have a realistic basis for your development? It might be unrealistic to expect the answer 'yes' to all of these questions, but you should get a positive answer to some of them. It is quite a useful idea to make a note of the things you learn in this way to help build the foundation for your own work. Some people keep a learning log in which they note what they have learned 'on the job'.
- The projects you work on. It is good to start on small projects where you can see the complete project lifecycle, even if you see it only at a superficial level, because it gives you a framework on which more detail can be hung later. Often, though, we are pitched into detailed work managing subprojects, but they too can be a good foundation. Write down what you have learned as you go along.
- Formal training. We cannot learn everything on the job; we need some inputs from outside about the things we do not know but need to know.
- Luck! There is an element of luck in all successful careers. People sometimes call it 'being in the right place at the right time'. If you are deep into a project when an exciting new opportunity arises, it is unlikely that you will be the one chosen to lead it. However, a world famous golfer in response to a spectator's remark, 'You had a lucky round today', said, 'Do you know, it's a strange thing, the more I practice, the luckier I get'. The lesson for project managers is two-fold: (1) keep working on your personal, professional development, and (2) be visible so that you do not get overlooked when new things come along.

One way that you can put all of these things together is by demonstrating your development through the project management qualifications you have. This does not mean that you should become a trophy hunter and aim for certificate after certificate; project management is a practical activity with very visible practical outcomes. You can, however, demonstrate the body of your project management knowledge through the qualifications you have. That is what this chapter is about: project management qualifications that say something about you. The chapter covers:

- The Project Management Institute
- The Association for Project Management
- The British Computer Society
- The APM Group
- The Australian Institute of Project Management

For all these bodies and their qualifications, you need to read the information on their websites that are listed in this chapter; for the first two, however, there is some additional information in the next chapter.

25.2 Project Management Institute (www.pmi.org.uk)

Five volunteers in Pennsylvania, USA, set up the Project Management Institute (PMI) in 1969, and at the beginning of 2004 it had over 125,000 members worldwide. Its qualifications are recognised across the world although it is strongly American. Project managers in many different sectors including aerospace, automotive, construction, engineering, financial services, IT, pharmaceuticals and telecommunications have qualifications from the PMI.

The PMI's *Guide to the Project Management Body of Knowledge* (BoK) has a worldwide reputation and is almost a global standard for project management. At the end of 2003 it was being revised for its third edition, and it is claimed that a million copies of earlier editions are in circulation.

There are two levels of qualification available through the PMI. These are the Certified Associate in Project Management, and the Project Management Professional. Both have an examination route for people with a degree and a route for those without a degree. Both examinations are based on the PMI BoK, are multiple-choice examinations and are not methodology-specific. Neither has an oral component.

For the Certified Associate, the routes are:

- Degree plus 1,500 hours (around 35–40 weeks) of project management experience in two years and the multiple-choice examination.
- No degree plus 3,000 hours of project management experience over four years and the multiple-choice examination.

For the Project Management Professional, which PMI says measures 'the application of knowledge, skills, tools and techniques' used in project management, the examination is four multiple-choice examination papers amounting

Project initiation 8.5%

Project planning 23.5%

Project execution 23.5%

Project control 23%

Project closing 7%

Professional responsibility 14.5%

Knowledge tested

Project initiation
- Determine project goals
- Determine deliverables
- Determine process outputs
- Document constraints
- Document assumptions
- Define strategy
- Identify performance criteria
- Determine resource requirements
- Define budget
- Produce formal documentation

Project planning
- Refine project
- Create work breakdown structure
- Develop resource management plan
- Refine time and cost estimates
- Establish project controls
- Develop project plan
- Obtain plan approval

Project execution
- Commit resources
- Implement resources
- Manage progress
- Communicate progress
- Implement quality assurance procedures

Project control
- Measure performance
- Refine control limits
- Take corrective action
- Evaluate effectiveness of corrective action
- Ensure plan compliance
- Reassess control plans
- Respond to risk event triggers
- Monitor project activity

Project closing
- Obtain acceptance of deliverables
- Document lessons learned
- Facilitate closure
- Preserve product records and tools
- Release resources

Professional responsibility
- Ensure integrity
- Contribute to knowledge base
- Apply professional knowledge
- Balance stakeholder interests
- Respect differences

Figure 25.1 PMI qualification examination content

to 200 questions to be taken in 4 hours. The pass score is 137. The examination content and percentage of questions set at the end of 2003 are illustrated in Figure 25.1.

25.3 Association for Project Management (www.apm.org.uk)

The Association for Project Management (APM) describes itself as 'the leading project management authority in the UK', and, if you are interested in a generalist, UK-based qualification, this might be more useful than those of the PMI. At the end of 2003 the APM had just over 13,000 individual and 250 corporate members. There are branches throughout the UK.

The APM offers four levels of qualification. At the base level is the Introductory Certificate in Project Management and this is open to anyone interested in starting a career in project management or wanting to understand the principles of project management. The syllabus covers a wide spread of planning and scheduling, communications, quality management, teamwork, resource management, risk management, handover and review. It is designed to be taught over two days by accredited training providers, and is examined by a 60-question, one-hour, multiple-choice test. Beyond this introductory level are three further qualifications:

- The Associate grade, which is the next level up, is a foundation-level, knowledge-based qualification. It is aimed at project team members and project office staff with up to two years' project management experience and assesses their breadth of knowledge of all areas of project management, including strategic, commercial, technical, organisational and people aspects. There is a one-hour multiple-choice test and a two-hour essay-based examination paper. Around 6,000 people held this qualification at the end of 2003.

- The Practitioner Qualification is for people with three to five years' experience of managing 'non-complex projects' who can demonstrate their ability to manage a complete project as a key component of a large-scale project. The assessment process takes three days and includes a written examination, observed and assessed groupwork and an interview. Candidates are assessed against 30 project management criteria.

- At the most senior level is the Certificated Project Manager for people with substantial experience and who are skilled at managing complex multidisciplinary projects with multi-stakeholder interests outside the organisation. Assessment is in three stages. Stage one is the submission of a detailed CV describing the projects managed, a self-assessment form and a précis of a sample project. Stage two is a 5,000 word project report based on the précis. Stage three is an oral examination.

25.4 British Computer Society (www.bcs.org.uk)

Qualifications in project management are organised by the Information Systems Examinations Board (ISEB) division of the British Computer Society. The qualifications are focused on the needs of practitioners in IS/IT projects and extend from foundation to advanced levels.

- For professional staff in programme and project support offices, there are two certificates, at Foundation and Advanced levels. Training is provided by accredited training providers with 24 hours of training required for the Foundation level and 32 hours for the Advanced level. Candidates for the Advanced level must hold the Foundation certificate.
- The Foundation examination is a 45-question multiple-choice test, and for the Advanced level there is a two-hour written paper and an oral test.
- In project management, qualifications are provided at three levels. Announced in November 2003, the Foundation Certificate in IS Project Management is designed for anyone involved in or affected by IS/IT projects. Accredited training providers will run training courses and there will be a one-hour multiple-choice examination

The next step up is the ISEB Project Management Certificate that has already been taken by 6,000 people. The assessment and qualification process is shared between accredited course providers and the ISEB, with course providers offering a minimum of 80 hours of training. There is a three-hour written examination set and moderated by the ISEB but marked by the course provider. Success in the written paper leads to an oral examination lasting about 45 minutes with two ISEB appointed external examiners. This is a popular and valued qualification for IS/IT projects. The syllabus includes:

- An overview of project management, including strategy, the project lifecycle, project organisation and ethical considerations.
- Managing plans.
- Managing people and other resources.
- Managing the development and delivery of project products.
- Managing quality.
- Managing change.
- Managing risk.

Beyond this lies the ISEB Diploma in Project Management, which is intended for experienced project and programme managers.

25.5 APM Group (www.apmgroup.co.uk)

The APM Group was originally the trading arm of the Association for Project Management but became an independent organisation in 2000. It is primarily a UK-based organisation and in the context of this chapter is best known for the accreditation of training organisations and the organisation of examinations in PRINCE and PRINCE2® on behalf of the UK Office of Government Computing. These examinations are very popular and the qualification is clearly of value in the IS/IT marketplace.

- At Foundation level the measure is whether or not candidates can act as informed members of a project management team using PRINCE2®. Assessment is by a closed book, multiple-choice examination of 75 questions to be answered in one hour.
- At Practitioner level the focus is on using PRINCE2® to manage a project and being able to adapt PRINCE2® to different project circumstances. There is a three-hour, open book, written examination.

25.6 Australian Institute of Project Management
(www.aipm.com.au)

Originally set up in 1976 as the Project Managers' Forum, the Australian Institute of Project Management (AIPM) now offers certification and qualification at four levels, three of which are part of its Registered Project Manager (Reg PM) framework. The entry-level certificate prepares people for involvement in project management and is a knowledge rather than a competence award and so not part of the Reg PM framework. Entry into the grades of associate, member and fellow are by application and based on education, training and length of experience in project management.

The Institute is active in the development of the Asia-Pacific Federation of Project Management representing eleven regional nations.

25.7 Summary

We would recommend that you seek some qualification once you are close to becoming a project manager or have started out in project management. How do you decide which qualifications to choose? There are four conclusions that you might like to consider:

- If you are working in a project support office, take the ISEB qualifications at Foundation and Advanced levels.
- If you expect to be managing IS/IT projects then sit the examinations at Foundation and Practitioner levels offered by the ISEB.
- If you see project management as your life, you will want to evaluate the APM and the PMI and choose the one that fits you best.
- Wherever you are, if you are using PRINCE2®, then you will find the APM Group qualification valuable.

Whichever route you take, good luck. There is a world of opportunity for good project managers.

26 Bodies of knowledge and standards

26.1 Introduction

In this last chapter we introduce some places where project managers can go to learn more about their craft – or art, or science, or whatever you want to call it – and to find guidance on what to do and how to do it.

Our discussion falls into two categories: bodies of knowledge and standards. Bodies of knowledge are compendia of what a project manager needs to know and be able to do; standards are guides to the best ways of doing it.

The two main professional bodies for project managers are the Association for Project Management, based in the UK but with support from other parts of the world, and the Project Management Institute, which is based in the USA and has a widespread presence elsewhere. Each has developed a body of knowledge which, although they are similar in principle, do differ greatly in detail.

For standards, we need to go to the British Standards Institution (BSI) and its international counterpart the International Organisation for Standardisation (ISO), based in Geneva. The BSI has a standard for general project management, BS 6079, and the ISO has ISO 12207 'Information Technology – Software Lifecycle Processes'. In addition, quality has been a recurring feature of this book, so we also look at the two main standards relating to that: ISO 9000 'Quality Management Systems – Fundamentals and Vocabulary' and ISO 9001 'Quality Management Systems – Requirements'. Finally, because organisations today have to take more seriously their responsibilities towards the environment, we cover ISO 14001.

We cannot in the space available examine any of these works in detail. Rather, our aim is to sketch out their main features and recommend that you contact the relevant organisations for more information.

26.2 Bodies of Knowledge

Association for Project Management

The APM's body of knowledge (BoK) was first published in 1992 and the current (fourth) edition appeared in 2000. It is described in a small booklet or can be downloaded from the APM website (www.apm.org.uk). The BoK is divided into seven sections:

414

1 *General* – explaining the context of project management and defining some basic concepts.

2 *Strategic* – explaining how project management fits in with business strategy and its relationship to other issues such as value management, risk management, quality management and health and safety.

3 *Control* – the methods for breaking down the work, budgeting, resource management, change control, earned value management and information management.

4 *Technical* – managing the technical definition of a project, including requirements management, estimating, value management and configuration management.

5 *Commercial* – business case, marketing and sales, finance, procurement and legal awareness.

6 *Organisational* – the lifecycle of a project, organisation structures and roles.

7 *People* – the interpersonal side of project management, topics including communication, teamwork, leadership, managing conflict, negotiation and managing people.

Each section contains an overview of the topics covered, a slightly more detailed treatment of each topic, and references to relevant publications. There are additional references at the end of the BoK. The APM BoK is not a detailed document, nor is it intended to be. Instead, it provides a valuable survey of the world of project management and a set of good references for those wishing to research any particular topic in more detail.

The syllabi for the APM's range of professional qualifications are based on the BoK.

Project Management Institute   The PMI's BoK is contained in its publication *A Guide to the Project Management Body of Knowledge*. It is available in hardback, paperback and on CD-ROM, and all three can be ordered from the PMI website (www.pmi.org). In addition, the books can be ordered from booksellers. The content of the PMI's BoK is summarised in Figure 26.1.

The PMI BoK is rather more detailed than its British counterpart from the APM and it contains more guidance on how to do things, as opposed to what to do. For each of the Project Management Processes, for example, there is a definition of the inputs, techniques and outputs that are relevant.

The syllabi for the PMI professional qualifications are based on its BoK.

26.3 Standards

BS 6079   BS 6079 is the British standard on project management. It was last reissued in 2002 and has three parts:

■ BS 6079-1:2002. This is the actual *Guide to Project Management* and covers project management, management techniques, management operations, organisation, budgeting, forecasting, purchasing and trading standards.

Figure 26.1 **PMI's body of knowledge**

- BS 6079-2:2002. This is a supporting vocabulary and provides a comprehensive glossary of project management terminology.
- BS 6079-3:2002. This is the *Guide to the Management of Business-related Project Risk*; it was a new addition to the standard in 2002.

In total, the standard provides a comprehensive guide to the conduct of projects. Because it is generic, some of the material is not directly relevant to IT project managers and some of the terminology can create difficulties; for example, BS 6079 uses the term 'implementation' to mean 'doing the work' or 'developing the product', whereas in IT this is usually used in the more restricted sense of putting a developed system into live operation. Nevertheless, BS 6079 does encapsulate a lot of best-practice ideas, containing, for example, model templates for project plans, an explanation of the work breakdown structure approach, discussions of cost patterns in projects and material on investment appraisal and earned value analysis.

The standard is expensive but can be ordered online at www.bsionline.co.uk.

ISO 12207 ISO 12207 is entitled *Information Technology – Software Life Cycle Processes*. As the name suggests, it is concerned with providing a process model for software development. The resultant lifecycle is therefore more directly applicable to IT projects than that in BS 6079, although it is quite simple to establish parallels between the two.

The main elements of the software lifecycle defined in the standard are:

- Acquisition.
- Supply.
- Development (subdivided into requirements elicitation, system requirements analysis, system architectural design, software requirements analysis, software design, software construction, software integration, software testing, system integration, system testing and software installation).
- Operation.
- Maintenance.

In addition, the standard describes 'supporting lifecycle processes' such as documentation, configuration management, quality assurance, verification, validation, joint review (between the project stakeholders), audit, and problem resolution.

Necessarily, the standard does not provide detailed guidance on how to do any of these things but it does establish what needs to be done and why.

ISO 12207 can be downloaded on payment of the appropriate fee from the ISO website (www.iso.ch) and it is also available from the British Standards Institution.

ISO 9000   ISO 9000, last revised in 2000, explains the basic concepts of quality management and quality management systems. It sets out the principles of quality management, explains the requirements for a quality management system and defines the vocabulary used in quality management.

The standard can be downloaded on payment of the appropriate fee from the ISO website (www.iso.ch) and it is also available from the British Standards Institution.

ISO 9001   Where ISO 9000 sets out the principles of quality management, ISO 9001 provides a more detailed description of how a quality management system should work. This covers:

- Senior management commitment to the operation of a quality system.
- Provision of suitable resources to carry out the work.
- Recruitment and training of competent people.
- Establishing an infrastructure.
- Providing a suitable working environment.

ISO 9001 is focused on putting in place a suitable framework within which products can be developed and delivered. It also promotes the concept of continuous process improvement.

ISO 9001 can be downloaded on payment of the appropriate fee from the ISO website (www.iso.ch) and it is also available from the British Standards Institution.

ISO 14001   ISO 14001 covers the establishment of an environmental management system. Clearly, having such a system is of great importance in projects such as oil exploration and building nuclear power stations. But all projects have some sort of environmental impact, even IT projects, which seem to generate a lot of paper and also involve items such as computers and laser toner cartridges for which thought has to be given to careful disposal. Interestingly, the structure of the environmental management system is similar to that of the quality management system, and ISO 9001 does have a comparison of the two areas.

The standard can be downloaded on payment of the appropriate fee from the ISO website (www.iso.ch) and it is also available from the British Standards Institution.

Further reading

British Standards Institution (2002), BS 6079, *Project Management Parts 1–3*, BSI

Dixon, Miles (ed.) (2000), *Body of Knowledge*, 4th edn, Association for Project Management

International Organisation for Standardisation (2000), ISO 9000 *Quality Management Systems – Fundamentals and Vocabulary*, ISO

International Organisation for Standardisation (2000), ISO 9001 *Quality Management Systems – Requirements*, ISO

International Organisation for Standardisation (2002), ISO 12207 *Information Technology – Software Life Cycle Processes*, ISO

International Organisation for Standardisation (1996), ISO 14001 *Environmental Management Systems – Specification with Guidance for Use*, ISO

Various (2000), *A Guide to the Project Management Body of Knowledge*, Project Management Institute, Pennsylvania, USA

Glossary

Acceptance criteria Established (ideally) at the start of a project, these define the tests that will be applied to see whether the customers should accept the finished product or service from the suppliers.

Activity network A diagram showing the various project activities, put into a logical sequence, and showing the *dependencies* between activities.

Balanced Business Scorecard Devised by Kaplan and Norton, the BBS enables an assessment to be made of an organisation's performance. Unlike many performance measures it does not rely solely on financial indicators.

Baseline A term used in *configuration management*. A baseline is a 'snapshot' of a configuration item, 'frozen' at some point. The very first baseline will be established by the specification for the item and subsequent baselines will occur when there is an important change in how the item is represented as it is transformed in the design and coding process.

Benefits management An approach to managing a project, including its implementation and the subsequent use of the IT system, in such a way as to try to ensure that the business benefits are achieved. This might involve, for example, refusing to delay a project or not adding features which cannot be cost-justified and which might erode the planned benefits.

Benefits realisation The process of checking, after a project has been completed, that the hoped-for business benefits have been achieved.

Business assurance *See* Project assurance.

Capability Maturity Model A methodology for the development and improvement of an organisation's software development process. The model describes a five-stage evolutionary path of an increasingly organised process.

Change control The process of managing changes – or proposed changes – to the scope of a project in a controlled fashion, involving identifying the change, assessing its impact and making an informed decision on whether to proceed with it or not.

Checkpoint A checkpoint is one of the regular *control points* in a *PRINCE2®* project. Control is exercised through the checkpoint meeting which is conducted either by the *project manager* or the project assurance team. The meeting provides the information used to measure actual progress against planned. The output from the meeting is a checkpoint report.

CMM *See* Capability Maturity Model.

Competitive advantage This describes the dominance that an organisation has in its marketplace over its competitors. Organisations develop *strategies* to gain control and to defend their position.

Concession An *off-specification* which is accepted by the *project board* without insisting on the defect being corrected.

Configuration item A configuration item is a component in a configuration or larger product. Thus a computer system will have a functional specification, program specifications, test plans, programs, subroutines and so on. It is necessary to know the current version of each configuration item and, through *configuration management*, which items fit together to form the entire system.

Configuration management The process of identifying and controlling changes to *configuration items*. In essence, configuration management ensures that components fit and work together and that the current state of a system, for example, is known in relation to the components which make it up. Version control is an important aspect of configuration management.

Control points *PRINCE2®* defines a number of control points of which the principal ones are: project initiation, *mid-stage assessment*, *end-stage assessment* and *project closure*.

Cost/benefit analysis The process of identifying and, where possible, quantifying the costs of undertaking a project and its expected benefits, with a view to determining whether the project can be justified.

Critical path analysis (CPA) Sometimes known as network analysis, CPA is a method used in the scheduling of project tasks. It shows the *dependency* between tasks so that the critical path – the path that must be followed if the project is to complete on time – can be identified.

Critical success factors The resources, capabilities, skills and competences that organisations have that enable them to develop a competitive advantage in their marketplace.

Dependency If one task has to be completed before another can begin, or one *product* must be available before another can be started, there is said to be a dependency between them. Dependencies therefore constrain the order in which a project must be executed.

Discounted cash flow (DCF) A method for appraising the value of capital expenditure by predicting the streams of cash flows – in and out – during the lifetime of a project and adjusting flows in future years so as to bring them to represent the current value of money.

Earned value analysis A method of assessing progress on a project which takes account not only of what has been done (or spent) to date but also what value has been achieved for that effort or expenditure.

End-stage assessment A major *control point* within a *PRINCE2®* project. The *project manager* needs to make a formal presentation to the *project board* and there is an opportunity to re-appraise the project to ensure that it is still likely to meet its business objectives. The project board must give explicit authority for the project manager to move to the next stage of the project.

ESA *See* End-stage assessment.

Exception plan An exception plan is produced by the *project manager* whenever it is apparent that the *tolerances* assigned to the project are likely to be exceeded. The exception plan can be produced at project, stage or team plan level and, if approved, becomes the revised plan for the remainder of the project or stage.

Exception report A report prepared by a *project manager* if it is likely that the project's *tolerances* will be exceeded. It explains how the situation has arisen and, through the *exception plan*, shows how the stage or project will be completed.

Executive The senior member, and chair, of a *PRINCE2®* project board. The executive is the owner of the project's business case and is responsible for ensuring that it meets its defined business objectives.

Five forces model This model can be used to assess the influence that IS can have to alter the relative importance of the five forces that impact an organisation as set out in Michael Porter's competitive analysis model. These forces are direct competition, the power of suppliers, the purchasing power of customers, the threat of new entrants to the marketplace, and the threat of alternative products or services.

Fixed-price One method of contracting for a project, whereby the supplier offers to carry out a set specification of work for an agreed sum of money. If the work costs more than expected, the supplier bears the cost; if it costs less, he enjoys a higher profit. Adopting a fixed-price contract has the effect of placing the financial risk for the project on the supplier. See also *Time-and-materials*.

Functional (organisation) structure The simplest form of business organisation, whereby the organisation is divided into functional areas (for example, marketing, operations and distribution), each function being managed by a specialist head.

Hierarchy of needs A theory of personality that describes five groups of needs that influence our behaviours. These are physiological needs, safety needs, social needs, the need for esteem, and self-actualisation.

Highlight report A regular report produced by the *project manager* for the *project board*. The report details progress to date, problems encountered and plans for the next reporting period. The highlight report is based on information gained from *checkpoint meetings*.

Impact analysis Connected with *configuration management*, this is the process of assessing the impact of making a change to the existing (or evolving) system.

Internal rate of return (IRR) Used in the appraisal of capital expenditures, IRR is an interest rate that gives a net present value of zero when applied to a projected cash flow. It is the interest rate, that, when applied to the project, makes the present values of the cash outflows and inflows equal. The IRR can then be compared with the cost of capital for the project.

IS steering committee The body in an organisation that is responsible for setting the information systems strategy. It therefore identifies opportunities to use IT to further the organisation's business objectives.

IT executive committee This group is responsible for initiating individual projects that support the IS strategy. For each project, it appoints the *project board* and sets the project's terms of reference.

Johari's window A model for helping people to understand the differences between our view of ourselves and the view that other people have of us.

Matrix (organisation) structure A form of organisation structure, whereby a cross-divisional structure such as a project structure is superimposed on a functional organisation.

Mid-stage assessment This is an optional *control point* in a *PRINCE2®* project. A mid-stage assessment can be called for at any time by the project board and may be required where, for example, significant problems have occurred on the project or where the stage itself is rather long and waiting for the *end-stage assessment* may lead to a loss of control.

MSA *See* Mid-stage assessment.

Net present value (NPV) This is the difference between the present values of the cash outflows of a project and the present values of the cash inflows, all future cash flows being adjusted to reflect the present-day value of money.

Network diagram A diagram showing the sequence and *dependencies* between the activities or deliverables on a project. Sometimes also known as a PERT chart (PERT = Programme Evaluation and Review Technique).

Off-specification One form of *project issue* whereby a system, or part of a system, fails to meet its specification.

PBS *See* Product breakdown structure.

PERT chart *See* Network diagram.

PESTEL This is an acronym for a process used in environmental analysis during the development of *strategy*. It stands for an assessment of the Political, Economic, Socio-cultural, Technical, Environmental and Legal circumstances that may affect a strategy. It is sometimes spelled PESTLE.

PFD *See* Product flow diagram.

PID *See* Project initiation document.

PPSO *See* Project and programme support office.

PRINCE PRojects IN Controlled Environments, a method that supports many aspects of project management. The current version of the method is known as *PRINCE2®*.

PRINCE2® A project management methodology of eight processes developed by the UK Government and now used internationally. It replaced *PRINCE*.

Product A deliverable from a project. It may be input to, or the output from, a project process. In *PRINCE2®*, products may be: management products (such as the project plan) that are associated with the control of the project; or specialist products which make up or lead to the final deliverable. Some authorities also distinguish between user (or external) products, which are delivered to the customer at the end of the project, and project (or internal) products which are developed and used by the project team en route to the final deliverables.

Product breakdown structure (PBS) A hierarchical decomposition of the *products* of a project from the overall deliverable (for example, a computer system) to its component parts.

Product description A definition of the purpose, composition, derivation and quality criteria that apply to a *product*. The product description acts as a specification for those developing the product of what it is, what are its components and how its *quality* will be tested.

Product flow diagram (PFD) A *network diagram* showing the transformations that turn *products* into other products. The diagram shows the sequence in which the project's products must be developed.

Programme A programme has various definitions but the most common one is a portfolio of projects that, together, help to achieve a common set of business objectives.

Programme and project support office (PPSO) A person or, more likely, group of people, who provide administrative support to one or more projects.

Programme director The person charged with managing a series of projects as a programme. The programme director will delegate overall control of individual projects to *project boards* and, through them, to *project managers*.

Programme executive A group set up to manage a programme of work. It has three roles: the programme manager (responsible for the day-to-day coordination of the projects on behalf of the *programme director*); the business change manager (author and guardian of the business case for the programme); and the design authority (who ensures the consistency and compatibility of the various projects that make up the programme).

Project assurance On a *PRINCE2®* project, the *project board* has a responsibility to ensure that the project meets its objectives in terms of its business purpose (the role of the executive), the user's needs (the role of the senior user) and the technical requirements of the suppliers (the senior supplier). The process of doing this is called project assurance and it is usually delegated to a project assurance team who regularly check the three aspects of the project on behalf of the project board.

Project board In a *PRINCE2®* project, the body charged with responsibility for delivering a single project. The project board has three roles represented (though it may have more, or less, than three members): the *executive*, the *senior supplier* and the *senior user*. The project board delegates day-to-day control of the project to a *project manager*.

Project closure The formal end of a *PRINCE2®* project. The *project manager* prepares a project closure notification to inform all parties of the end of the project and the project must be accepted by the *project board*.

Project initiation document (PID) A document that brings together all the information needed to start the project, including for example:

- Terms of reference
- Acceptance criteria
- Project organisation and responsibilities
- Project plan
- First stage plan
- Definition of the business case
- Risk assessment
- Product descriptions.

The PID must be approved by the *project board* as the *project manager*'s authority to start work on the project.

Project issue Any issue that needs to be managed within the project, including *off-specifications* and *requests for change*.

Project manager The person given day-to-day control of a project under the delegated authority of the *project board* or *sponsor*. In a *PRINCE2®* project, the project manager exercises control within *tolerances* set by the project board.

Project office *See* Programme and project support office.

Project (organisation) structure A form of organisation whereby a dedicated team, containing all the skills needed, is put together to carry out a specific project. When the project is over, the team is disbanded.

Quality 'The totality of features and characteristics of a product or service that bear on its ability to satisfy stated or implied needs' (ISO 8402:1991).

Quality review A formal inspection of a product to check its compliance with the quality criteria defined in the *product description* (see definition).

RAD Rapid application development is an approach to software development that sees software being developed through a series of iterative stages generally involving the use of prototypes and high, active user involvement so as to speed up the development process.

Rapport Developing rapport is the skill of building an harmonious relationship with someone else, mostly in a work context but also socially.

Request for change A formal method of proposing and controlling a modification to the specification of the product required.

RFC *See* Request for change.

Risk acceptance Allowing a risk to happen because there are no feasible or affordable countermeasures.

Risk assessment The process of estimating the likelihood (probability) of occurrence and scale of impact of identified risks.

Risk avoidance Measures aimed at reducing the likelihood of identified risks occurring. Cf. *Risk mitigation*.

Risk log *See* Risk register.

Risk management The process of identifying and assessing the risks faced by a project and of putting in place actions to avoid, or mitigate the effects of, those risks.

Risk mitigation Measures aimed at reducing the impact of identified risks, if they occur. Cf. *Risk avoidance*.

Risk owner Someone tasked with taking the actions needed to avoid or reduce the impact of a risk.

Risk profiling A process of examining a project with a view to gaining an understanding of the level of risk associated with it and, perhaps also, with various ways that the project can be tackled.

Risk register A repository of the information recorded about the risks on a project, also known (especially in the *PRINCE2®* method) as a risk log.

Risk transfer Taking measures to shift the impact of a risk on to somebody else.

Senior supplier On a *PRINCE2® project board*, the senior supplier represents the interests of those who are developing the product or service of the project.

Senior user On a *PRINCE2® project board*, the senior user represents the interests of those who will use the product or service being developed.

Sensitivity analysis With regard to a *discounted cash flow* calculation, trying alternative discount rates to see how much effect a change in rate has on the profitability of a project.

Situational leadership A style of leadership; a recognised and useful leadership model. A situational leader has different leadership styles according to the situation and in particular according to the need for direction or support to be given to those being led.

Sponsor (project sponsor) The person who 'owns' a project from a business perspective and who is (usually) responsible to the organisation for the achievement of the project's business case. In a *PRINCE2®* project, the sponsor role usually equates with that of the *executive*.

Stage *PRINCE2®* recommends that, to maximise control, a project be conducted as a series of stages. At the end of each stage, progress and the continued viability of the business case should be checked before moving to the next stage. This is good practice for non-PRINCE2® projects, as the organisation's commitment to the project is limited and graduated.

Stakeholder Individuals or groups who are affected by the activities of an organisation or a project.

Steering committee A committee set up to give overall guidance about the direction of a project. It takes decisions on matters outside the scope of the *project manager's* responsibility. *Project board* is a more modern term for this activity.

Strategy Strategy defines the future direction of an organisation and the actions it needs to take to achieve its goals.

SWOT A model for assessing the Strengths, Weaknesses, Opportunities and Threats that face an organisation. It is used during the assessment of strategy.

Team manager A person responsible for managing one of a possible number of teams who are contributing towards a project. The team managers report to the *project manager*.

Team spirit The spirit or camaraderie of a group that makes everyone want to succeed together. The recipe that enables the group to perform to a level of performance higher than is thought possible.

Time-and-materials One method of contracting for a project, whereby the supplier charges the customer on the basis of the amount of work done. This is useful where the scope of work cannot be defined adequately in advance but it has the effect of placing the financial risk on the project on the customer. *See also* Fixed-price.

Tolerance When a *project board* delegates day-to-day control of a project to a *project manager*, it also sets *tolerances* within which they must operate. For example, the budget may be defined as £500,000 plus or minus £50,000 and the timescale as one year plus or minus one month. As long as the project manager can keep the project within these tolerances, he or she retains control; but if it appears that the tolerances are likely to be exceeded, specific project board authority must be sought via an *exception report* and *exception plan*.

Total quality management (TQM) A structured and comprehensive approach for the improvement of product and service quality through continuous refinement in response to regular feedback.

Value engineering An approach to managing projects where, once the objectives have been agreed, the effort is directed to meeting them at the minimum cost.

Value management An approach to managing projects that endeavours to uncover and reconcile the differing views of stakeholders and to finding a solution that satisfies the majority of their concerns.

Virtual team Virtual teams are teams that never or rarely meet, yet function perfectly well through the use of a network of communications and carefully constructed work methods and team development processes.

Work package A set of information related to the creation of one or a set of *products* by a team or individual. The work package is a 'contract' between the *project manager* and whoever is developing the product.

Index